In the Shadow of Vesuvius

In the Shadow of Vesuvius

Views of Naples from Baroque to Romanticism 1631-1830

Electa Napoli

The following staff from Electa Napoli
have contributed to this catalogue:

Editorial Office
Silvia Cassani

Art Director
Valentina Lepore

Layout
Valentina Lepore
Enrica D'Aguanno

Technical co-ordination
Angelo Mombelli

Published in Italy

In the Shadow of Vesuvius
Views of Naples from Baroque to Romanticism 1631-1830

Accademia Italiana delle Arti e delle Arti Applicate
London, 27 October - 27 November 1990

This exhibition is under the gracious patronage
of Her Majesty Queen Elizabeth II
and His Excellency Francesco Cossiga
President of the Italian Republic

The Exhibition
«In the Shadow of Vesuvius»
has been promoted by
the Ministry of Foreign Affairs - Rome
the Ministry for the Artistic and Cultural Heritage - Rome
and coordinated by
the Superintendence for Historical and Cultural Heritage - Naples

Scientific Committee
Giuliano Briganti
Cesare De Seta
Alvar González-Palacios
Alfonso E. Pérez Sanchez
Wolfgang Prohaska
Pierre Rosenberg
Nicola Spinosa
Lindsay Stainton

Organizing Committee
Boris Biancheri
Rosa Maria Letts
Francesco Sisinni
Nicola Spinosa
Alessandro Vattani

Executive Committee
Brigitte Daprà
Elisabetta Kelescian
Rossana Muzii
Lilia Rocco
Mariella Utili

Organization of the Exhibition
Rebus S.r.l.
Naples - Turin
Accademia Italiana delle Arti e delle Arti Applicate
London

Design of the Exhibition
Arch. Lucio Turchetta

We wish to thank for the contribution:
Regione Campania
IRI Group

Essays:
Giuliano Briganti
Nicola Spinosa
Lindsay Stainton

Entries:
[L.Am.] Luisa Ambrosio
[P.B.] Paul Bédarida
[M.I.C.] Maria Ida Catalano
[B.D.] Brigitte Daprà
[A.G.-P.] Alvar González-Palacios
[W.K.] Wolfgang Krönig
[S.M.G.] Silvana Musella
[R.M.] Rossana Muzii
[A.P.] Annalisa Porzio
[N.S.] Nicola Spinosa
[L.S.] Lindsay Stainton
[M.U.] Mariella Utili

Photographs:
Photographic Archives of Naples
the Superintendence for Historical and Cultural Heritage - Naples

Translation of the catalogue
Stella Cragie

Translation of the credits
Rebus

Bibliography:
Ornella Agrillo
Sergio Liguori
Giovanna Barrella

List of Lenders
Accademia delle Belle Arti, Naples - Banca Commerciale Italiana, Milan - Banco di Napoli - Birmingham Museum and Art Gallery - Deputazione del Tesoro di San Gennaro, Naples - Fundacion Casa Ducal de Medinaceli, Siviglia - Galleria Palatina, Palazzo Pitti, Florence - Galleria Sabauda, Turin - Ian Woodner Family Collection - Lord Montagu of Beaulieu - Marylebone Cricket Club, London - Museo di Capodimonte, Naples - Museo di San Martino, Naples - National Museum of Wales, Cardiff - Scottish National Portrait Gallery, Edinburgh - Soprintendenza per i beni Ambientali, Architettonici, Artistici e Storici, Caserta - Soprintendenza per i Beni Ambientali e Architettonici, Naples - Tate Gallery, London - The Ashmolean Museum, Oxford - The British Museum, London - Victoria and Albert Museum, London

Acknowledgements
Emilio Acerna, Giuliana Alecce, The Duke of Buccleuch, Filippo Carli, Marina Causa Picone, Ian Craft, Marco Chiarini, Giuseppe Dalla Vecchia, Antimo D'Amodio, Michele De Capua, Romualdo De Juliis, Michela Di Macco, David Edmond, Giorgio Focas, Federico Forquet, Vanda Frizzi, Gabriella Grossi, Hazlitt Gooden & Fox, Gianmarco Jacobitti, Susan Lambert, Mario Manuli, Antonio Maria Marocco, Don Ignacio de Medina y Duque de Segorbe, Giovanni Messe, Rosetta Mosco Agresti, William Mostyn Owen, The Duke of Northumberland, Charlotte Oppè, Denys Oppè, Sandra Pinto, Julie Ronald, Don Antonio Sánchez González, L.B. Sanderson, Nicholas Serota, Giovan Battista Sersale, Timothy Stevens, Duncan Thomson, Giorgio Visocchi, Christopher White, David Wilson

Among the interesting cultural events which will be attended by the President of the Italian Republic, Francesco Cossiga, on his state visit to Britain, will be the exhibition on landscape painting entitled «In the Shadow of Vesuvius», which will definitely be one of the highlights of his visit.
This exhibition is in a sense a tribute to the friends of Italy who contributed to making the fortune of the Grand Tour of Italy.
It was above all visitors from Northern Europe who were instrumental in spreading the image of our country, and making it popular from shore to shore, all over the world. The majority of travellers were British, and a great many of the scenes painted of Italy, the Bel Paese, were of the Naples area.
It was Naples – in early times called Parthenope and Neapolis – which fired the imagination. This ancient world, still visible today with its churches and palaces, streets and squares, and above all its sea and sky, has always been a perfect setting, both unique and varied, for Vesuvius with its plume of smoke. And the imagination has responded to all this beauty through the lyrical media of poetry, music and painting, translating these scenes into the sublime sensations experienced during visits to Naples.
This exhibition revives that magic moment when heart and head become one and take in the complex and contradictory realities of Naples – her great history, beautiful landscapes but also the drama of everyday life.
These foreign visitors have returned among us. The sight of these works conjures up visions of the British painters in Naples, some staying longer than others, who were active for about a hundred years from the mid-18th. to mid-19th. century, guests of Sir William Hamilton and Neapolitan aristocrats. A particularly significant contribution was made by great artists like Richard Wilson, Wright of Derby, Thomas Jones, John Robert Cozens, Francis Towne and first and foremost Joseph Mallord William Turner, whose presence in Naples was fundamental for the rise of Neapolitan landscape painting some years later. The School of Posillipo, as this movement was called, produced romantic work, full of luminosity and colour, whose major exponents were Anton Pitloo and Giacinto Gigante and whose paintings are a fitting climax to this London exhibition.
However, we feel sure that this exhibition will go far beyond the artistic creativeness elicited by the theme of Naples. Visitors will sense that Art is the messenger of Love, expressing beauty inspired by the good, authentic values of life.

Francesco Sisinni
Director of the Superintendencies for the Environment, Architecture, Archeology, Art and History

It is now two hundred years since Sir William Hamilton, the British Envoy at the Bourbon court in Naples, was eagerly collecting paintings of the city and surrounding area. So that his fellow countrymen could also appreciate the fine works he had painstakingly collected, he sent some of the paintings back home, hoping that they would encourage the English to come and visit the Gulf of the Sirens.
England was already on friendly terms with Naples; the Neapolitan patriots exiled in London were made very welcome, as were Mazzini and Panizzi, the latter being given the great honour of directing the Library of the British Museum. Gladstone's disapproval of the behaviour of the Bourbon government resulted in the English giving assistance to Garibaldi. One of the factors which drew the English to Naples was certainly their admiration of the Campanian landscape, the charm of the Roman and Greek ruins at Pompeii and Paestum, and the tranquillity of Capri.
It was Hamilton again, one of the first in Europe to do so, who was responsible for making known these places and all their history. His picture gallery at Palazzo Sessa, the mansion where he lived for thirty years during the reign of King Ferdinand IV and Queen Caroline, boasted works by Titian and Guido Reni. However, the pictures which he liked best and which particularly pleased his foreign friends were the scenes of the Kingdom of Naples, the eruptions of Vesuvius, and scenes of popular life – the prototypes of the great 19th. century school of Neapolitan landscape painting. This splendid exhibition with the romantic title «In the Shadow of Vesuvius» was housed in Castel Sant'Elmo, a castle dominating the city and was visited by thousands of people who found it a source of infinite pleasure. This same exhibition is now about to be presented in London and will echo age-old emotions, evoking the nostalgia of the Grand Tour travellers who were so attached to this area. Many of the paintings on display belonged to Sir William, while others were commissioned by him from famous artists, others again he gave as presents to English friends as a «souvenir» of their stay or sent home to show the beauty of the Bay of Naples and Vesuvius, whose «shadow» was then the reddish hue of lava producing a spactacle which Hamilton could see from his terrace almost every evening. Visitors to the exhibition will also be able to admire the same scenes, part of this inspiring collection and the result of long and hard work on the part of the Superintendence for Historical and Cultural Heritage-Naples in collaboration with government agencies and art historians.
The Campanian Regional Government has been promoting cultural initiatives for some time now, and these are aimed at incentivating the social and economic aspects of Naples – this ancient land of Ulysses and the Sirens, philosophy, music, opera buffa; and home of Giambattista Vico, Benedetto Croce, Pergolesi, Paisiello, Cimarosa, Enrico Caruso and world-famous love-songs. So the idea of bringing together for the first time a large collection of some of the loveliest views of the area, from public and private collections all over Europe was approved wholeheartedly. Britain has provided some of the most beautiful works, a number of which have not been exhibited before, and which were taken back home by refined cultivated travellers and art-lovers, like Sir William Hamilton.
Those visiting the exhibition in London unfortunately will not be able to see in these pictures Campania as it is now – the passing of time affects everything. Nevertheless, we are committed to protecting the beauty of these legendary places in Campania and shall continue to do so. Centuries of history may in some way have spoilt the original charm of the landscape, but we are fortunate enough to have these magnificent paintings, carefully collected over the years, which will always testify to its beauty. As has been said, many of these come from British museums and collections, and we should like to take this opportunity of thanking the British Government and people for their loans, and the care with which they have preserved these unique views of Campania.
We hope that when the descendants of those great travellers visit Naples they will not be too disappointed. Rest assured, we shall do our best to give them as warm a welcome as they received in Sir William's time, that unique man who loved Naples so much that he expressed the wish of finishing his days «in the shadow of Vesuvius» – an everlasting tribute to the beauty of Naples and his love for Southern Italy.

Ferdinando Clemente di San Luca
Head of the Campanian Regional Government

The exhibition «In the Shadow of Vesuvius» was originally held in Naples between May and July this year and was highly acclaimed. The exhibition is now in London, and this is certainly no coincidence.

The original exhibition stressed the connection between Naples and the many foreign artists who visited the city, many of whom were British. Naples, the capital of the Kingdom of the Two Sicilies, was renowned for encouraging the spreading and exchange of culture across her borders, as a great European capital should do. The IRI, representing the largest group of Italian industries, has been present in Naples through a wide range of activities – electronics, shipbuilding, steelworks, telecommunications, transport, information technology, all of which are characterized by a particularly high standard of technology. The IRI is the sponsor of both the Naples and London exhibitions, the former reflecting the desire to preserve the history of this great city, and the latter testifying to an international commitment, made even more fitting by the birth of the European Single Market, which is just round the corner.

The very theme of the exhibition – great «views» of the city and bay – suggests far more though than mere collection of works of art, however rare, unusual and fascinating they may be. The «veduta» implies insight into the relationship between man and nature, city and country, man and history, great architecture and back alleys, all of which are part and parcel of today's new-found love of «the land».

The authoritative essays in the catalogue give a particularly vivid picture of Naples in the 18th century, and especially at the turn of that century. The result is a colourful portrait of Anglo-Italian society set in the fertile cosmopolitan cultural climate of the Enlightenment, though firmly rooted in their respective national traditions.

Among the great collectors and patrons of the arts are singular figures, who encouraged generations of artists. Here was a blending of experience which derived from the continual comparisons between these foreigners' own world and another one, so radically different in its customs and landscapes as to inspire the frequent depictions of mythological subjects, which were particularly popular at the time.

Nature and history, interest in volcanoes and earthquakes, and the classical world are the favourite themes of British landscape painting, which achieved such a complex stature and significance in Naples.

The links between Britain and the Kingdom of Naples were not only artistic: there were strong commercial connections too. Naples was the farthest point south on the Grand Tour for many rich young travellers. These connections were born of the extraordinary progress achieved in the British textile industry and in the field of mechanics, and which were to contribute to the beginnings of industry in Southern Italy in the early decades of the 19th century, and in particular to the newly built railway between Naples and Portici, the first one in Italy, full of symbolic importance.

The Naples exhibition was seen by the IRI as an encouragement to the Neapolitans to reflect on their great history, not in provincial or nostalgic terms but rather as a way of underlining that unique role the city played in Italy and abroad. The London exhibition pays tribute to the stimulating and fertile influence that British politics, economics and culture exerted on the laborious process of the development and emancipation of our country, and above all of the South.

The works gathered in this room are, then, a revisitation of Neapolitan history, both high and low cultures, in the warm and luminous tones of landscapes now world-famous. First and foremost though, these works stand to signify the heartfelt wish of our industrial group, the sponsor of both exhibitions, that the great European market will be the perfect occasion to renew the traditional bonds of friendship between our two countries in a climate of collaboration shortly to become a more complete integration.

Franco Nobili
Chairman of the IRI

Contents

Landscape Painting and Naples

Giuliano Briganti

Three Italian cities in particular are linked to the history of landscape painting – Rome, Venice and Naples, though other cities were also renowned for their beauty. The height of fame of this art form – the 18th. century – was synonymous with travels and the Grand Tour, and at this time landscape painting became a genre in its own right. It was undoubtedly influenced in the choice of different viewpoints and perspectives, in the «rules» establishing how the views were to be depicted and in the variations that were possible, by some of the most significant aspects of these three cities and by the period itself.
To explain this better, some considerations should first be made concerning the development of the landscape genre. In Venice, unlike Rome and Naples, landscape painting was very much the highest expression of local art (back in the 15th. and 16th. centuries certain distinctive landmarks had already been used as themes) and as is well known in the 18th. century it achieved particular distinction within the framework of genre painting mainly due to Antonio Canal, better known as Canaletto, who gave landscapes a new modern expression – an innovation which was developed by his nephew Bellotto. In Rome and Naples though, 18th. century landscape painting originated above all from Northern European culture which had close links with cartography. These origins were to give landscape painting that love of precision and perspective that would last for many a year.
A view is what one sees, said Roberto Longhi so succinctly forty years ago about that singular view of Piazza Pasquino in Rome, painted by the Genoese artist Sinibaldo Scorza in 1627. What one sees: in Longhi's words, «in this new faithful depiction a street can now be precisely what it is – a fragment of reality... while shadow falls on the buildings one by one, people put on their hats and the knife-grinder and the paper-vendor carry on with their jobs. Here is no map of the city». This faithfulness to reality would lead to the striking realism of that view of Palazzo Gravina in Naples by Viviano Codazzi, an artist from Bergamo, though the climax of this art form was to be reached by Velazquez not long later in his two views of Villa Medici painted during his second stay in Rome, in which reality takes shape from that fleeting encounter of light and objects in a flash of creativity. Here reality, captured just as it is coming into existence, is life itself. Yet despite this, it cannot be stated that this kind of vision is the origin of 18th. century topographical views, or of the landscape genre.
In the early pictures of the city in the 15th. century, and particularly in the 16th. and 17th. there are sweeping panoramas or bird's eye views which are the prototypes of landscape painting. In the transition from cartography to painting the stress lies on reality which materializes through a meticulously descriptive medium with the addition of figures, animals or ships which make the picture more lifelike. The panoramic view was used by the 16th. and 17th. century Northern European artists for the purpose of showing where the most important monuments of ancient Rome lay within the city walls, though these views were sometimes very realistic like the one painted by Maarten van Heemskerck from Monte Caprino in 1534, or the even clearer bird's eye views of 1550 by Anton van den Wyngaerde of the Baths of Costantine. However, these pictures covering 360° did not open the way to landscape painting as such, but rather the circular panoramic views of the 18th. century, and particularly those of the 19th. with their central observation point.
It was really the views like the one by Hendrick van Cleve around 1550 of Colle Oppio seen from very high up at an almost unreal angle which was to herald the birth of landscape painting, or a view of Naples by Jan van Stinemolen in 1582 seen from a double viewpoint. These views had «a high horizon like the Flemish use, whose landscapes are majestic scenes rather then specific views» as Giulio Mancini so aptly remarked around 1625. That kind of scene, from a viewpoint which was practically impossible to reach (at least before the invention of Montgolfier's hot air balloon) was able to show many more things – buildings, squares, streets, gardens, old ruins than the more conventionally angled pictures, where the scene rarely had any lifelike quality due to the contrived perspectives used, clearly taken from the technique of map-making. In the latter, reality was definitely not «what one sees», because one could not really perceive it, but rather what the artist wanted to make visible, to define and describe. The relationship between cartography and landscape painting has been studied by Cesare De Seta and Gianni Romano, who has written an extremely interesting essay on landscape looking at this relationship in the framework of the great cultural and historical events which have decided how one should see certain aspects of the real landscape and how to react to the landscape in art.
So it is the maps of the city and the use of notes *about* reality and not the direct contact with reality (with «what one sees») which are the basis of views seen from above where the landmarks emerge as they really are, while little attention is given to the rest of the city (buildings without history). At that time maps were not even drawn to scale on the basis of exact measurements, and consequently they were little more than mere descriptions of the city seen from the zenith, where each building and monument was reproduced axonometrically.
So in a sense there is an organic development in the history of views of the city – almost a continuous line starting with maps and topographical materials with buildings drawn in perspective, moving on to bird's eye views, then close-ups of places of interest but always seen from a higher than normal viewpoint, finally coming closer and closer to a more lifelike portrayal. This line of development can be seen quite clearly in the history of the Neapolitan landscape starting with the Tavola Strozzi, which was probably the work of a cartographer-cum-painter active in the second half of the 15th. century, and continues with the views by Pieter Brueghel, Jan van Essen and Didier Barra. Barra's views dated 1647 would appear to be his personal version of the map by Alessandro Baratta of 1629, but in its turn it was used as a model by mapmakers, for example Stopendael's map of 1653. The trend progresses with views by Gaspar Van Wittel, Antonio Joli, Hendrick Van Lint, Gabriele Ricciardelli and Pietro Antoniani. There is no doubt in my opinion, that it is precisely this line of development and iconographic motivation which are the distinctive features in the depiction of Neapolitan landscapes.

Let us return for a moment to the introduction, which considers how the various pictorial requirements of the cities conditioned the different kinds of views making up this genre. Unlike Rome – city of *mirabilia* where the main themes chosen by landscape painters were mostly single monuments or groups of them (in the late 17th. century Van Wittel was to influence this genre for a great many years by his choice of viewpoints and composition) – Naples increasingly owed her fame to the extraordinarily beautiful position she enjoyed at the centre of the Bay. So it is no coincidence that the most popular view, starting with the Tavola Strozzi and continuing right up until the late 18th. century, was the panoramic view from the sea of the city lying along the coast, dominated from above by Castel Sant'Elmo and the Charterhouse of San Martino, with the focus of attention on Castel Nuovo, the city centre and the port nearby. A veritable «scenic majesty» as Mancini once described it. Van Wittel's favourite view which depicted the port and was also painted by other artists, should perhaps be considered as a close-up or rather a detail taken from the central part of that familiar scene. Neither in Venice nor in Rome, where the rules of landscape painting had been established by Van Wittel who had started out in 1675 as a map-maker to the «engineer» Cornelis Meyer, did the great panorama born of the map-drawing technique last for so long as in Naples. Here landscape painters like Tommaso Ruiz, Hendrick Van Lint or Johann Greevenbroek continued throughout the 18th. century to propose the same general view of the city which appears in the Tavola Strozzi and until the genre of landscape painting declined it was the city viewed from high up which prevailed, and made the combination of coastline, sea and urban landscape so impressive, seen from the right or from the left.

The 18th. century was undoubtedly one of the most prosperous and fertile periods of Naples' history, and she owed her fame as one of the most fascinating European cities to the incomparable beauty of the Bay, the ruins of Pompeii and Herculaneum which brought to light two entire cities covered in lava and ash by the eruption of Vesuvius in 79 A.D. and which were an inexhaustible source of works of art and information about antiquity, and last but not least Vesuvius. These three elements represented the basic leitmotivs of 18th. century art – the Picturesque, Classical and Sublime.

So it was in this century that Parthenope swiftly gained fame, with the spreading of landscape painting and the study of places where Nature's beauty was ennobled by the presence of what Man had built and the traces of past greatness. The Picturesque was represented by Nature, generous to Man and magnificent in its variety of forms; the Sublime was seen as Nature overwhelming the onlooker and filling him with awe with its unpredictable force; the Classical was the highest point that art could reach, and encouraged by «philosophical ideas» aroused interest in the amazing manifestations of Nature, searching for the causes and studying the effects. For this reason that incomparable display of art, landscape and spectacular natural phenomena which could be seen all along the coast from Capo Miseno to Punta Campanella, Baia to Herculaneum and Pompeii, the Phlegrean Fields to Vesuvius, from Ischia to Capri and which comprised such varied sights as fire and water, luxuriant vegetation and dry hardened lava beds, the frightening and the peaceful, liberally scattered with traces of Classical art and architecture could be appreciated in the 18th. century as never before. In fact, Naples fully deserved her reputation as one of *the* places to visit on the Grand Tour by «enlightened» foreign travellers.

The creation of a new sentimental and intellectual climate which was so typical of the Enlightenment was generally speaking due to the contribution and encouragement of foreign residents and travellers who had brought to Naples their love and spirit of observation, sense of aesthetics, curiosity for science and antiquity, and it was quite natural that all should be reflected in landscape painting, even directly affecting it. However, the old type of bird's eye view was still being produced with an increase in the number of viewpoints, the inclusion of Vesuvius as a background to the general views of city, with an extension north towards the Phlegrean Fields, or looking out to sea from the city, or with Capri and Ischia, and for these sweeping views maps still continued to be the inspiration. But alongside tradition new ideas were blossoming, inspired by the Picturesque – a genre where Carlo Bonavia excelled following in the footsteps of the great Vernet – the Sublime which inspired Pierre Jacques Volaire in his views of Vesuvius erupting by night, and the Classical with the first views of Paestum and Pompeii. All these subjects were to enrich Neapolitan landscape painting, which had previously been almost exclusively based on the city itself.

The history of landscape painting underwent a remarkable transformation from 1750 onwards, as the curiosity and interest shown by people tended to be directed to more specific features of the landscape. Elsewhere I have written that the real *invitation au voyage*, was the longing to travel which stimulated our 18th. century ancestors and was the driving force behind the Grand Tour. One of the strongest desires of the Enlightenment was to widen one's knowledge, to get out and about, physically not through the pages of a book, leaving behind what was familiar – in a sense, a search for freedom. Travelling was a kind of geographical experience which saw landscape painting not only as a precious object to take home as a souvenir, but as a record, something to be studied. This is how a particular kind of painting took shape, which left its mark on Naples too – the landscape painting of the artists who travelled around Europe and Italy above all (but also in the Near East), along the most beaten tracks of the Grand Tour, a favourite with collectors of antiquities too.

Inseparable from their sketchbooks or leather-cased folios and their folding seats, whether alone or in company of rich fellow travellers and their learned guides and friends, or as part of a group headed by architects and men-of-letters, they sketched whatever caught their eye on their travels, or whatever they were asked to draw, and they finished their drawings and made watercolours or oil paintings of them in their studios or while resting at an inn. Travelling artists, like Kniep who was accompanying Goethe on his journey through Italy, or Giovan Battista Lusieri who worked in Greece for Lord Elgin, also left some wonderful views of Naples. No less beautiful were the illustrations for Saint-Non's *Voyage Pit-*

toresque de Naples et Sicile by the artists who were travelling with Vivant-Denon. Their work is characterised by a spirit of observation which is very similar to painters who were in Naples on a more permanent basis, like Volaire, Pietro Fabris (who illustrated Sir William Hamilton's *Campi Phlegraei*) and above all Philipp Hackert, an artist who contributed more than any other to changing the appearance of Neapolitan landscape painting. However, right up until its decline this genre remained faithful to what was considered its essential requirement – visual description, even in its highest expressions, like the beautiful views by Claude Joseph Vernet. There were superb exceptions to the rule, of course – Naples by night, illuminated by amazing flashes of light by Wright of Derby, or the wintry, solitary, oppressive views of Naples by John Robert Cozens, all visions which are far removed from the cultural environment in which the 18th. century topographical view had developed. However, it is not until the work of Thomas Jones, that lonely, introverted artist and the enchanting realism of his views of sunny Neapolitan rooftops and terraces in the still blue noonday light that one can really say that a view is none other than «what one sees».

Landscape Painting in Naples – From a Portrait of the City to Scenes of Strong Emotion

Nicola Spinosa

Landscape painting in Naples has been correctly identified by modern critics as beginning in Gaspar Van Wittel's first visit to Naples in 1700, in his light and lustrous portraits of the city which he made for the viceroy of the period, the Duke of Medinaceli. Van Wittel's clear-cut views and his vibrant use of colour can be considered the first modern contribution to Neapolitan landscape painting decades before the city reached the peak of its fame and prosperity under Charles and Ferdinand of Bourbon. Half a century later, Joseph Vernet was to take up the challenge once more, and this is when landscape painting as we know it really began.

The earliest pictures of Naples (15th. and 16th. centuries) are seen from a limited number of viewpoints – from the front, the sea, above or from a bird's eye view, painted on panels, canvas and on vellum. They are a meticulous and detailed portrait of the city, where it is possible to trace the slow progress of urban development by means of the different interpretations of perspective, the change in viewpoints and visual field and the wide-ranging social and cultural transformations. By the 18th. and 19th. centuries, the artists began to specialize in new viewpoints, for example from the east or west, or from the hills of Castel Sant'Elmo and Capodimonte, but they also began to look further afield to the Phlegrean Fields, the Amalfi and Sorrento coasts and Paestum, turning their attention to new themes like the countryside, villages, ruins, sea-shores and hills, to complement the urban landscape of Naples. These themes also became popular due to the awakening of interest throughout Europe in the Mediterranean landscape, and in science and archeology. The aim was now to find a way of interpreting through images the emotional reaction produced in the onlooker by such places and sights.

Until recently art historians and critics have given particular importance to historical development and the pictorial techniques used to depict the city, neglecting the relationship between the quality of the work, the perception of the landscape and the models and techniques chosen. It would perhaps have been more useful to discover how these artists were able to portray so well that vast and deep human experience composed of culture and sentiment, perception and emotion, the individual and the collective, which emerged so strongly from behind their masterly use of brushwork. Relationship and influence (on the part of clients) are always valuable if one wants to understand the forerunners of landscape painting and learn more about it in the 18th. and 19th. centuries.

Our survey starts back in the 15th. century, and attempts to identify the models, interconnections and variations of the urban «portrait» without losing sight of the style, period and attribution of the paintings.

The Tavola Strozzi (c. 1465) is usually seen as being the first landmark in «modern» views of Naples, and it is the most complete picture extant of Ferrante of Aragona's famous capital – an objective and analytical representation of the city's buildings, which is more typical of the Northern European townscapes. Generally speaking, pictures of this kind were painted for official purposes, at least until the mid-17th. century. Some other significant works of the same kind were painted by Pieter Brueghel, François de Nomé, Didier Barra and Jan van Essen between the 16th. and 17th. centuries.

The urban landscape showing details of the city or its surroundings painted during the «naturalist» period under the influence of Caravaggio can be seen in some works by Scipione Compagno, typified by the substantiality of Nature; or in the irresistible attraction of the eruptions of Vesuvius felt by certain Northern European artists and again in works by Viviano Codazzi and Domenico Gargiulo (nicknamed Micco Spadaro), who treated the landscape with the sensitivity of more modern painters. Codazzi stressed the perspective of ruins or town and country residences seen by the eyes of the onlooker, complete with figures by Aniello Falcone or Domenico Gargiulo. These views were not dictated by any topographical technique or specific model and developed their own naturalistic interpretation of the theme, even entering into the life of the inhabitants.

Between the end of the 17th. and the beginning of the 18th. centuries landscapes were inspired by the work of Salvator Rosa, in a Baroque and imaginary atmosphere, decorative and idealized. One artist who was able to inject concreteness and objectivity into a framework of classicism and solemnity (typified by Solimena's works) was the Dutchman Gaspar Van Wittel, whose pictorial innovations were a preview of the Enlightenment. He was called to Naples to undertake the task of depicting some famous places, like Largo di Palazzo (in front of the Royal Palace), Castel dell'Ovo, the port, the newly developed Chiaja district, Posillipo, Pozzuoli and the Sorrento coast.

The viceroy, the Duke of Medinaceli, had ambitious plans for Naples and ordered Van Wittel to record all the details as exactly as possible – there was officially no necessity as yet to actually capture emotions visually. Van Wittel is a synthesis of naturalistic experiences (Codazzi and the Roman Bamboccianti) and the typical cultural and technical qualities of the Dutch school. His work is a skilful process of visualizing reality through the use of perspective and sophisticated pictorial media which succeed in creating a brilliant, concrete and infinite visual emotion. He captures particularly well that extraordinary combination of nature and artifice in the city and the vast proportions of the views with immediacy and genuine beauty.

So in the 18th. century it was not so much the new ways of depicting the city that were to contribute to the development of landscape painting, but rather a different capacity for pictorial interpretation, especially of the impact with the amazing variety of landscapes to be found. The innovations by Gaspar Van Wittel though, were a closed chapter for many years, with only brief instances of good quality work emerging, like Falciatore and Coccorante, until the appearance on the scene of Vernet.

Vernet's compositions on canvas are so evocative that one feels one is part of a great natural theatre with all its human and everyday events, where the actors are drawn from both the poor people and the aristocracy. In his drawings and paintings the city is not only a group of buildings, streets and squares but a living organism which has to be penetrated, perceived and understood in all its overt and covert aspects.

Naples was now one of the places to visit for educated travellers on the Grand Tour, who were consumed by curiosity for «science», and it had become an independent kingdom with an «enlightened» court encourag-

ing urban development, the arts and crafts, and culture. Vernet was the first to produce a fascinating portrait of this great cosmopolitan stage with Vesuvius smoking in the background, and his beautiful scenic and decorative effects complement his spectacular use of light and colour.
At this time English painters were beginning to arrive in Naples, but also French, German and Austrian ones. Generally speaking, the Italians were not very interested in depicting townscapes (though there were some exceptions like Antonio Joli and Pietro Fabris) because they preferred those sacred and profane themes of a highly decorative nature which were ordered by their clients. Despite this, it was a Neapolitan painter - Carlo Bonavia - who between 1755-88 was to pick up where Vernet had left off, producing some very attractive views, in which he intensified the emotional impact, blending caprice and objectivity. The particularly high quality of his style, the luminosity of his colour and the skill at portraying physical phenomena strike the onlooker in very much the same way as Vernet does. Although Bonavia was influenced by Salvator Rosa like other local painters, his work was more imaginative and poetic when dealing with popular themes like ruins. In fact, he was to be the only Neapolitan who gained European recognition.
From now on, there was a new way of looking at nature, which was no longer faithful imitation but a lyrical surge of emotion. Aesthetics counted now, rather than the ethics of science. And this new conception of nature was to have a strong effect on a significant work of the times, the album *Voyage Pittoresque* by the Abbé de Saint Non, compiled between 1759 and 1781, which is a pictorial guide to Southern Italy, containing 170 illustrations of particularly fine quality.
One of the most interesting French artists in Naples was Pierre-Jacques Volaire, who became popular for his strongly emotive painting, his attractive use of colour, and his great skill in depicting the landscape. He did not follow the contemporary trend of scenic and decorative work, preferring to see his themes just as a foreign taveller to the area would, interpreting them in a blend of the picturesque and the sublime. He is most famous for his views of Vesuvius, usually at night-time in the moonlight. Vesuvius was fast becoming a favourite theme with artists and would be depicted in a wide variety of interpretations and from many different angles. After almost 500 years of inactivity the volcano suddenly came to life in 1631. Before this date there were very few pictures of Vesuvius, but even in the late 17th. century there was little pictorial innovation regarding this subject - Didier Barra, Scipione Compagno and Domenico Gargiulo among others, were more interested in linking the volcano with religious ritual typical of the Neapolitan area, or using the pictorial device simply to record volcanic activity. By 1770 though, Vesuvius had become an object of curiosity at home and abroad, on a par with Pompeii and Herculaneum, which aroused both admiration in onlookers (Goethe talked of «this superb spectacle») but also fear - «a new wonderful yet horrible sight». Vesuvius was, in fact, a perfect theme for a romantic interpretation, with its tongues of fire, lava flows and smoke, at once a heroic and diabolic image: «a new language of picturesque romanticism» as Benedict Nicholson said.
In 1774-75 Wright of Derby painted a fiery version of Vesuvius. While he was in Naples he met the British Ambassador Sir William Hamilton, the famous portrait-painter George Romney (Hamilton's guest) and the artist Thomas Jones. Wright of Derby painted several studies in oil, in gouache and watercolour, and his work can be said to mark the beginning of intense activity by a group of English painters, which was to conclude with the great Joseph Mallord William Turner in the early 19th. century. Wright chose famous subject like Virgil's Tomb, Posillipo and the Amalfi coast, portraying them realistically but also with genuine emotion. Thomas Jones, who was in Naples between 1778 and 1783, also produced some very fine work, mostly sketches in oil on paper from life, but his favourite subjects were not the popular ones of the time. He preferred buildings - terraces and roofs, unusual angles and views of the city. There is an extraordinary visual and emotional intensity in his work, to such an extent that it appears «modern», almost a forerunner of Corot's style, with bold viewpoints and perspectives reminiscent of photographic techniques.
The work of the English landscapists offered the first really modern and sensitive interpretation of this art form, subtly poetic yet rooted in the reality of the Mediterranean - nature and colour, light and emotion. It was the watercolourist John Robert Cozens who showed great skill in translating into luminous colour the countryside round Naples, from the Phlegrean Fields to Paestum, with swift, bold brushstrokes, producing a delicate effect yet pervaded by strong emotion.
Another interesting artist who preferred watercolour was Giovan Battista Lusieri (active in Naples between 1782-93) whose transparency distinguished him from the English school, but the overall effect was no less impressive. He liked large compositions covering two sheets of paper with sweeping views of the Bay of Naples or the Phlegrean Fields, exalting the natural beauty of these places through his light, sparkling colours. This crystalline clearness is more reminiscent of his contemporary, the German painter Philipp Hackert than the English, or of the gouaches by Saverio Della Gatta. Lusieri was immensely popular with Sir William Hamilton and Lord Elgin who ordered many pictures from him.
But not all clients wanted to experience the strong emotions engendered by the picturesque and sublime. There were many, like the court and certain foreign collectors, who simply wanted a record of significant events in Naples, religious and historical, or more frivolous ones like processions and entertainment, featuring the clergy and the nobility as protagonists. These pictures were deprived of any lyrical sentiment and stuck to a matter-of-fact representation of reality. This tendency was to develop in the 19th. century, when there was less motivation in the way of ideals, and would lead to the creation of a series of sentimental and banal stereotypes which would accompany the image of Naples for a great many years - the inevitable visual cliché.
Yet the first painters to indulge in this kind of style produced work which was both striking and good quality, like Antonio Joli. This artist from Modena worked for Charles of Bourbon and as a scene-painter at the San Carlo theatre from 1761 onwards. His versatility enabled him to paint both landscapes and «official» subjects, such as the departure of Charles

C.-J. Vernet, Naples from La Marinella. Alwhick, Duke of Northumberland's Collection.

C.-J. Vernet, Naples from Mergellina. Alwhick, Duke of Northumberland's Collection.

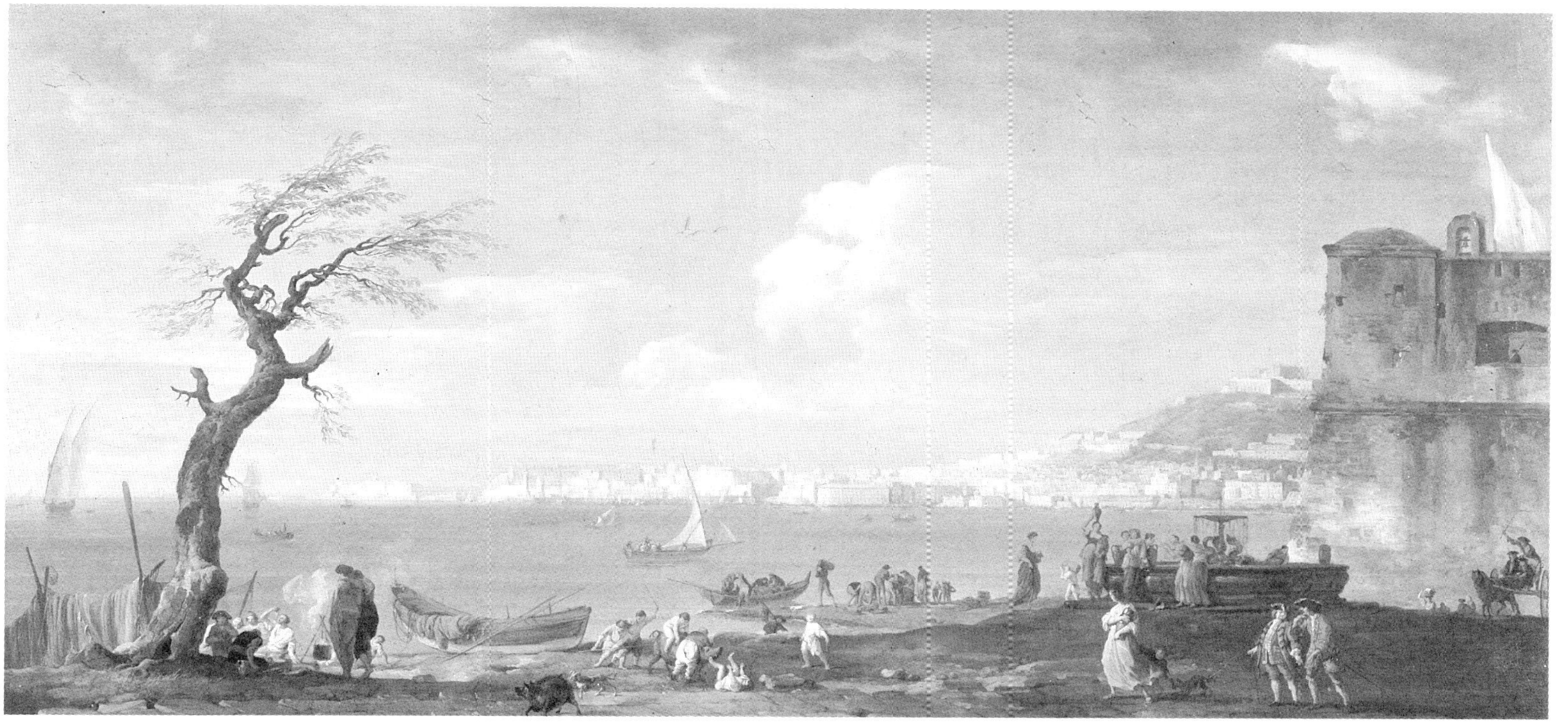

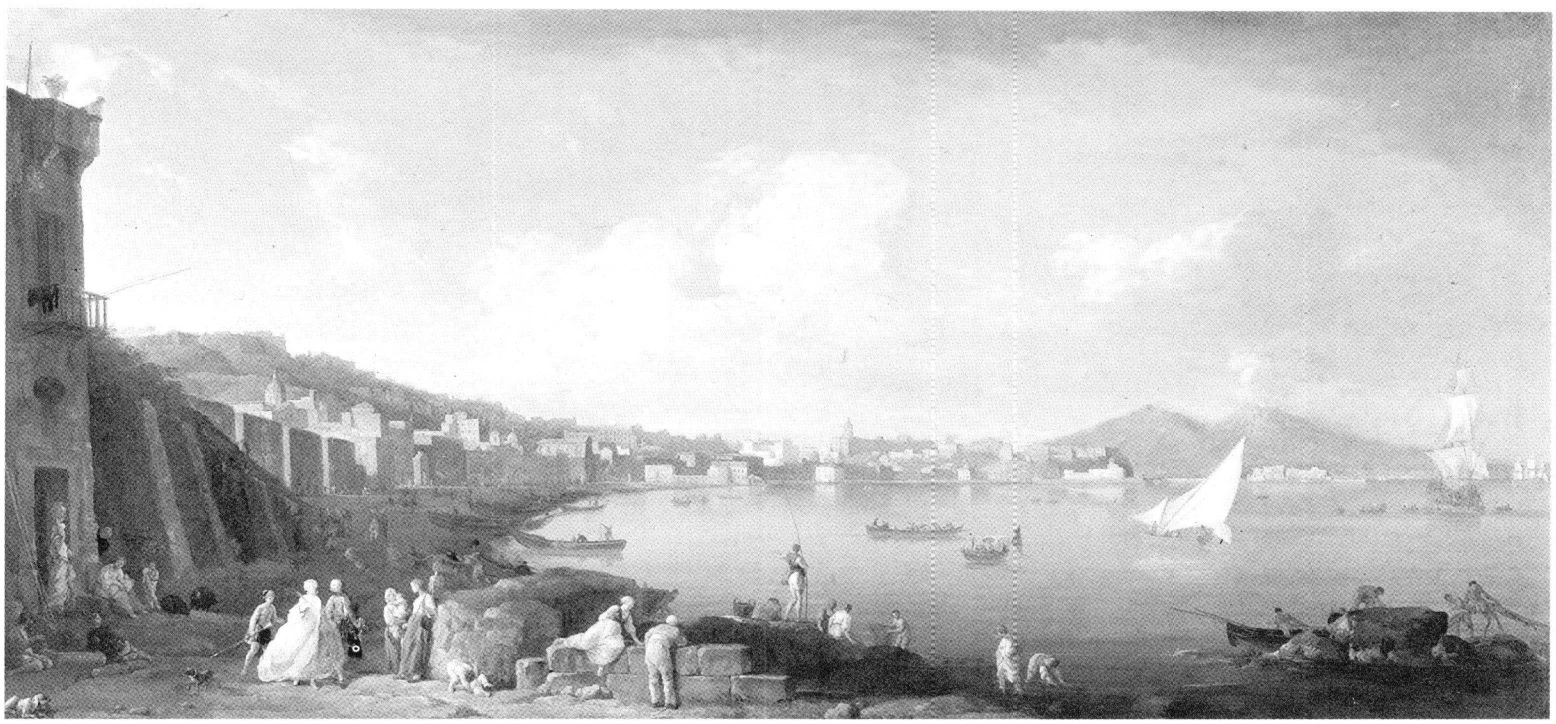

from Naples on his way back to Spain. Joli's main achievement was to depict an extraordinarily fertile slice of Neapolitan life – streets and palaces, churches and castles, ball-games, processions of boats or courtiers with the city in the background. His training in the style of Canaletto and his assimilation of Van Wittel's style induces a tendency to clear-cut images, a faithful use of perspective and a wealth of detail. His eye is penetrating but does not search for cultural, ideological or existential motivations.
For Lord Brudenell, another important patron, he painted landscapes which show his skill in portraying riches and rags with «enlightened» intelligence, and these works are undoubtedly of much better quality than his official portraits of the city.
Another painter, the Neapolitan Gabriele Ricciardelli studied in the Classical style and was successful in capturing a certain «watercolour effect» with soft pale colours, though he was never able to reach Joli's standard. Closer to Joli in intensity and brilliance is Pietro Fabris, especially in his urban views of ceremonies and court entertainment which were intended for an international market. His stirring renderings of folk themes is subtly reminiscent of genre painting and in particular Rossi, Bonito and Falciatore. He is a master at combining reality and fantasy in a Neapolitan landscape which is perceived with great lucidity and decorative brilliance worthy of no less a painter than Bonavia. His favourite subjects are scenes of everyday life in the suburbs or on the sea-front and he attracted clients from all over Europe, who were intrigued by the costumes and traditions of Naples. His style is pleasant to look at and easy to decipher, which contributed to his success, though at times he tended to fall into stereotyped work. His best paintings are those around 1775-80, in oil on canvas and gouache on paper. However, it is the gouaches painted for Sir William Hamilton's *Campi Phlegraei* (1776) which are his masterpieces, with their fortunate blend of scientific phenomena, visual emotions and Classical references. Hamilton was instrumental in bringing out the talent of this artist, with his refined, modern, uninhibited character. Fabris can definitely be considered one of the greatest landscape artists of the first half of the 18th. century, a forerunner of the picturesque and sublime, a style which was to reach its fame with Hackert and the English landscapists.
Two artists who follow in the footsteps of Joli and Fabris are Saverio Della Gatta and Alessandro D'Anna. Della Gatta's work in particular is of high quality, with bright luminous colour but in the delicate hues of gouache and watercolour, again reminiscent of Lusieri. Very popular with collectors of Neapolitan paintings today, Della Gatta and D'Anna both specialised in genre scenes of Vesuvius and scenes inspired by folklore. These themes, unfortunately, were to be heavily exploited in following years for sale to tourists as souvenirs of Naples, resulting in a decline in technique, style and content.
But before this tendency took root, and at the same time as Fabris was producing his best work, Neoclassicism reached the height of its popularity, interpreted to perfection by Philipp Hackert. Modern criticism has been perhaps unduly severe about this painter, rating him no more than a trite mannerist, limited by Neoclassical stylemes.
However, Hackert's entire Neapolitan production was the result of experience gained in Europe and Rome in particular, in the Classicist tradition. Hackert though, was quite opposed to the romantic trend developed by the English. He preferred to penetrate the physical manifestations of the nature he saw before him and discover its secrets, then translate his impressions through a medium of simplification and purification into their essential forms – an almost arcadian interpretation, revisited with the spirit of the Enlightenment.
Obviously Hackert's penetrating approach excluded any spontaneous production of impressions, also because he felt that emotions should not be fleeting or purely sentimental. His work required a deep knowledge of history, careful planning and study, even the taking of notes about the physical properties of his subjects. All this was necessary for the transmission of the authenticity and solemnity, the truth and simplicity of the Classical image – a picture of life from life, the ideal of eternal tangible beauty, distilled in his views ranging from the Phlegrean Fields to Sorrento, Caserta, Paestum, Capri and Ischia.
His use of oil or gouache produced a new visual clarity, nothing like the technique of the elegant Vernet, the picturesqueness of Volaire, the sublimity of Wright of Derby, the rarefied luminosity of Thomas Jones, the atmosphere of Cozens or the delicate transparencies of Lusieri. Hackert is definitely emotion though, but controlled through skilful technique and pure erudition.
A close friend of Hackert's was the great Goethe, and not surprisingly they both had the same views on painting – they disdained tradition, folklore and easy sentiment, insisting that the landscape should be reproduced as faithfully as possible, even if paradoxically the result often seemed more unreal than real. After the flight to Palermo of Hackert's patron Ferdinand IV during the short-lived Neapolitan Revolution in 1799, Hackert left Naples with Tischbein, a fellow painter, thus decreeing the end of this extremely significant period of art in Naples.
In 1794 the Swiss artist Ducros fled to Naples from Rome, where he had been accused of conspiracy. Prevalently an engraver and watercolourist, Ducros specialised in landscapes and he had already gained fame in Rome with his views of the surrounding countryside. Initially trained to depict ideal landscapes, he was also influenced by the startlingly modern ideas of Piranesi. Ducros manipulates reality and objectivity, combining them with imaginary topography, and Nature which is «larger than life». With his exuberant and uncontrollable vegetation, covering the ruins and continually encroaching on them, he seems to be saying that what man has made counts for nothing in comparison with Nature. Active in Naples until 1805, he was also strongly influenced by the Sturm und Drang movement. In fact his work on Neapolitan themes, which are seen by the majority of artists as havens of repose and tranquillity, are contorted by Ducros into disturbing, passionate sights, dictated by the violence and brute force of Nature. His watercolours (often touched up with tempera or varnish) can be said to interpret that restlessness of the emotions, that visual immediacy which ends up by countering any optical or sentimental pleasure, which was so typical of the successful mythical representations of Neapolitan landscapes.

J.B. Camille Corot, Vesuvius.
Paris, Louvre.

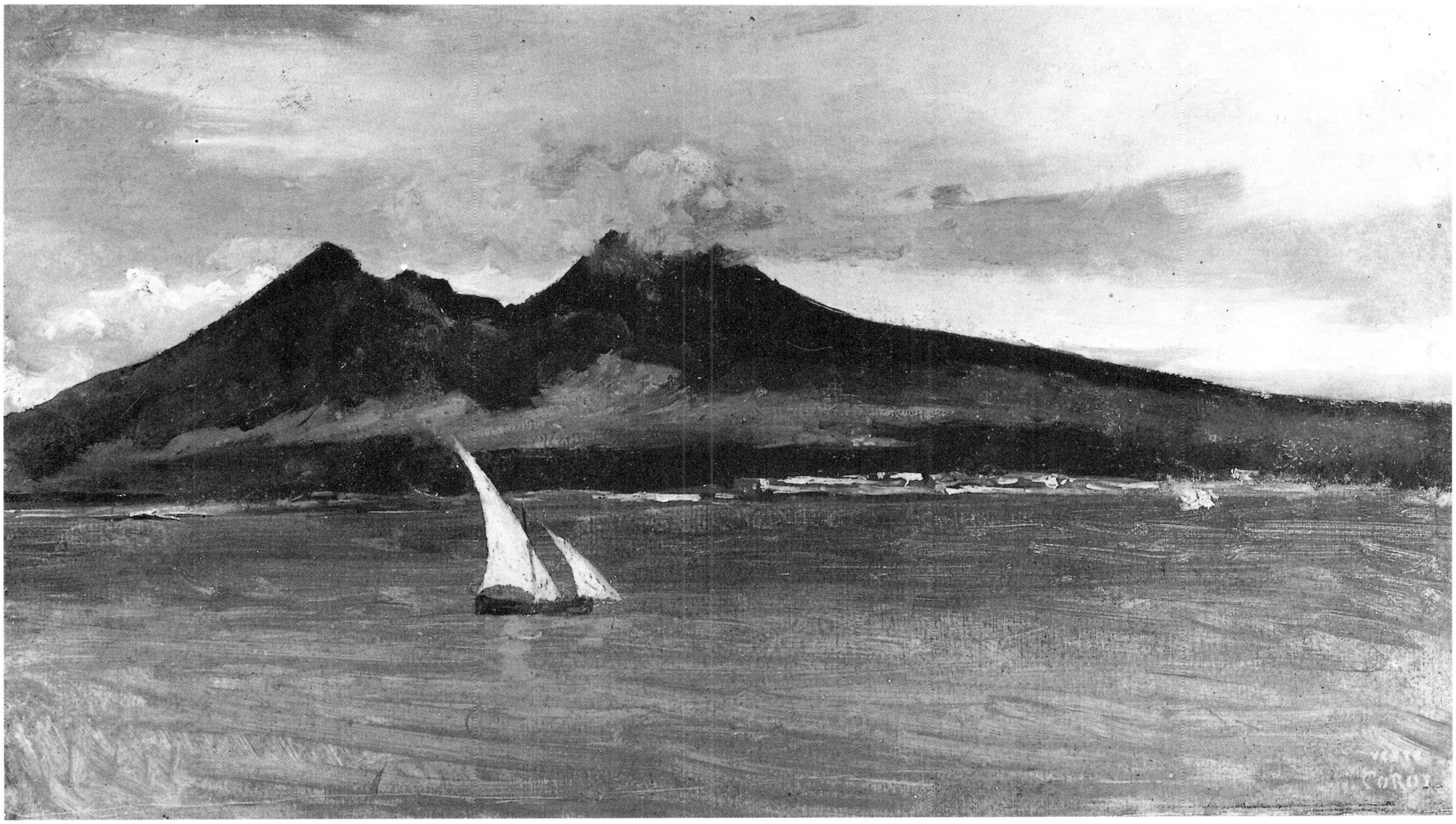

Under Joseph Bonaparte and Murat, foreign painters still flocked to Naples, especially from France, following what was now the established tradition of sophisticated, erudite landscapes, at times conventional in taste but nevertheless full of light and atmosphere.
Anton Sminck Van Pitloo is usually considered the first exponent of the Posillipo School. In the early 19th. century, this Dutch artist learned much about landscape painting from Dahl and Catel, in particular how to get over that overwhelming natural beauty of the area in innovative terms of romantic intensity. The classicist, idealised landscape was now a thing of the past, with the stress on free expression, unconventionality and play on light. Pitloo succeeds extremely well in modifying the traditional view of Naples, but without cutting himself off from past experiences, as he recognised how important the «atmospherics» of the English landscapists were and how vibrant the luminosity of Dahl.
The Russian Schedrin was also working in Naples during the decade 1819-28, and was the first of a series of Russians who came to paint the splendours of Posillipo and Sorrento. To a certain extent Schedrin's style is similar to Pitloo's and for this reason he is sometimes considered as being part of the Posillipo School, also due to his picturesque representation of natural beauty, the intensity of his sentimental insight and the great variety of light and atmosphere.
However, the most significant artist of the Posillipo School was undoubtedly Giacinto Gigante, who had studied landscape painting with Pitloo and Huber. Despite his training in the purely illustrative technique of topography, around the 1830's Gigante was already producing pieces of work of such lyricism as to make him one of the greatest romantic landscape artists. He was not only able to put into practice what he had gleaned from the English school – the picturesque emotion of the impressions evoked by the sunny Mediterranean – but also to use elements typical of much earlier painters, like Micco Spadaro or Salvator Rosa, perhaps even from Ribera's works of around 1635.
Another exponent of the Posillipo School, the Italianised Fleming Frans Vervloet, around the same time as Gigante was painting landscapes from life, creating his own interpretation of vibrant soft hues. He also worked «en plein air» and «sur nature», transferring his impressions directly on to canvas, board or paper, thus capturing a fleeting moment, a strong emotion.
Two other great artists who contributed to the modernity and intensity of the Posillipo School were Turner and Corot. Turner was in Naples in 1819 to record the landscapes between the Phlegrean Fields and Paestum, with his idiosyncratic use of dramatically unconventional angles and atmospheres. His paintings were displayed in Rome in 1828 and no doubt were seen by Pitloo and the young Gigante.
Corot is recorded in Naples between 1817-21 and again in 1828, when he painted a set of views of the Bay of Naples with great essentiality and immediacy, and with immense visual emotion through the medium of spots of light and pure colour. This must have impressed Gigante and Pitloo, giving them interesting new ideas.
From the mid-19th. century onwards, the theme of Naples and the surrounding area as a «portrait» in the collective imaginary was now pretty much exhausted, after having offered so much in the way of surges of emotion, bright strokes of colour, transparency and continuously changing atmosphere. So perhaps it is no coincidence that the downward trend in the image of Naples was to herald the city's slow and inevitable decline as a centre of European culture.

«Classic Ground»: British Artists in Naples in the 18th and 19th Centuries

Lindsay Stainton

In 1783 the twenty-three year old William Beckford [1] published a book chiefly devoted to his impressions of Italy with the haunting title *Dreams, Making Thoughts and Incidents,* a phrase that is also expressive of the reactions of those British artists who visited Naples during the eighteenth and early nineteenth centuries. One of the most extraordinary personalities of his era, Beckford was a romantic traveller and recluse, who became a legendary figure in his own lifetime, first for his extravagance as a collector and as the builder of Fonthill, second for his extravagance of character, particularly as revealed in his oriental tale *Vathek,* published in 1787, a fantasy that has exerted a powerful influence on many admirers. In the context of the present exhibition, however, he is most significant as one of the major patrons of John Robert Cozens (1752-1797), arguably the most important British landscape artist to work in Italy in the eighteenth century: in 1782 Cozens accompanied Beckford to Naples, where he found the inspiration for a number of his finest works, the visual counterparts to Beckford's *Dreams, Making Thoughts and Incidents.*

The lure of Italy was a critical factor in the development of British landscape art. Although not the first landscapist to work in Italy (J. R. Cozens's father, Alexander, was in Rome in 1746), Richard Wilson was the first to crystallize the image of the country as «Classic ground» [2] and to evoke that heightened sense of emotion which the sentient visitor experienced in places hallowed by classical associations or of renowned beauty. Wilson visited Naples briefly two or three times during his years in Italy, sketching subjects and later developing them into paintings encapsulating a vision of the area that was to influence British artists until the 1820s.

Trained originally as a portrait painter, Wilson had travelled to Italy in 1750 where under the influence first of Zuccarelli and then of Vernet he turned to landscape. His response to Italy (where he stayed until 1756 or 7) and that of his patrons was generated above all by a knowledge of and profound admiration for the history, civilization and landscape of the country's classical past. *Lake Avernus,* c. 1760, painted shortly after he returned to England, expresses these sentiments. The countryside around Naples was associated above all with the poetry of Virgil: from a viewpoint close to the grotto of the Cumaean Sibyl where, according to Virgil, Aeneas had descended into the underworld, the spectator looks across the lake and the Gulf of Pozzuoli to Capri in the far distance. Wilson's audience would have understood such associations without any necessity for him to make an overt reference in the title of the painting. The tranquillity of the extensive landscape and the muted, harmonious tonality suggest a sense of repose and meditation that seems to spring naturally from the subject but which Wilson has in fact carefully controlled. In this respect, Wilson's paintings derive their greatest force from subtle allusion to the work of Claude Lorrain. The composition of *Lake Avernus,* with its framing trees on the left, receding planes of light and shade and enormous expanse of sky, is in direct emulation of Claude; Wilson has drawn on a recognized tradition, thus linking his view of Lake Avernus not only with the classical past but also with an ideal golden age of pastoral art. Although not the first British artist to have made use of the pantheon of seventeenth century painters, Wilson was one of the earliest to recognize the potential of combining the depiction of a real place with the traditions of ideal landscape painting.

An important aspect of Wilson's influence, and one of the ways in which a knowledge of his subject matter and style were more widely disseminated, was his role as a teacher. Among his pupils was Thomas Jones, whose name is indissolubly linked with Naples. Born in 1742, a younger son of a Welsh landowning family, he had been intended for the church, but when his great-uncle who had guaranteed his education died intestate, he left Oxford without a degree and in due course became a pupil of his fellow countryman Richard Wilson. The paintings he exhibited before he went to Italy were, to judge from those that have survived, somewhat crude historical landscapes in the manner of his master, offering few clues to his subsequent development. He was thirty-four years old when he eventually arrived in Italy in 1776, fulfilling an ambition that had developed from his study of Wilson's paintings and drawings. As he was later to write, «I had seen and Copyed so many Studies of that great Artist Mr Richerd Wilson .... and was so familiarized with, & enamoured of *Italian* forms, that I enjoyed pleasures unfelt by my Companions» [3]. For some years, Jones was better known for the journal he kept in Italy than for his pictures. It is far from being a sophisticated piece of literature comparable with Goethe's *Italienische Reise,* but it is in its way a minor masterpiece. No other eighteenth century artist has left such a vivid account of daily life.

Jones writes about his friends, fellow artists and acquaintances, his attempts to attract patronage and his reaction to the countryside: «Every scene seemed anticipated in some dream – it appeared Magic Land» [4]. From its pages and from the paintings and drawings of Jones, J. R. Cozens, William Pars, John «Warwick» Smith and Francis Towne among others, it becomes apparent that the late 1770s and early 1780s was a point at which a new style – or rather, a new way of articulating a felt perception – developed among a group of like-minded people. It is above all the emotive interpretation of antiquity and landscape that differentiates the work of these artists from their continental contemporaries such as the technically brilliant but over meticulous Giovanni Battista Lusieri – a close friend and sketching companion of Jones in Naples – or the literal-minded Jakob Philipp Hackert.

Jones visited Naples for the first time in September 1778, staying for four months, partly at least to see an eruption of Vesuvius and partly to find new subjects for paintings. He travelled to Naples with the sculptor Giuseppe Plura and found lodgings on the Mole kept by a Swiss with an English wife, «drinking Punch, Dorchester beer, & living much in the English manner» [5]. He met up with his friend «Warwick» Smith, who had been in the city since March 1778. Little is recorded elsewhere about Smith's personality, so it is amusing to glimpse from the *Memoirs* the two men on 29 October sketching the newly erupted Vesuvius after «climbing up on all fours», refreshing themselves «with Eggs & Bacon & a flask», or on another occasion attending the Teatro Nuovo. At the end of December, the Earl-Bishop of Bristol and Derry arrived in the city, accompanied by the architect John Soane, and after an early-morning interview with Jones, who «found him combing and adjusting a small single curl which was fixed by a String to his own Short Hair» [6], he ordered two large pictures, «A View on the Coast of Baia including M. Vesuvius & ye Islands» and «A View of the Rock at Terracina (a Storm)». Jones fared less well with another visitor, Sir Thomas Gascoigne, who found fault with him for not preparing mineral pigments or bleaching his canvases like Hackert» [7]. Nor, on this visit, did he make the acquaintance of Sir William Hamilton. The *Memoirs* show that Jones spent the greater part of his time sketching from nature in the environs of Naples. A watercolour such as that of *The Gulf of Salerno* made in November 1778 is typical of his style at this date and provides a context for the oil sketches he was to paint during his second visit to Naples. Characteristic of Jones is the utterly straightforward rendering of what he sees – the scrubby, rocky terrain in the foreground, the landmarks carefully identified, the exact location and date noted: a visual equivalent to his journal. Indeed it is this very directness that is so appealing and was to be such a striking element in his oil sketches. The bright, clear blues are a reminder that Jones's watercolours remained unknown and unseen outside his family until 1954, away from exposure to light.

Jones's chief motive in returning to Naples in May 1780, where he was to stay until he returned to England in 1783, was chiefly in the hope of attracting the patronage of Sir William Hamilton, the influential British Minister in Naples from 1764 until 1800, whose reputation as a patron, collector and scientific investigator of Vesuvius made his salon at the Palazzo Sessa an essential port of call for those on the Grand Tour as well as for artists seeking contact with, and recommendation to, potential patrons. Jones arrived with an introduction to Hamilton from John Coxe Hippisley[8], but although he was received with great courtesy, the Minister did not visit Jones's studio until August 1782, and probably only then because his guest William Beckford had just been to inspect Jones's work. It may have been at the suggestion of J. R. Cozens that Beckford visited Jones, who, to his great distress, was out when he called, and subsequently «never was able to procure a sight of that Gentleman». Not until April 1783, only a few months before Jones left Italy, did Hamilton buy a painting, a large vew of the *Campi Phlegraei from the Camaldoli,* for 50 guineas, and in May he then allowed Jones to use the billiards room in the Palazzo Sessa to paint in until his departure. Although Hamilton's painting is no longer identifiable, an earlier view, dated 1780, is one of several similar subjects painted by Jones in Naples. Some of these may never have reached their intended owners, for between 1784 and 1798 he exhibited a number of Neapolitan views at the Royal Academy, unflatteringly described by Joseph Farington (a former fellow-pupil of Wilson) as «dull – like china»: perhaps Jones had absorbed into his style something of Hackert's porcelain-like finish. An additional reason for Jones to move to Naples was that he had fallen foul of the two principal manipulators of the Anglo-Roman art market, Thomas Jenkins and James Byres, and therefore seems to have decided to start afresh in Naples. However, Byres's Neapolitan counterpart, the *cicerone* Clarke, seems to have behaved in an equally obstructive manner towards Jones, deliberately omitting to mention his presence in Naples to potential patrons. An encounter with Hackert, who already enjoyed considerable favour at the court of Ferdinand IV and Maria Carolina, was an icy affair: Hackert did not relish the prospect of competition, and treated Jones to a somewhat patronizing appraisal of his abilities. Jones, for his part, had no sympathy with Hackert's style of painting: «(his) minute finishing, which ... was more congenial to his own taste, who like most German Artists, study more the Minutiae than the grand principles of Art», and thoroughly disliked Hackert's haughty manner. «I may here observe that there never was, perhaps, a man who was more endowed with the talent of making people believe that he was the greatest Genius that ever existed» [9].

Jones led a comparatively isolated existence in Naples, ignored by most of his countrymen, or at least by those with influence. A poignant passage in his *Memoirs* describes his feelings, and shows also his fundamental resolve to make the best of his situation and apply himself to his art. «The depression of my Spirits was such, that I endeavoured avoiding as much as possible those places where I was most likely to meet them [fellow Englishmen] – The greater part of my Excursions aboad were mournful and solitary – The various picturesque Scenes of Nature had still their charms, & I made Studies of them with ye same Ardour as ever – it was the immediate pleasure of the Moment – not from any Expectation of a future pecuniary Recompence, for the feeble glimmering hopes that remained of that sort were dying fast away – After the first Emotions of my Mind had a little subsided, & I had made a Calculation that my present Commissions were more than Sufficient to support me, in frugal stile of living, three years longer in Italy – a calm resignation ensued – which brightened up by degrees into a Gleam of Happiness» [10].

Hower, his *Memoirs* do show that he established a small circle of friends in the city, among them several artists, including Giovanni Battista Lusieri and «Don Luigi Micheli», described by him as a Roman born painter, who arranged for him to attend life classes at a private Academy organized within the precincts of the Royal Palace by the influential Marchese Venuti, while his acquaintances included the elderly Giuseppe Bonito, Pierre-Jacques Volaire, Michael Wutky and Angelica Kauffman. Among the most pleasurable events were the visits of William Pars (one of his oldest friends) for a few weeks in 1780 and again in the summer of 1781, and Francis Towne in March 1781. Jones describes their sketching expeditions, and the pleasure that he took in being able to «conduct (them) to many picturesque Scenes of my Own discovery, entirely out of the common road of occasional visitors, either Cavaliers or Artists[11]. Sufficient watercolours by each of these artists survive to enable a comparison of their different approaches (although it should be noted that while Naples inspired Jones's finest work, Pars's most striking watercolours are those of Alpine scenery, exhibited in 1772, and Towne's are those painted in Rome and the Alps 1780-1781). Pars's Neapolitan watercolours are tranquil and picturesque. Towne took a different approach. His answer to the problem of generalizing from nature was given in terms of line and pattern – he abstracted his landscapes from nature. Towne never achieved any wide success in his lifetime: he was already forty when he visited Italy in 1780 and his return to England the following year he once more took up life as a provincial drawing master. Having failed to be elected to the Royal Acade-

Thomas Jones, Naples from Phlegrean Fields. Private collection.

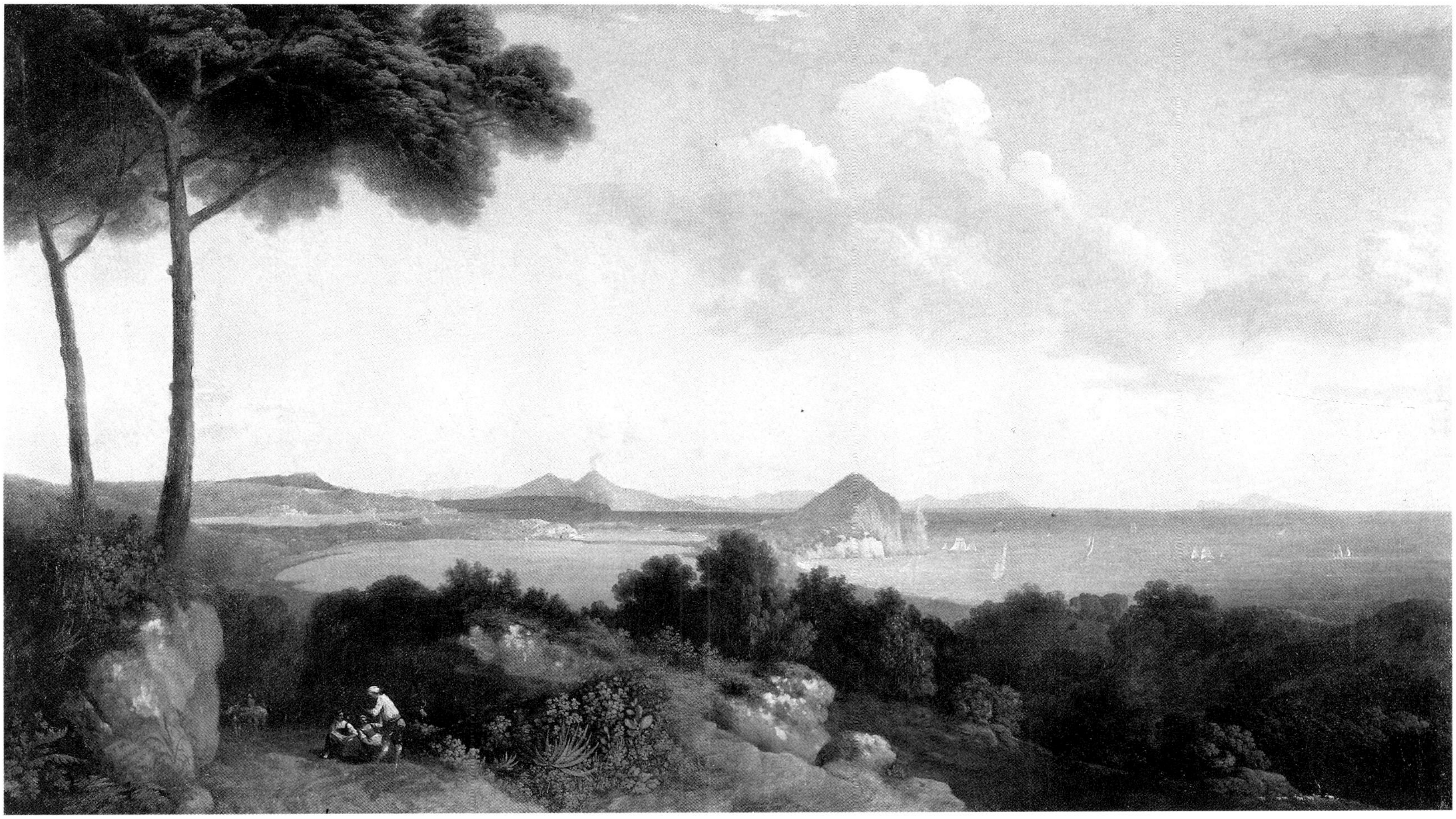

my he held his own one-man exhibition in 1805, but this bold gesture went almost completely unnoticed. In 1816 he bequeathed the drawings he had made in Italy to the British Museum, but it was not until this century that his idiosyncratic linear style, dependent on bold pen outlines and flat washes of colour, came to be appreciated [12].

The most remarkable achievement of Jones's second Neapolitan visit, oil sketches, date from 1782-1783. In 1954, around fifty, to use his own words, «studies in oil on thick primed paper - after nature» appeared at auction in London. These revealed Jones as one of the most original artists of the eighteenth century - «a sporadic genius» [13] as he has been described. It is instructive to compare Jones's Neapolitan sketches with Pierre Henri de Valenciennes's exactly contemporary sketches of Rome. While Valenciennes' preoccupation is on the whole with the transient effects of light and atmosphere, Jones analyzes the relationship between forms with almost geometric precision and clarity. Of a few simple elements - the crumbling walls of two characterless houses, punctuated by shuttered windows and scaffolding holes, some nondescript vegetation in the foreground and a strip of sky - he has distilled the essence of the city in which he lived but which was ignored as unworthy of attention by any of his contemporaries. The beautifully calculated and near-abstract placing of the elements of the composition finds its nearest analogy in a certain type of ultra-sophisticated modern architectural photography. The question is when and where Jones learned to make sketches of this sort, which are not preparatory studies for larger paintings but works complete in themselves. One answer might be «in Rome», where the tradition among French artists of sketching directly from nature in oil was long established. In the 1750s Vernet followed this practice[14], as Valenciennes was later to do. Although he had first come to Italy in 1777, it was only after a visit to Paris in 1781, where he had the opportunity to study briefly with Vernet, that he began to make oil sketches on his return to Rome[15], in which he developed a means of rendering what Constable later described as «the Chiaroscuro of Nature». There is no mention of Valenciennes in Jones's *Memoirs,* and in any case by 1782 Jones was living in Naples. It is true that in Naples Jones knew Volaire and his work, but his limited range of subject matter can hardly have been much of an inspiration to Jones [16]. Richard Wilson, Jones's master, had known Vernet in Rome, but there is no evidence that he ever followed Vernet's precept, as recorded by Sir Joshua Reynolds - «paint from nature instead of drawing» [17]: he seems always to have recommended to pupils his own practice of drawing from nature in black and white chalks on tinted paper. While it was with difficulty that Jones set aside Wilson's compositional formulae - indeed, in his public oil-paintings he never did - he seems to have discovered for himself the technique of the oil sketch. As early as 1770 he records making such studies from nature, and at least one such view of Penkerrig, his father's estate in Wales, is dated 1772 - that is, four years before he went to Italy[18]. His interest in apparently featureless buildings and rooftops probably began in Rome, to judge from a study now at Yale[19], which however lacks the wonderful clarity and precision of his Neapolitan sketches. However, the immediate impetus for Jones's choice of subject matter was quite simply what he saw from the window or *lastrica* of the various studios he rented. In July 1782 Jones's friend J.R. Cozens arrived in Naples in the entourage of his patron William Beckford. Capricious, vain, demanding, erratically brilliant, Beckford almost literally drove Cozens mad. In later years he was to refer to Cozens as that ungrateful scoundrel [20] and refused to subscribe to the fund instituted to support Cozens in the mid 1790s, but while they travelled together he seems to have valued Cozens's ability to express in visual form those sentiments of poetic melancholy that suffuse his own letters and travel-journals. Seven of Cozens's sketchbooks from this tour survive[21] so that we can follow their progress from England in May 1782 through Germany and Switzerland to northern Italy, travelling via Verona, Venice, Padua, Ferrara and Rome to Naples. Here they stayed as guests of Sir William Hamilton, first at Posillipo and then at Portici. After two months, Beckford, restless and depressed by the death of Lady Hamilton (not the famous Emma, but his first wife, Catherine) who had been kind and sympathetic to him, left Italy for Switzerland. Cozens stayed behind in Naples for three months before returning to Rome, as Jones put it, «[Beckford's] draughtsman Cozens once more a free agent and loosed from the shackles of fantastic folly and Caprice» [22]. A sharp and disagreeable light, however, is thrown on his position by a remark in a letter from Sir William Hamilton to Beckford: «Cozens passed a day with me here. The vermin plays a good stick upon the violoncello, which was a fine discovery ... He has made some charming sketches but I see from his book that he is indolent as usual»[23]. This remark may in fact have been occasioned by Cozens's physical frailty: in 1778 Jones noted his poor health, and shortly after arriving in Naples in July 1782 Cozens was ill for almost a month with the fever that killed Beckford's music master. Free of his obligations to his patron. Cozens was able to please himself. He sketched in the city and in the surrounding countryside, building up a store of motifs from which he later developed his watercolours. He travelled south to Vietri, where he noted the soft light of evening and a violent storm (although he must also have had in mind Vernet's shipwreck paintings) and on to Salerno and Paestum. Of all the British artists who visited this region in the eighteenth century it was Cozens who gave the fullest pictorial expression to his dream-like recollections of the landscape. Sometimes a sense of desolation or melancholy seems to pervade a composition, as in the watercolour of a shepherd's hut between Naples and Portici, in which a dejected figure evokes the viewer's empathy. Another watercolour, painted in 1790, long after he had returned to London, is quite different in mood, and is among the starkest and boldest images in his oeuvre: the sheer precipice of the Castel S. Elmo, almost like an Alp, has a sublimity that makes it one of his most extraordinary achievements. Perhaps here he reflects something of Jones's understanding of spatial relationships and his fascination with architectural form. More than any other artist before Turner, Cozens was gifted with the power of imparting the highest imaginative significance to a subject by subduing its topographical content and enhancing its pictorial and emotional elements.

In 1783, both Jones and Cozens returned to England. Jones, who had been in Italy for almost seven years, had begun to suffer from what was called the «Swiss malady» – homesickness. Nevertheless his departure from Naples was tinged with sadness, and as his ship set sail on the evening of 3 August, «I remained on deck, and with a heavy heart contemplated the grand & beautiful scene ... till Night drew her Veil over all – I bid a last Adieu and with a sigh retired below» [24]. Cozens, who had spent nine months in Rome after leaving Naples, travelled overland to England via Switzerland, where he called on Beckford, perhaps to discuss the series of finished watercolours he was painting for him. For the next ten years or so he painted watercolours derived almost exclusively from sketches made in Switzerland and Italy. In 1794 he began to show serious signs of mental instability and died in 1797, in the care of Dr. Monro – a link with the next generation, for Monro was one of J.M.W. Turner's earliest patrons, setting him to copy Italian subjects by Cozens, which were to be a potent influence on his developing style.

It was not until 1819, after the conclusion of the Napoleonic Wars, that Turner first visited Italy, but it would be no exaggeration to say that this experience was the culmination of his career to date and the greatest single influence on on his subsequent development. Since the 1790s many of his most important works had been connected with the art and landscape of the country, and he was thoroughly steeped in the knowledge of Claude, Dughet and Rosa as well as his more immediate precursors Wilson and Cozens. In c. 1798 an early patron, the antiquarian Sir Richard Colt Hoare, commissioned Turner to paint a picture of *Aeneas and the Sibyl: Lake Avernus*[25], based on a drawing he himself had made in Italy in 1786. The style of this, Turner's first Italian subject and the earliest of four paintings devoted to this theme, was not unnaturally inspired by the example of Richard Wilson. The theme, implying the lurking horrors of death and the underworld beneath the beauty of visible nature, had a long lasting appeal for Turner, who returned to it not only in a reworking of the subject for Colt Hoare in 1814[26] but also in his two most important paintings to have been inspired by the landscape and associations of the area, *The Bay of Baiae* [27], 1823, and *The Golden Bough*[28], 1834. Colt Hoare had travelled extensively in Italy and Sicily and besides being widely read in classical literature and history had himself written several works describing his tours, including *Hints to Travellers in Italy*, 1815, a copy of which Turner owned. It was perhaps he who introduced Turner to two important books, *Select Views in Italy*, 1792-1796, illustraded by engravings after John «Warwick» Smith (see *Naples from Sir W.H's Villa*), and *A Tour through Italy*, 1813, by the Rev. J.C. Eustace, these Turner studied in detail in 1818, marking thumbnail copies of all Smith's illustrations in a sketchbook and copying out passages from Eustace's book[29]. His interest in visiting Italy was further stimulated by a commission he had undertaken to illustrate James Hakewill's *Picturesque Tour of Italy*[30], 1818-1820, and perhaps most importantly by the publication in 1818 of Canto IV of Byron's *Childe Harold's Pilgrimage*. His own vivid sympthy with the Italian scenes he visited in 1819 was heightened by what Byron had written: Turner felt that Byron had defined in an important way what it was that he, Turner, had to say about Italy. He made this clear when he used this Canto as the source of quotations appended to several of his paintings in Royal Academy catalogues in subsequent years. By the summer of 1819, Turner had definitely decided to visit Italy, and it can only have been a happy coincidence rather than a deciding factor that Sir Thomas Lawrence should have written from Italy in June to a friend in London: «in Mr. Turner, it is injustice to his fame and to his country, to let the finest period of his genius pass away ... without visiting those scenes which, if possible, would suggest still nobler images of grandeur and beauty than his pencil [brush] has yet given us, and excite him to still greater efforts than those which have already proved him the foremost genius of his time» [31]. While Rome was to be his chief objective, Naples was scarcely less important[32]. He was to spend just over a month from mid october to mid November, exploring the city and its environs, a region by now familiar to him at second hand but which he was anxious to see for himself. Intensely secretive by nature, Turner only infrequently let slip personal information and we do not know for instance where he stayed in Naples. However, a good idea of his travels is provided by the drawings in four small sketchbooks and by a handful of studies in watercolour [33]; from these it is apparent that he visited almost all the chief sights of the region. Although misleadingly labelled by Turner himself, the *Gandolfo to Naples* sketchbook is in fact mostly devoted not to his journey from Rome, but to Naples and its more immediate environs – the architecture of the city, the Bay seen from the heights above the city, Vesuvius (a shower of hot ash spattered over several pages), Pozzuoli, the Bay of Baiae, Cumae and Lake Avernus, including several sketches of precisely the view that he had already twice painted before seeing it himself in 1819. He had hoped (like Wright of Derby in 1774) [34] to see a spectacular eruption of Vesuvius, but this occurred after he had returned to Rome, and his watercolours of the volcano seen across the Bay, among the most exquisite studies he made during this trip, show only a plume of smoke, an ever present reminder of «tranquillity tinged with terror» [35].

Vesuvius Angry, had been painted before Turner left England. Further afield, Turner's sketchbooks show that he made an expedition to Paestum, where he seems to have had Piranesi in mind as he sketched the majestic temples and like Cozens before him, returned to Naples by way of the rugged Sorrentine penisula, making pages of tiny sketches from the boat in which he travelled. Herculaneum and Pompeii too attracted his keen eye, and he devoted around thirty pages of sketches to record his impressions of these celebrated sites.

Perhaps the chief characteristic of the way in which Turner worked in Italy in 1819 was his factual approach to everything he saw. His early training as a topographical draughtsman firmly established the way in which he was to work throughout his life, gathering information (sometimes also jotting down odd memoranda to himself), which he would subsequently use as the basis for finished watercolours and paintings. His visit to Naples in 1819 was to inspire two great paintings, *The Bay of Baiae, with Apollo and the Sibyl* (Tate Gallery, London), exhibited in 1823, and *The Golden Bough* (Tate Gallery, London), 1834. With the *Bay of Baiae* Turner returned to a theme that had long fascinated him, the passage of time and the decay of beauty. The subject was taken from Ovid's *Metamorphoses:* the Cumaean Sibyl, loved by Apollo, was granted by him one request.

Taking a handful of earth she begged to live as many years as there were grains of dust, and thus she slowly wasted away. Turner places Apollo and the Sibyl, still young and beautiful, in a landscape once the *resort* of the ancient Romans, but by the eighteenth century almost completely overgrown and ruined, now a desert ... destined to expiate in ages of silence and desolation the crimes of the last degenerate Romans [36], a perfect example of beauty, that like the Sibyl's, was to pass away. The landscape setting is characteristically made up of real and imagined elements. The background was closely based on pencil sketches made in 1819, and it is possible that the small oil study (Tate 05330) was made in preparation for this painting. The middle distance and foreground however were purely imaginary, as Turner was quite prepared to admit. What he was painting was not a naturalistic landscape, but a subject picture concerned with glory and decline, the lost greatness of Imperial Rome.

Similarly *The Golden Bough* is not primarily a landscape, although the setting is again Lake Avernus. Arguably more Claude-like in conception, Turner here depicted an idealized Italy, made up of many separate elements and far removed from reality, a landscape of complex allusion and significance. His continuing interest in subjects inspired by classical antiquity during the 1830s, in contrasting subjects such as *Ancient* and *Modern Italy*, 1838, to some extent separated him from his fellow artists. In 1832, *The Library of the Fine Arts* commented that «the heroes of antiquity and their Virtues are now quite out of date», and recommended leaving the depiction of ancient history to the French. This sentiment seems to have been borne out to a considerable extent, to judge from Royal Academy catalogues of the period, when classical subjects were outnumbered by Italian genre scenes or fanciful depictions of Neapolitan banditti, and visitors to Naples began to lay aside guidebooks based on classical texts and ancient histories, preferring to admire the quaint apperarance of local country-people or the picturesque corners of the old city. Turner, however, continued to pursue his own long-established themes, intensely conscious of Byron's lines:

«– and now, fair Italy!
Thou art the garden of the world.
Even in thy desert what is like to thee?
Thy very weeds are beautiful, thy waste
More rich than other climes' fertility:
Thy wreck a glory, and thy ruin graced
With an immaculate charm which cannot be defaced».

(*Childe Harold's Pilgrimage – Italy,* Canto IV, XXVI)

Turner's visit to Naples in 1819 continued to haunt his imagination for the greater part of his life.

[1] William Beckford (1760-1844). Gay Chapman, *Beckford*, London 1937, remains the standard biography.
[2] « For whereso'er I turn my ravish'd Eyes Gay Gilded Scenes and Shining Prospects rise.
Poetick Fields encompass me around, And still I seem to tread on Classic Ground », Joseph Addison (1672-1719), *Letter from Italy*, London 1701.
[3] The Memoirs of Thomas Jones, ed. A.P. Oppe, *The Walpole Society*, Volume XXXII, London 1951, p.60. Abbreviated as Jones 1951.
[4] Jones 1951, p. 60.
[5] Jones 1951, p. 78.
[6] Jones 1951, p. 83.
[7] Jones 1951, p. 84.
[8] Brinsley Ford, « Sir John Coxe Hippisley: An Unofficial English Envoy to the Vatican », *Apollo*, Volume XCIX, June 1974, pp. 440-445.
[9] Jones 1951, p. 118.
[10] Jones 1951, p. 97.
[11] Jones 1951, p. 102.
[12] The first serious critical study of the artist was A.P. Oppe, « Francis Towne, Landscape Painter », *The Walpole Society*, Volume VIII, 1919-1920.
[13] Lawrence Gowing, *The Originality of Thomas Jones*, London 1985, p. 7.
[14] *Claude-Joseph Vernet*, catalogue by Philip Conisbee of an exhibition at the Iveagh Bequest, Kenwood, London, 1976, *passim*.
[15] *Painting from Nature*, catalogue by Philip Conisbee of an exhibition at the Fitzwilliam Museum, Cambridge and the Royal Academy of Arts, London, 1981, p. 23.
[16] Jones seems to have been somewhat unimpressed by Volaire's paintings: see Jones 1951, p. 107.
[17] James Northcote, *The Life of Sir Joshua Reynolds*, London 1819, Volume II, pp. 90-91.
[18] *Penkerrig*, oil on paper, dated 1772, Birmingham City Museums and Art Gallery.
[19] See *English Landscape 1630-1850*, catalogue of an exhibition at the Yale Center for British Art, New Haven, 1977, no. 48.
[20] *The Diary of Joseph Farington*, Volume III, September 1796 - December 1798, edited by Kenneth Garlick and Angus Macintyre, New Haven and London, 1979, p. 855.
[21] Formerly in the possession of Cozens's patron William Beckford, the sketchbooks descended to his daughter Susan, wife of Alexander, 10th Duke of Hamilton, with whose heirs they remained until their sale at Sotheby's, London, 29 November 1973. They are now in the Whitworth Art Gallery, University of Manchester.
[22] Jones 1951, p. 114.
[23] John Oliver, *Life of William Beckford*, London 1937, p. 126.
[24] Jones 1951, p. 125-126.
[25] Martin Butlin and Evelyn Joll, *The Paintings of J.M.W. Turner*, 2 vols., London and New Haven 1977, revised edition 1984, no. 34. The painting is in the Turner Bequest, Clore Gallery at the Tate Gallery, London.
[26] Butlin and Joll 1984, no. 226. The painting is in the Yale Center for British Art, New Haven.
[27] Butlin and Joll 1984, no. 230. The painting is in the Turner Bequest, Clore Gallery at the Tate Gallery, London.
[28] Butlin and Joll 1984, no. 355. The painting (not part of the Turner Bequest) is now in the Clore Gallery at the Tate Gallery, London.
[29] Cecilia Powell, *Turner in the South*, New Haven and London 1987, pp. 13-14. The copies of engravings after « Warwick » Smith and his transcription from Eustace are in Turner's sketchbook TR CLXXII now in the Clore Gallery at the Tate Gallery, London.
[30] Turner's illustrations for the *Picturesque Tour of Italy* are discussed in Cecilia Powell, « Topography, Imagination and Travel: Turner's relationship with James Hakewill », *Art History*, Vol. 5, no. 4, 1982, pp. 408-425. See also Powell 1984, p. 201, note 54.
[31] D.E. Williams, *The Life and Correspondence of Sir Thomas Lawrence, Kt.*, London. 1831, vol. II, p. 161.
[32] Powell 1984 discusses the importance of Turner's visit to Naples in 1819, and its longlasting influence on his work.
[33] The four sketchbooks, all in the Turner Bequest in the Clore Gallery at the Tate Gallery, London, are: *Gandolfo to Naples* (TR CLXXXIV), *Pompeii, Amalfi, Sorrento and Herculaneum* (TR CLXXXV), *Naples, Paestum and Rome* (TR CLXXXVI) and *Albano, Nemi, Rome* (TR CLXXXII).
[34] It is of particular regret that no works by Joseph Wright of Derby (1734-1797) could be included in this exhibition. However, his visit to Naples is discussed and illustrated in Benedict Nicholson, *Joseph Wright of Derby: Painter of Light*, 2 vols., London and New Haven 1968, and an exhibition devoted to Wright's Italian visit of 1773-1775 was held at Gainsborough's House, Sudbury in 1987.
[35] Kenneth Woodbridge, *Landscape and Antiquity: Aspects of English Culture at Stourhead 1718 to 1838*, Oxford, 1970, p. 85.
[36] J.C. Eustace, 1813, quoted by Powell 1984, p. 83.

Catalogue

Note

The illustrations are arranged in chronological order and the entries in alphabetical order. The measurements in the entries are in centimetres unless otherwise stated, and the height of the work precedes the width. The abbreviation pl. p. stands for the number of the page where the illustration appears of the painting referred to in the entry.

An asterisk * appearing in the entries indicates a work which cannot be exhibited for technical reasons, but which has been included in the catalogue for documentary purposes.

François De Nomé, View of Naples.
Naples, Dalla Vecchia Collection.

Didier Barra, View of Naples from the sea.
Milan, private collection.

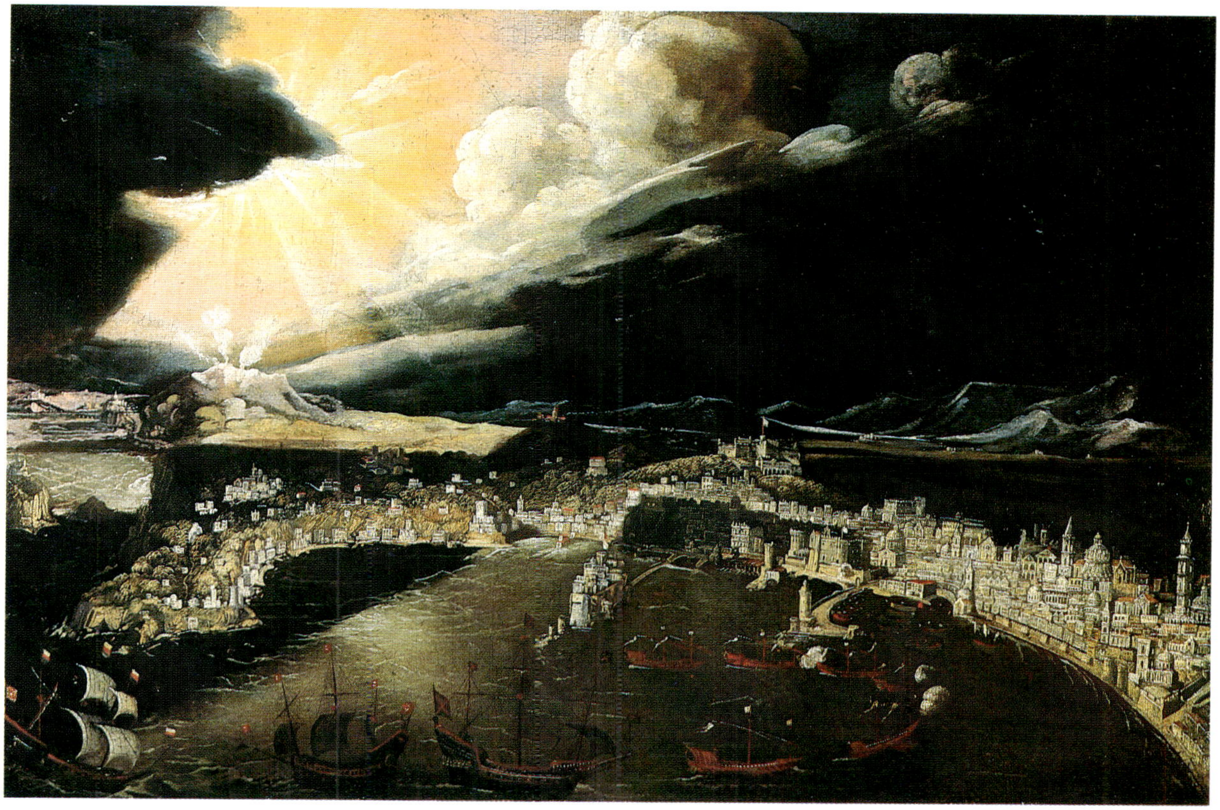

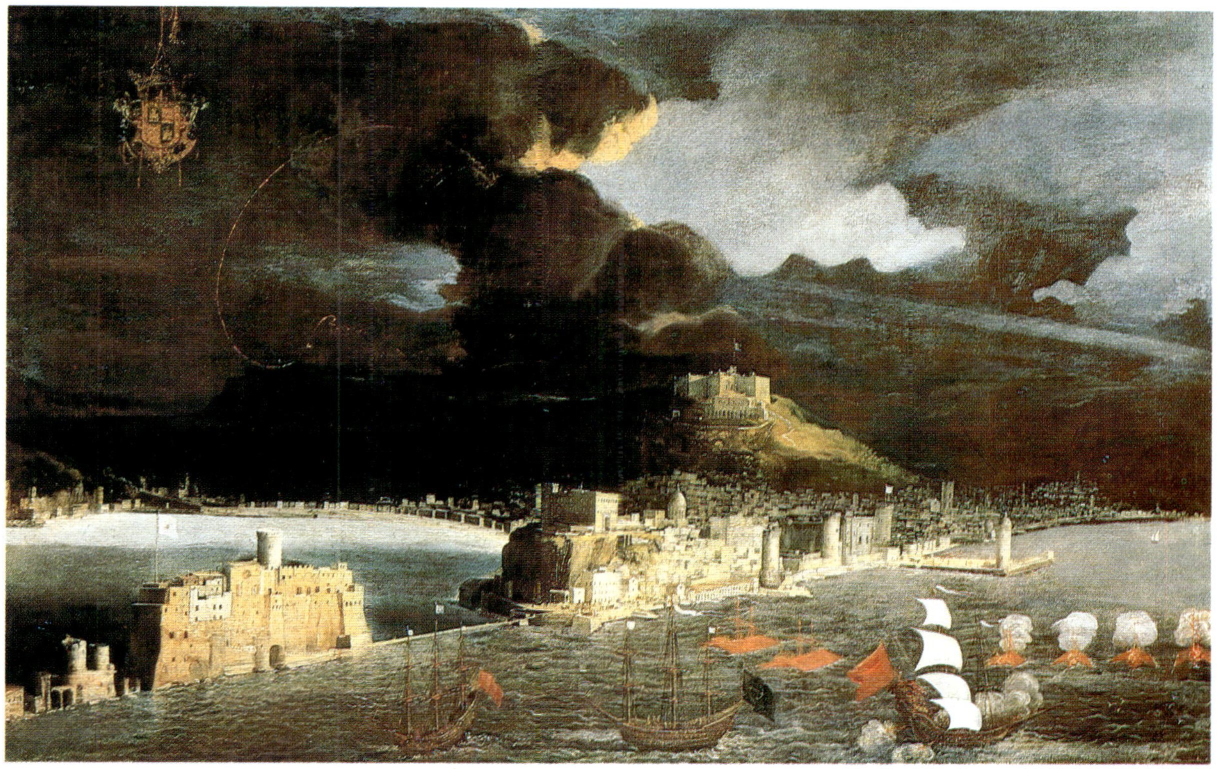

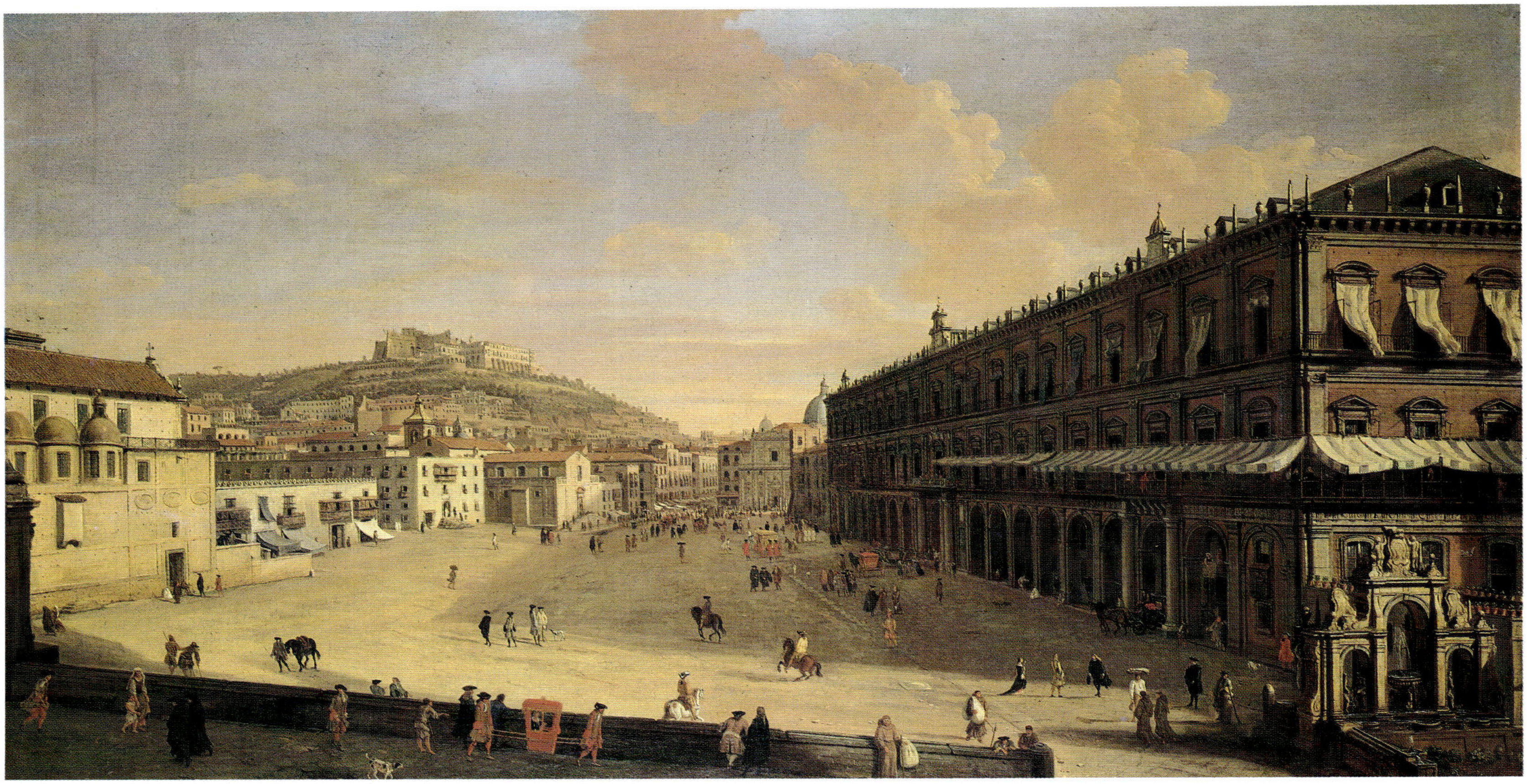

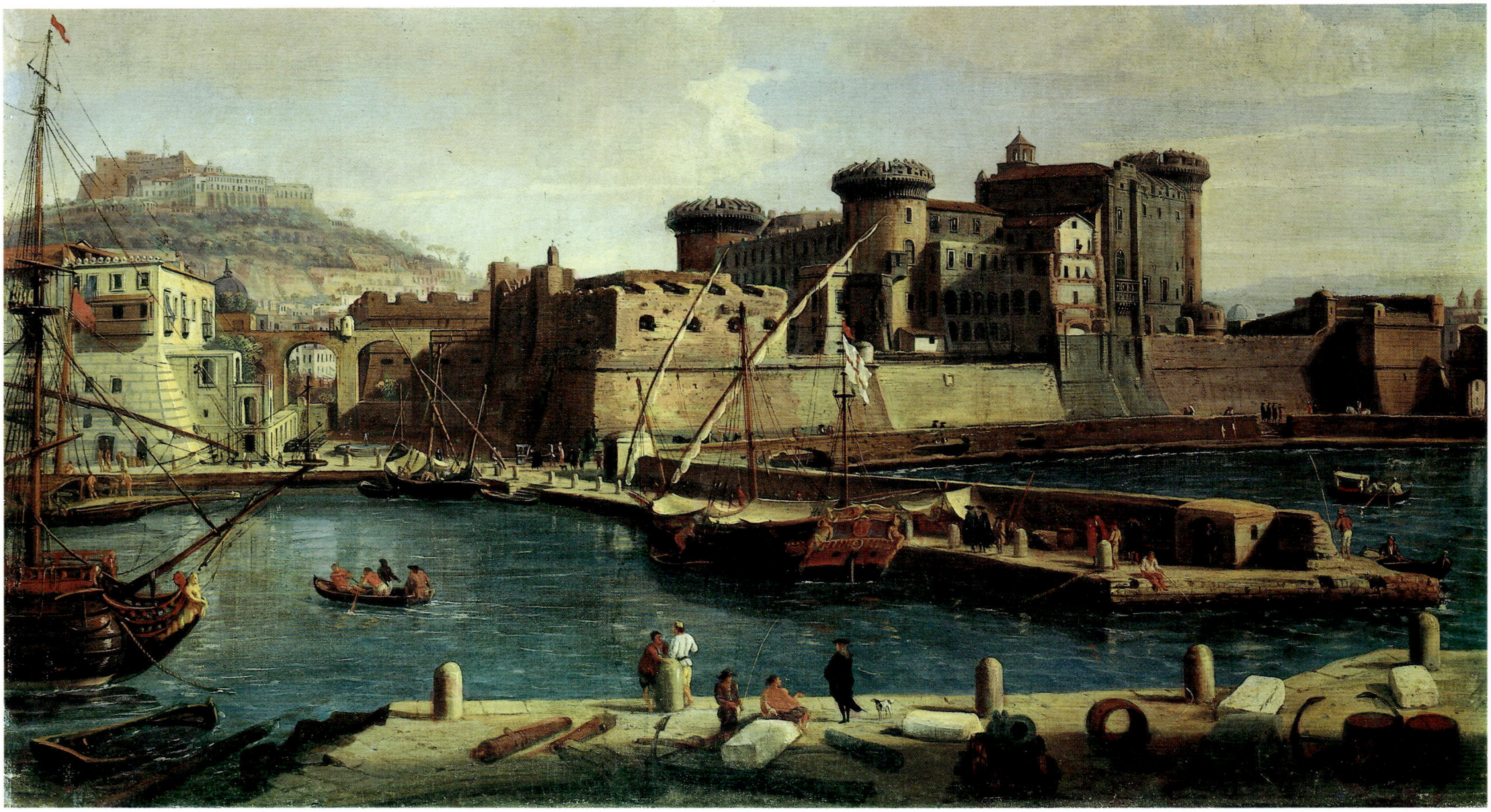

Gaspar Van Wittel, Largo di Palazzo. Milan, Banca Commerciale Italiana.

Gaspar Van Wittel, The Port. Naples, Museum of San Martino.

Gaspar Van Wittel, The Port. Turin, Galleria Sabauda.

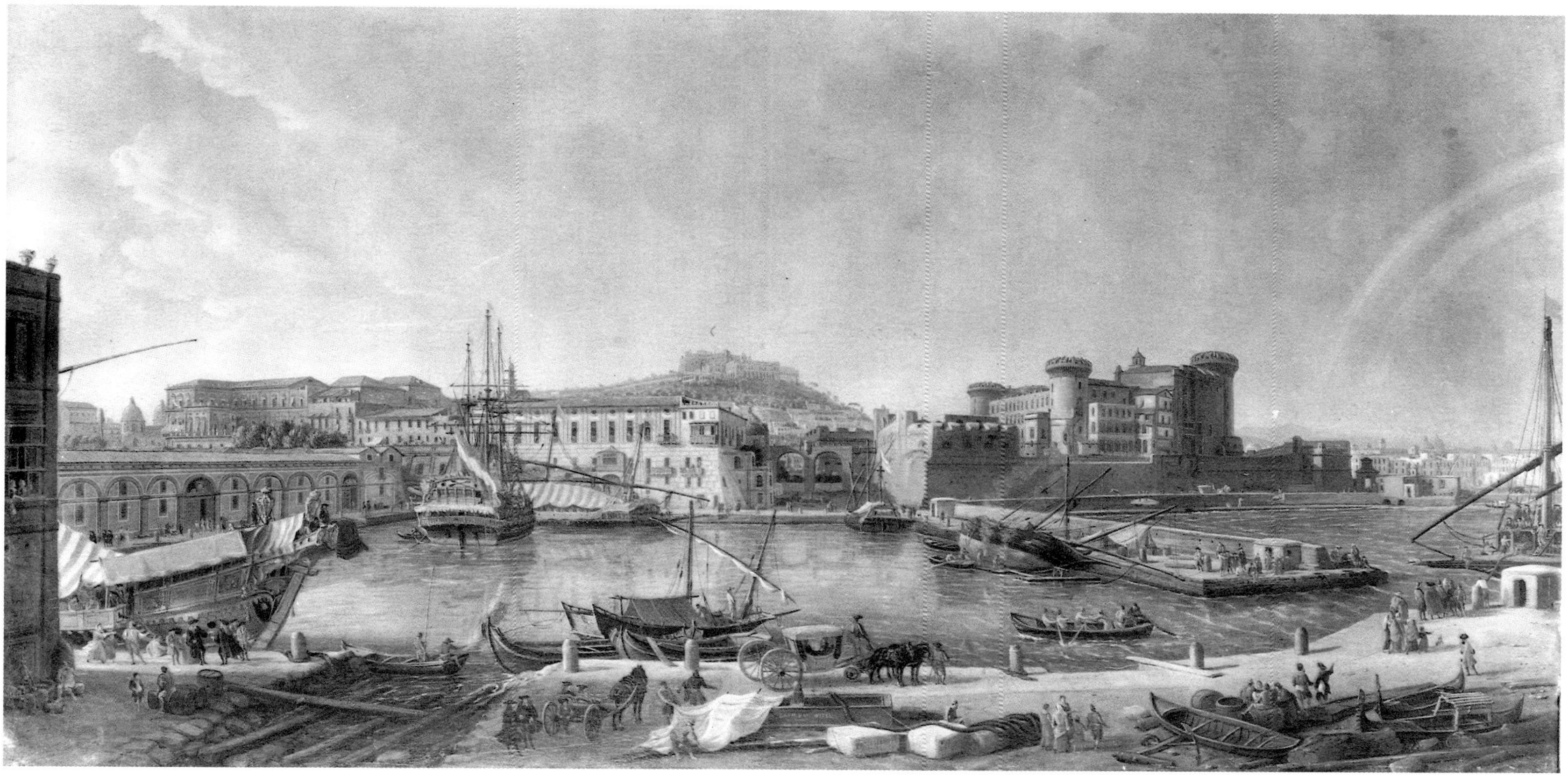

Gaspar Van Wittel, Naples from the sea. Florence, Palazzo Pitti, Galleria Palatina.

Gaspar Van Wittel, View of the Chiaia district towards Mergellina. Florence, Palazzo Pitti, Galleria Palatina.

Gaspar Van Wittel, Sorrento. Toledo, Hospital de Tavera.

Gaspar Van Wittel, The Hill of Pizzofalcone. Toledo, Hospital de Tavera.

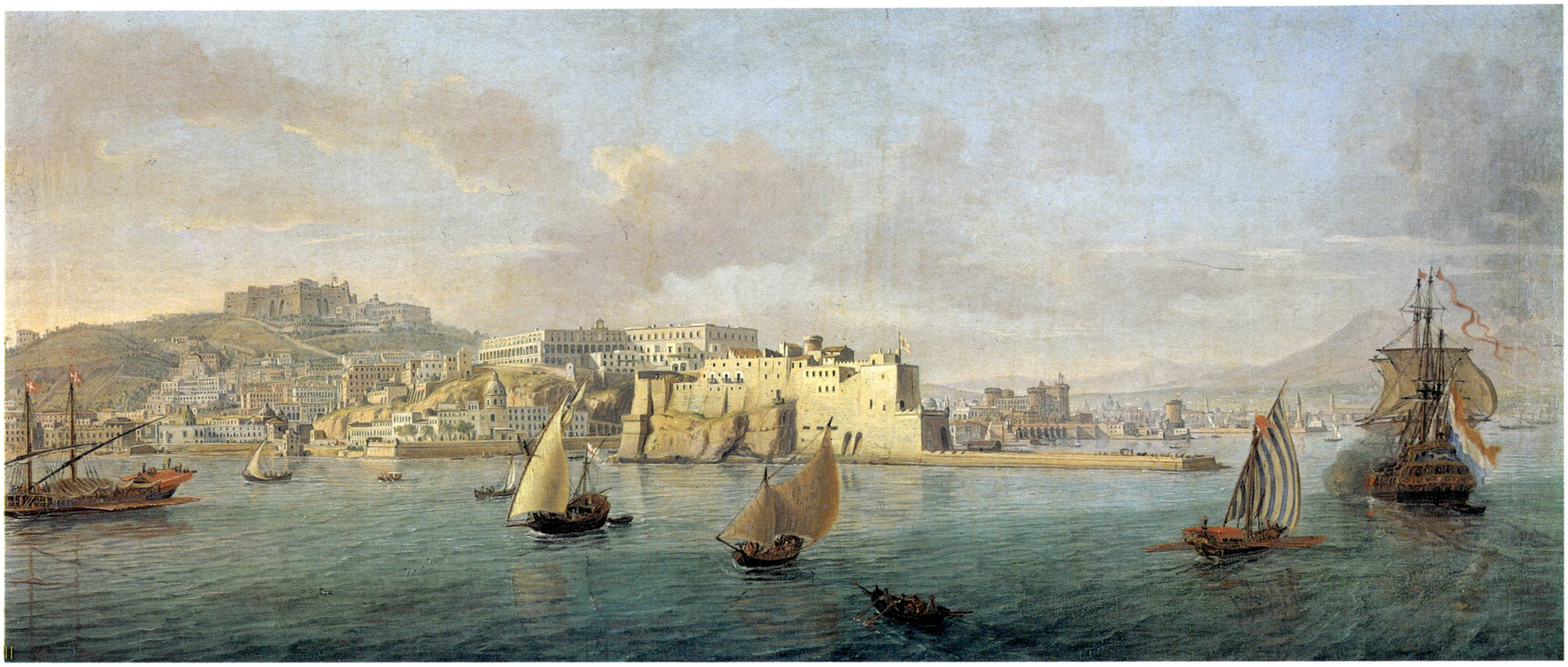

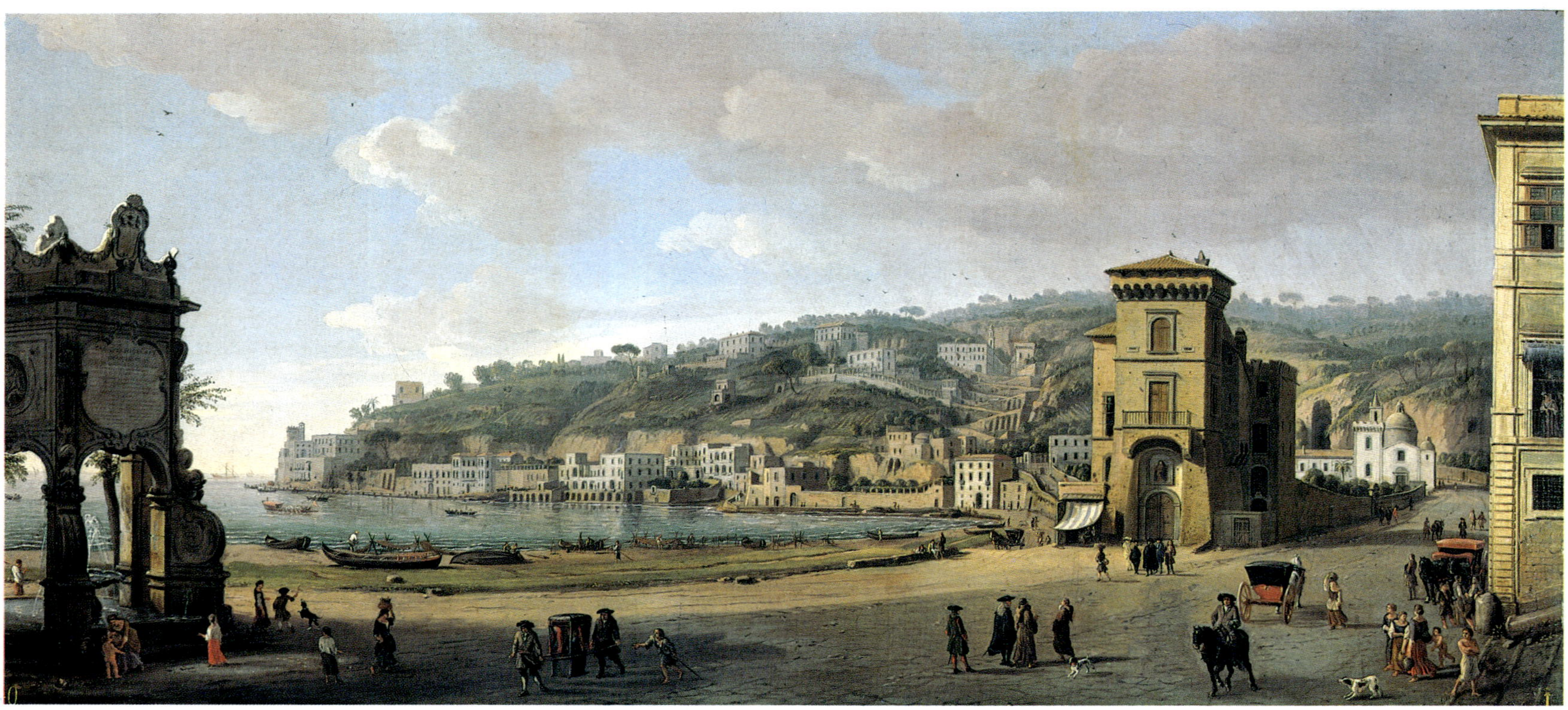

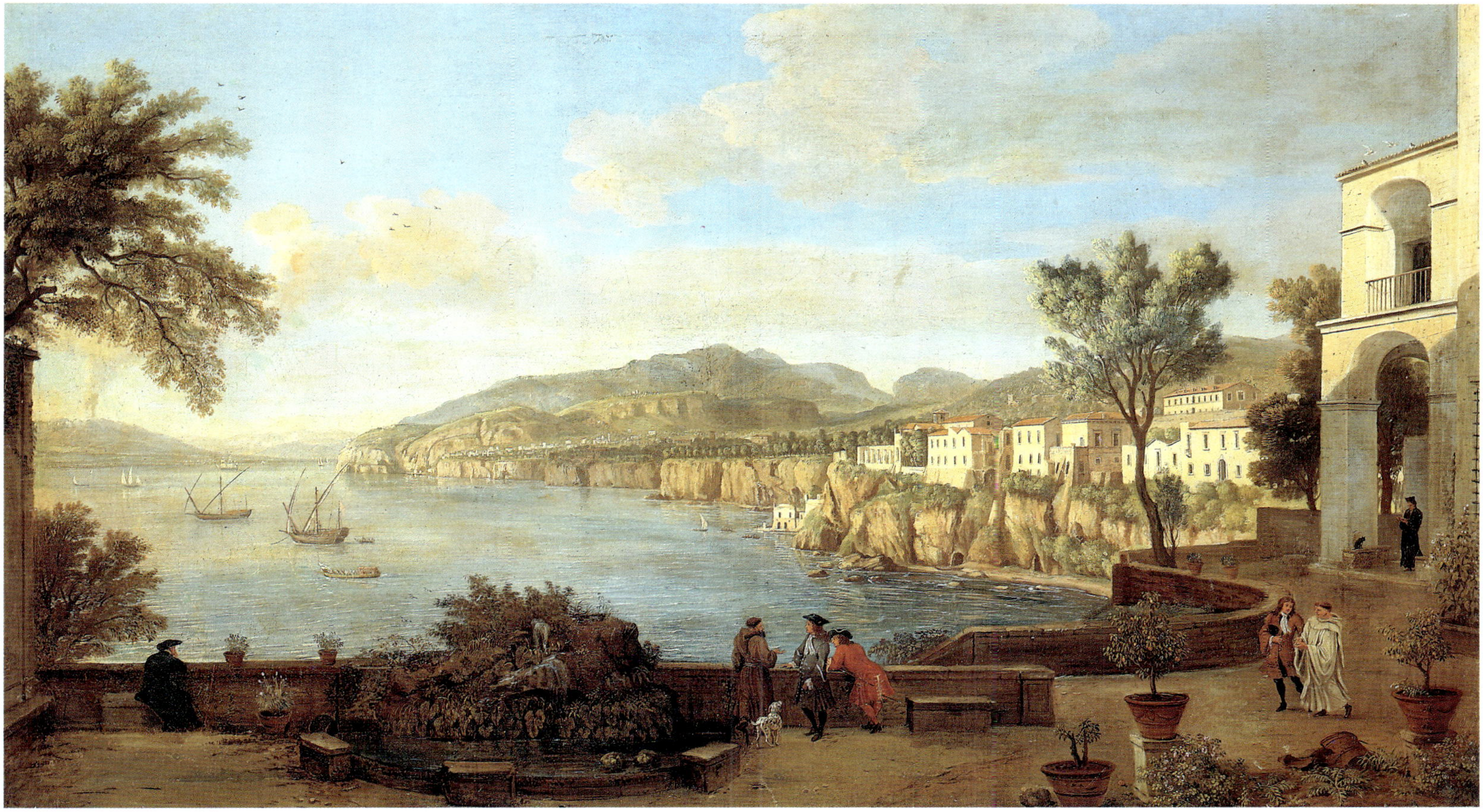

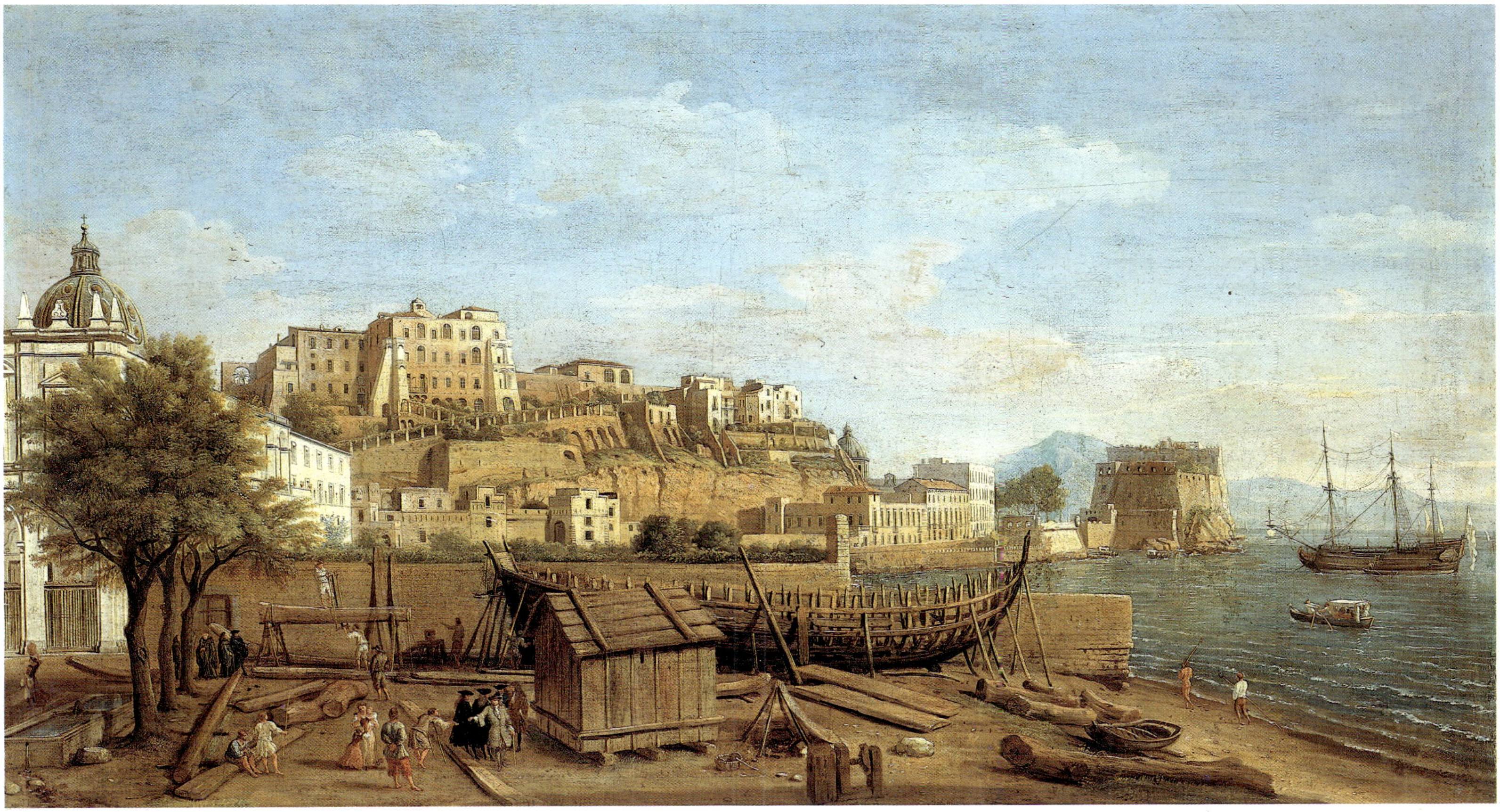

Gaspar Van Wittel, Chiaia from Pizzofalcone. Milan, private collection.

C.-J. Vernet, Charles of Bourbon hunting coots on the lake at Licola. Caserta, Royal Palace.

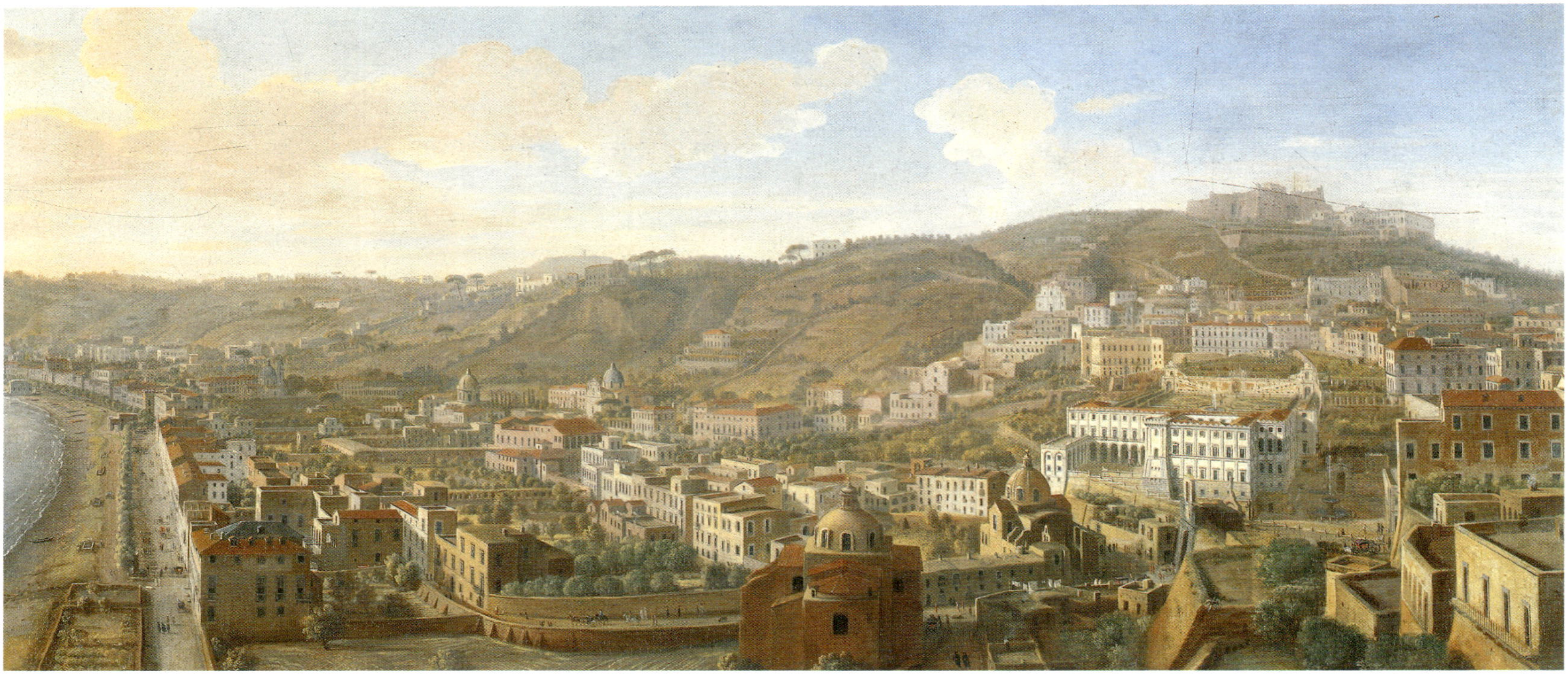

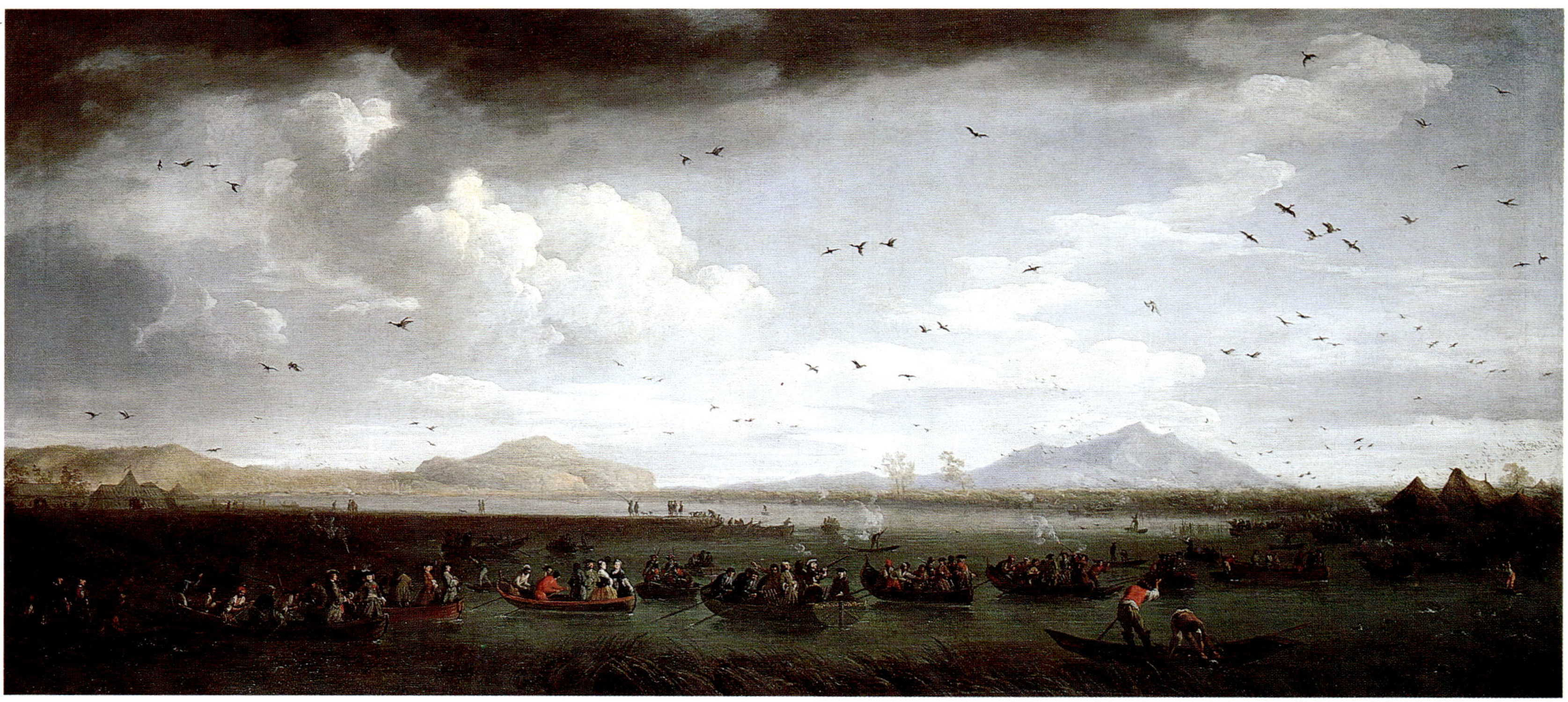

Antonio Joli, The Marketplace.
Beaulieu, Lord Montagu of Beaulieu.

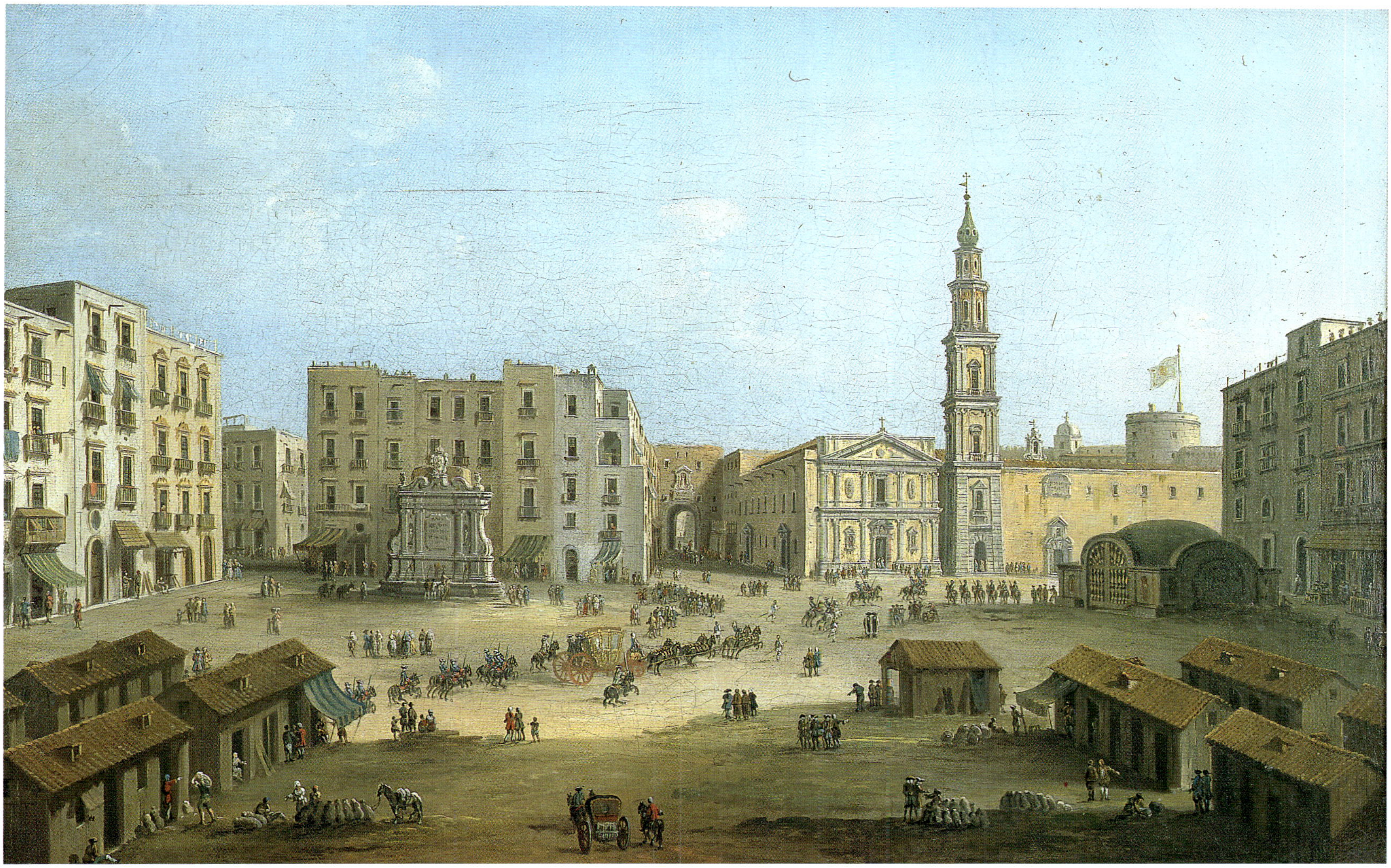

Antonio Joli, The Gate of Spirito Santo.
Beaulieu, Lord Montagu of Beaulieu.

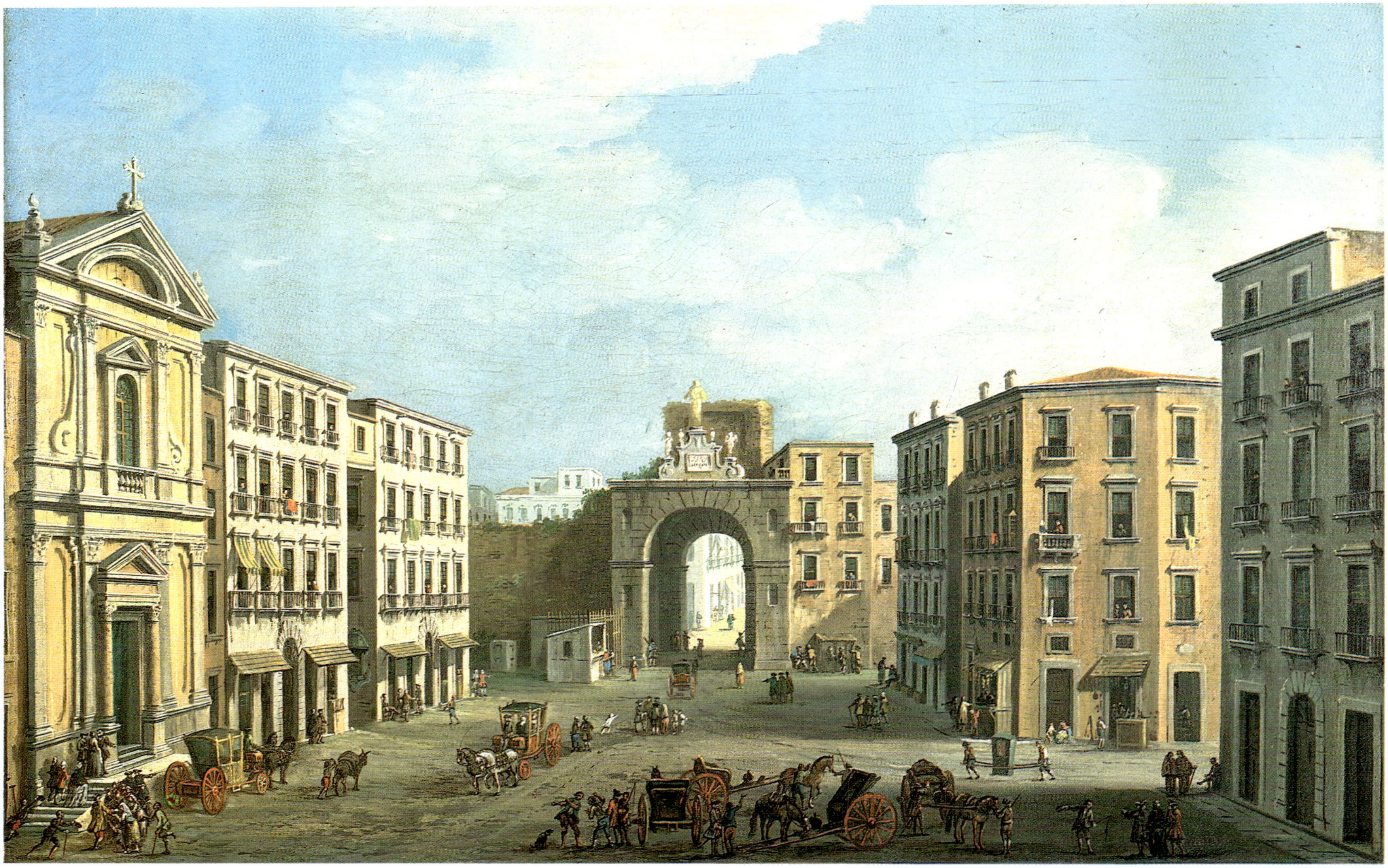

Antonio Joli, Largo San Gaetano.
Beaulieu, Lord Montagu of Beaulieu.

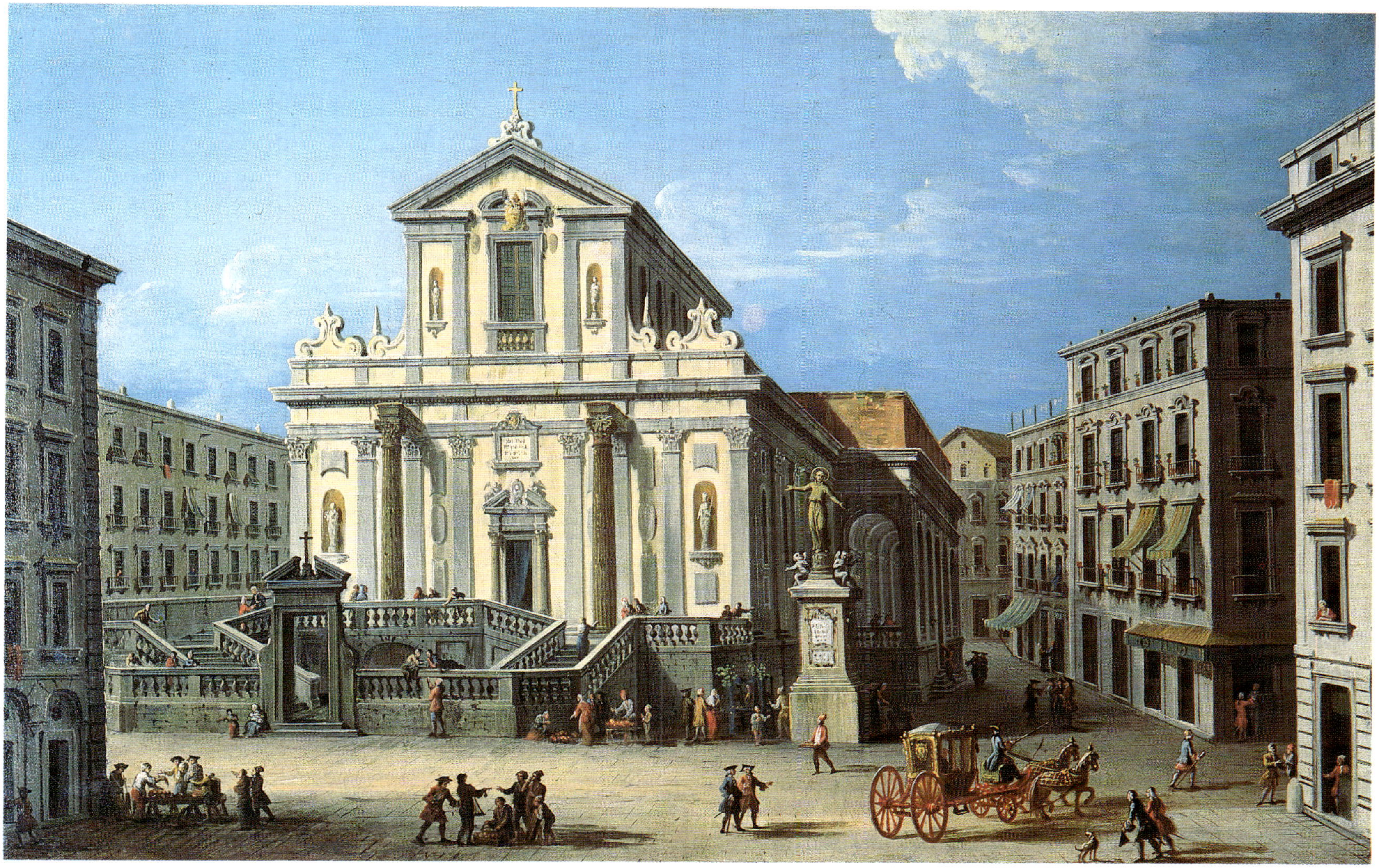

Antonio Joli, The street of Santa Maria di Costantinopoli. Beaulieu, Lord Montagu of Beaulieu.

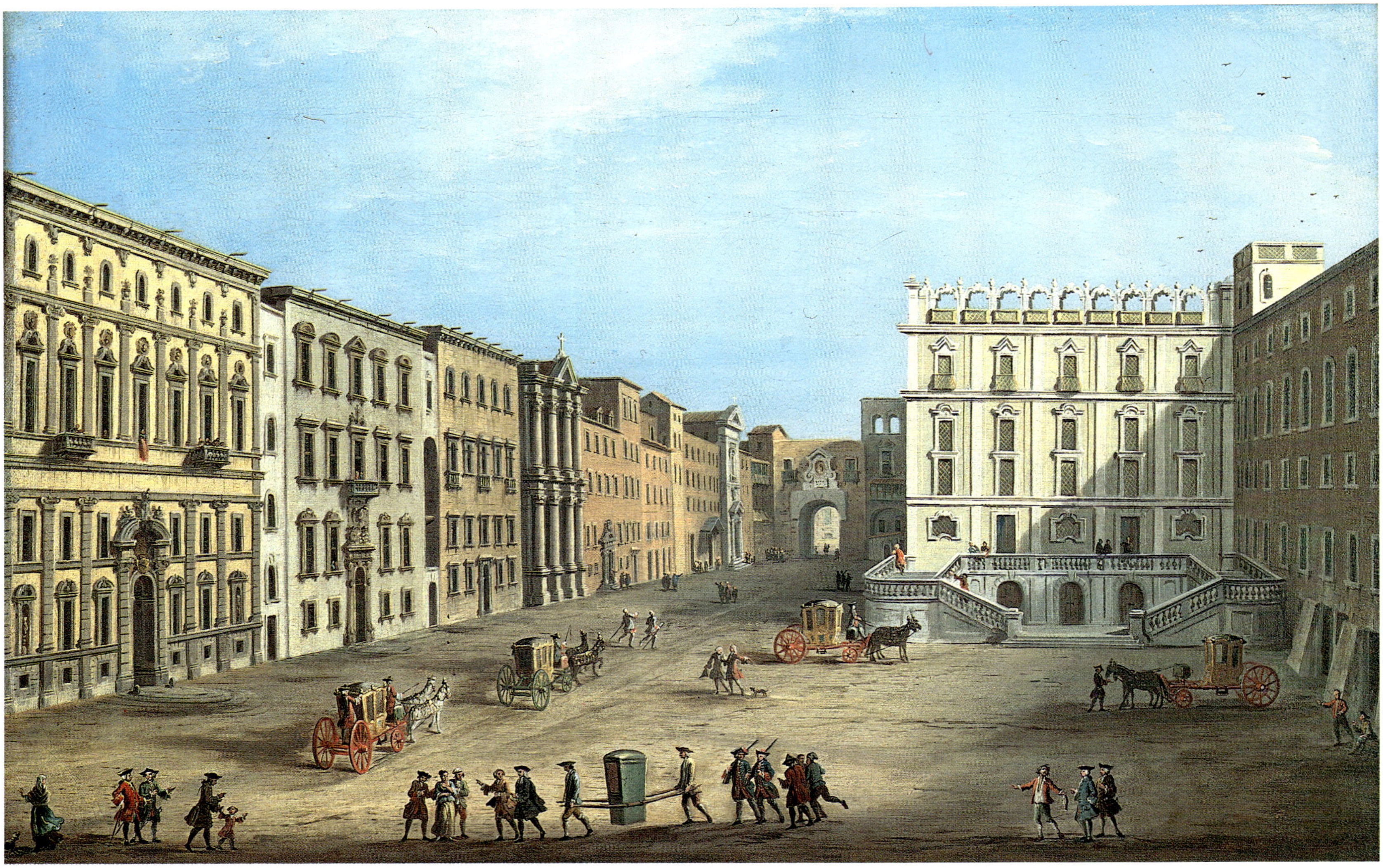

Antonio Joli, Naples from the port. Beaulieu, Lord Montagu of Beaulieu.

On the following pages:
Antonio Joli, The Royal Palace and Castelnuovo. Beaulieu, Lord Montagu of Beaulieu.

Antonio Joli, The street in front of the Royal Theatre of San Carlo. Beaulieu, Lord Montagu of Beaulieu.

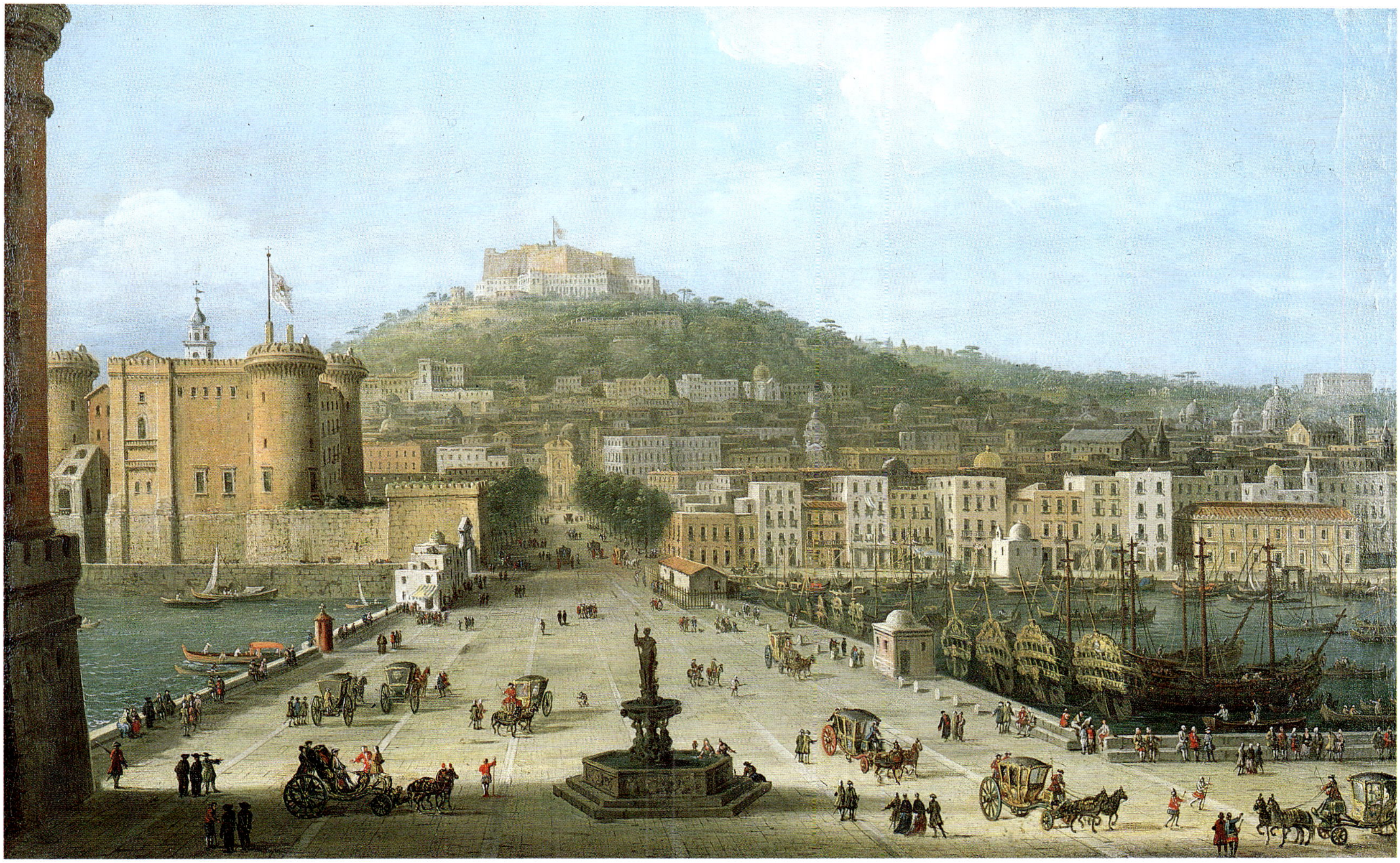

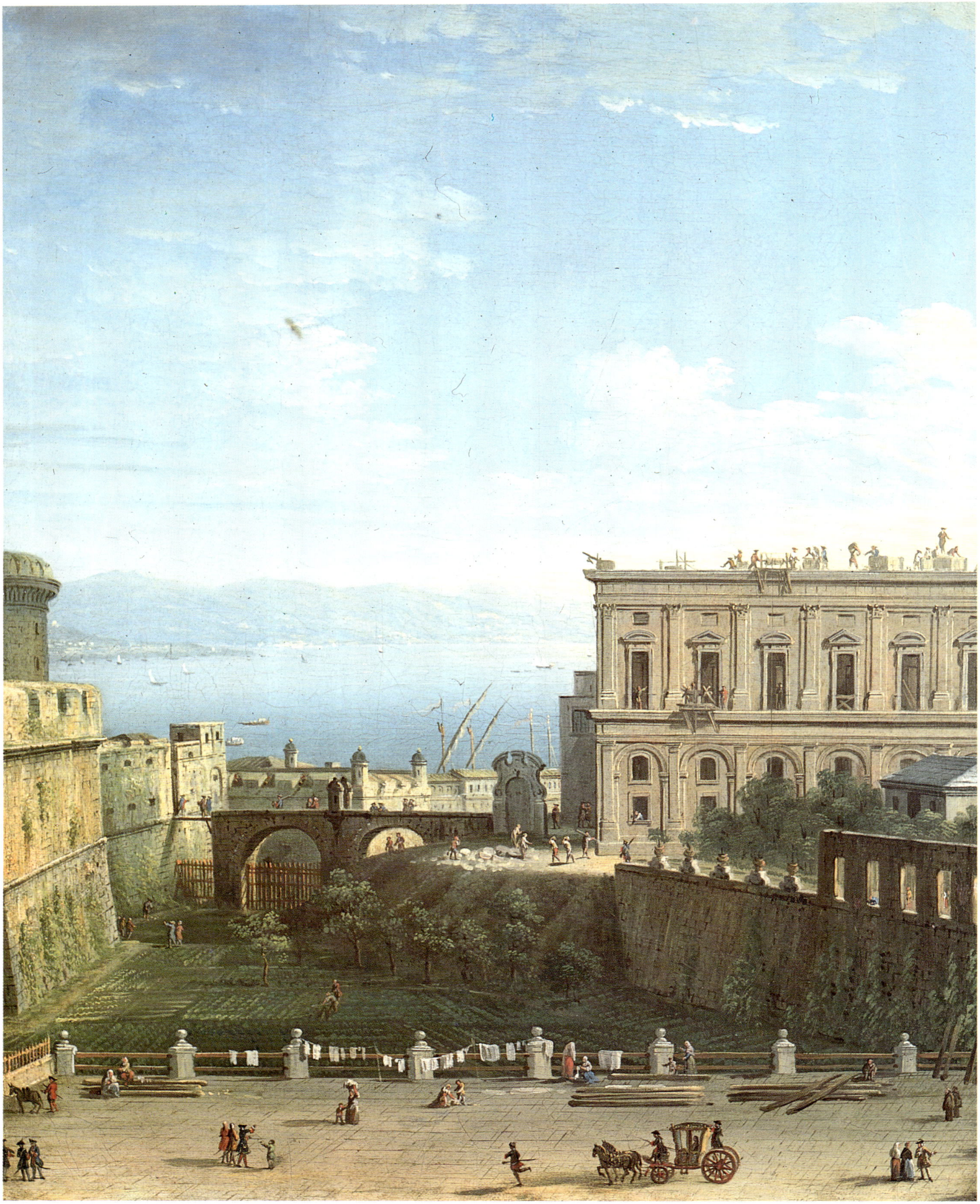

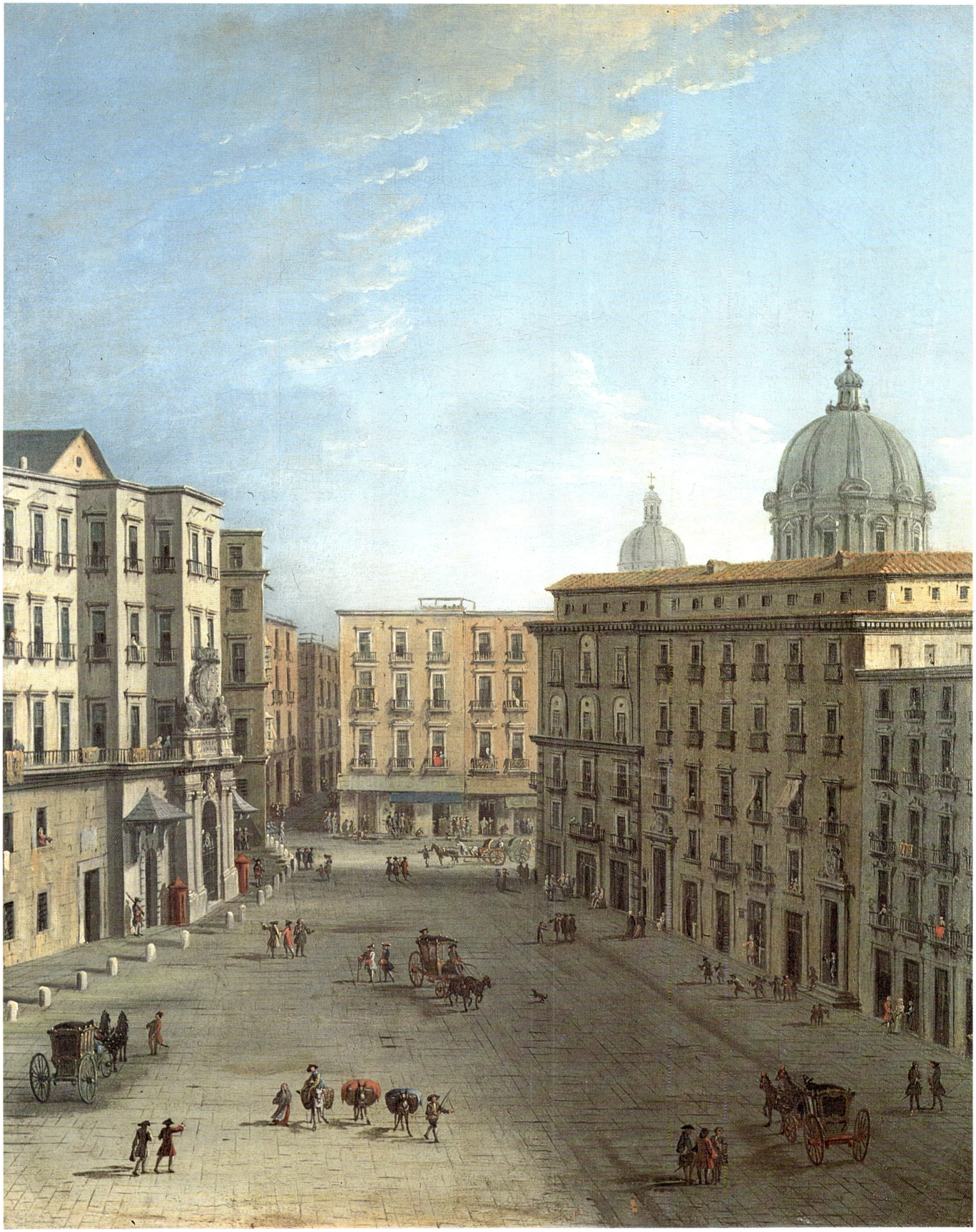

Antonio Joli, « Cuccagna » in front of the Royal Palace. Beaulieu, Lord Montagu of Beaulieu.

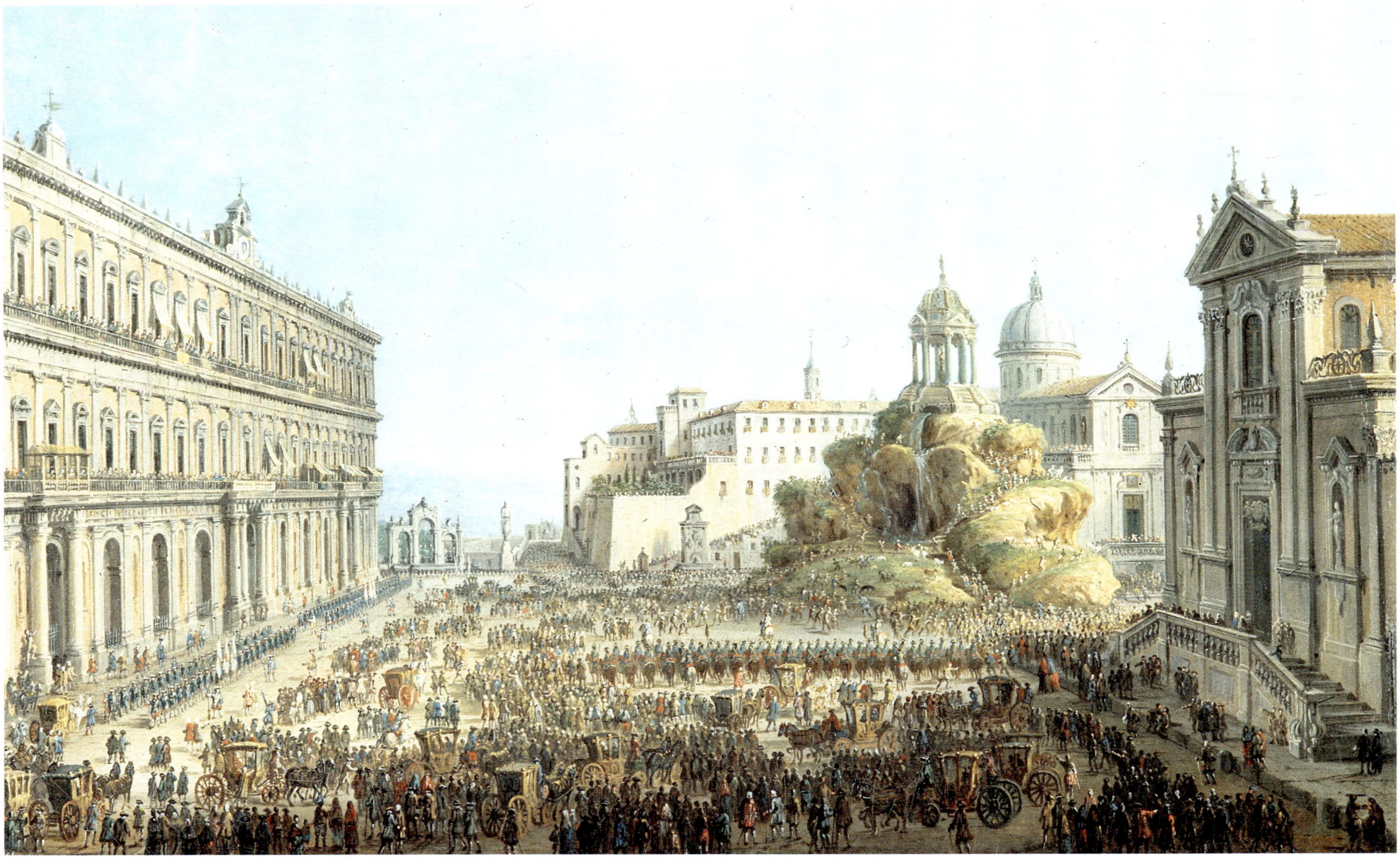

Antonio Joli, Carnival in front of Castel Nuovo. Selkirk, Bowhill, Duke of Buccleuch K.T.

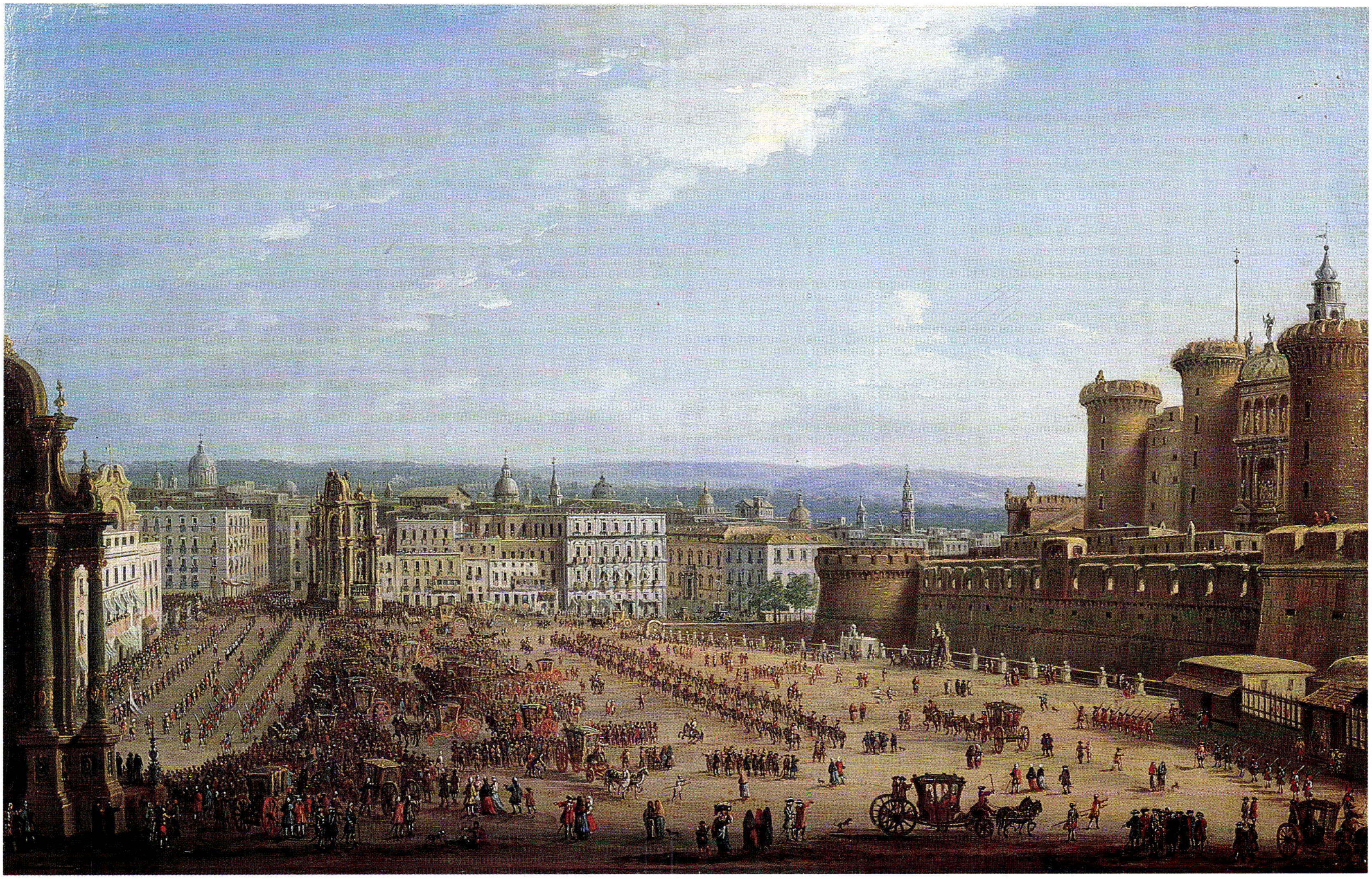

Antonio Joli, Largo San Ferdinando with royal carnival procession. Selkirk, Bowhill, Duke of Buccleuch K.T.

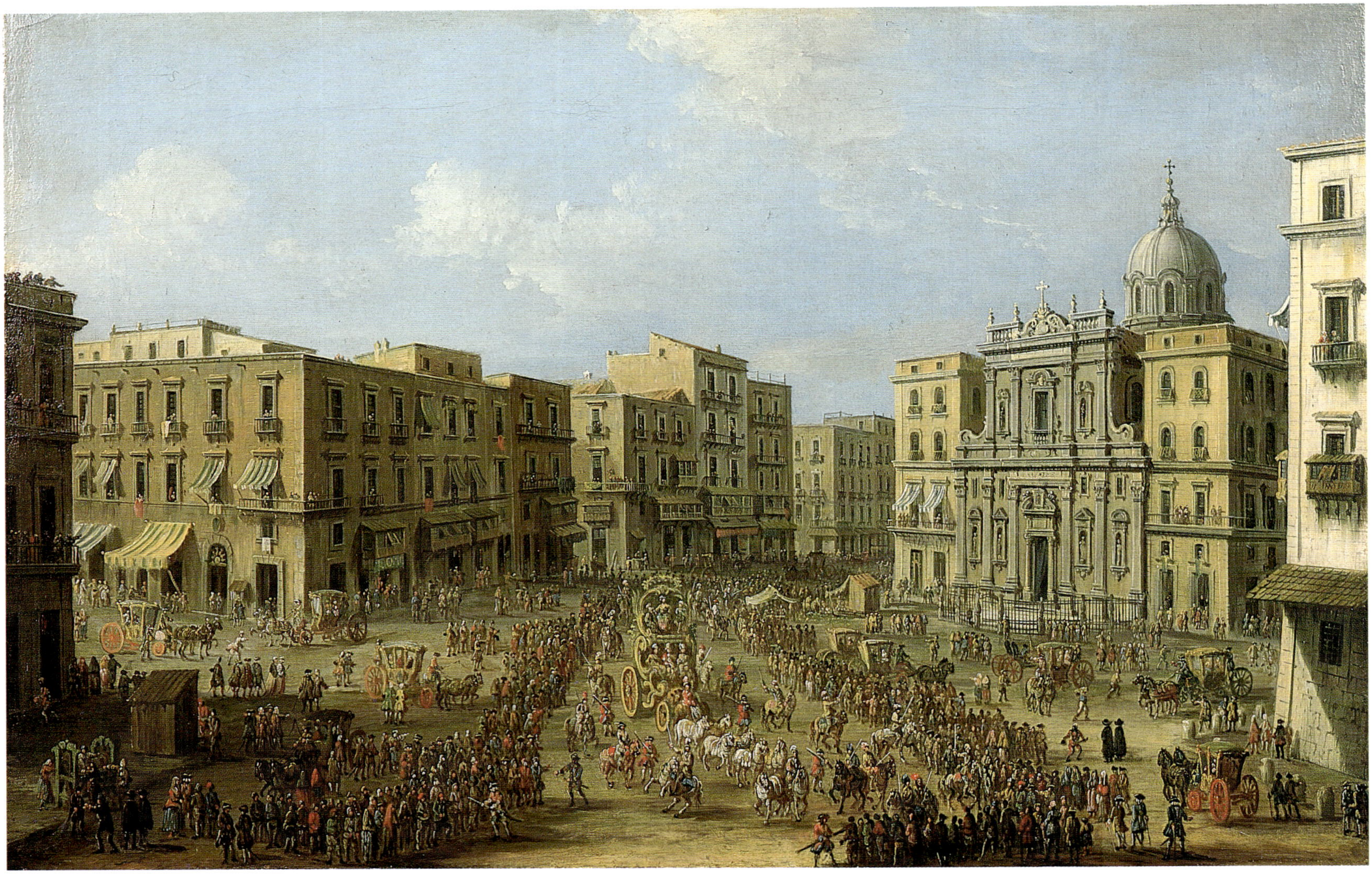

Antonio Joli, Plain of Paestum with the temples. Selkirk, Bowhill, Duke of Buccleuch K.T.

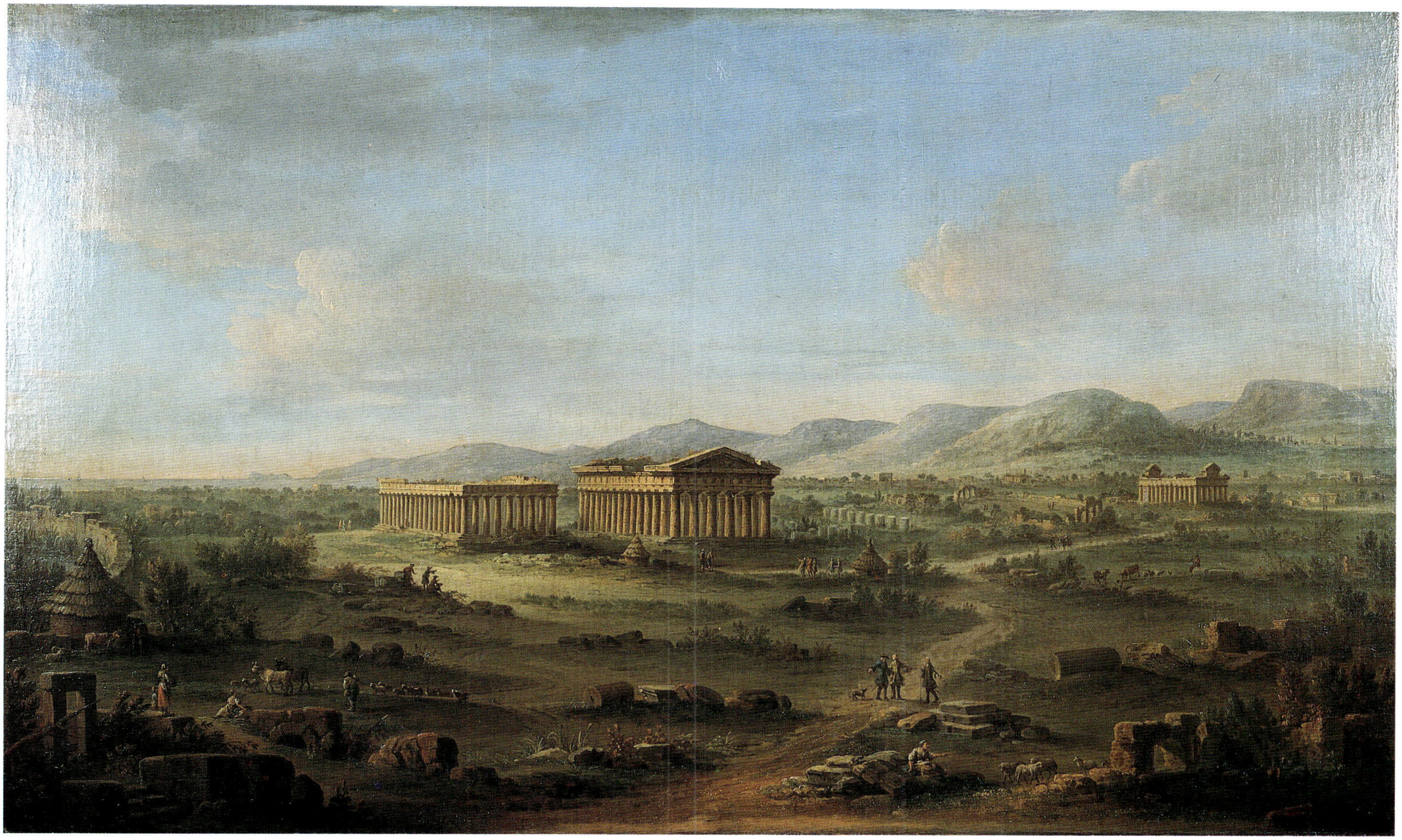

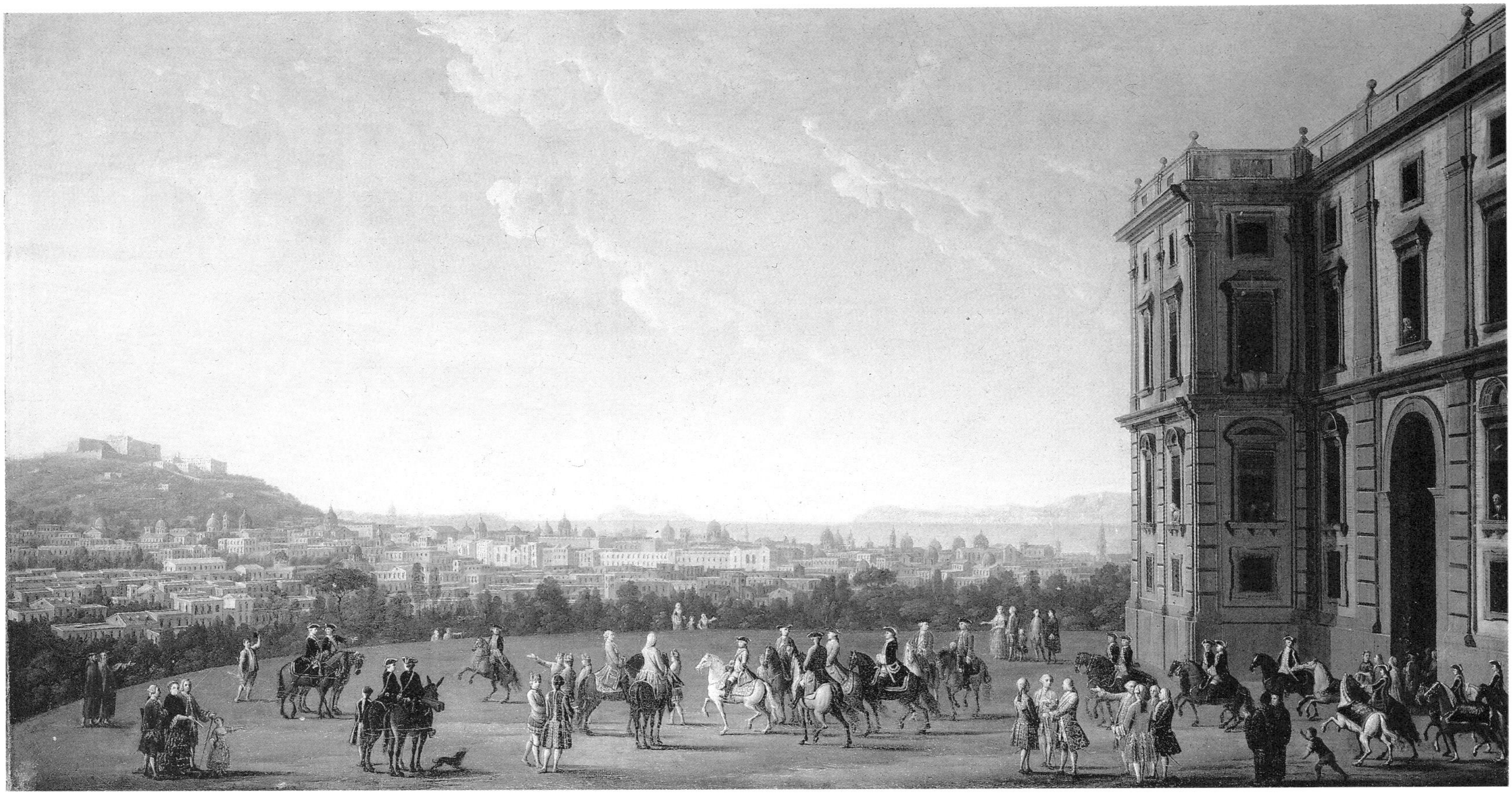

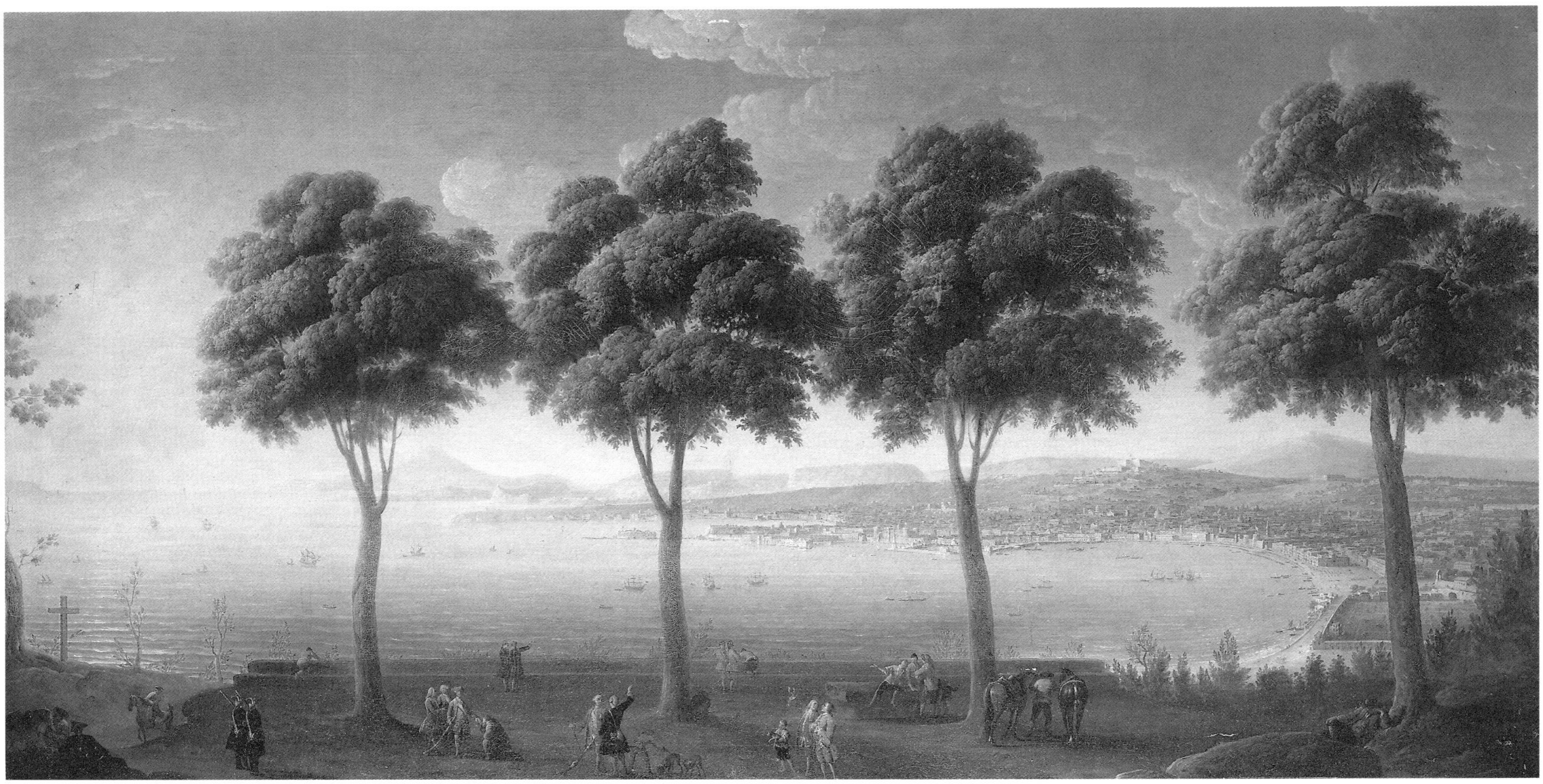

Antonio Joli, Ferdinand IV on horseback with the court at Capodimonte. Naples, Museum of San Martino.

Antonio Joli, The Bay of Naples from the slopes of Vesuvius. Naples, Museum of San Martino.

Antonio Joli, The Royal procession at Piedigrotta. Naples, Museum of San Martino.

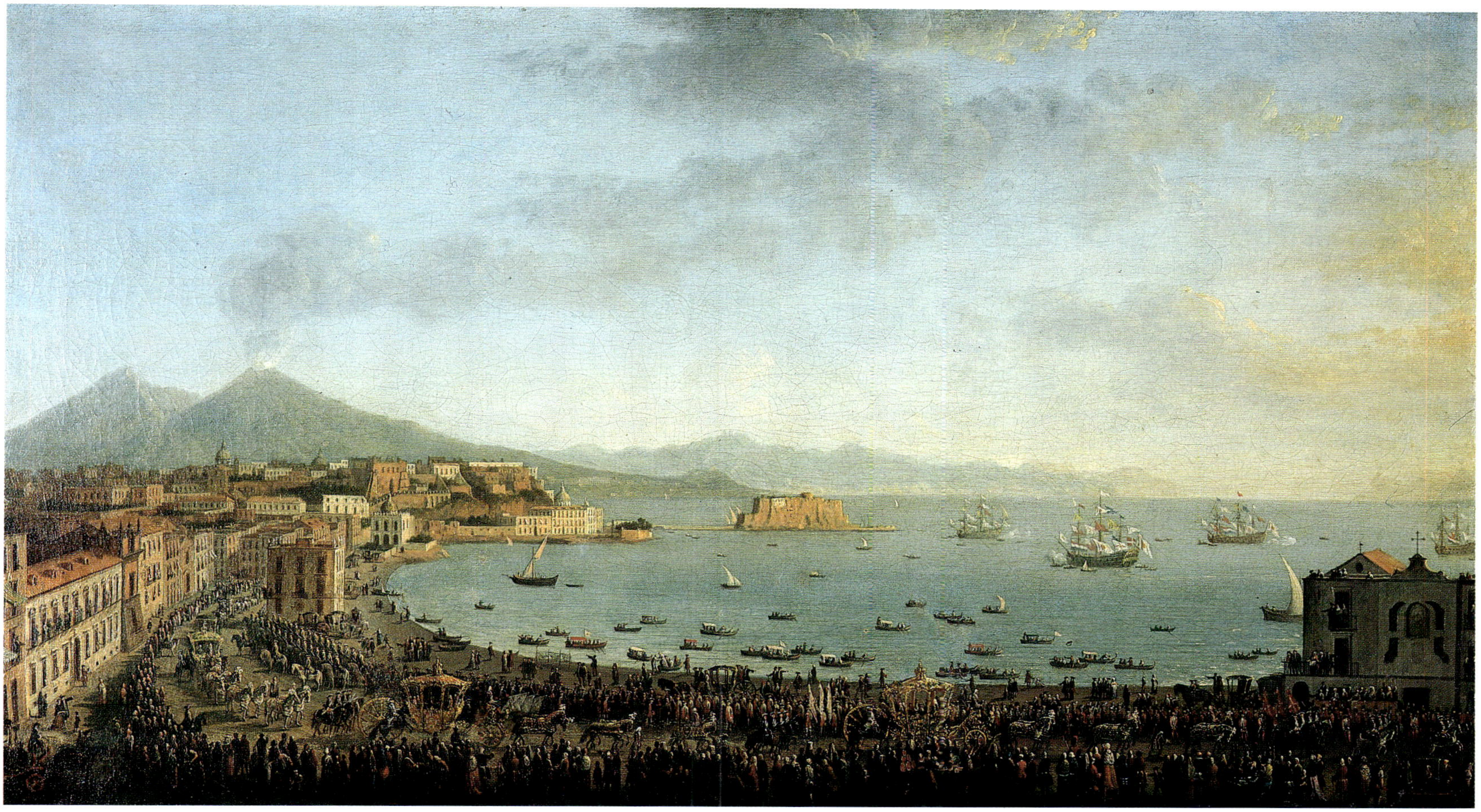

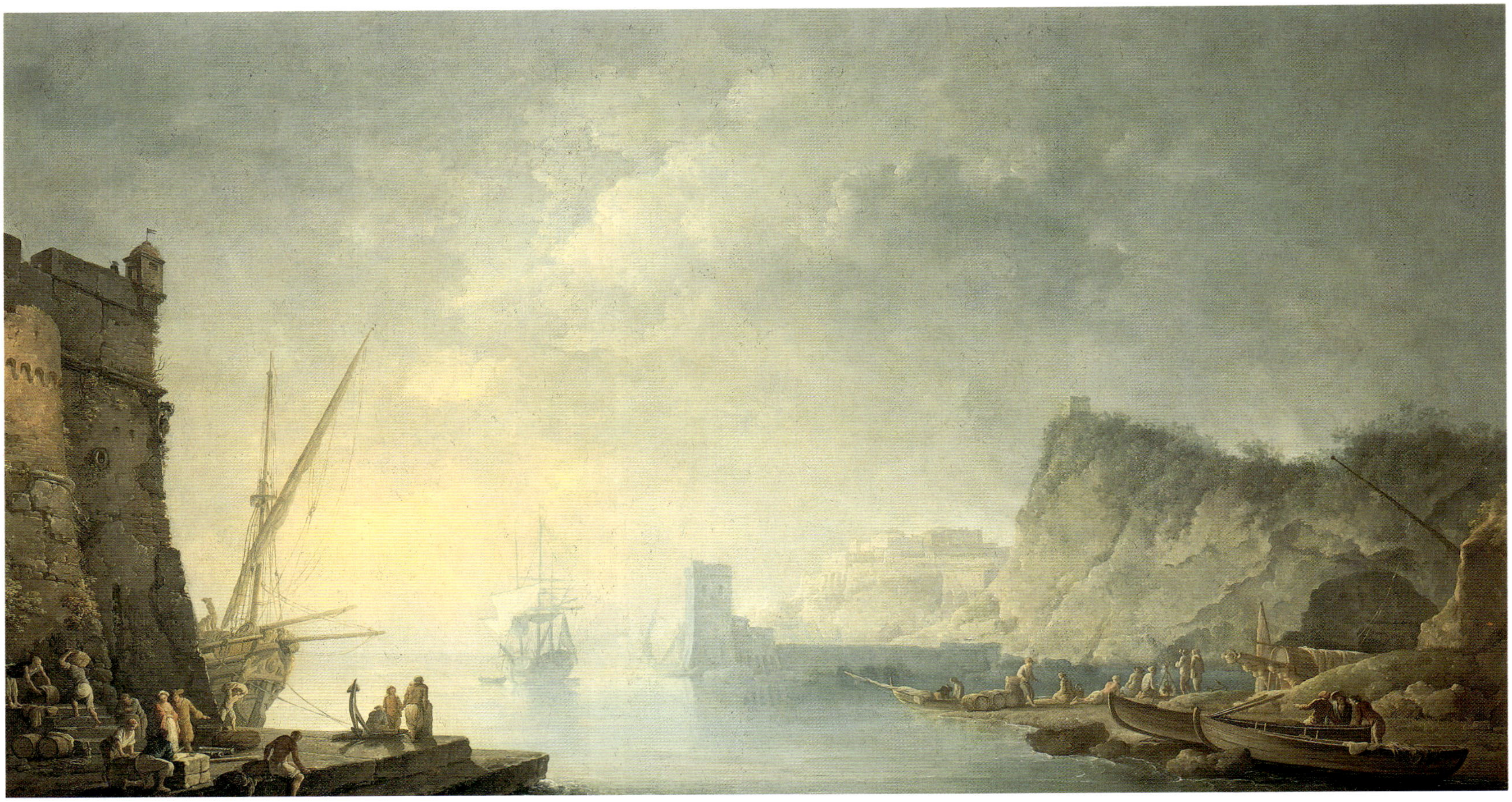

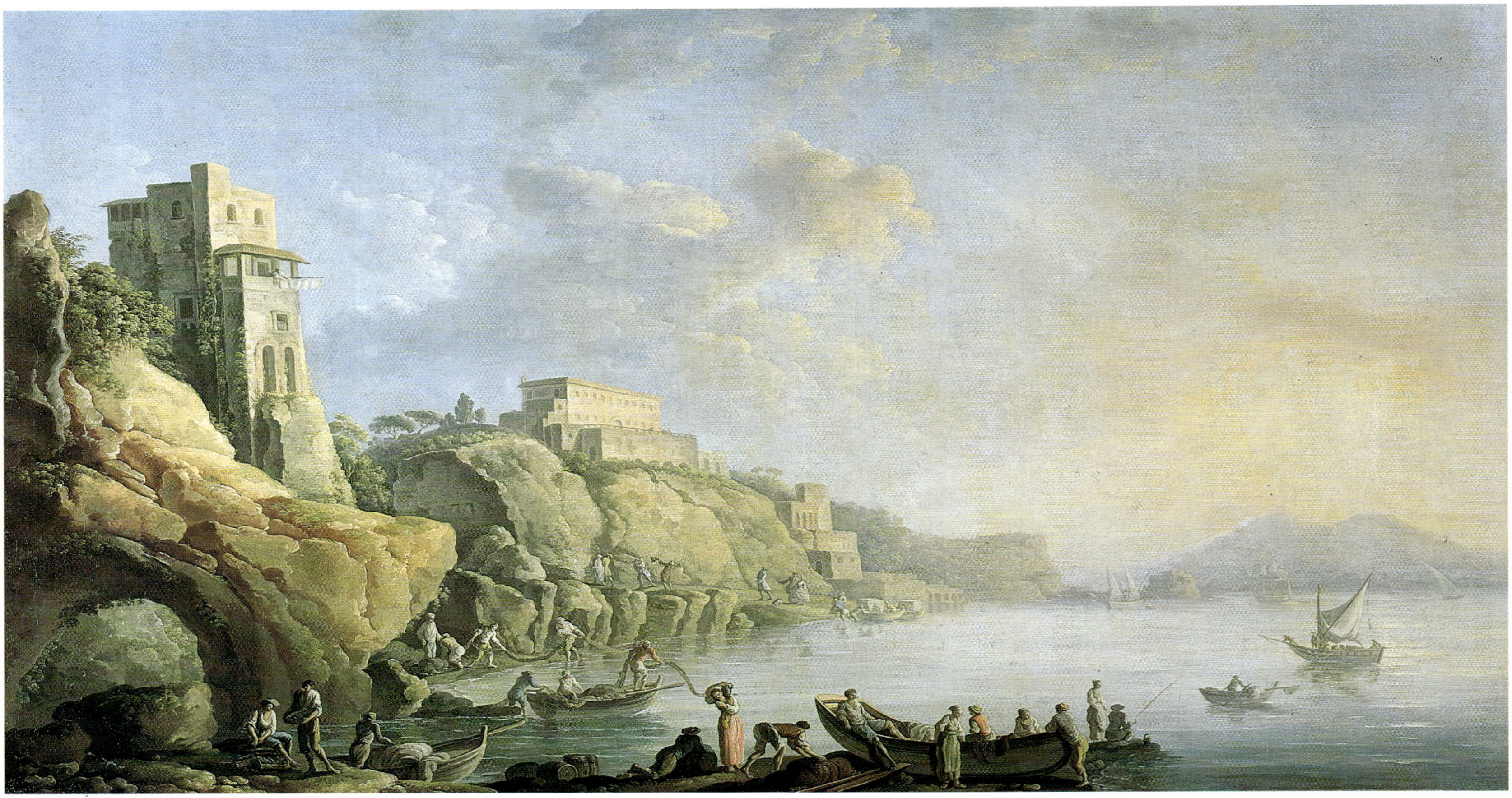

Carlo Bonavia, Coast Scene. Turin, private collection.

Carlo Bonavia, Lord Napier's Villa or Villa delle Cannonate. Rome, private collection.

Carlo Bonavia, Virgil's Tomb with Castel Sant'Elmo and the Charterhouse of San Martino in the background. Naples, D'Amodio Collection.

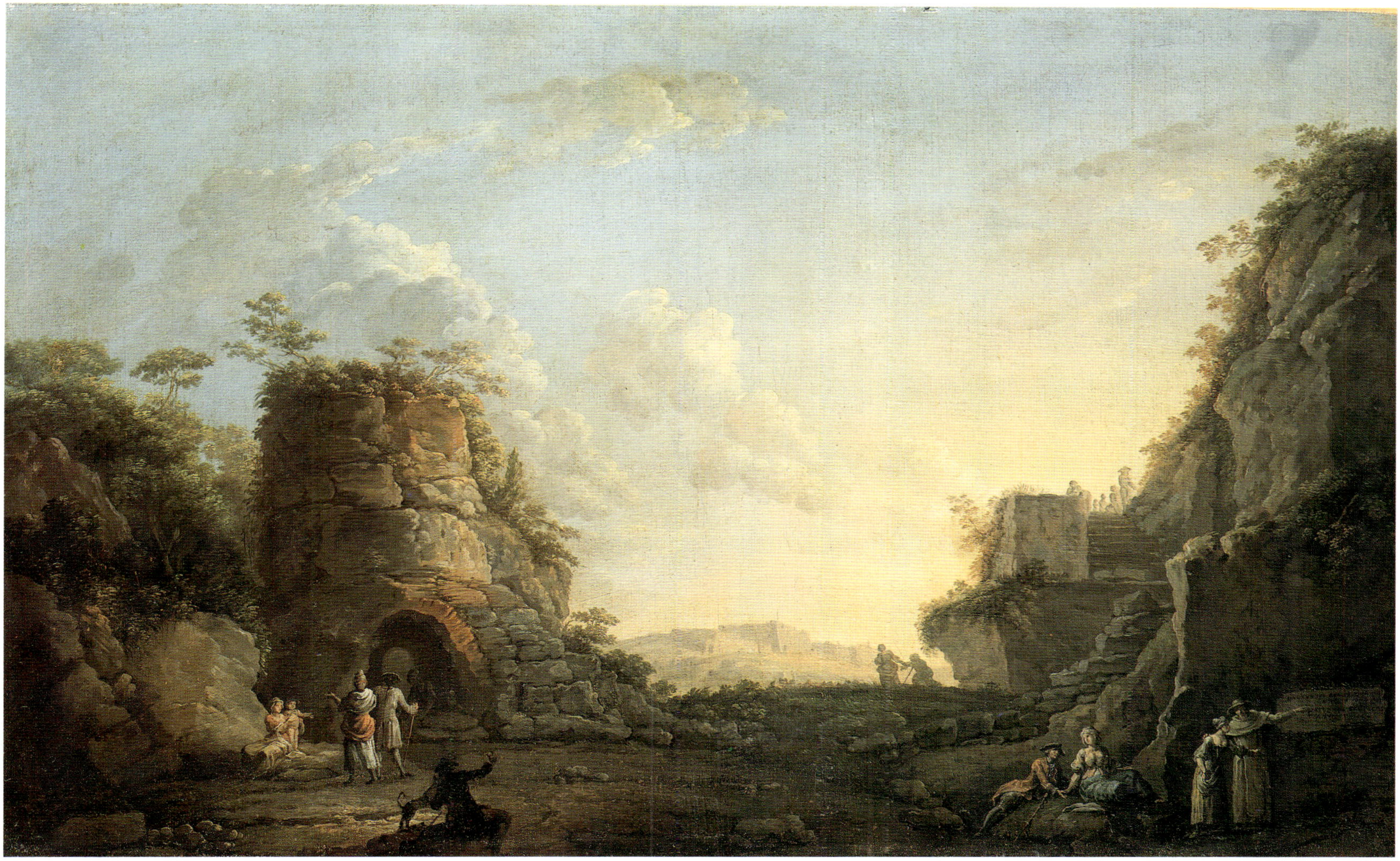

Carlo Bonavia, Eruption of Vesuvius from the Mole Lighthouse in the Moonlight. Beaulieu, National Motor Museum, Lord Montagu.

Carlo Bonavia, Coast Scene near Naples at Sunset. Naples, D'Amodio Collection.

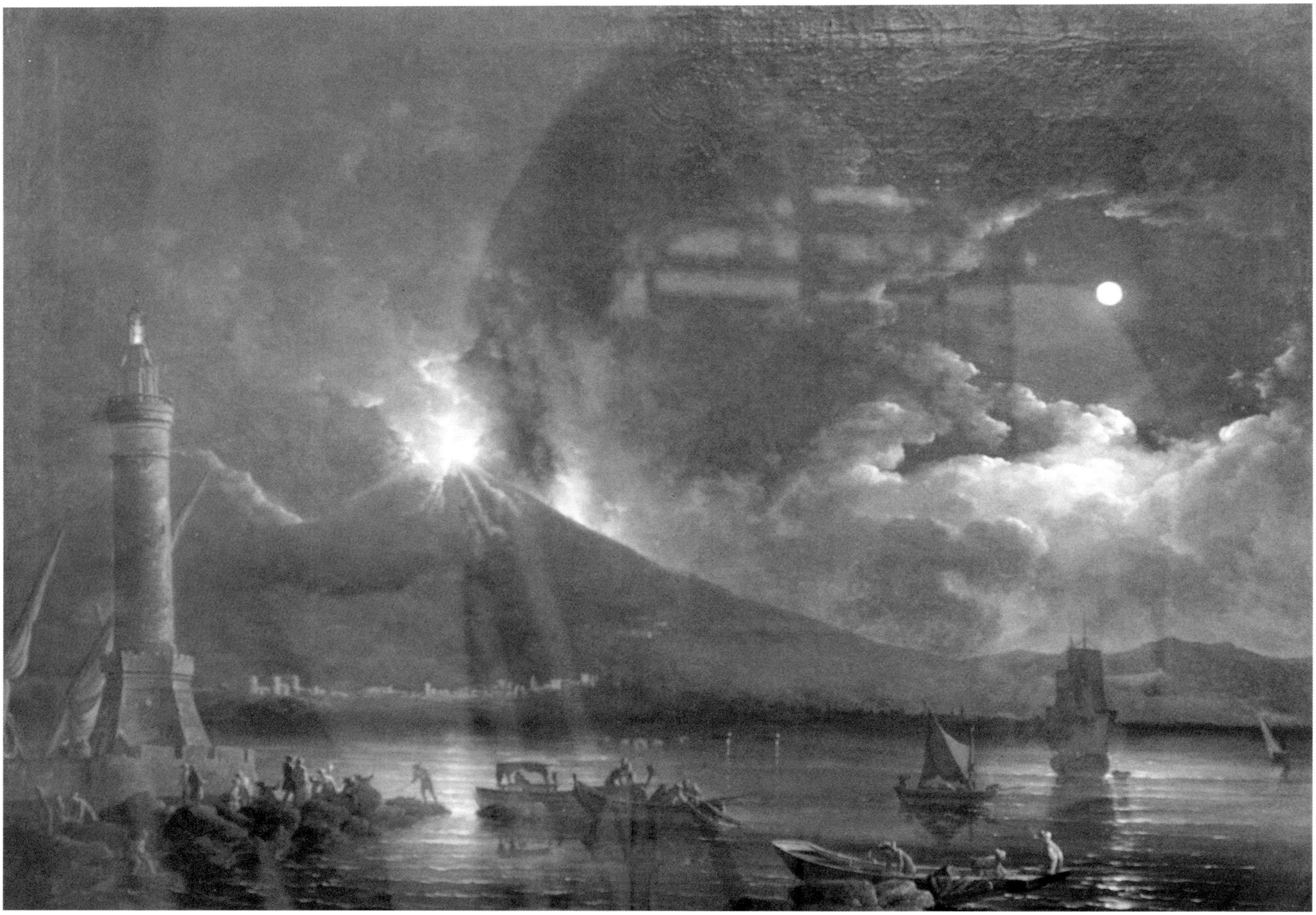

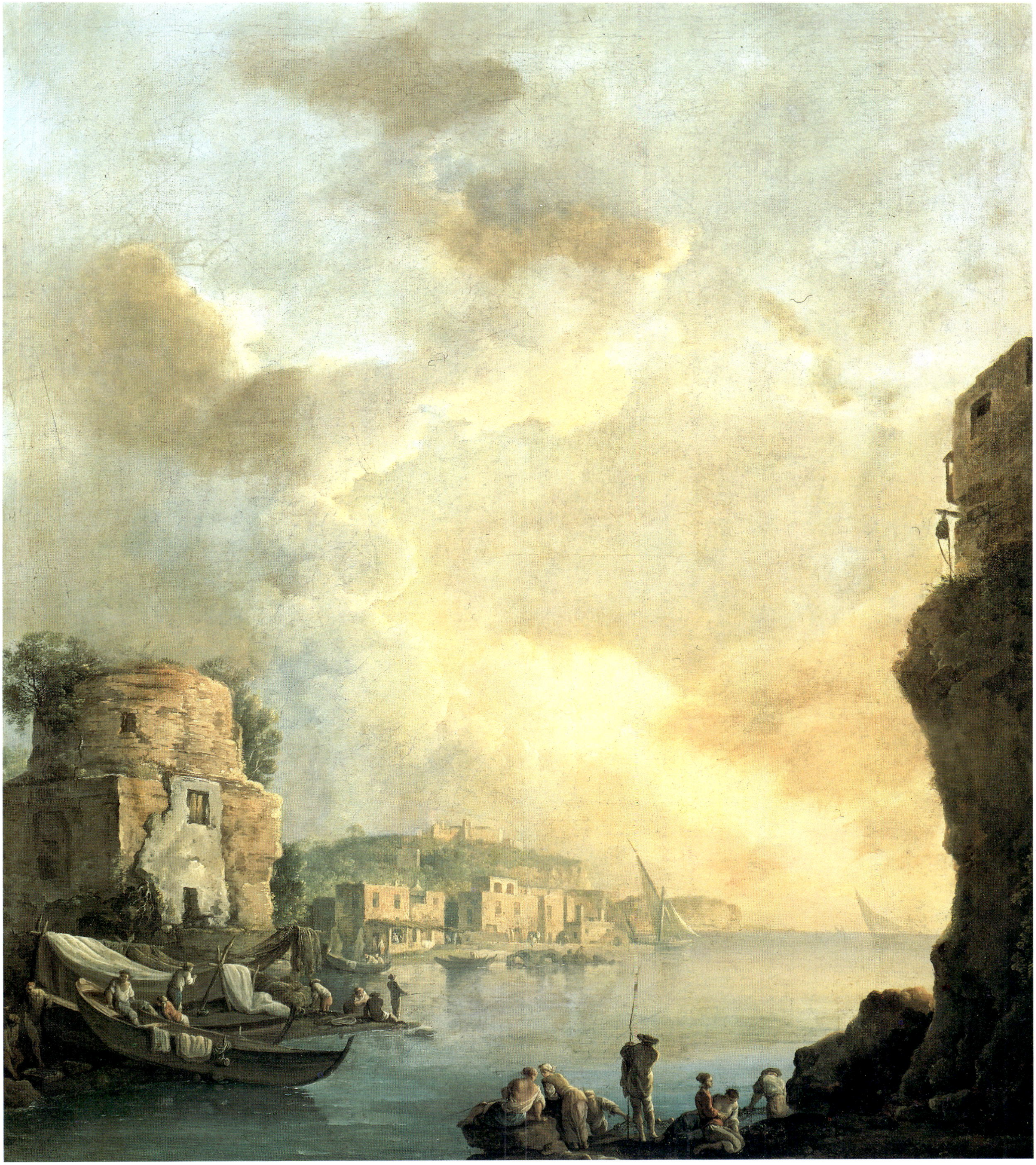

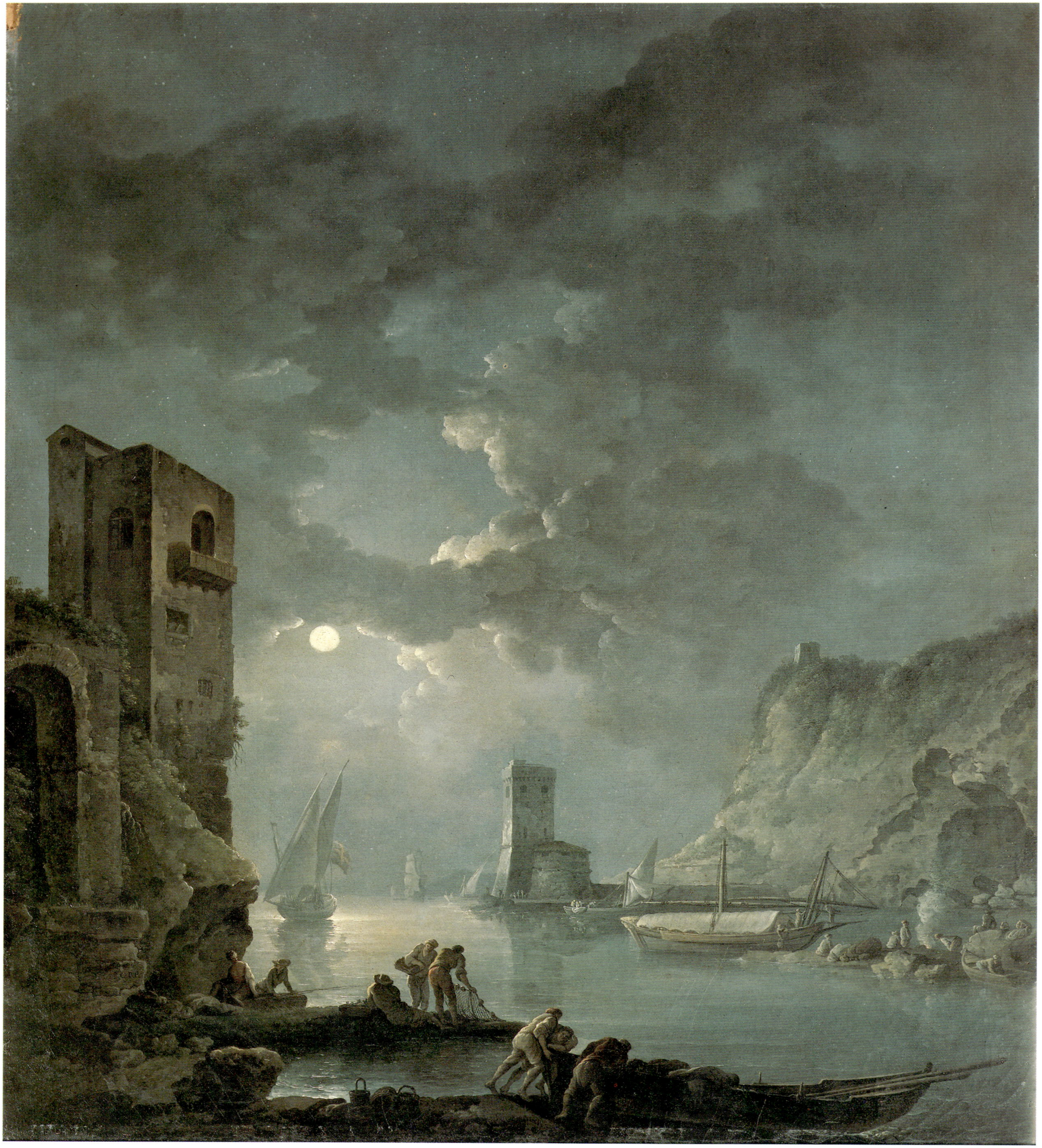

Carlo Bonavia, Coast Scene in the Moonlight. Naples, D'Amodio Collection.

Gabriele Ricciardelli, The Bay of Pozzuoli. Rome, private collection.

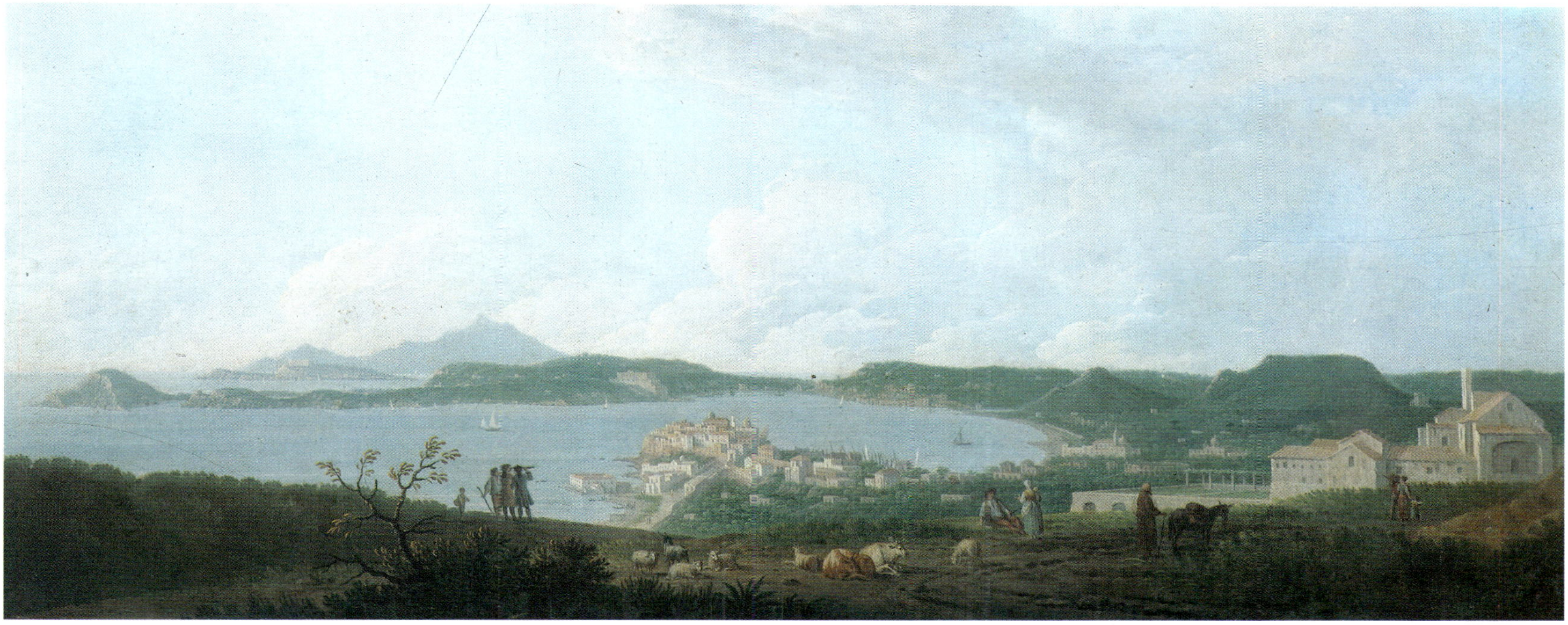

Pietro Antoniani, Eruptions of Vesuvius in 1767. London, William Mostyn-Owen.

Pietro Antoniani, View of Naples with the Eruption of Vesuvius. Naples, D'Amodio Collection.

P.-J. Volaire, Eruption of Vesuvius with the Bridge of the Maddalena. Naples, Capodimonte Museum.

P.-J. Volaire, Neapolitan seascape by night. Naples, Royal Palace.

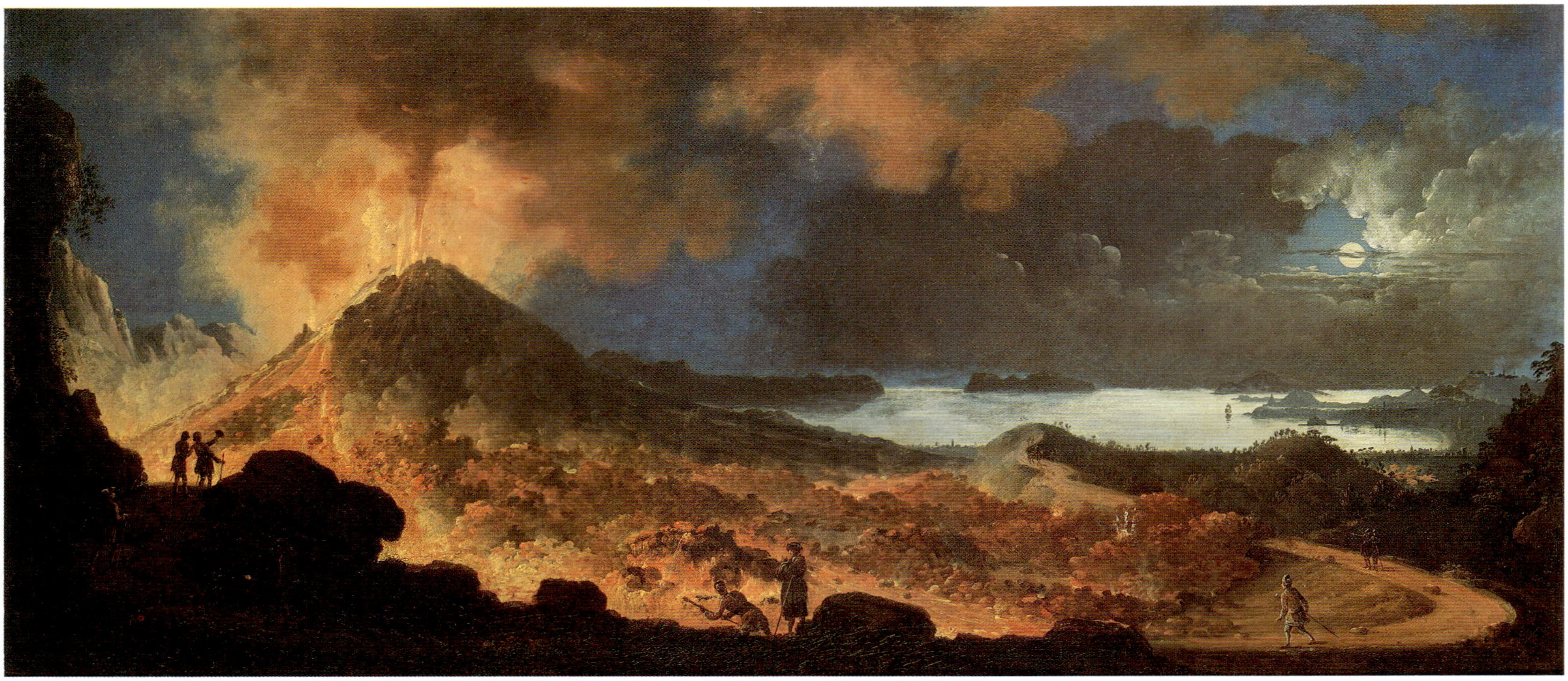

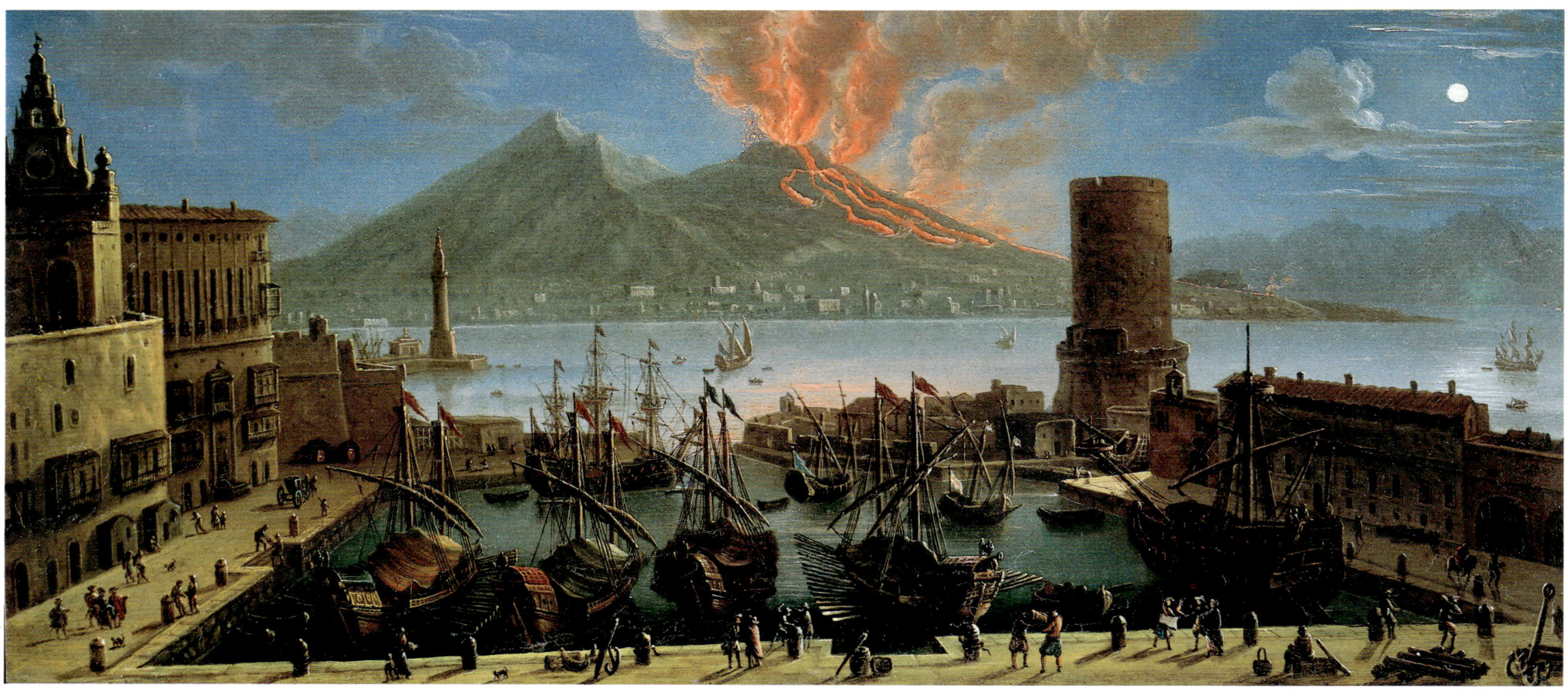

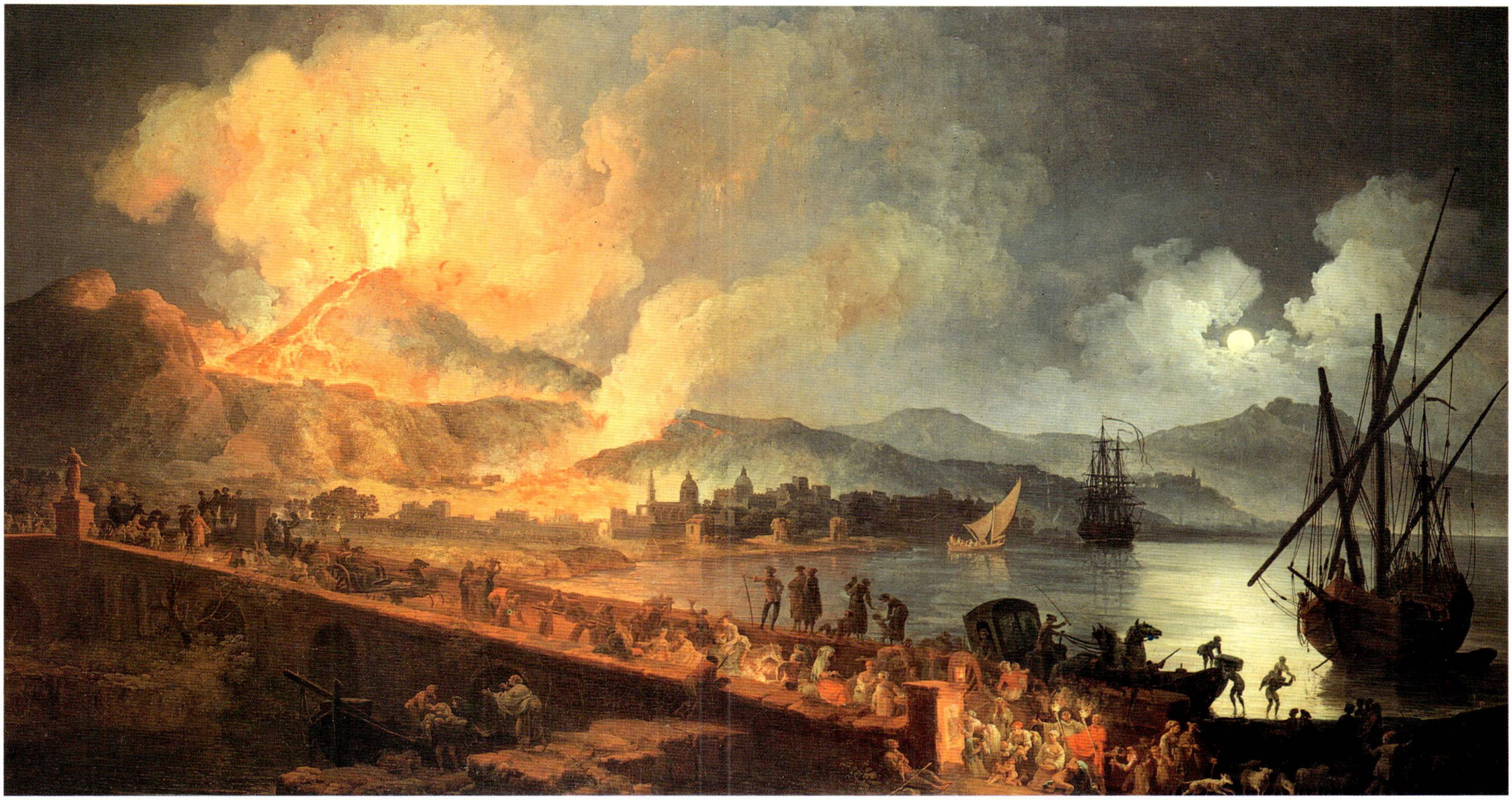

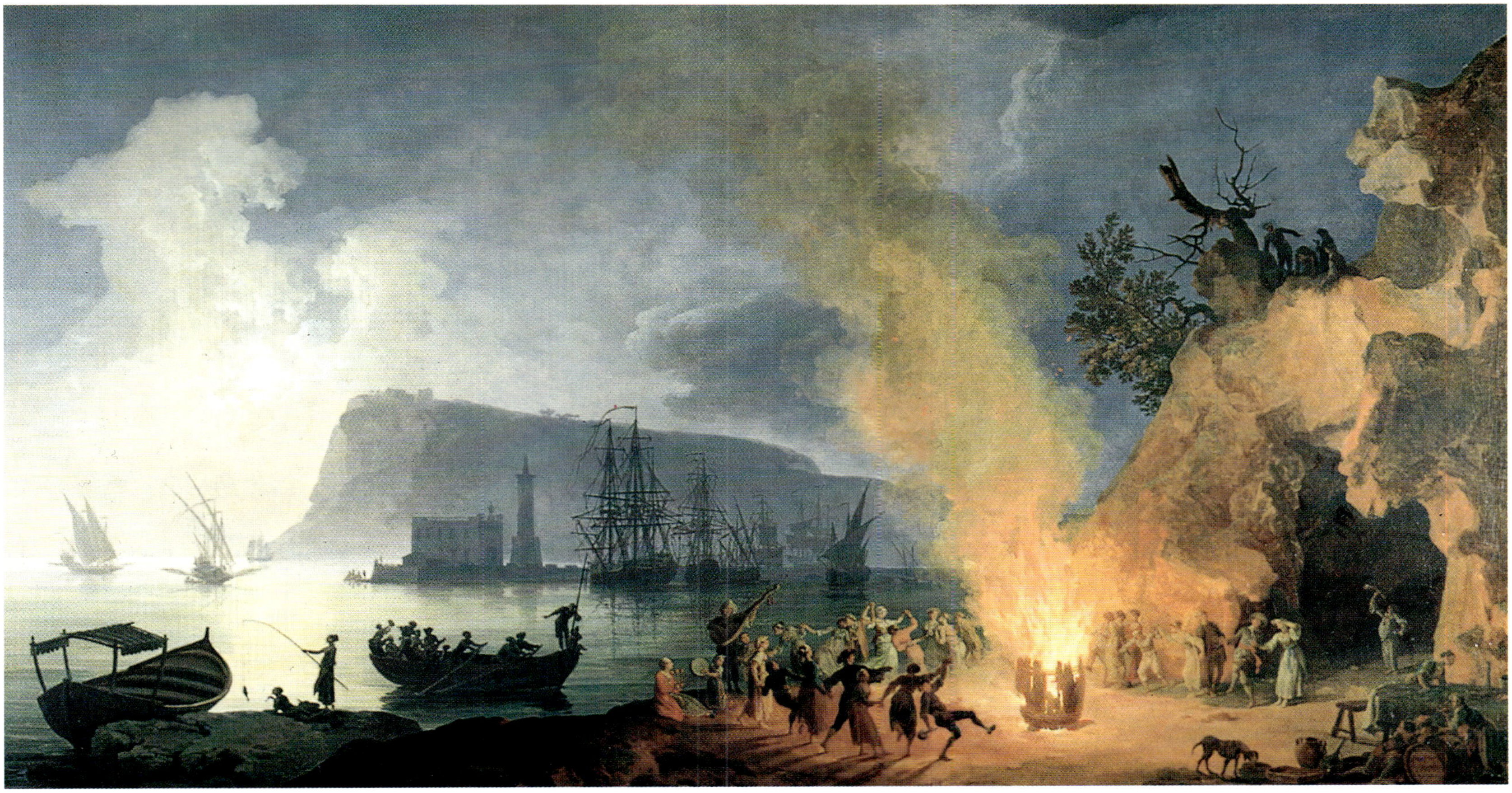

Richard Wilson, Lake Avernus. Tate Gallery, London.

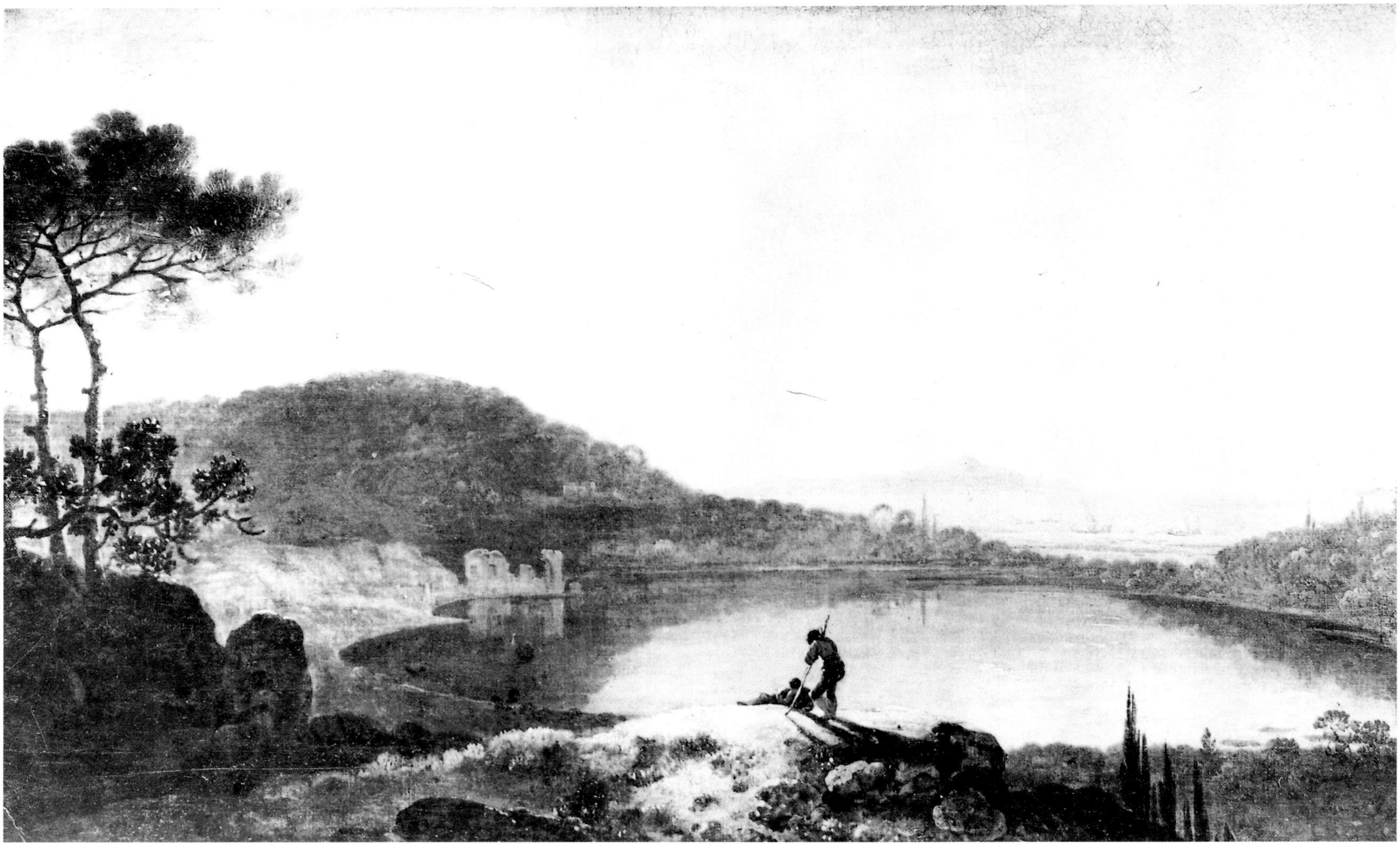

Joseph Wright of Derby, Vesuvius. Private collection, England.

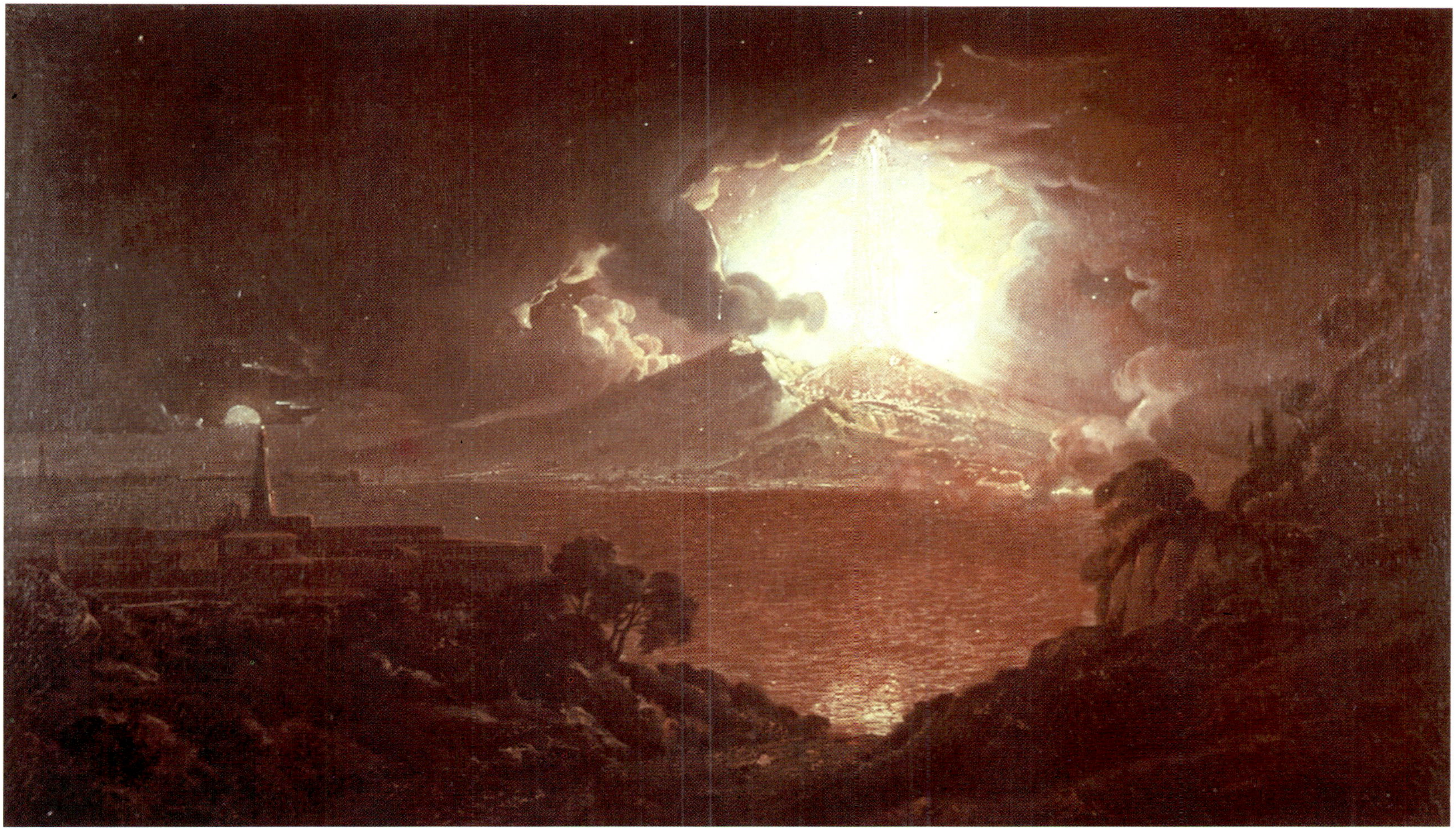

Thomas Jones, Houses in Naples. Trustees of the British Museum, London.

Thomas Jones, Rooftops in Naples. Visitors of the Ashmolean Museum, Oxford.

Thomas Jones, The Bay of Naples and the Mole Lighthouse. Private collection, England.

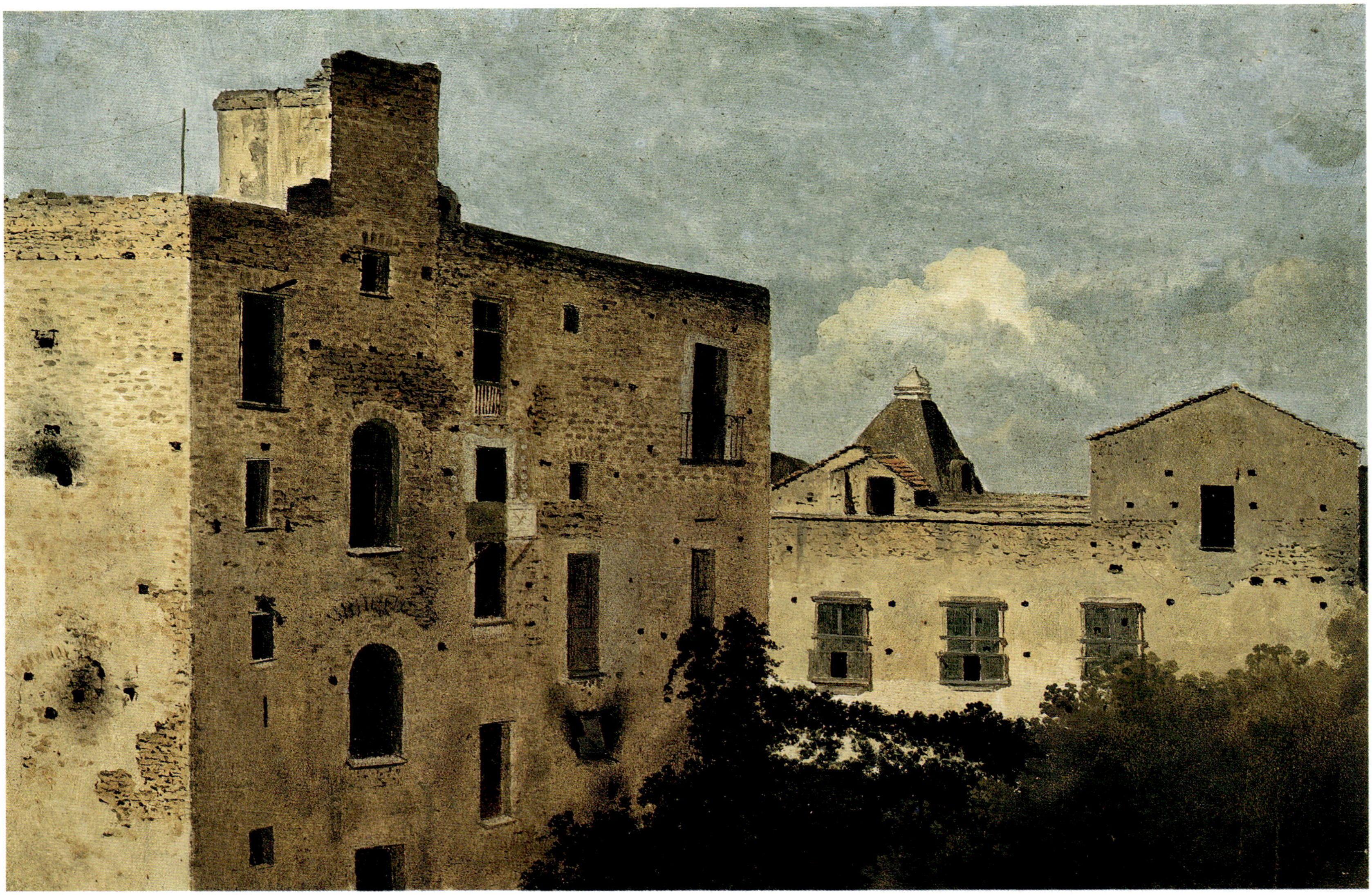

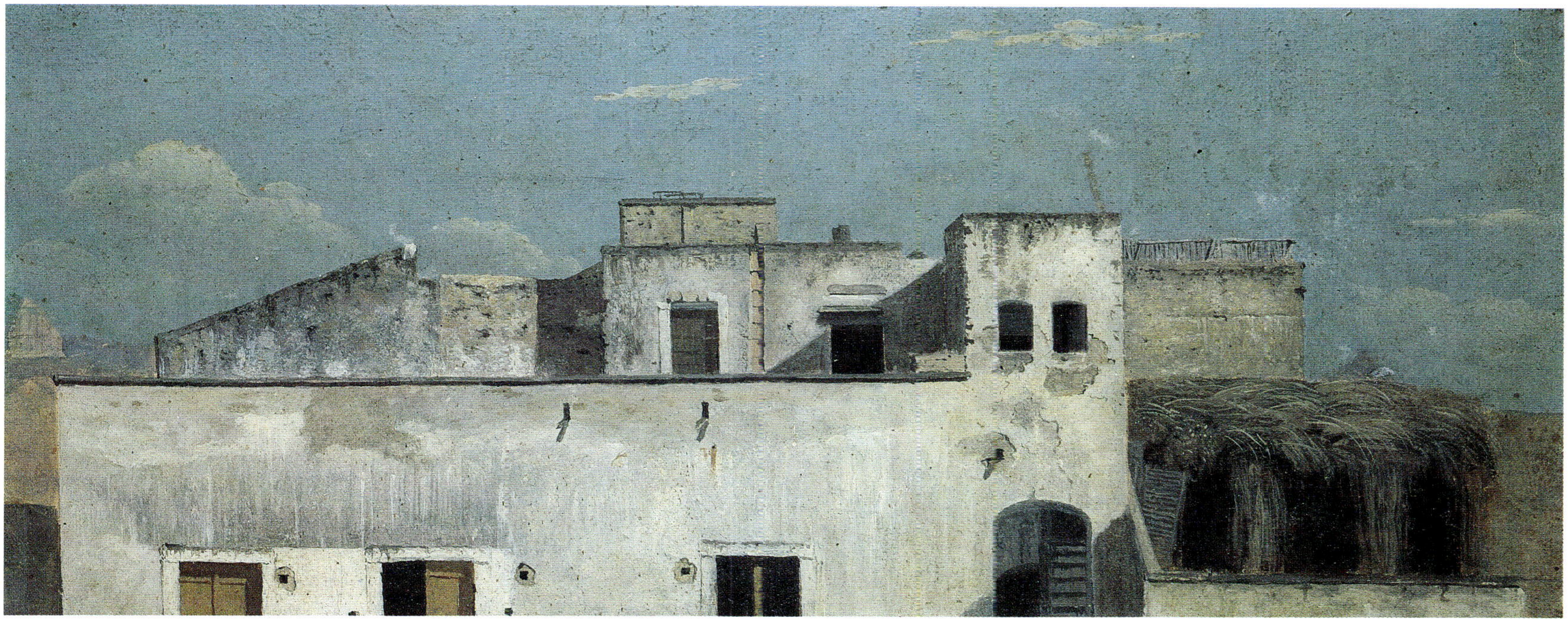

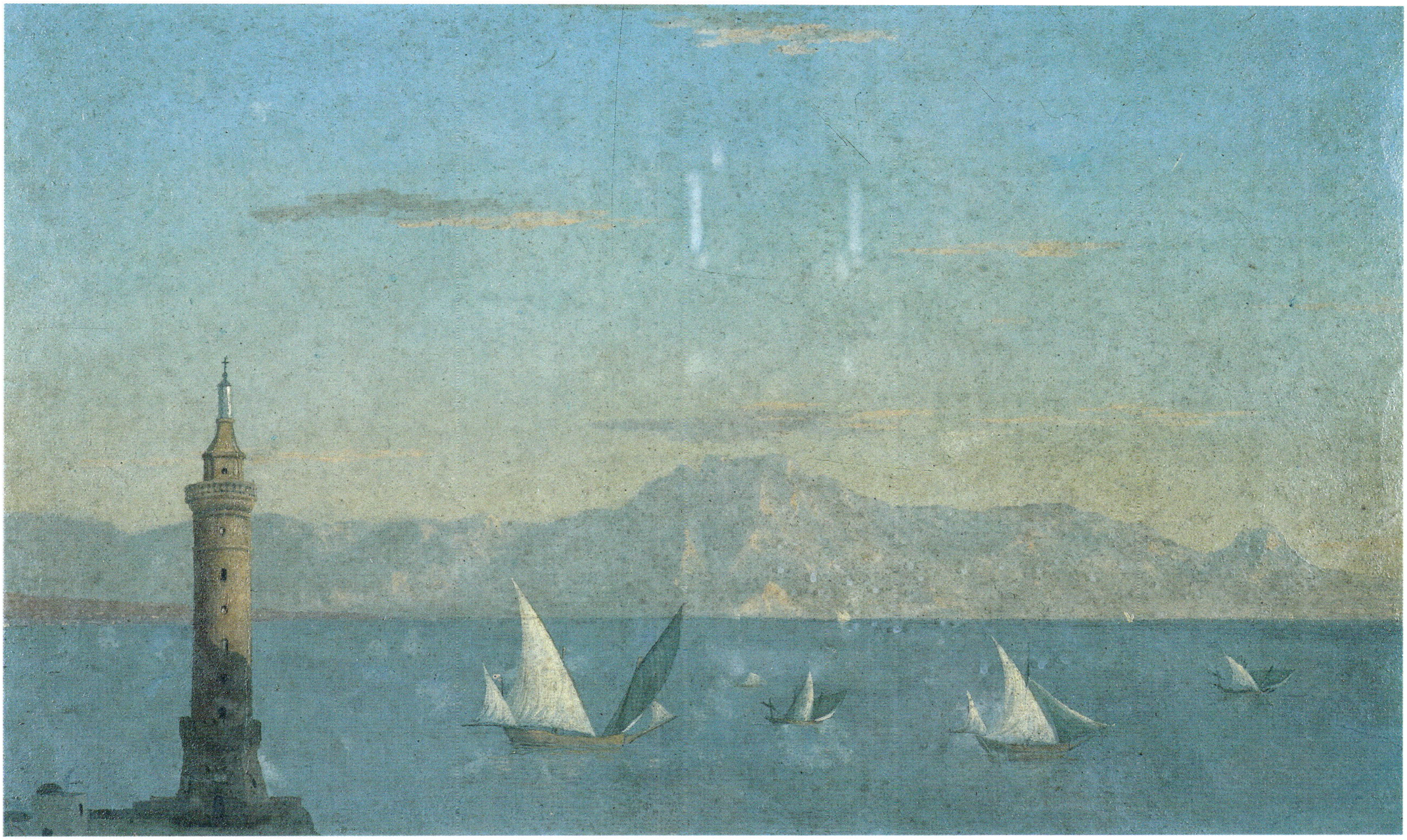

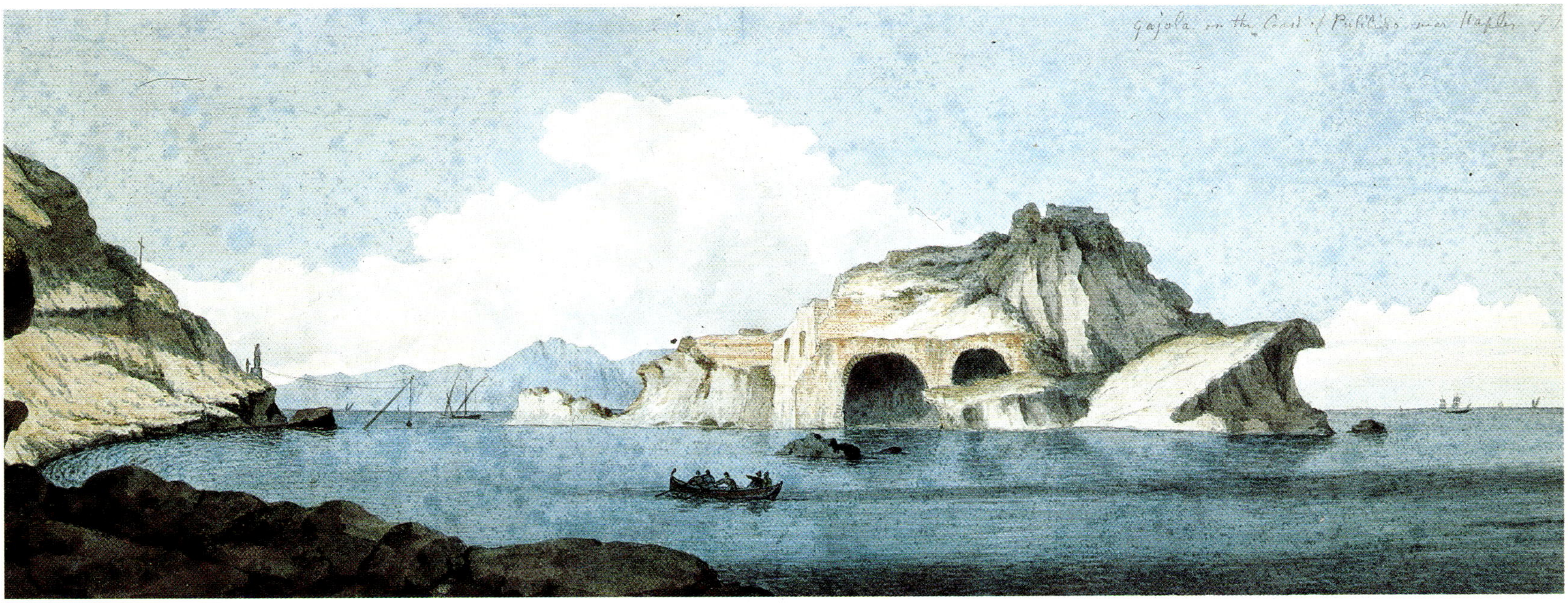
Gajola on the Coast of Pusilipo near Naples

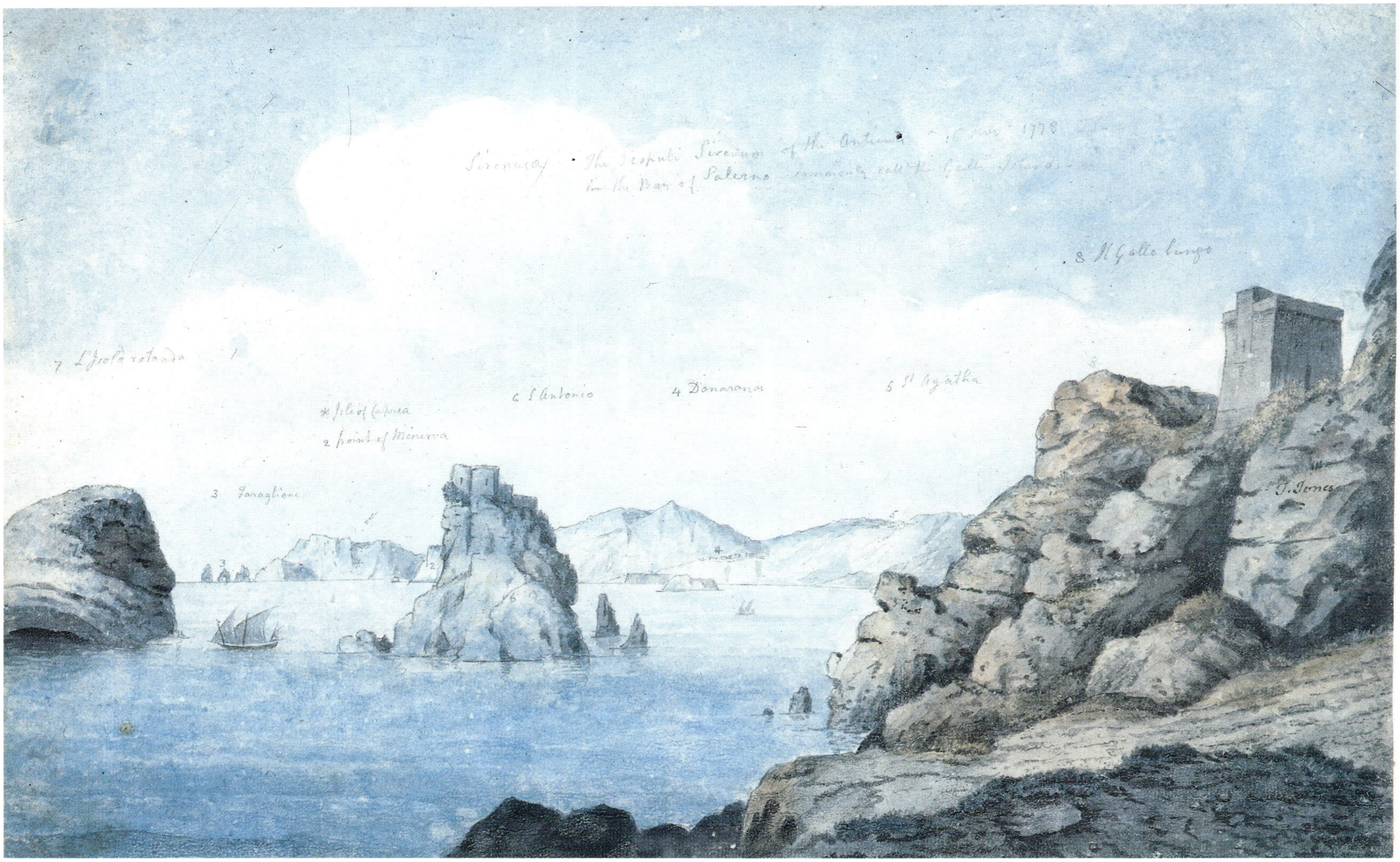
8 Il Gallo lungo
7 L'Isola rotonda
6 S Antonio
4 Donarana
5 St Agatha
* Isle of Caprea
2 point of Minerva
3 Faraglioni
T. Jones

Thomas Jones, Gaiola. National Museum of Wales, Cardiff.

Thomas Jones, In the Bay of Salerno. Trustees of the British Museum, London.

Thomas Jones, Landscape with dome. Birminghem City Museum and Art Gallery.

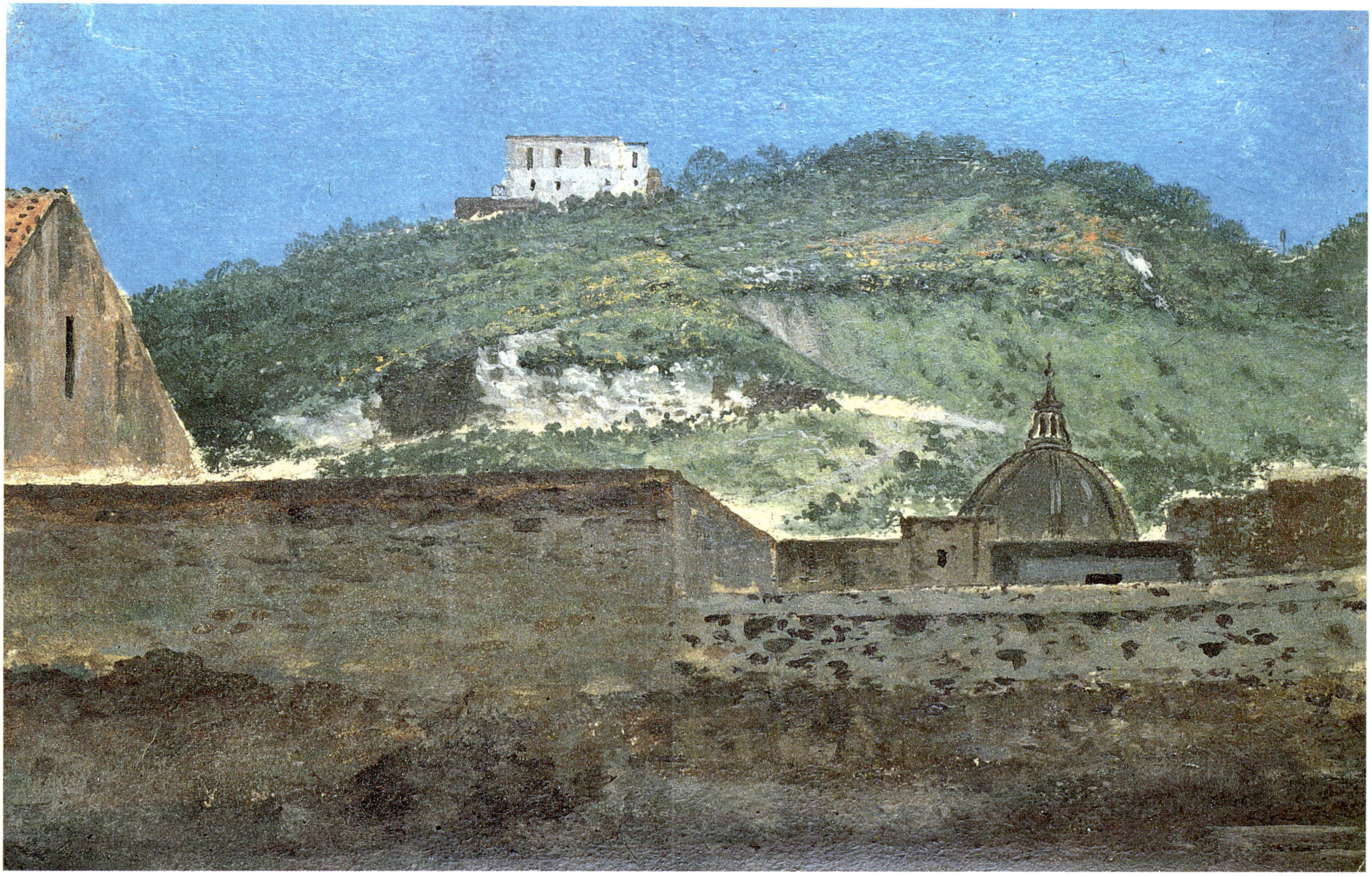

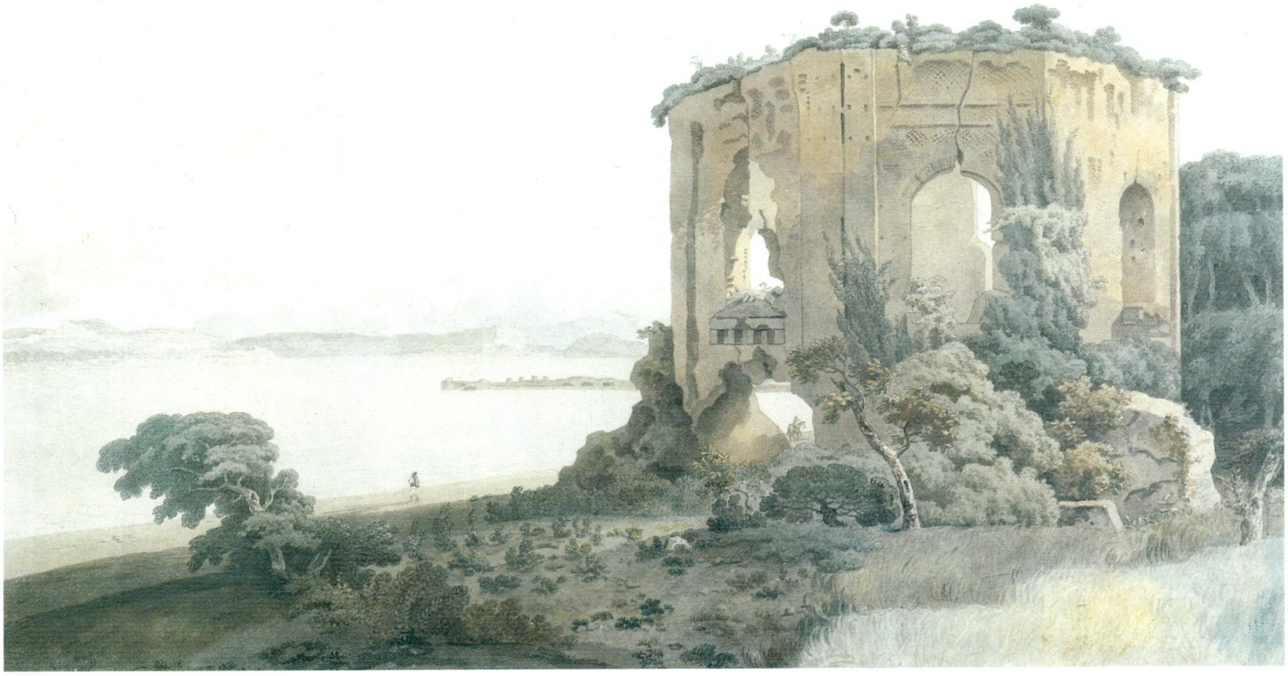

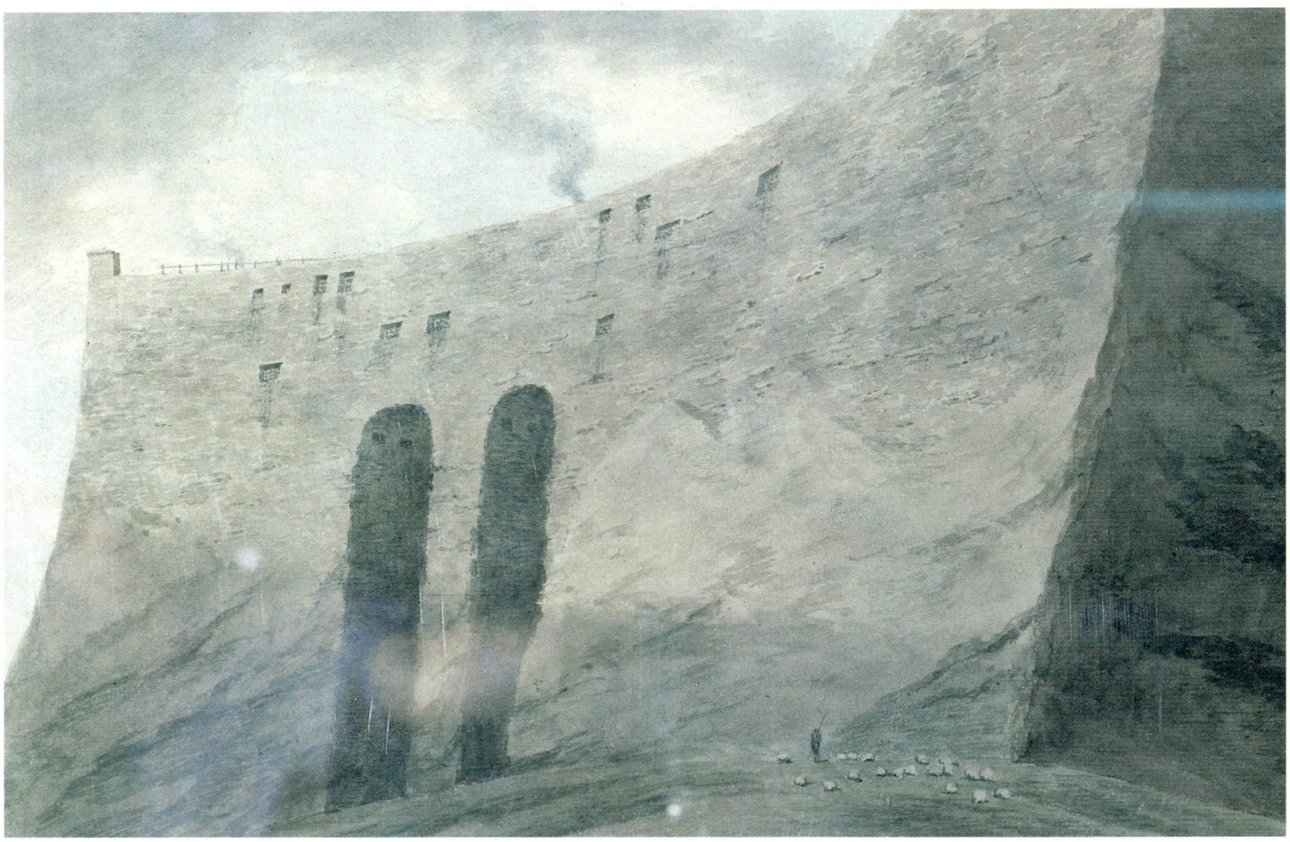

William Pars, The Temple of Venus, Bay of Baia. Birmingham City Museum and Art Gallery.

John Robert Cozens, Castel S. Elmo. Trustees of the British Museum, London.

John Robert Cozens, The Bay of Naples. Trustees of the British Museum, London.

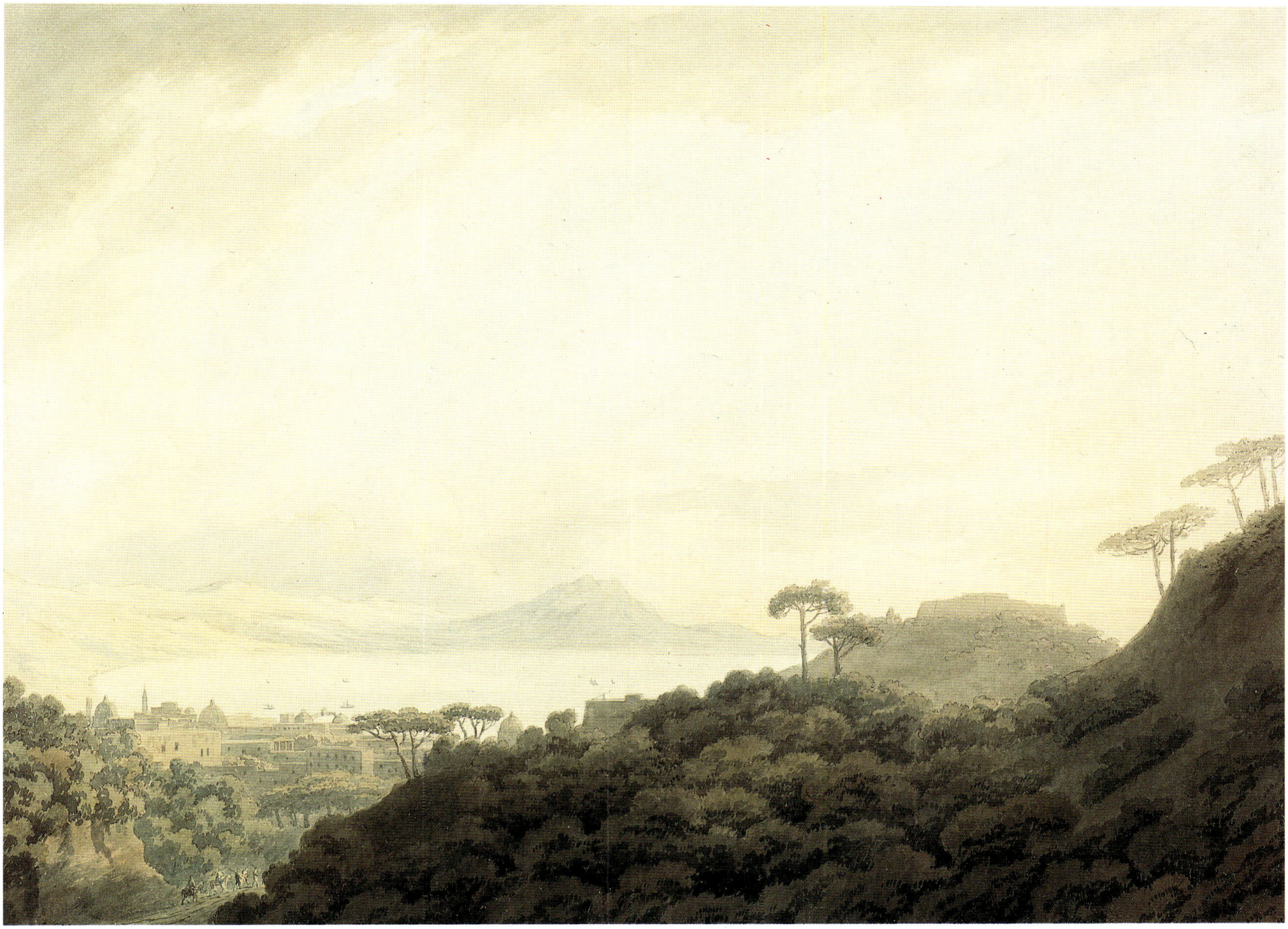

John Robert Cozens, Near the Mouth of the Garigliano. Trustees of the British Museum, London.

John Robert Cozens, Mare Morto, with the Islands of Procida and Ischia in the Distance. Trustees of the British Museum, London.

John Robert Cozens, Evening at Ratio with Vietri Beyond. Private collection, London.

John Robert Cozens, Coast Scene between Vietri and Salerno. Trustees of the Victoria and Albert Museum, London.

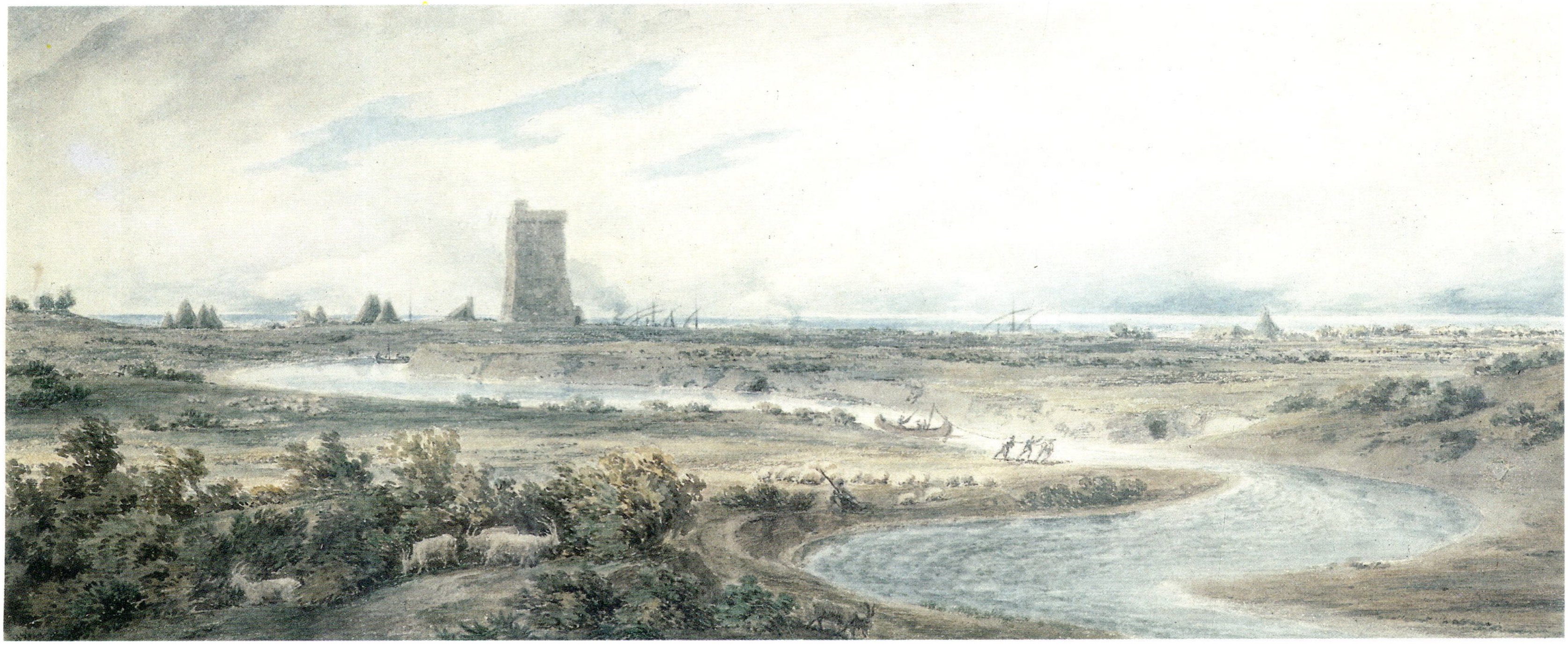

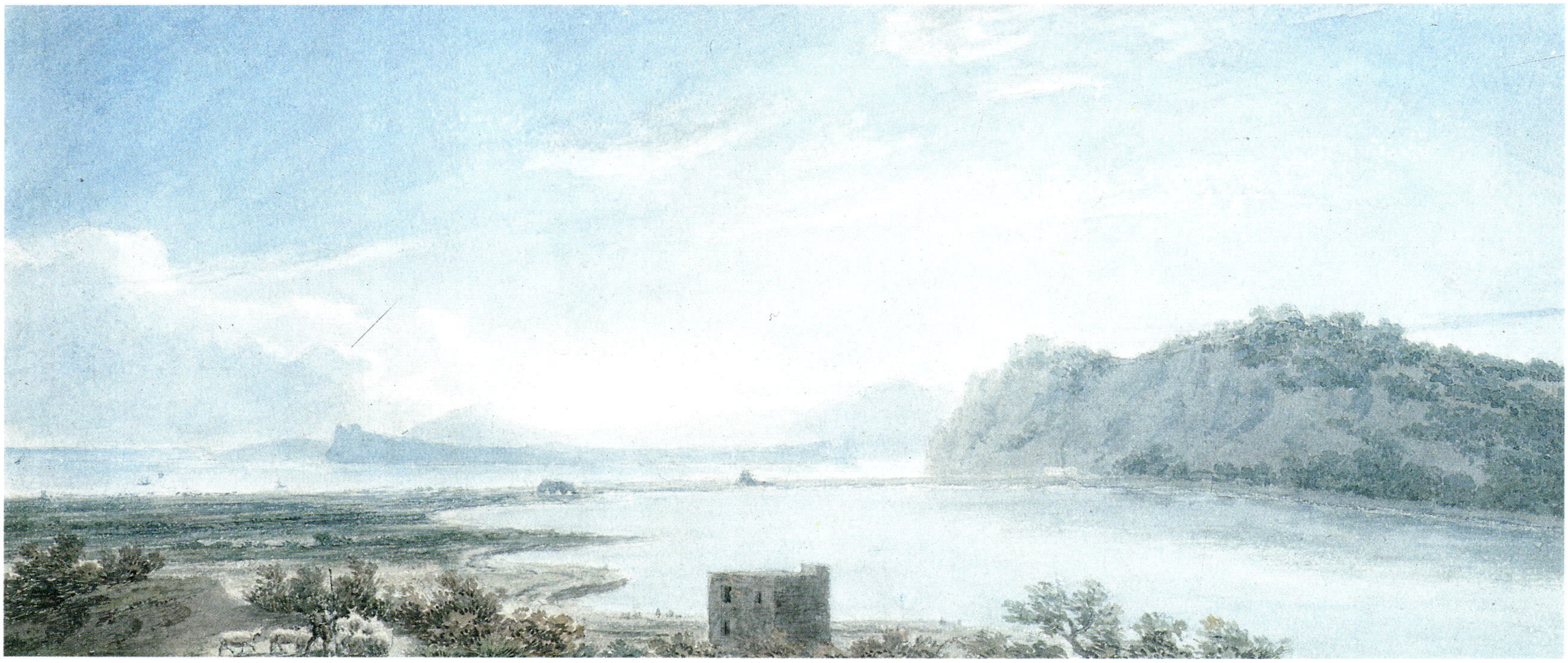

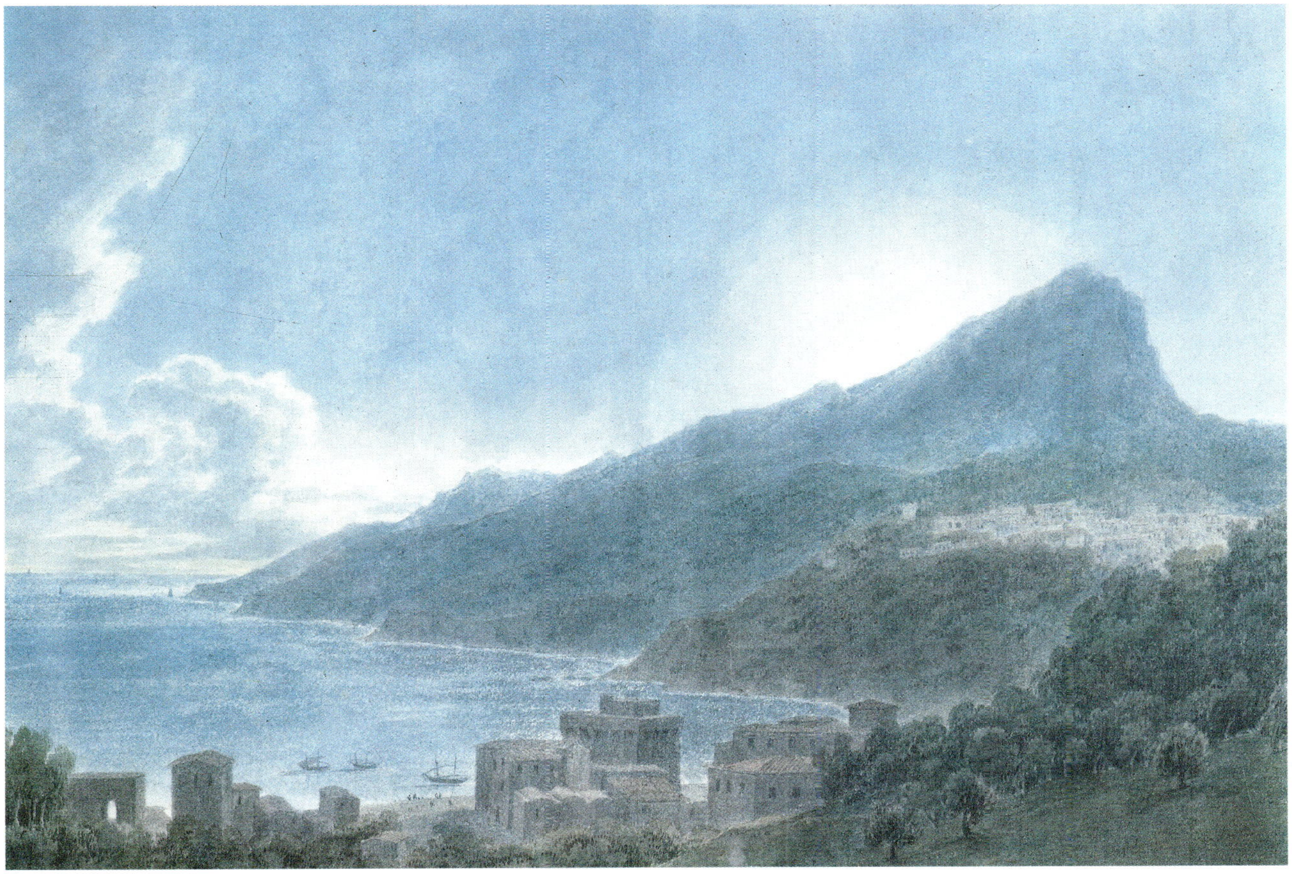

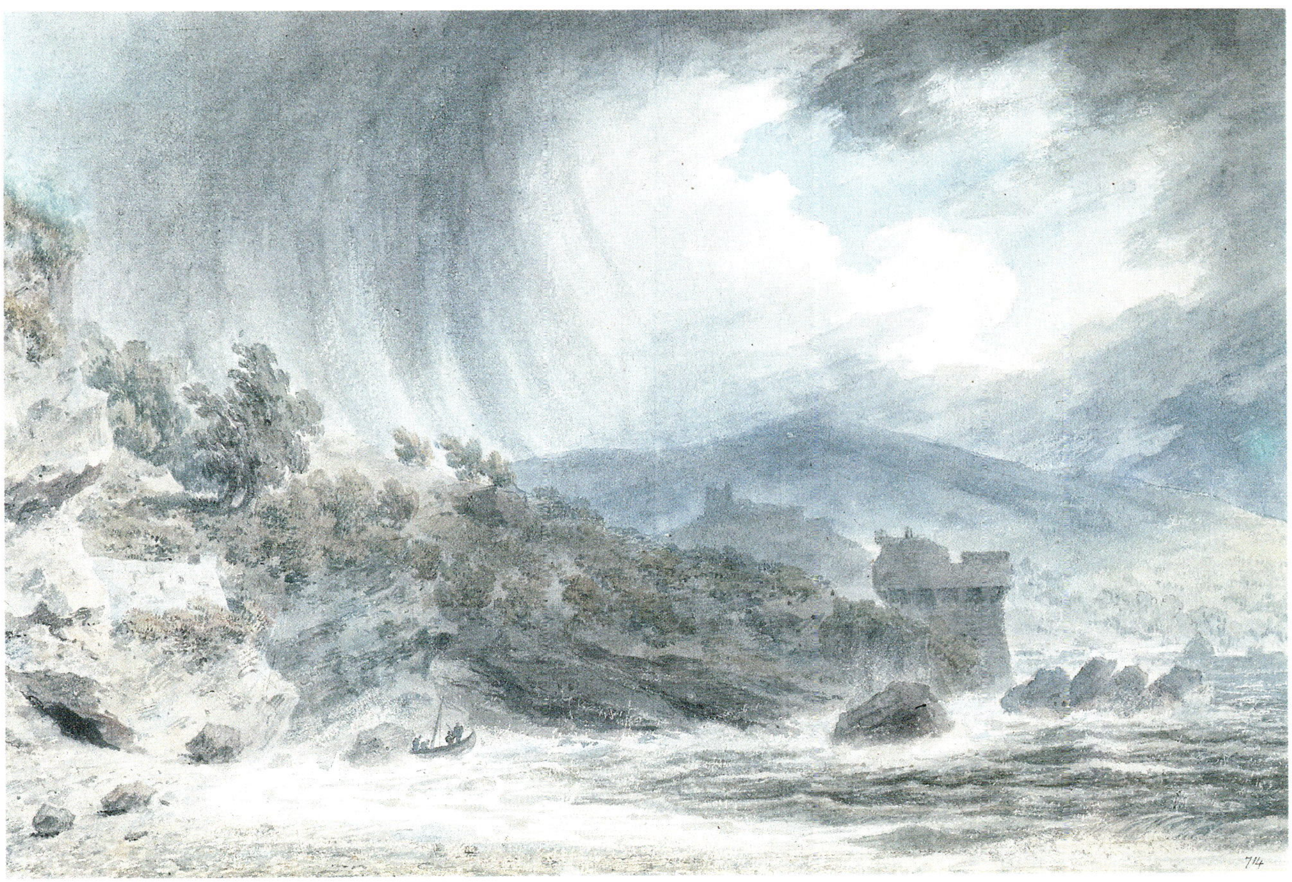
74

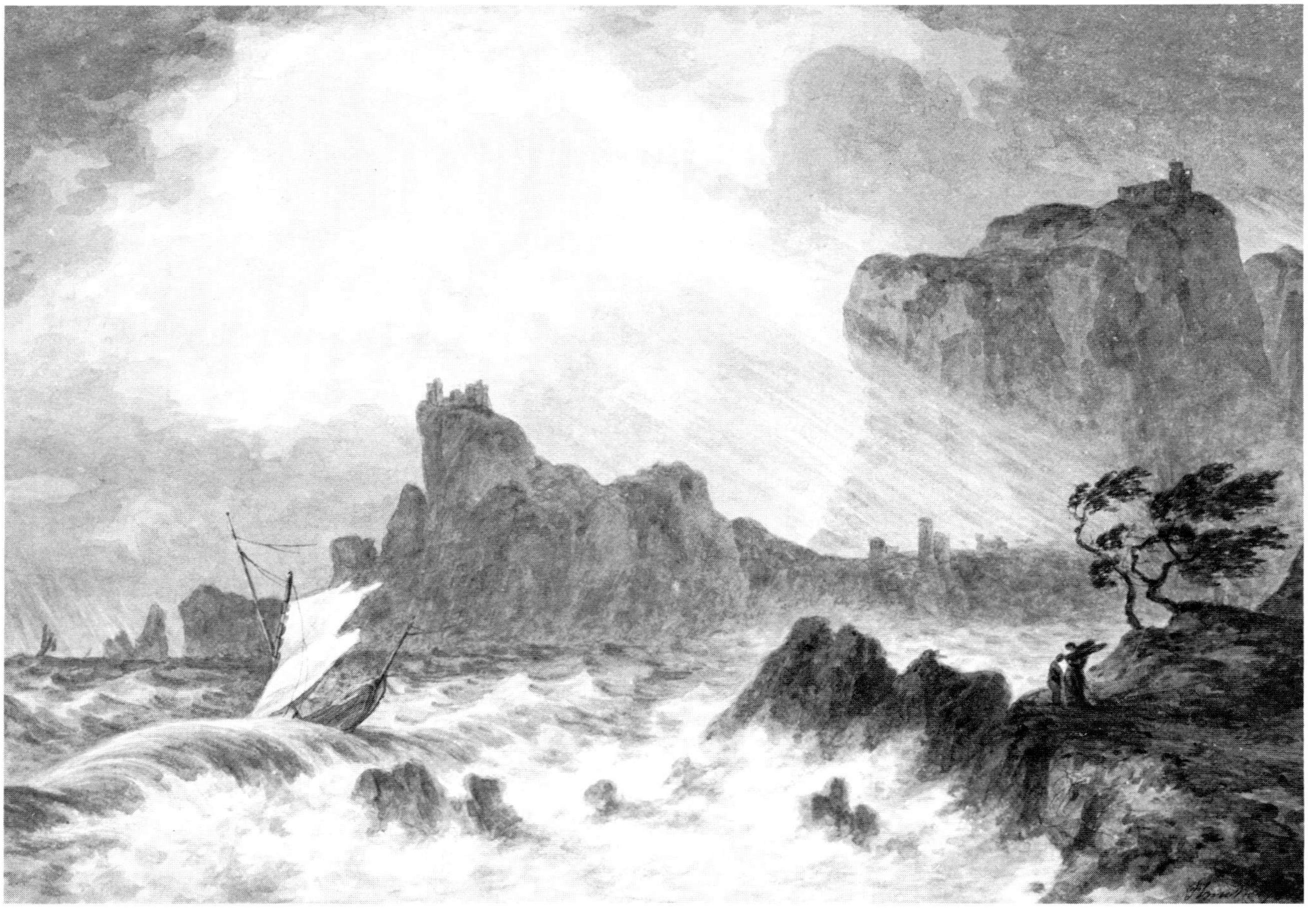

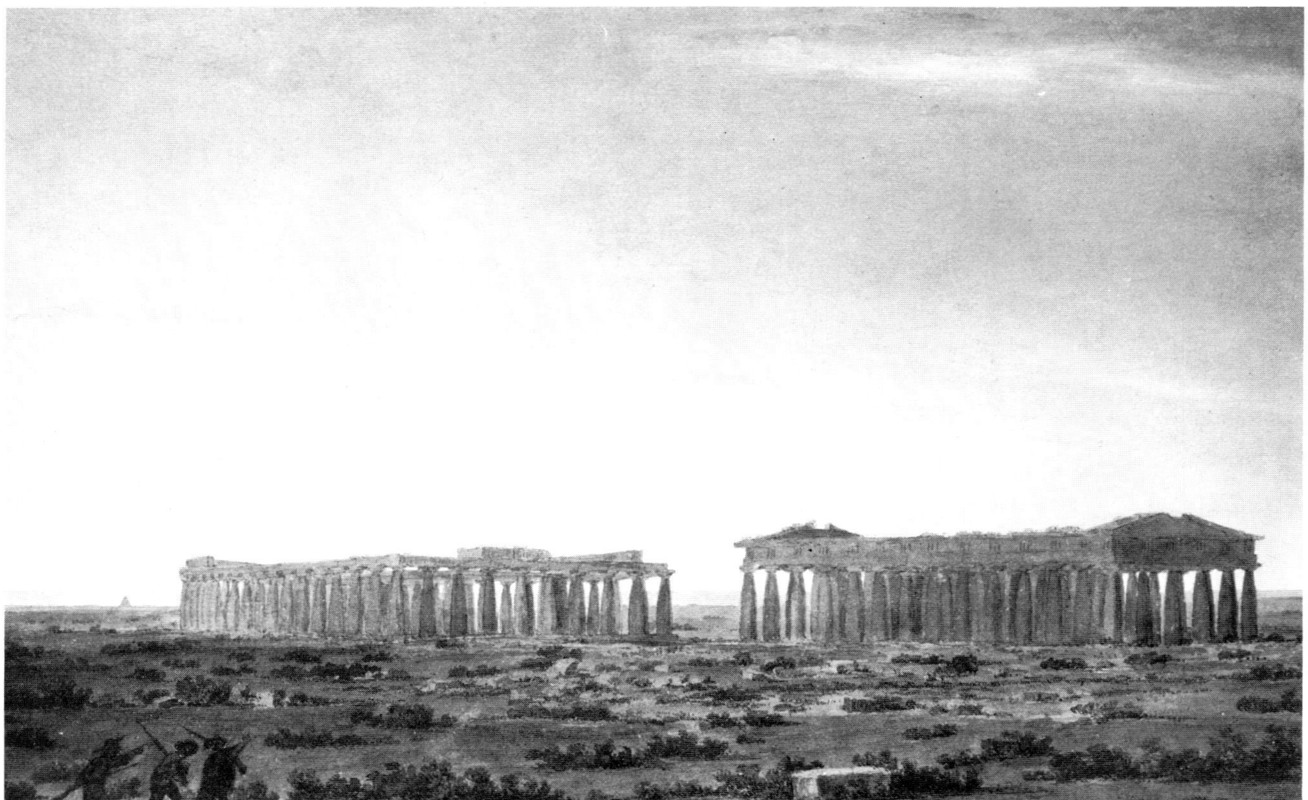

John Robert Cozens, Coast Scene between Vietri and Salerno: Storm Effect. Trustees of the Victoria and Albert Museum, London.

John Robert Cozens, The Two Temples at Paestum. Trustees of the Victoria and Albert Museum, London.

John Robert Cozens, A Shepherd's Hut between Naples and Portici. Trustees of the Victoria and Albert Museum, London.

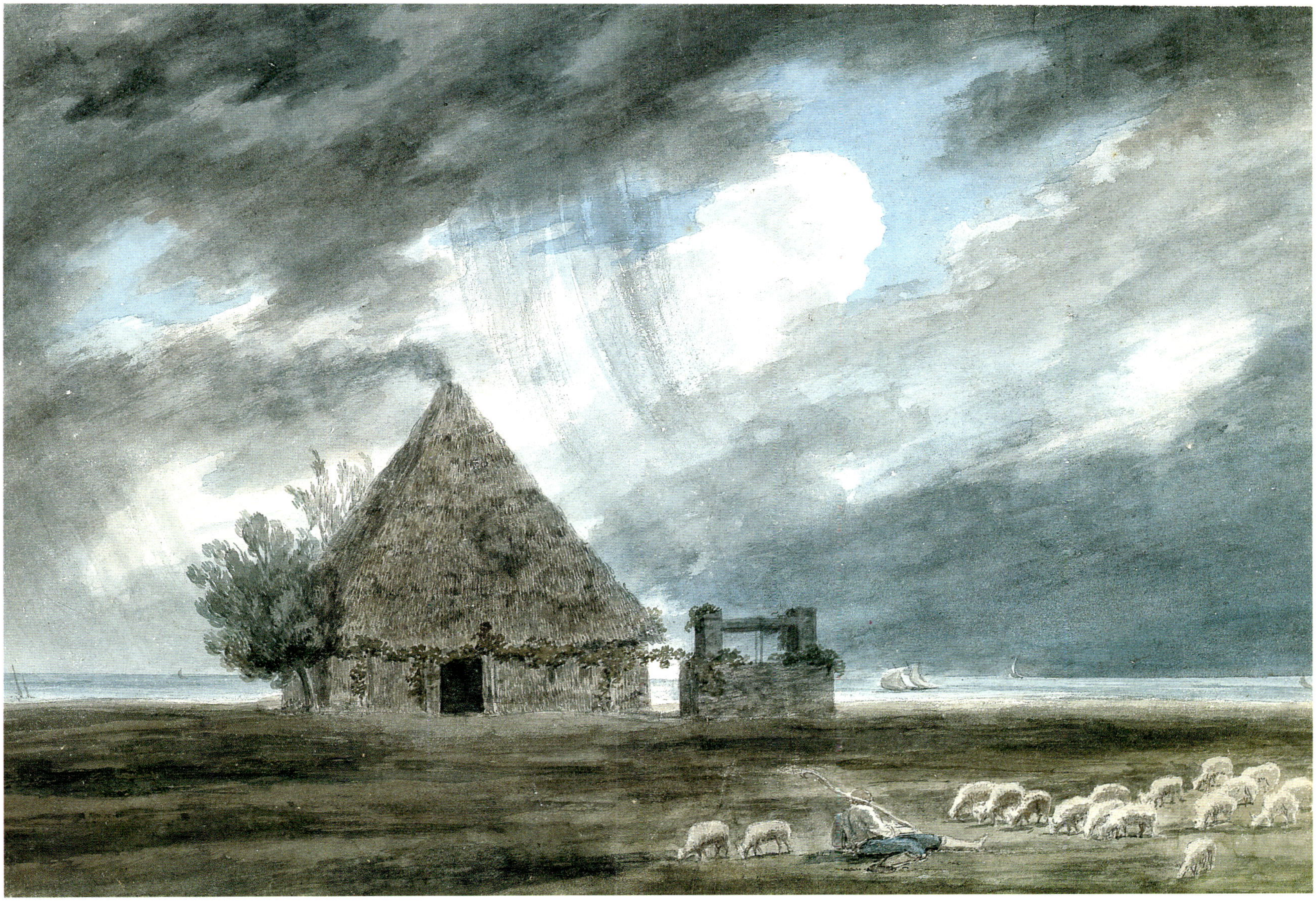

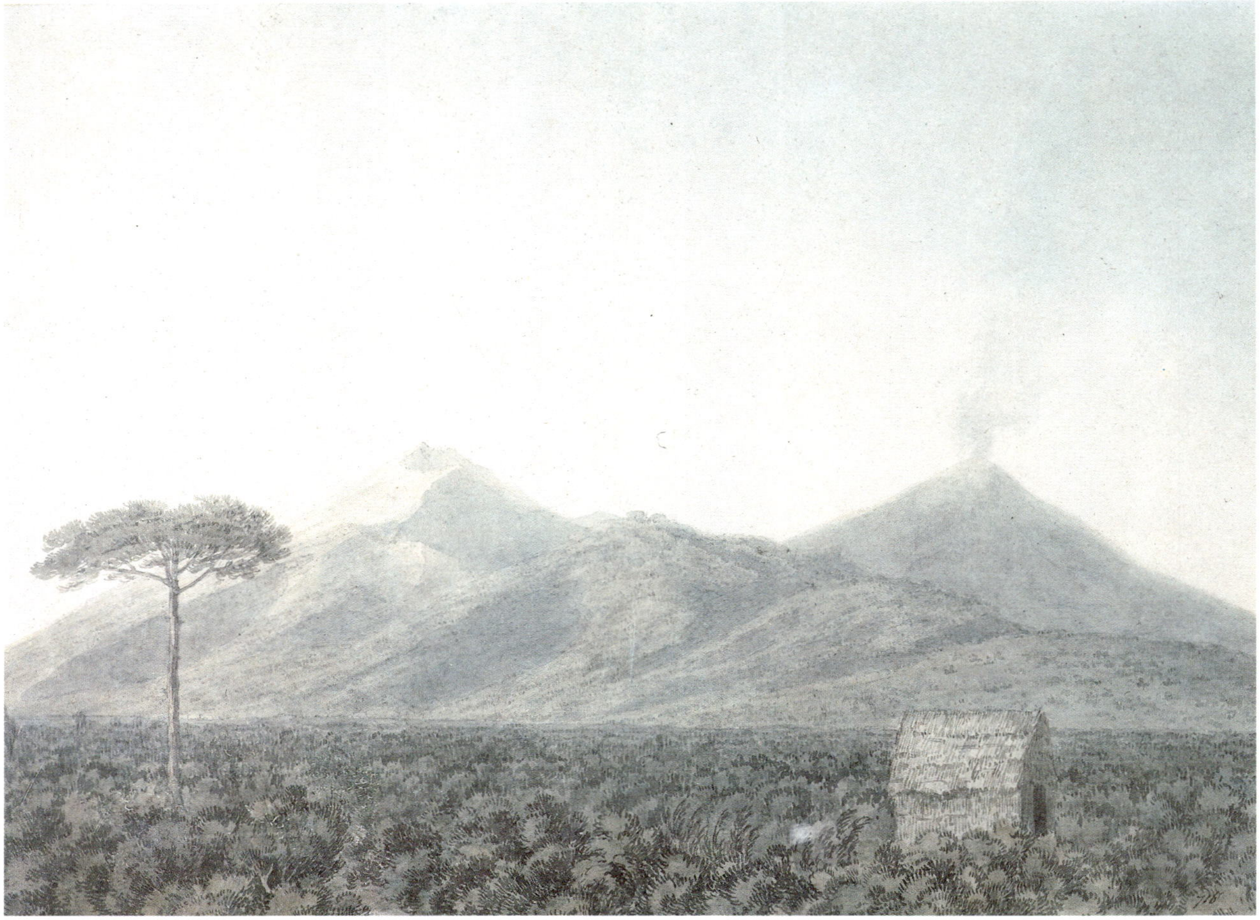

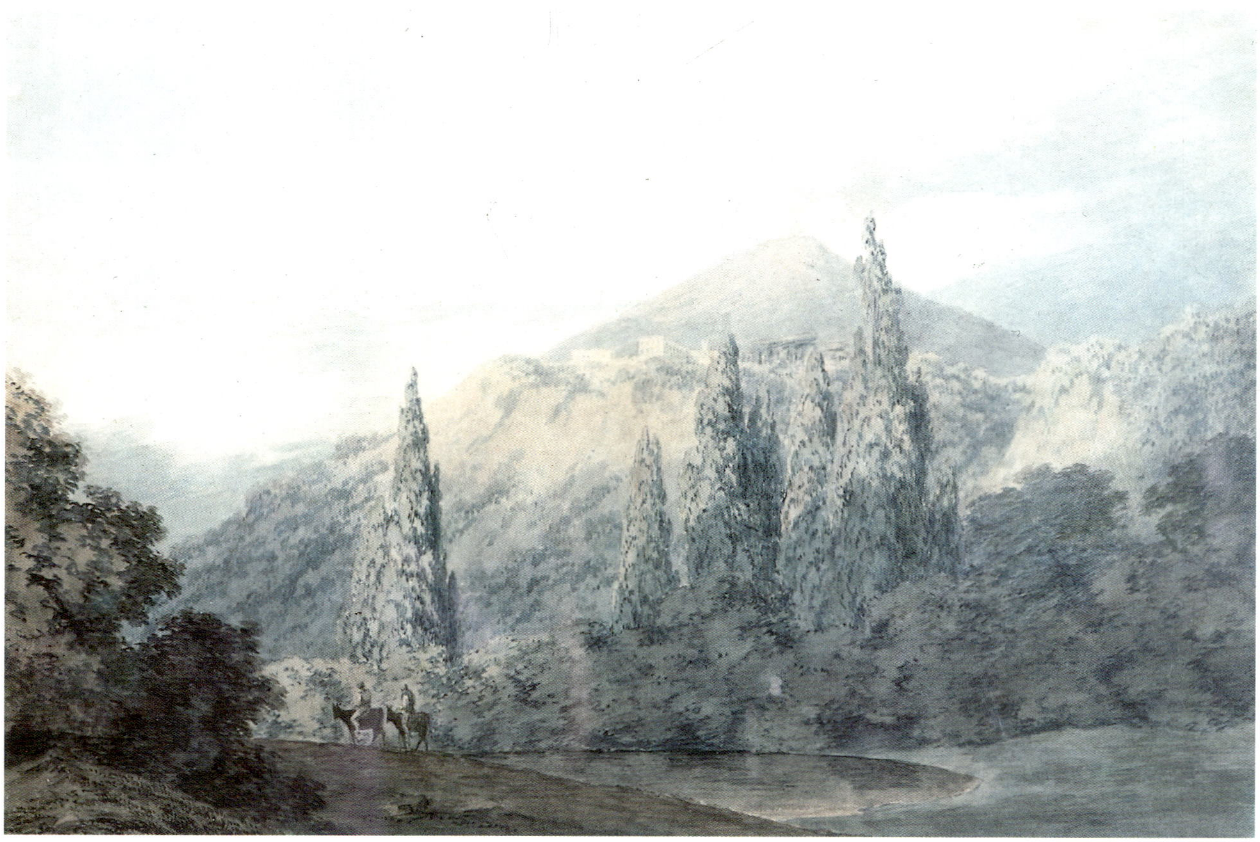

John Robert Cozens, Vesuvius from the Myrtle Plantation at Sir William Hamilton's Villa, Portici. Trustees of the Victoria and Albert Museum, London.

John Robert Cozens, Vesuvius. Trustees of the Victoria and Albert Museum, London.

John « Warwick » Smith, Naples from Sir William Hamilton's Villa at Portici. Birmingham City Museum and Art Gallery.

John « Warwick » Smith, Naples from Capodimonte. Trustees of the British Museum, London.

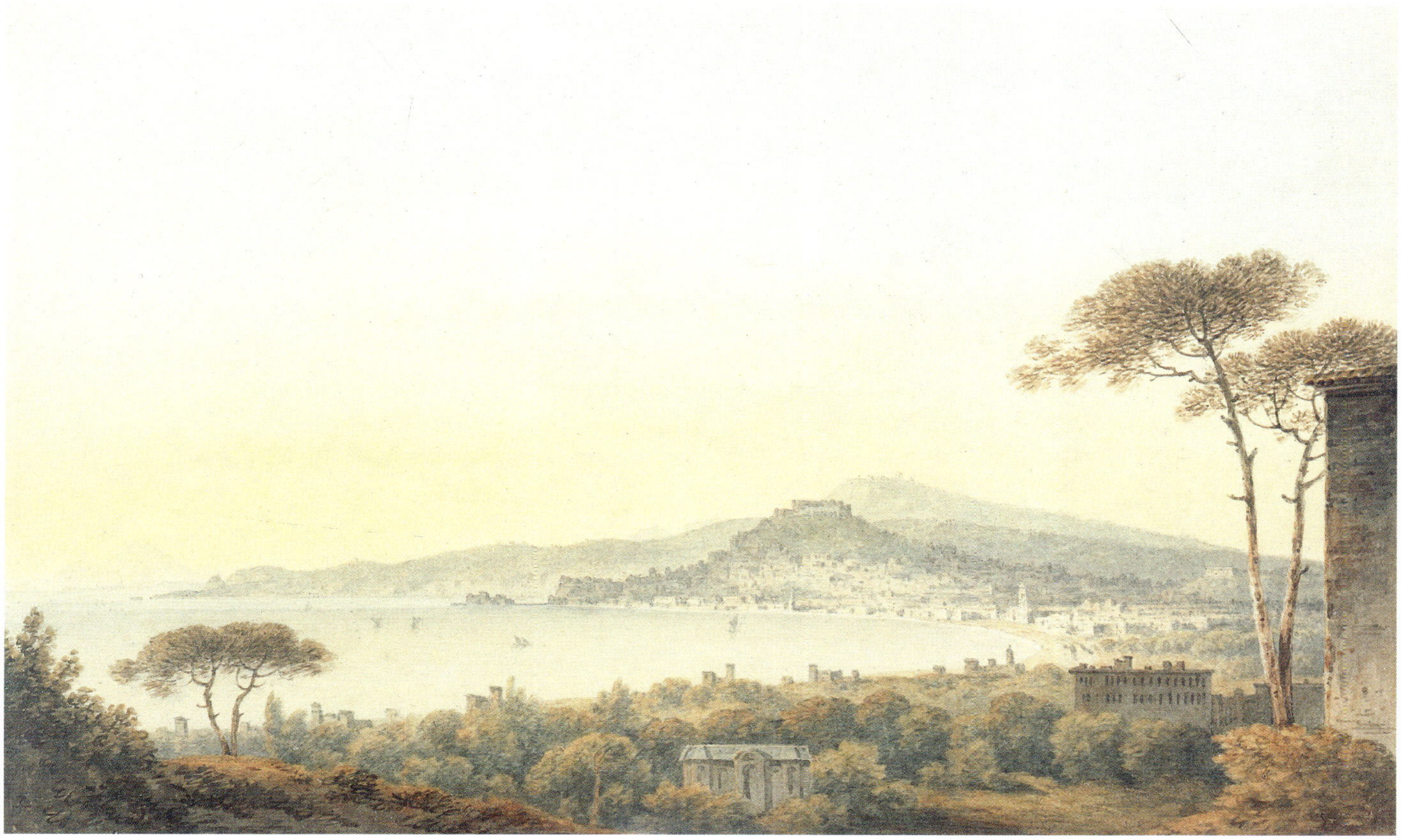

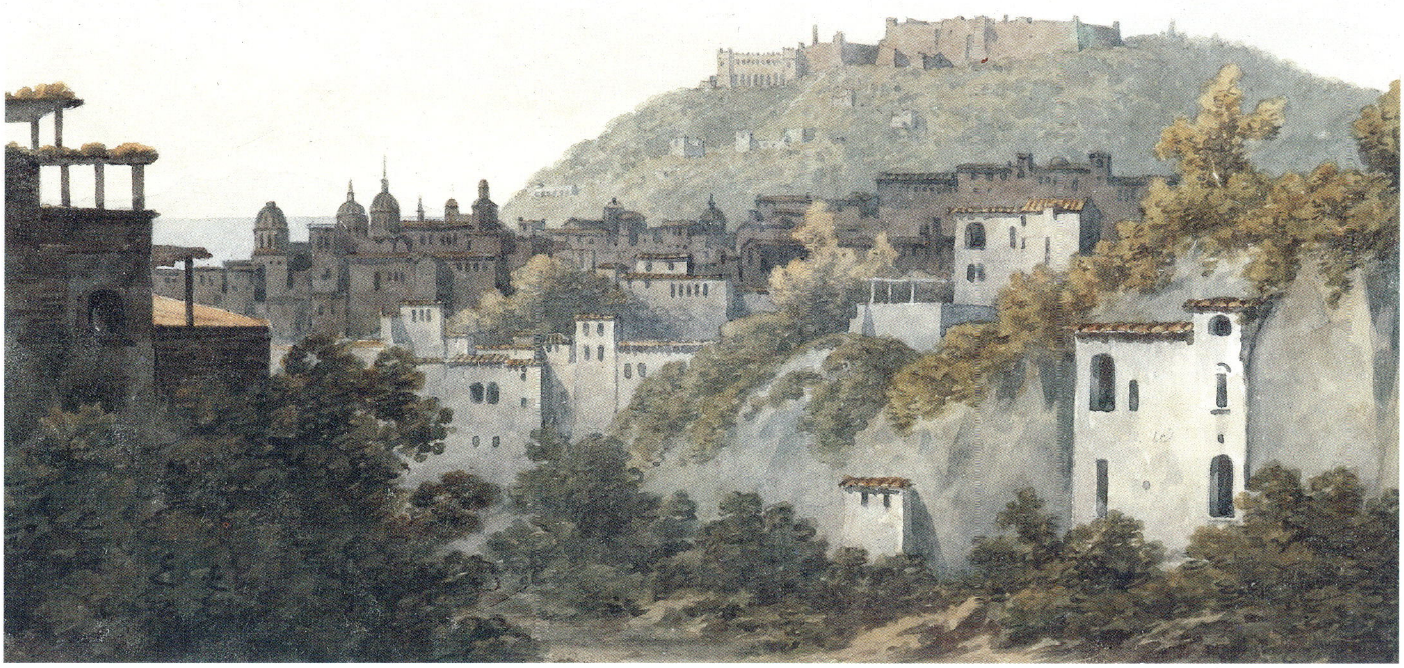

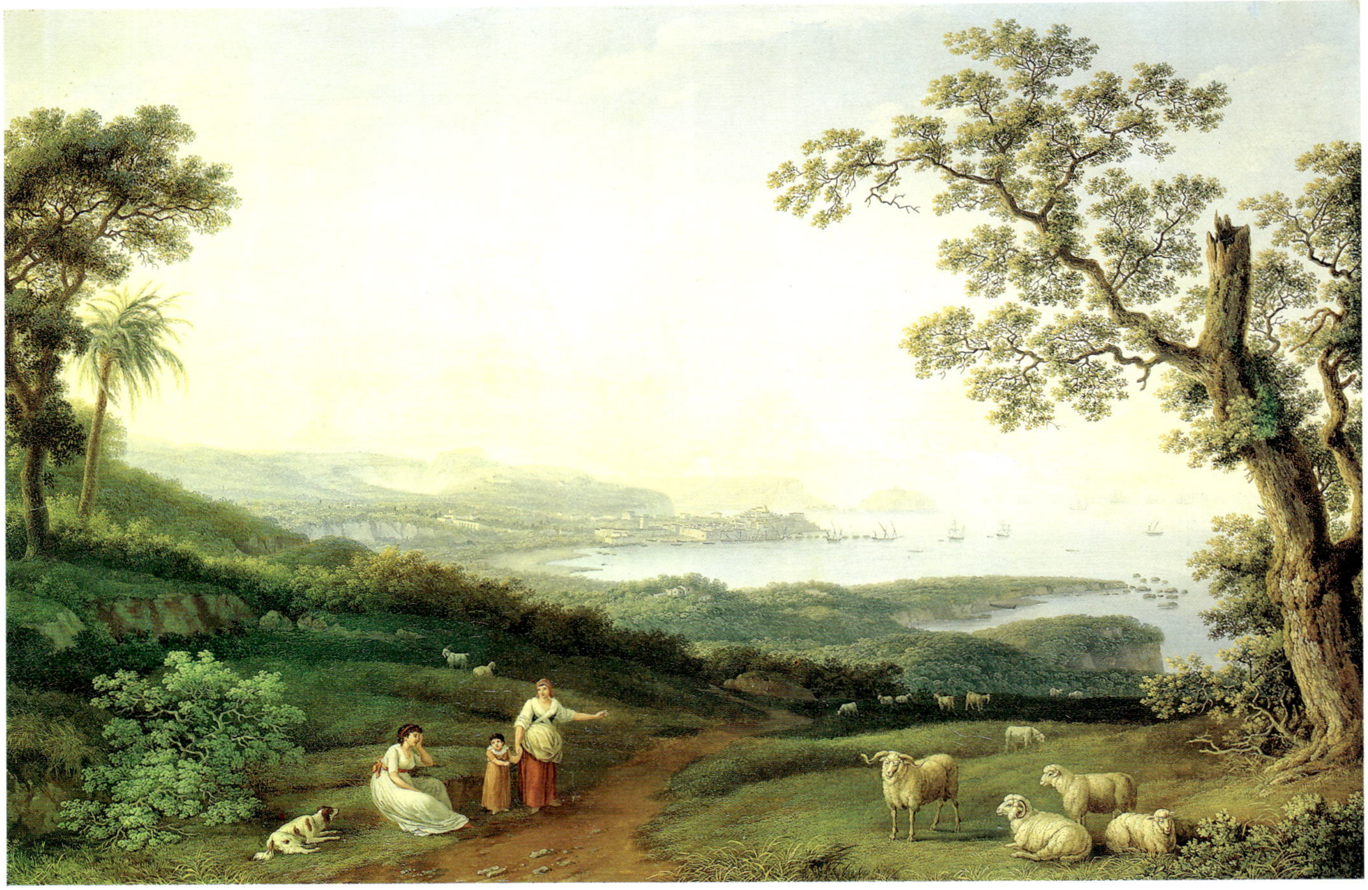

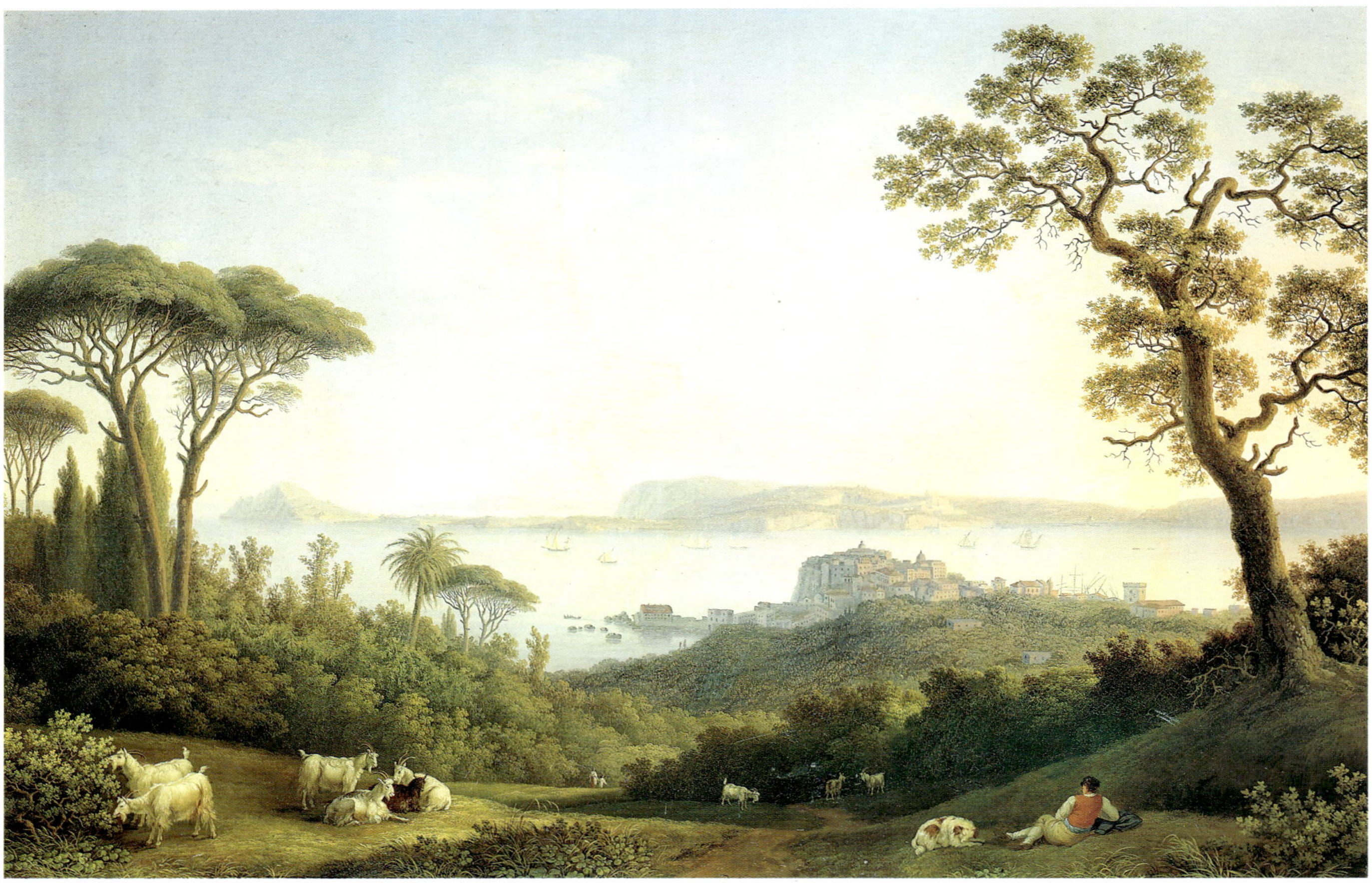

Philipp Hackert, The Bay of Pozzuoli at Dawn. Naples, private collection.

Philipp Hackert, The Bay of Pozzuoli at Dusk. Naples, private collection.

Philipp Hackert, Ferryboat on the Sele River. Caserta, Royal Palace.

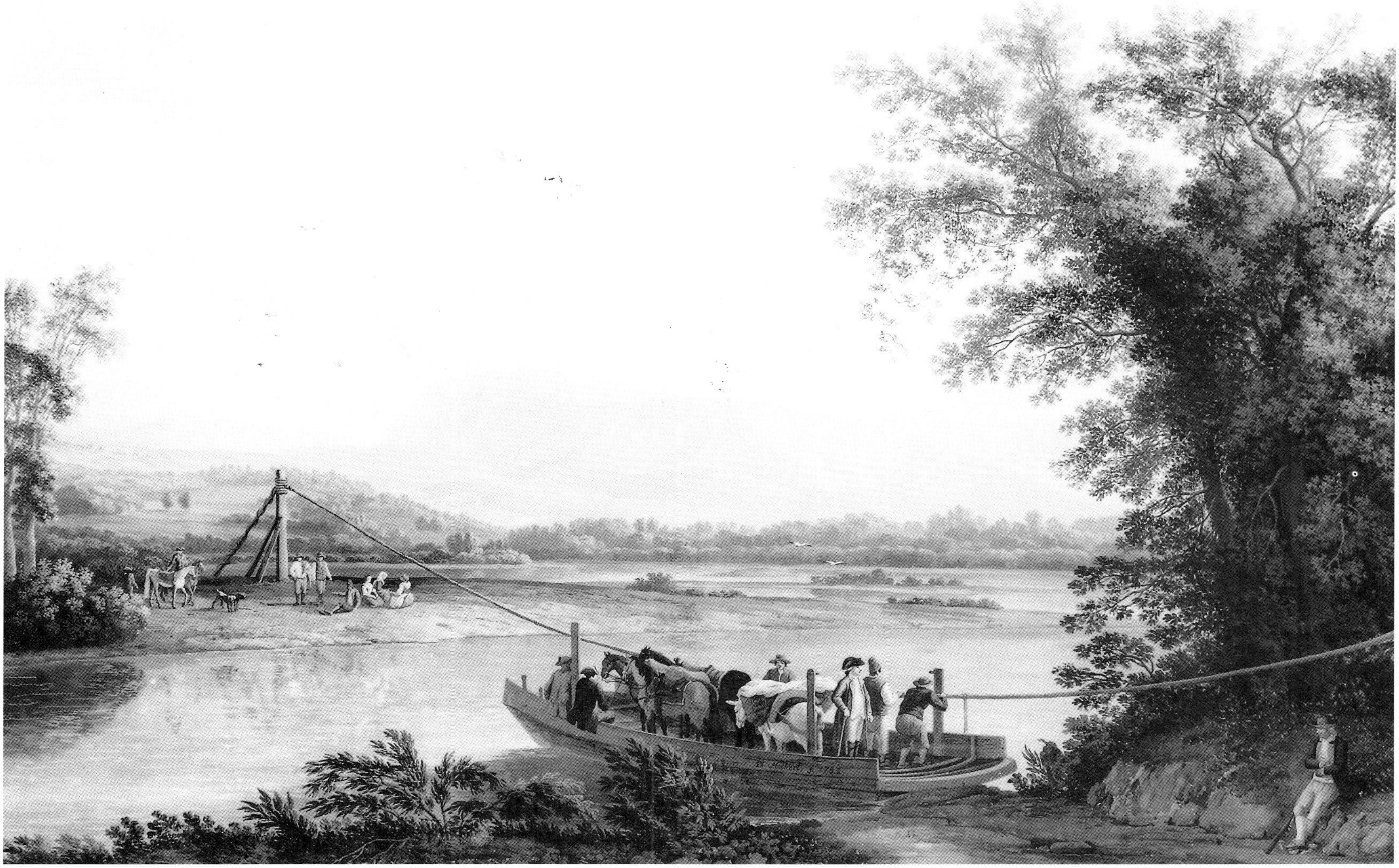

Philipp Hackert, The English Garden at Caserta. Caserta, Royal Palace.

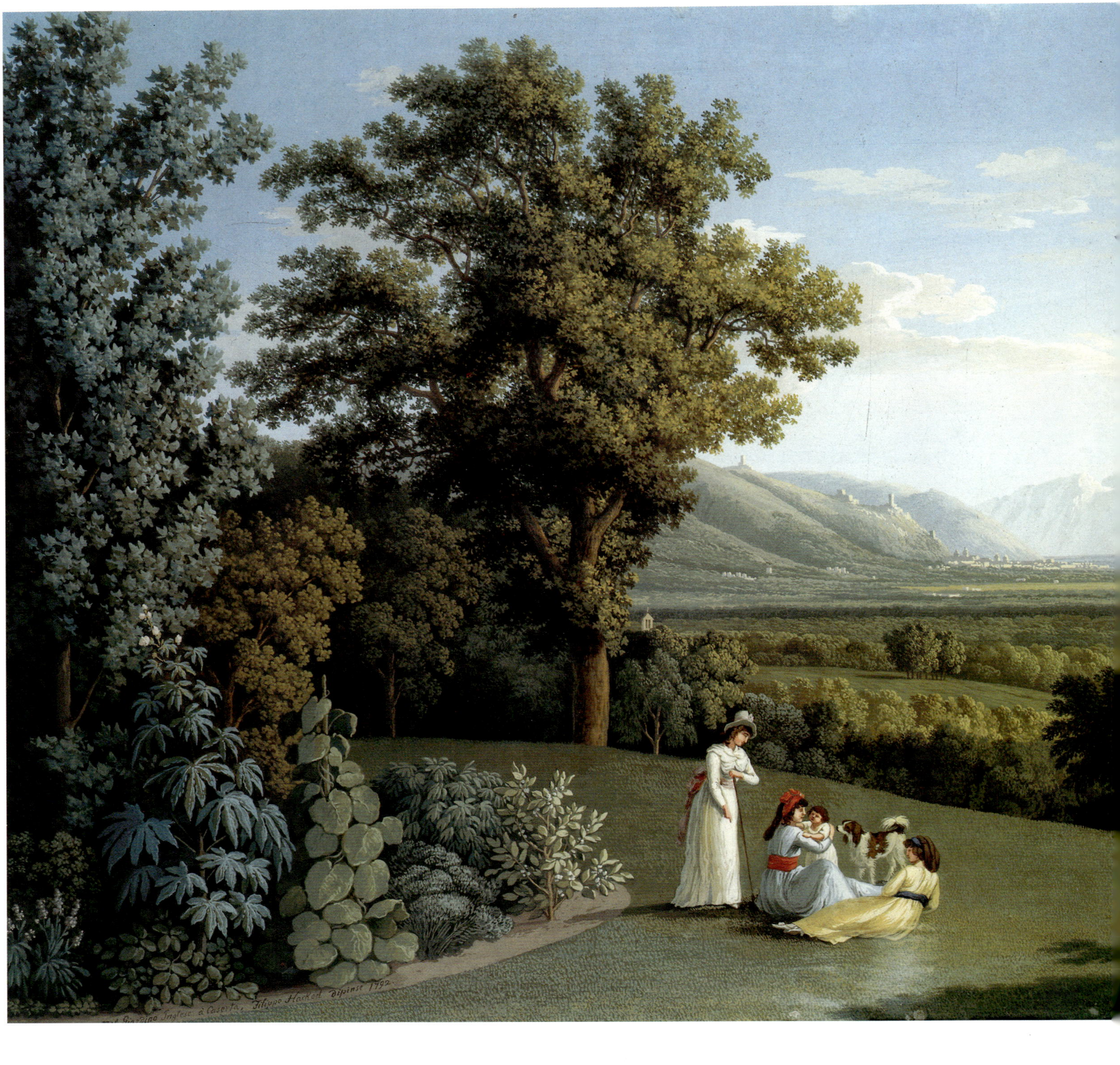

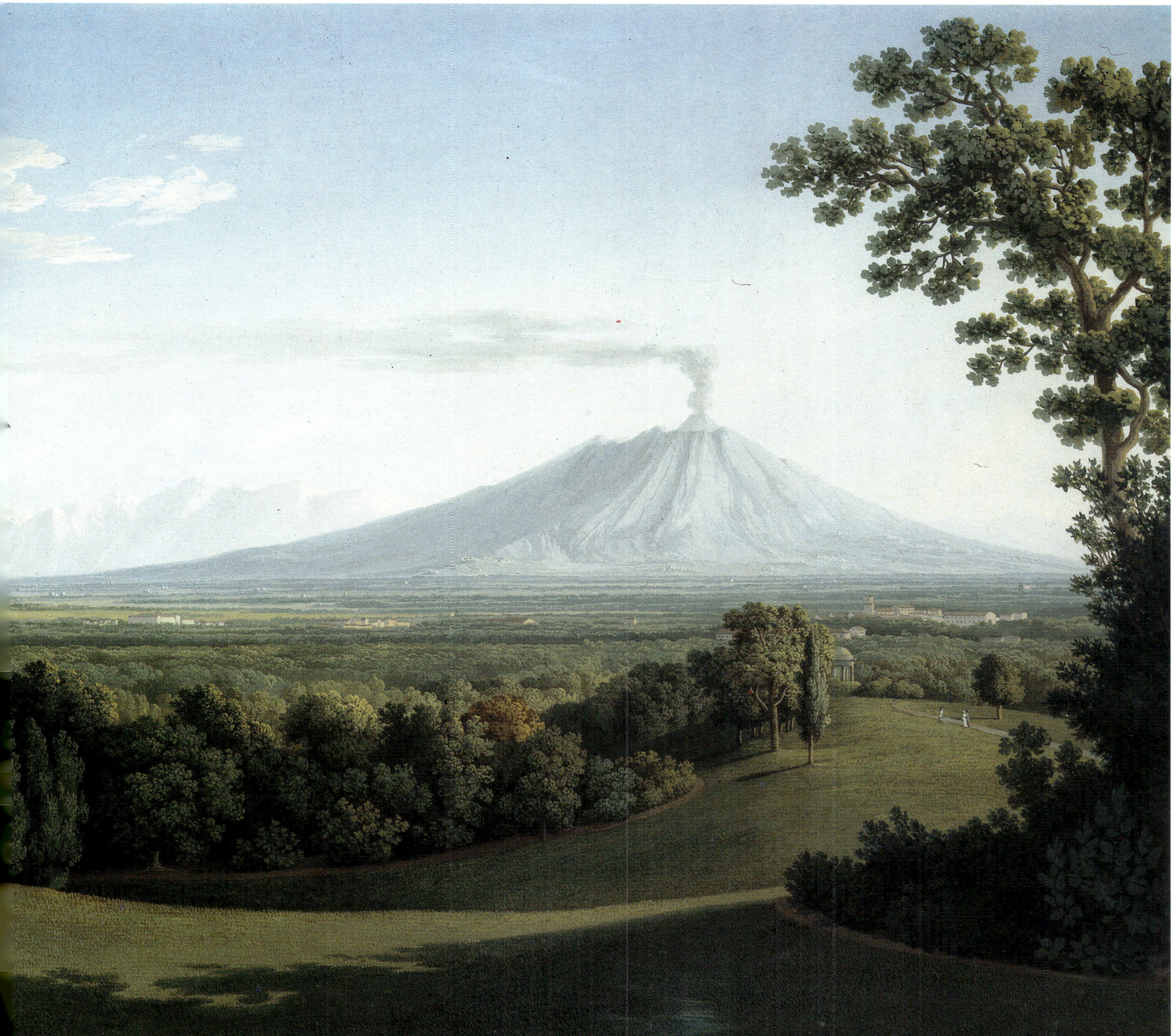

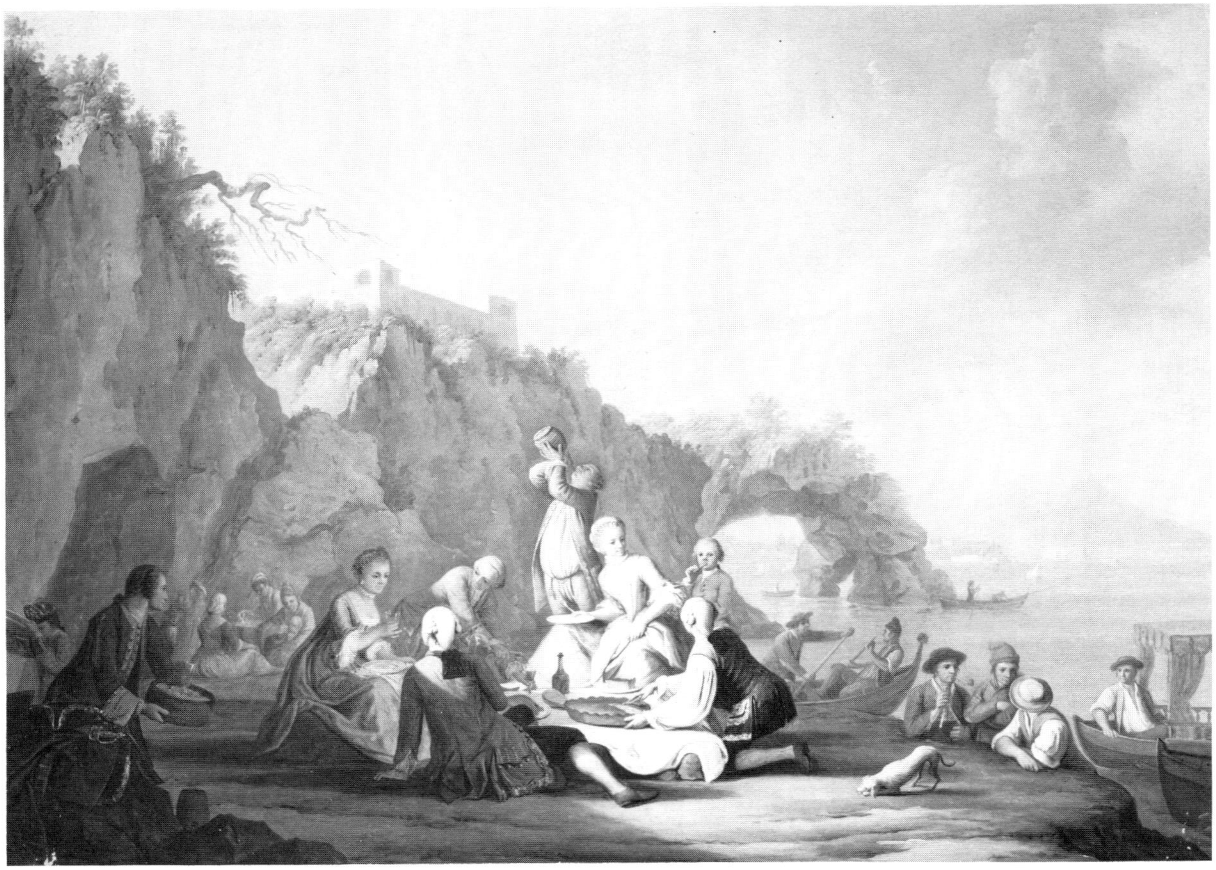

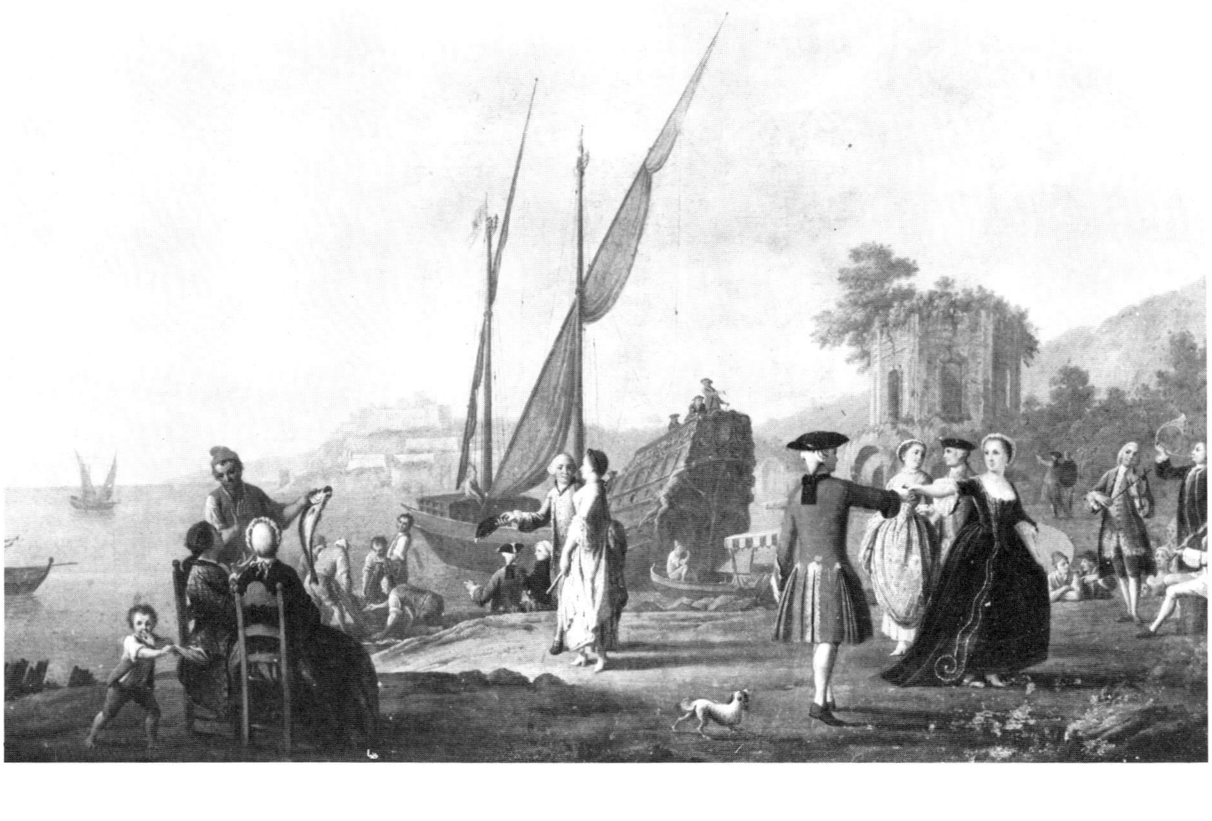

Pietro Fabris, Picnic at Posillipo. Caserta, Royal Palace.

Pietro Fabris, Minuet at Baiae. Caserta, Royal Palace.

Pietro Fabris, Sellers of Victuals along the Via della Marinella. Naples, private collection.

Pietro Fabris, A Tarantella with Posillipo in the background. Naples, private collection.

Pietro Fabris, The Procession of Royal Ships at Palazzo Donn'Anna. Naples, private collection.

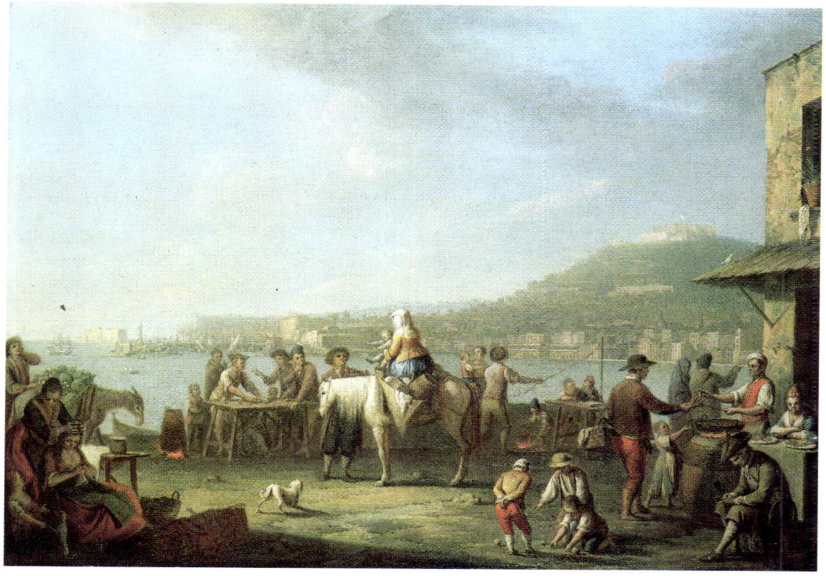

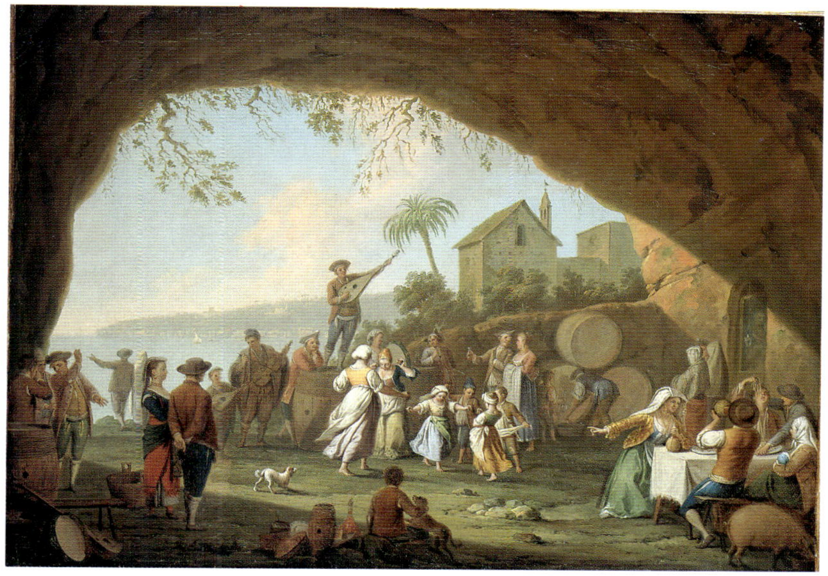

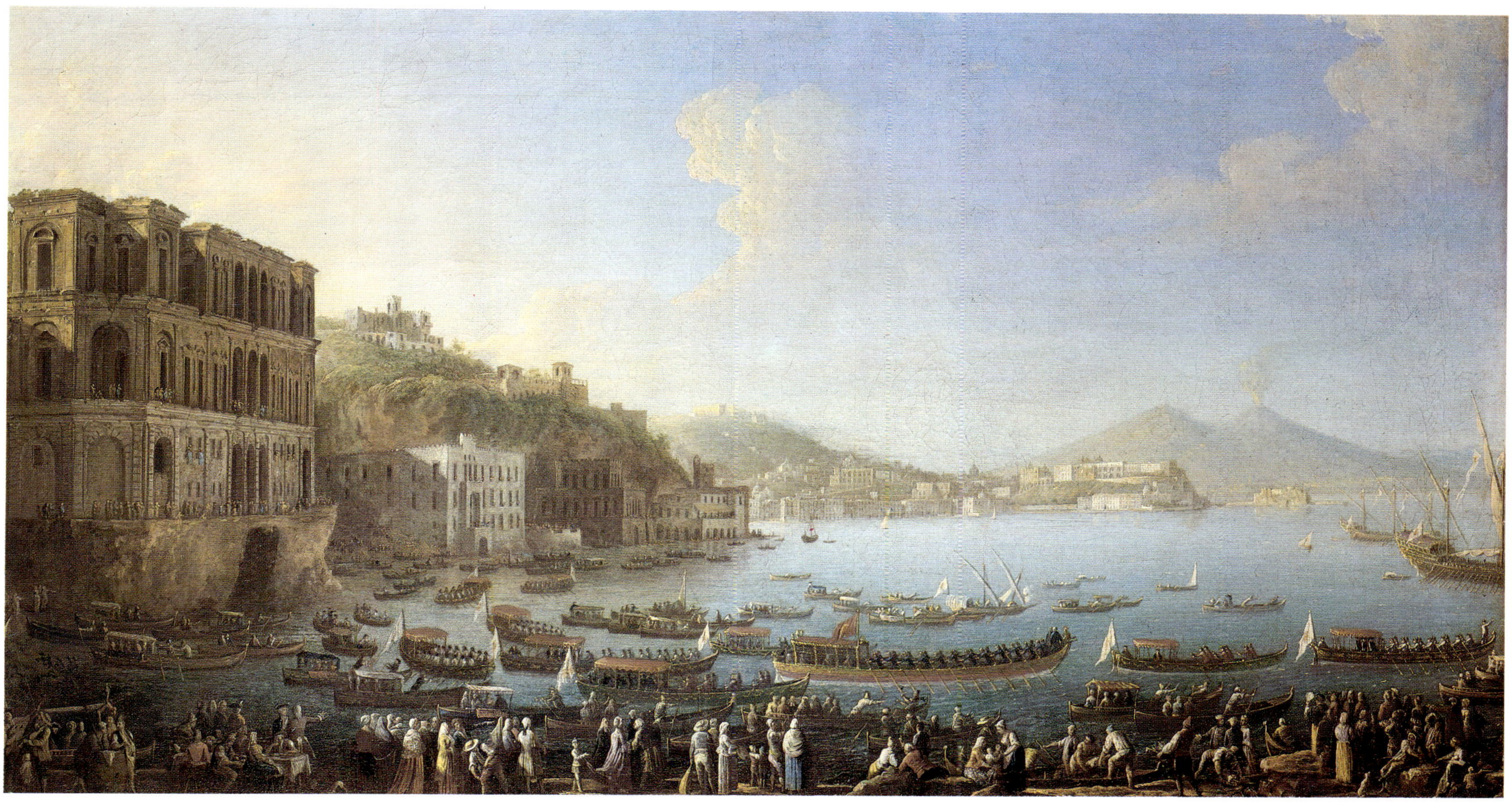

Pietro Fabris, The Ball Game. London, Marylebone Cricket Club.

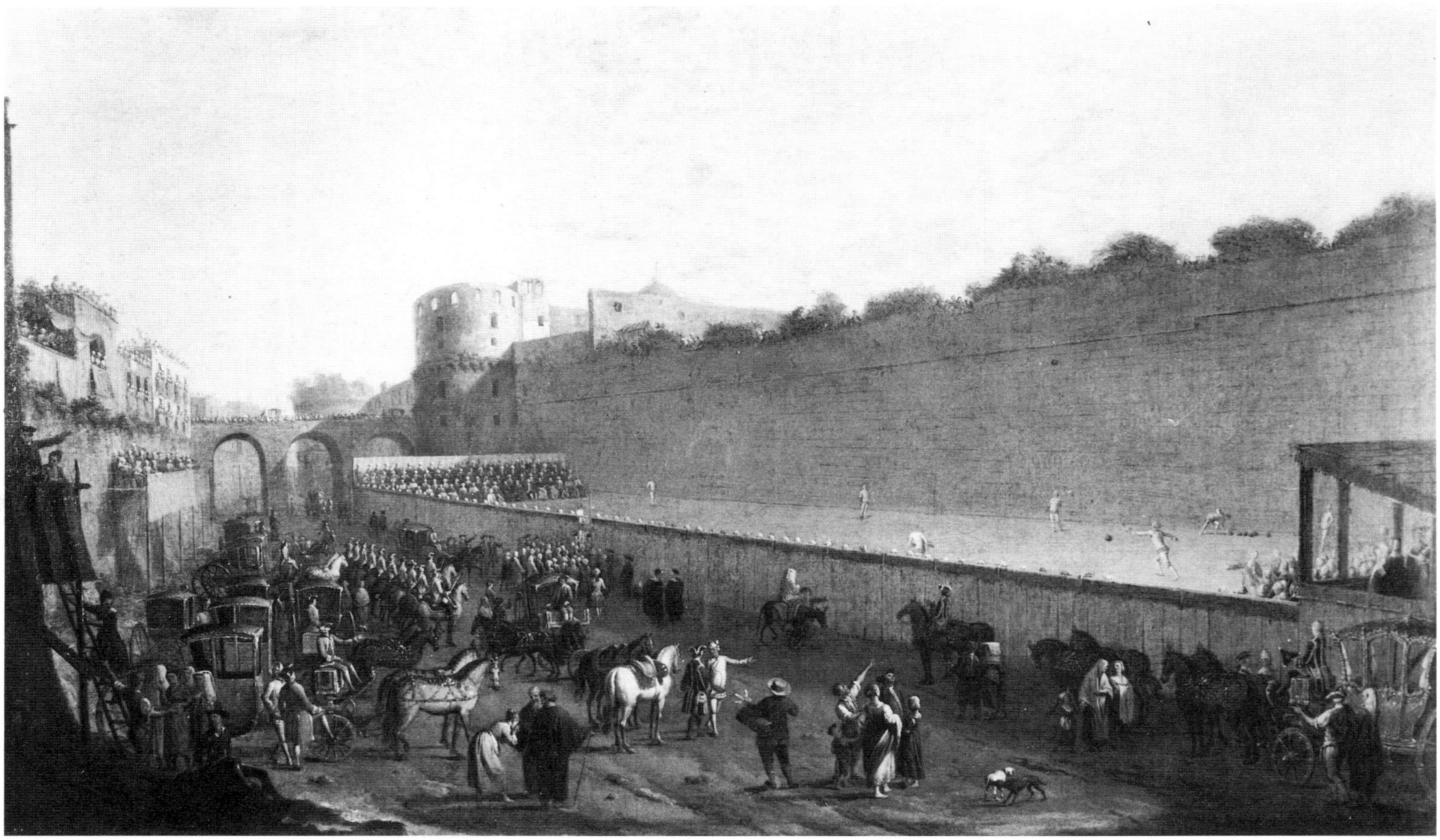

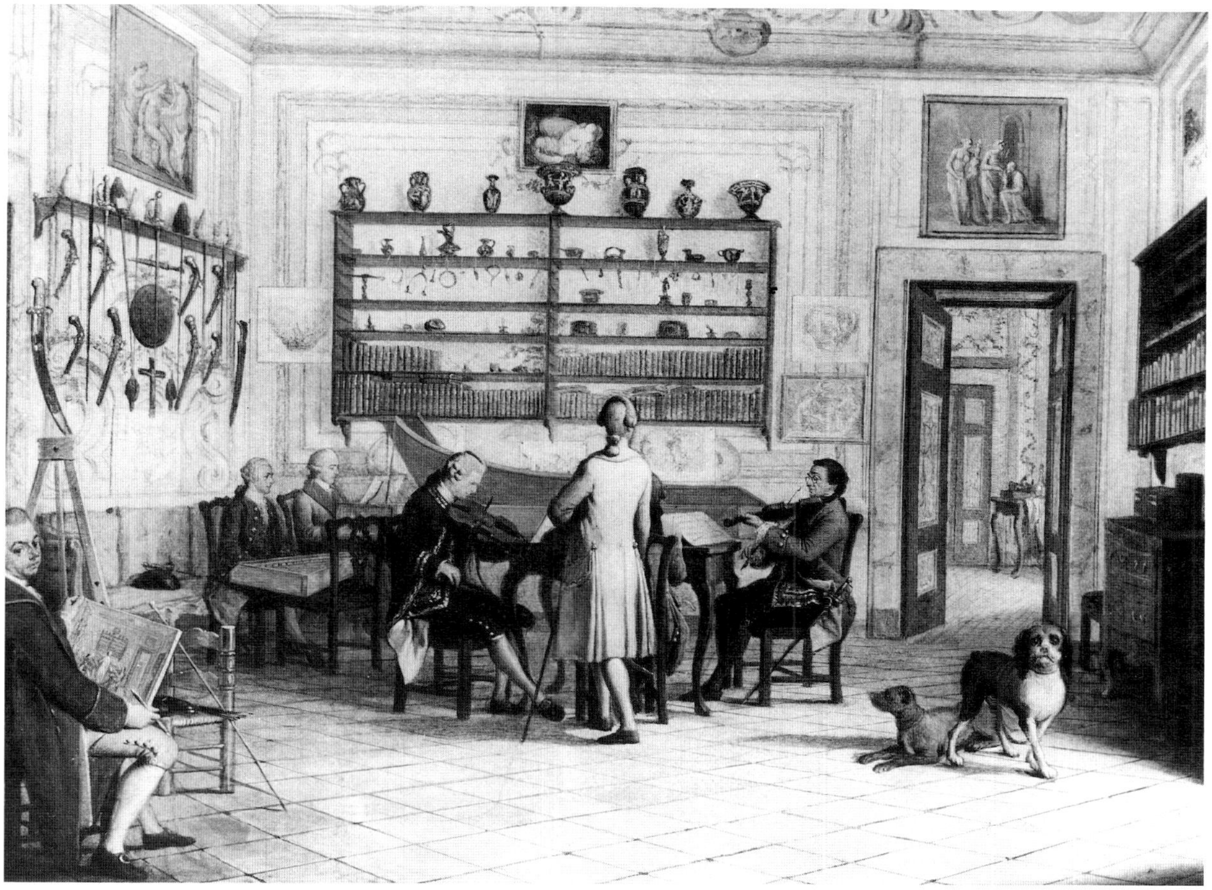

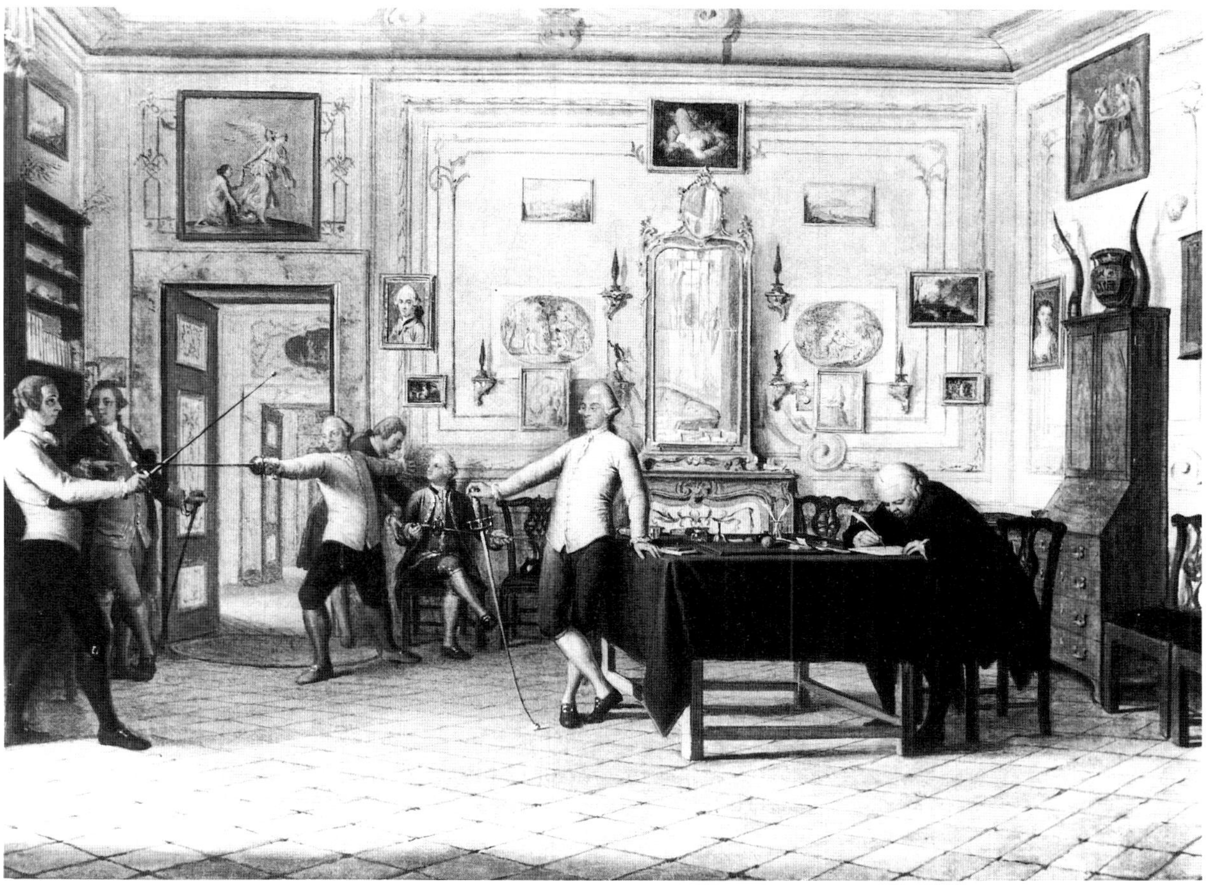

Pietro Fabris, Drawing-room in the Apartment in Naples of Lord Fortrose with a Group of Musicians. Edinburgh, Scottish National Portrait Gallery.

Pietro Fabris, Drawing-room in the Apartment in Naples of Lord Fortrose with a Group of Fencers. Edinburgh, Scottish National Portrait Gallery.

Giovan Battista Lusieri, Naples from Mergellina. United Kingdom, private collection.

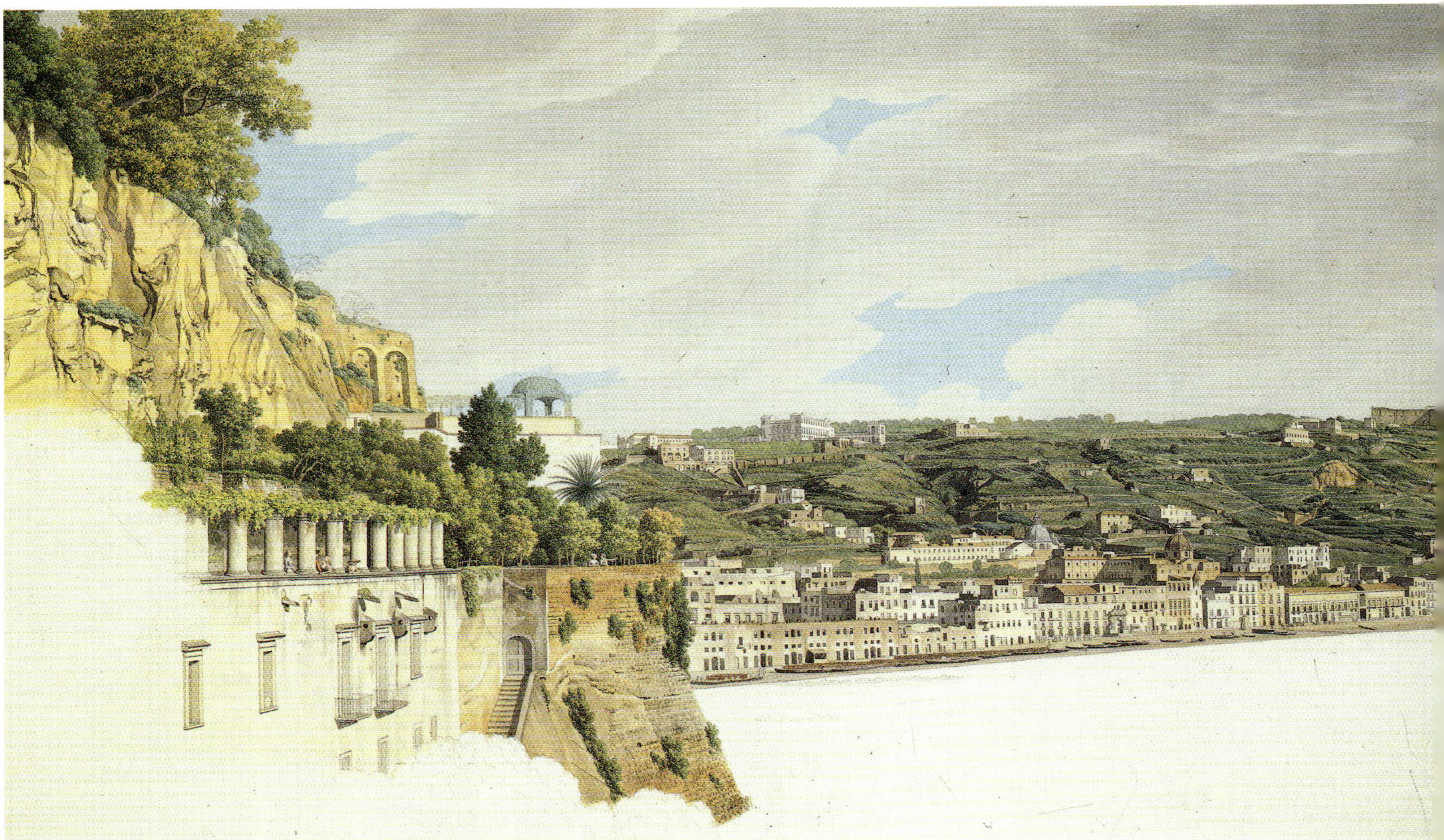

Giovan Battista Lusieri, Naples from Mergellina. New York, the Woodner Family Collection.

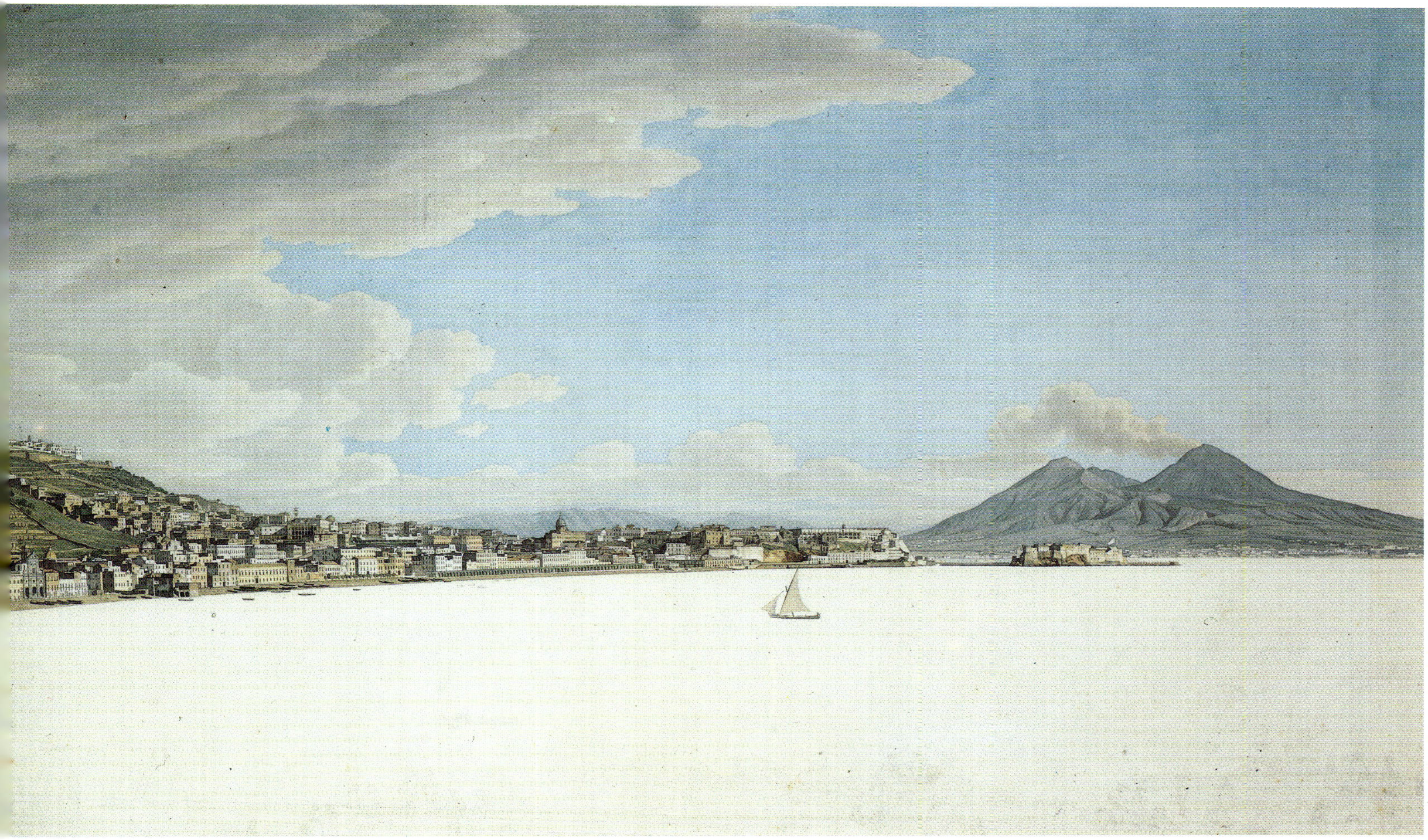

Giovan Battista Lusieri, Naples from Portici. United Kingdom, private collection.

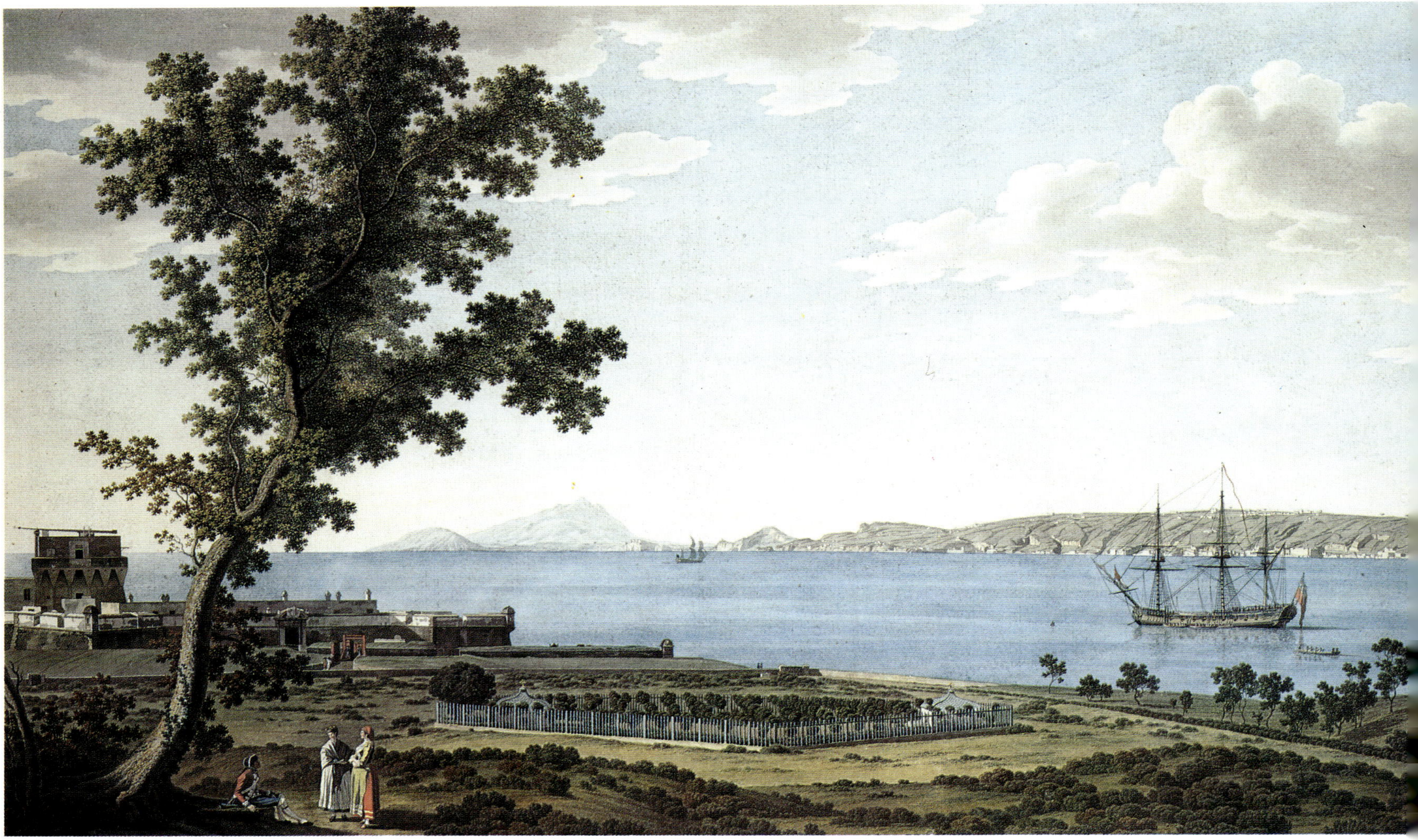

Giovan Battista Lusieri, Posillipo from Portici. United Kingdom, private collection.

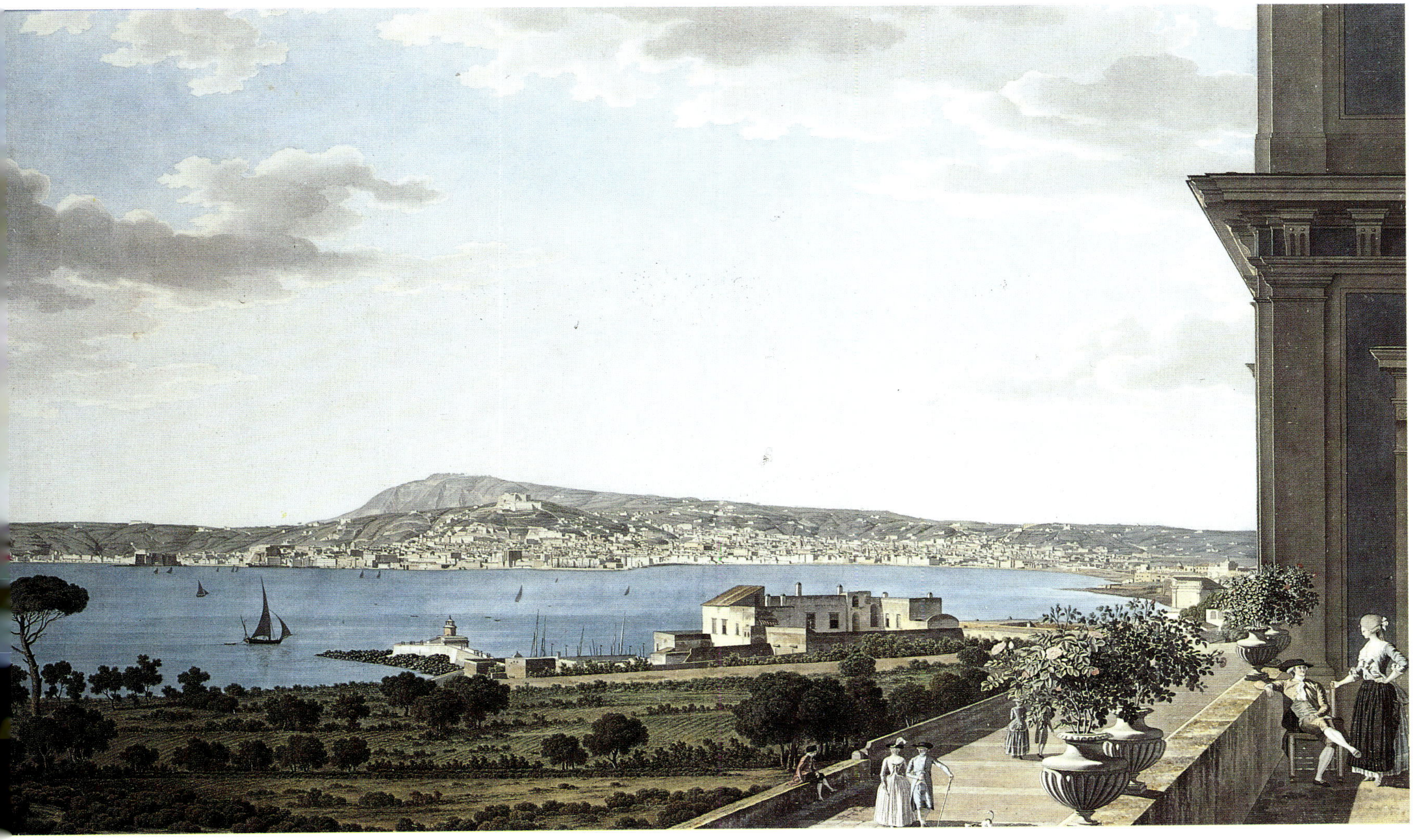

Giovan Battista Lusieri, Vesuvius erupting at night. Naples, private collection.

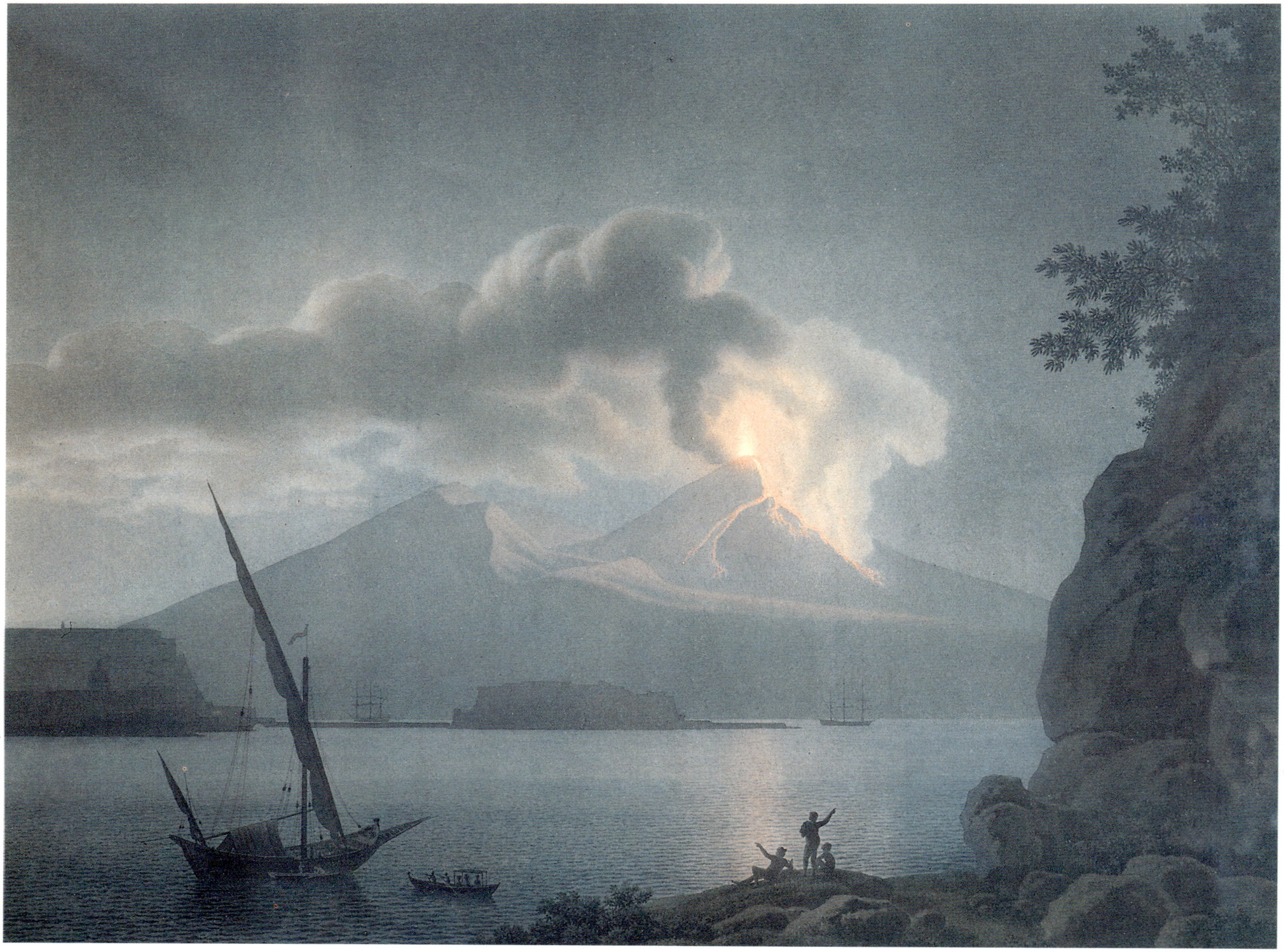

Saverio Della Gatta, Naples from Portici.
Rome, private collection.

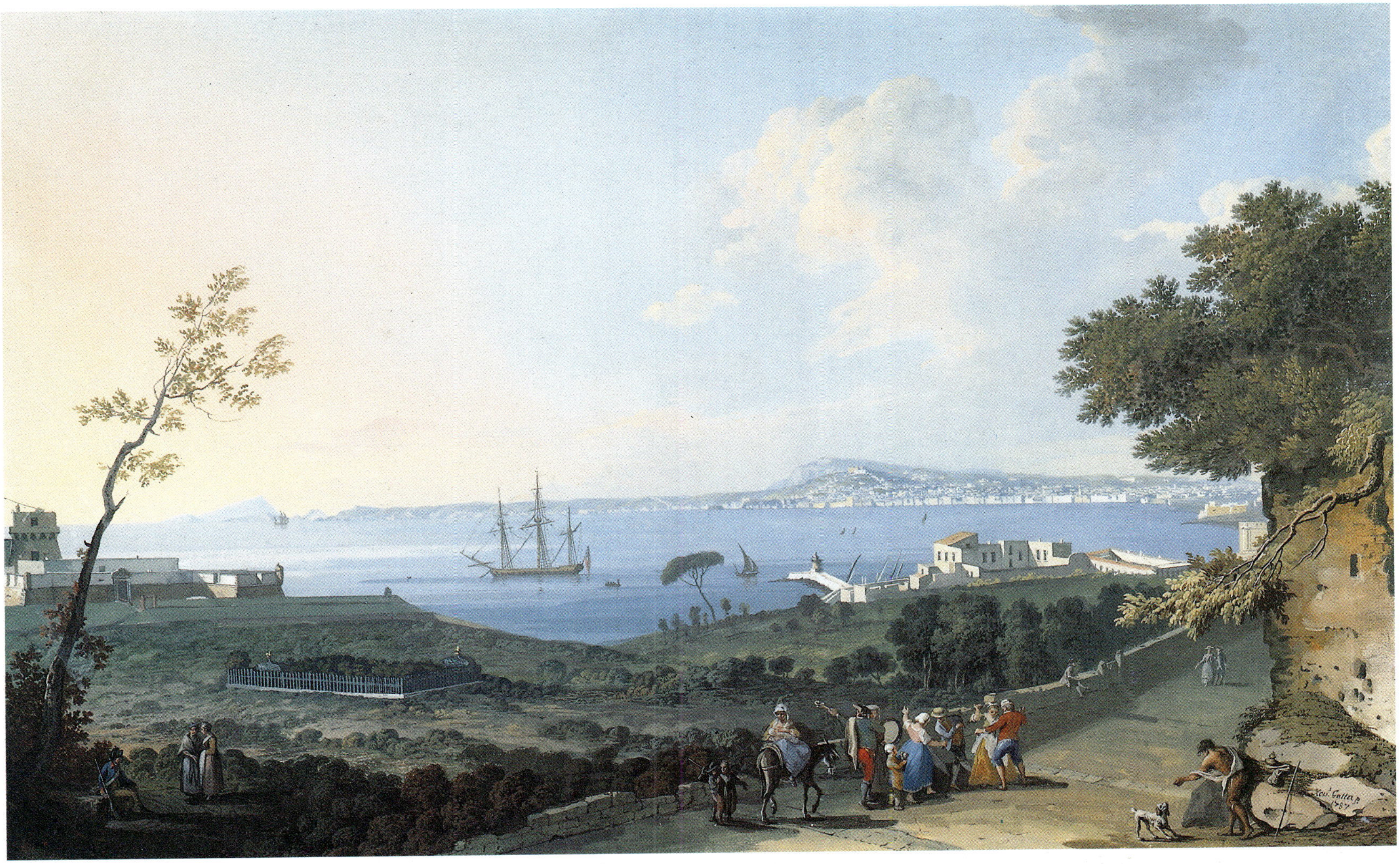

A.L.R. Ducros, Nisida from Posillipo.
Naples, private collection.

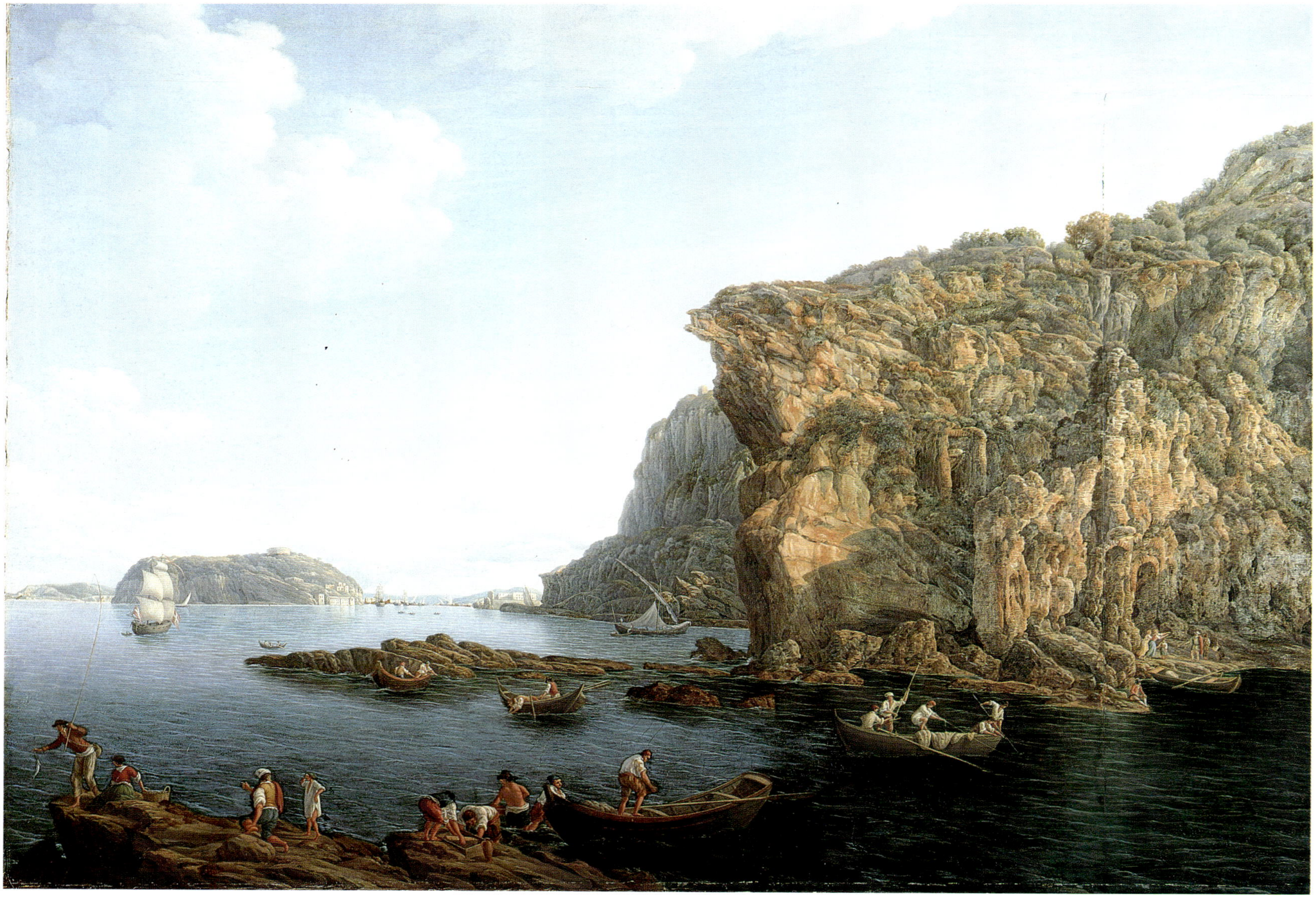

A.-L.-R. Ducros, Posillipo seen from Palazzo Donn'Anna. Naples, Museum of San Martino.

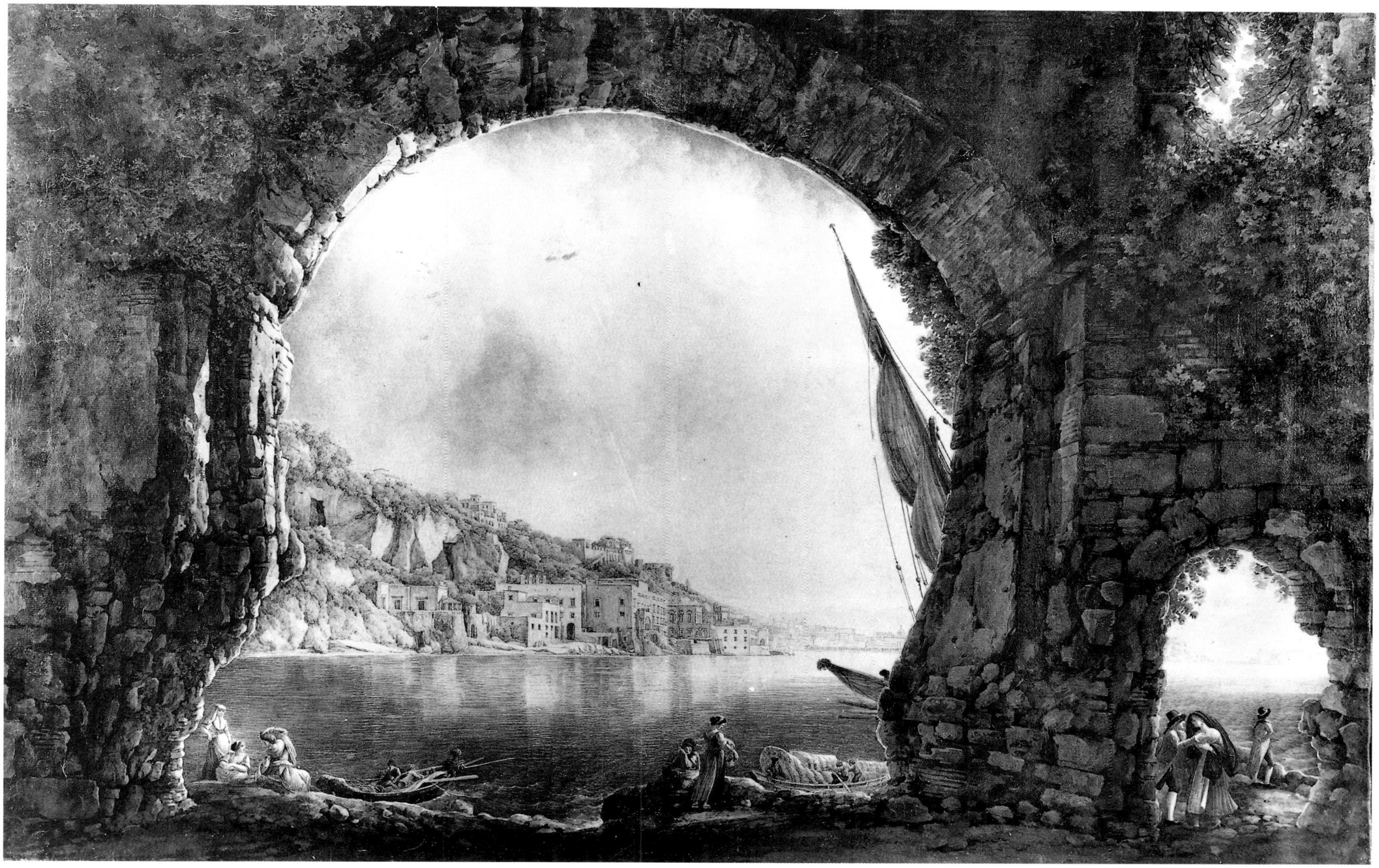

A.L.R. Ducros, View of Villa Acton at Castellammare. London, Hazlitt, Gooden & Fox Ltd.

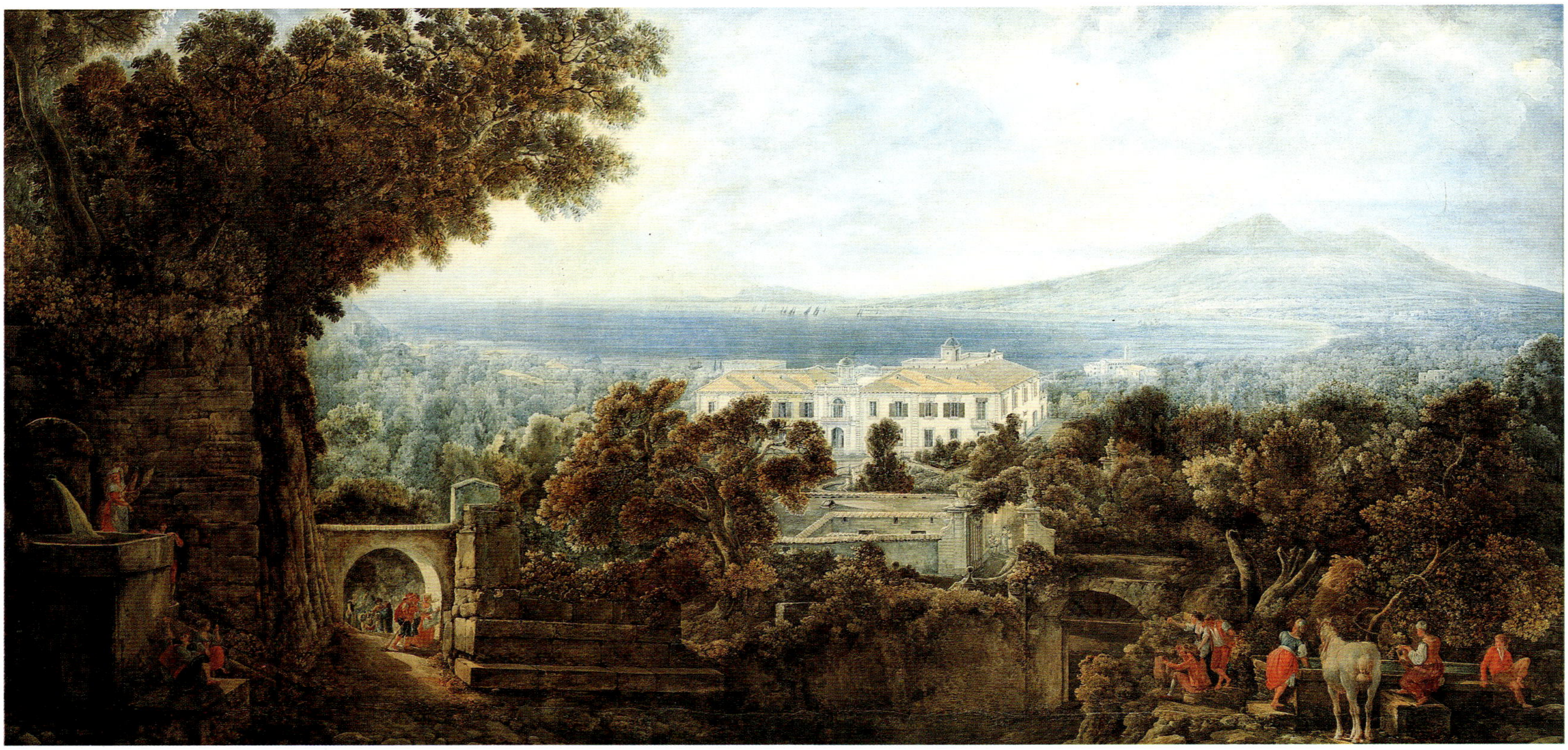

Francis Towne, The Palazzo Donn'Anna. Trustees of the British Museum, London.

On the following pages:
Francis Towne, Near Naples. Trustees of the British Museum, London.

Francis Towne, The Descent from Capodimonte, Trustees of the British Museum, London.

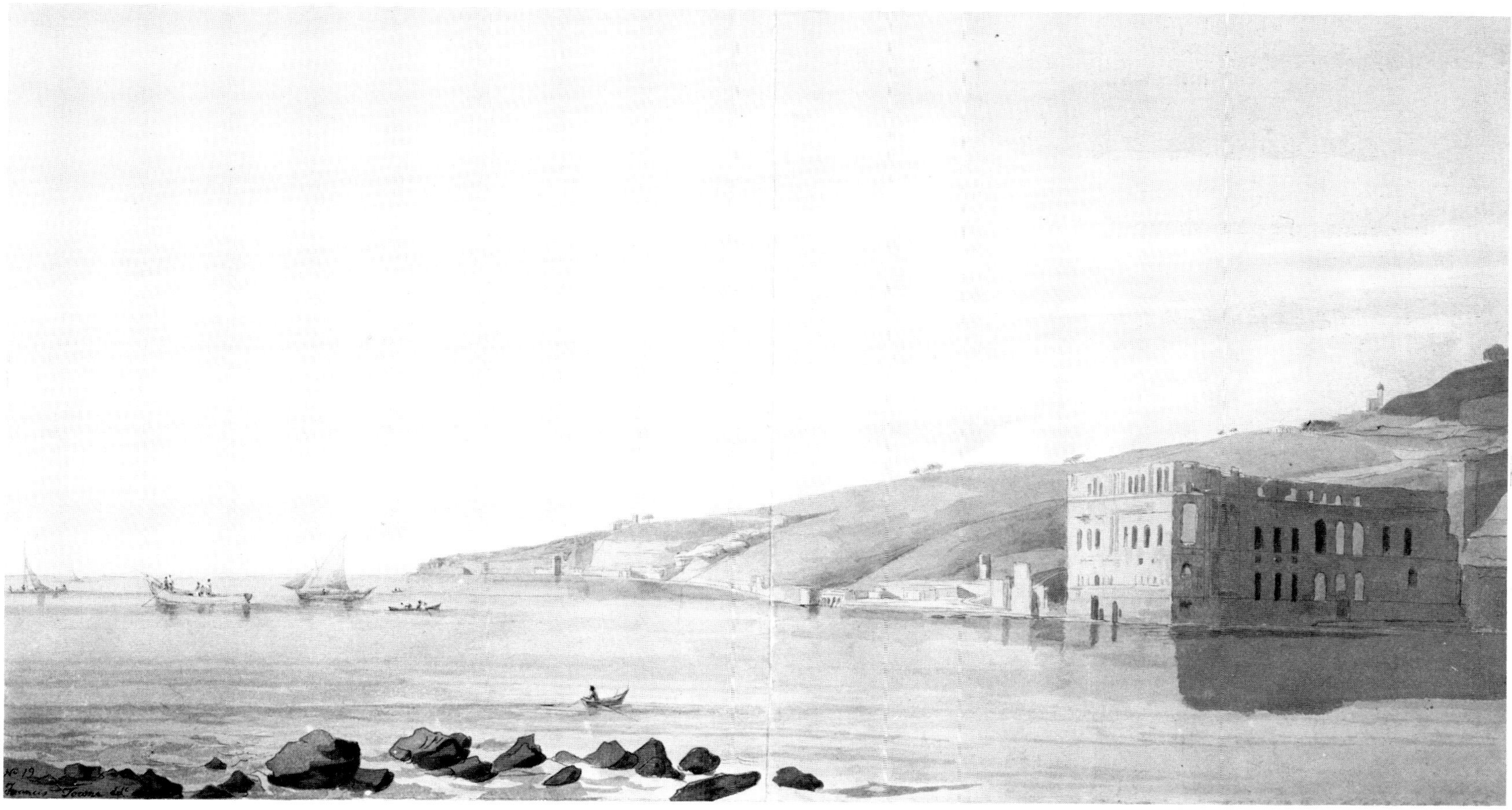

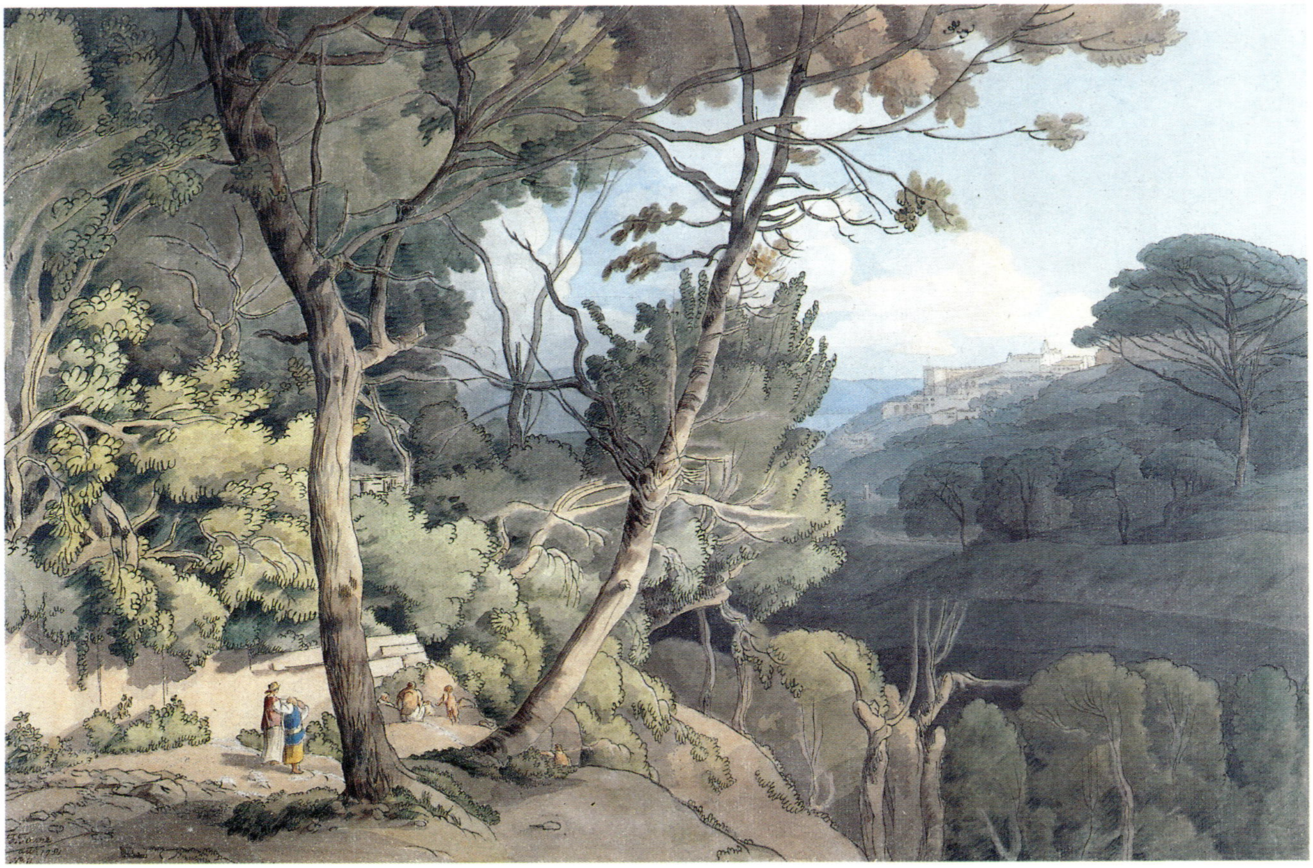

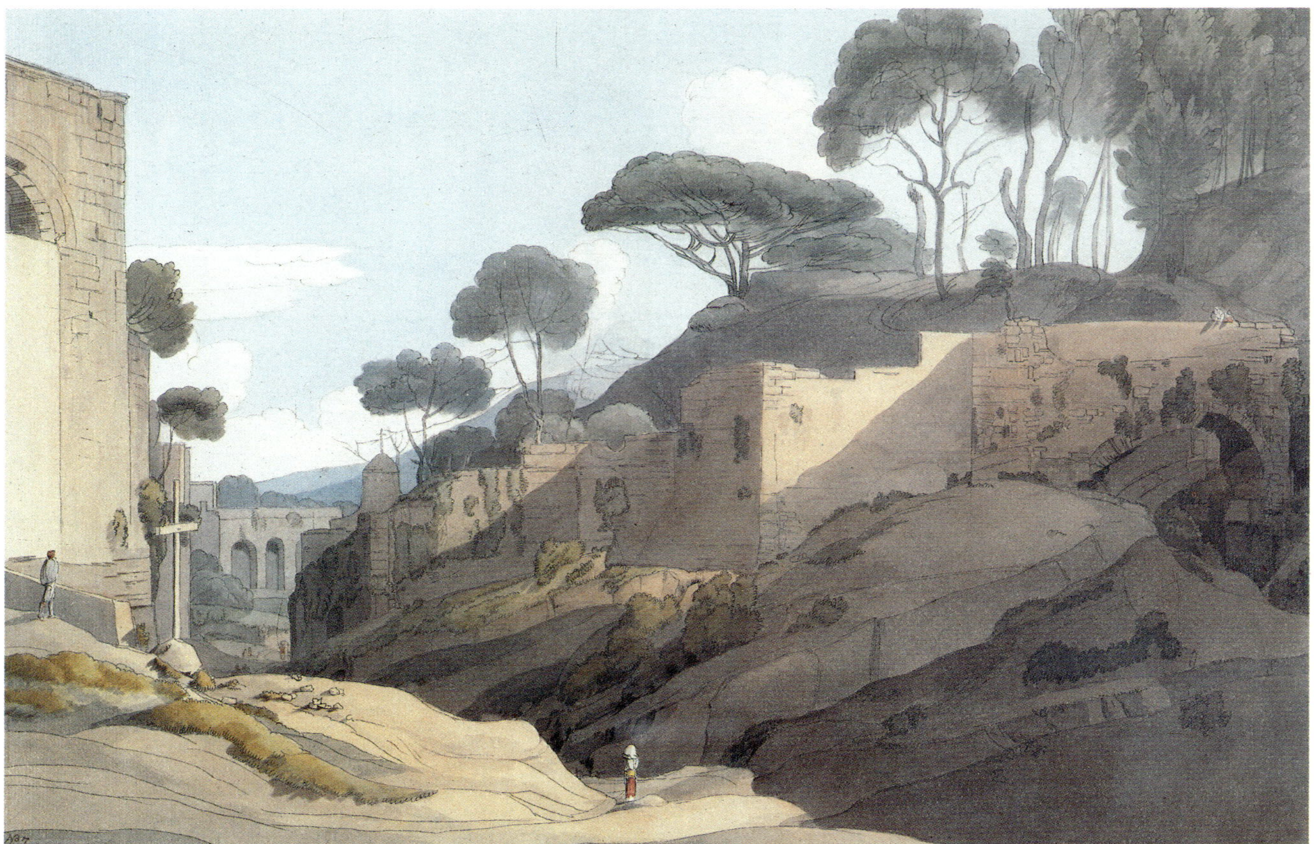

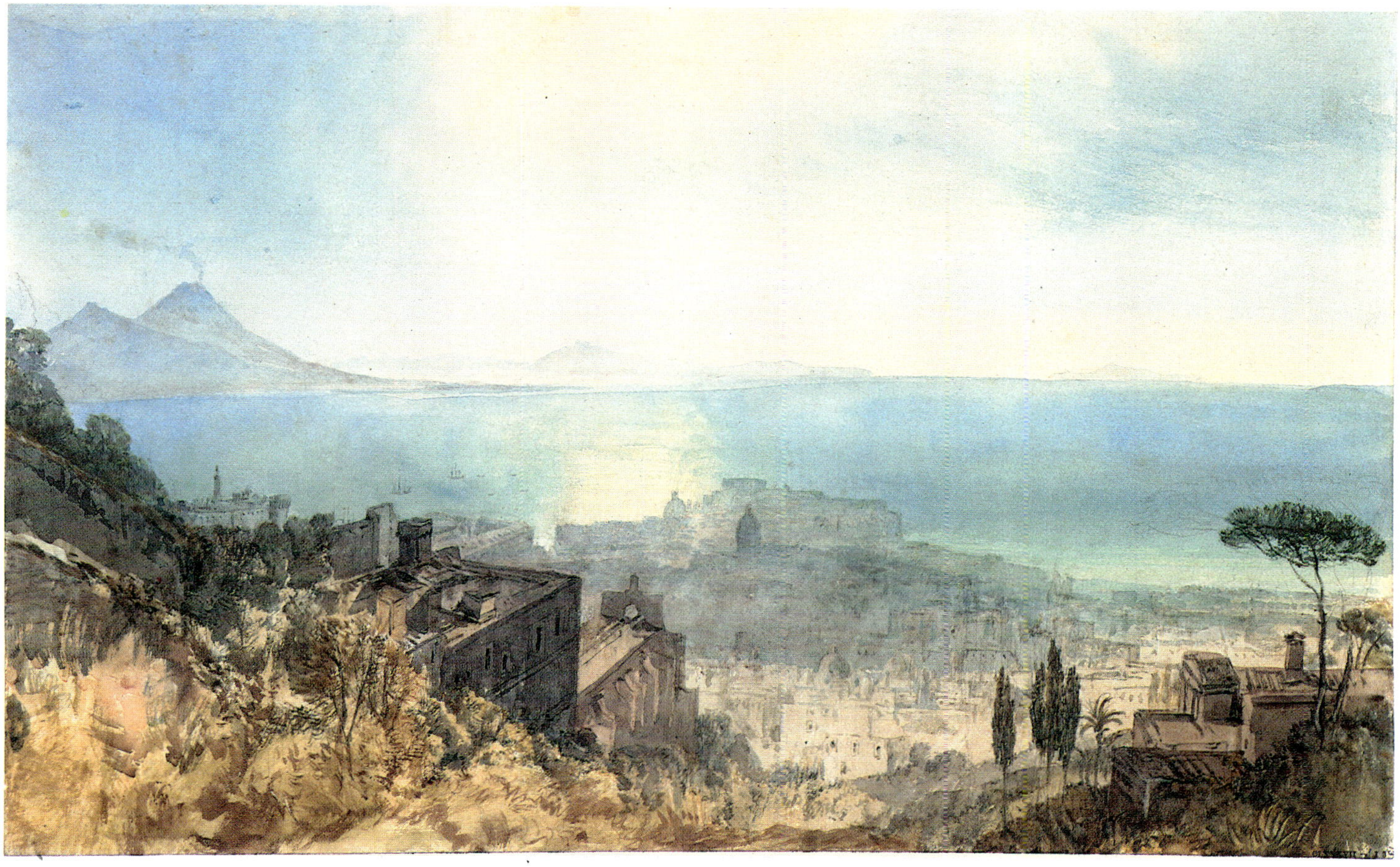

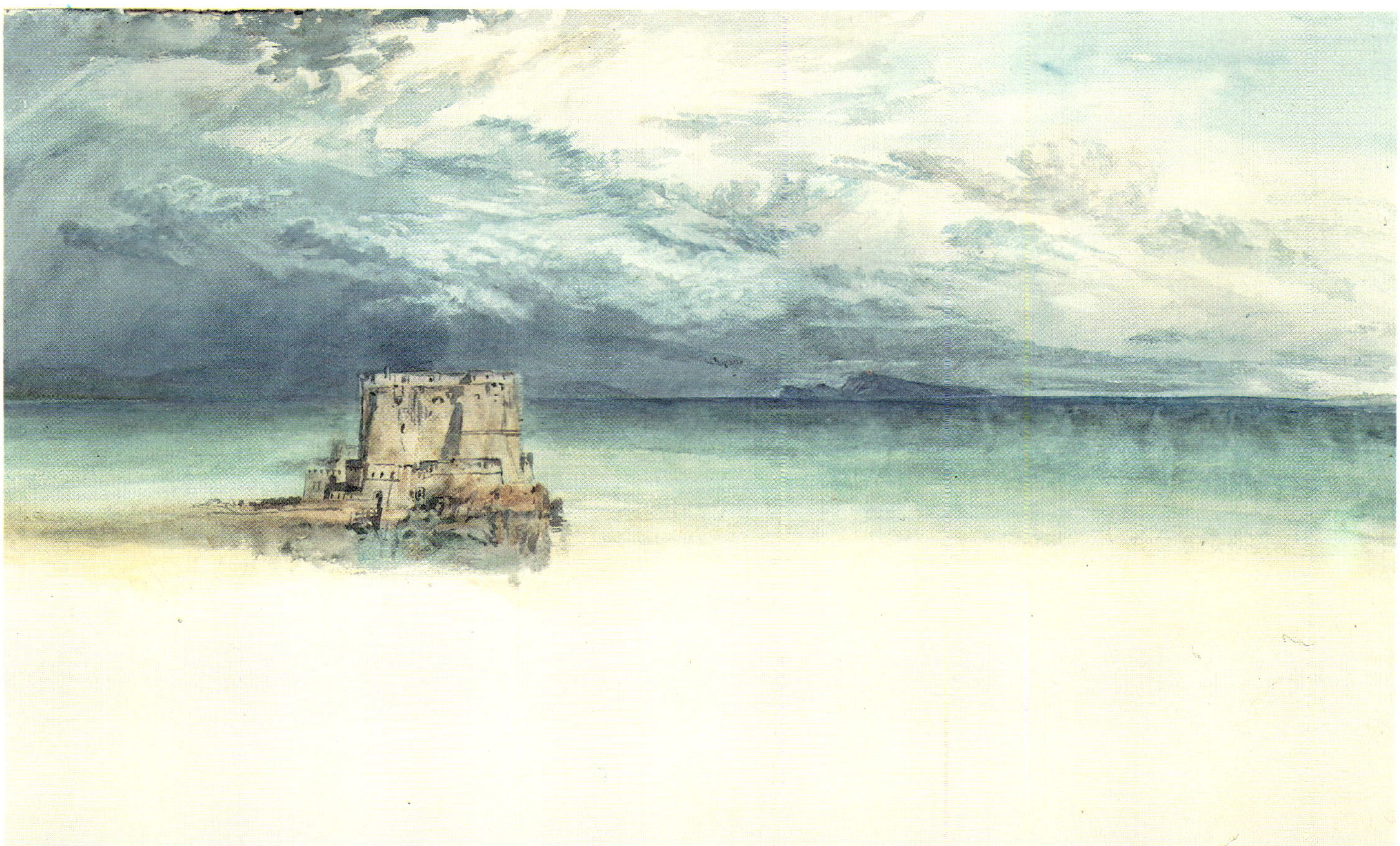

On the previous pages:
J.M.W. Turner, The Bay of Naples and Vesuvius. Tate Gallery, London, Turner Bequest.

J.M.W. Turner, Capri from Naples, with the Castel dell'Ovo. Tate Gallery, London, Turner Bequest.

J.M.W. Turner, Vesuvius. Tate Gallery, London, Turner Bequest.

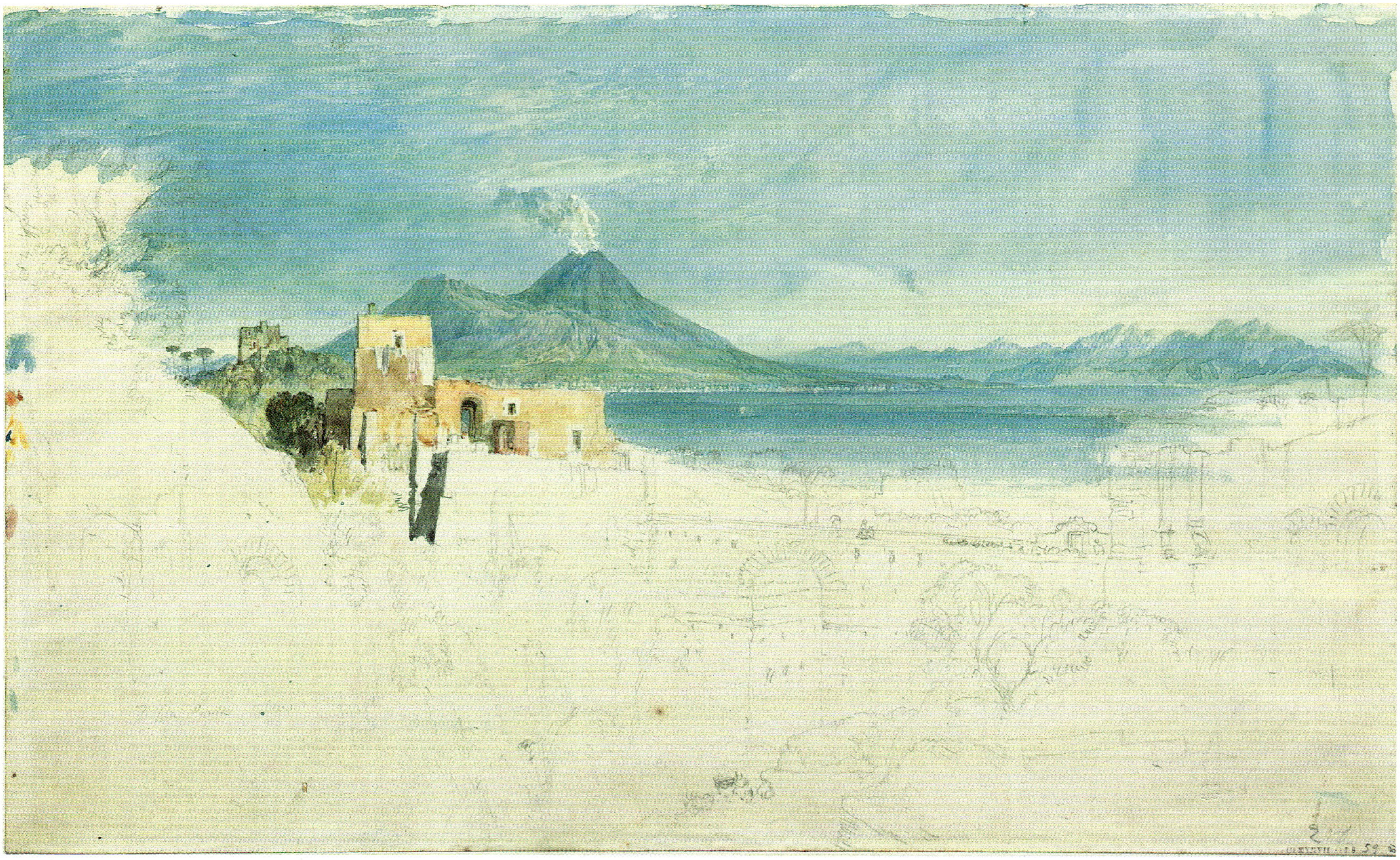

J.M.W. Turner, Coast Scene near Naples.
Tate Gallery, London, Turner Bequest.

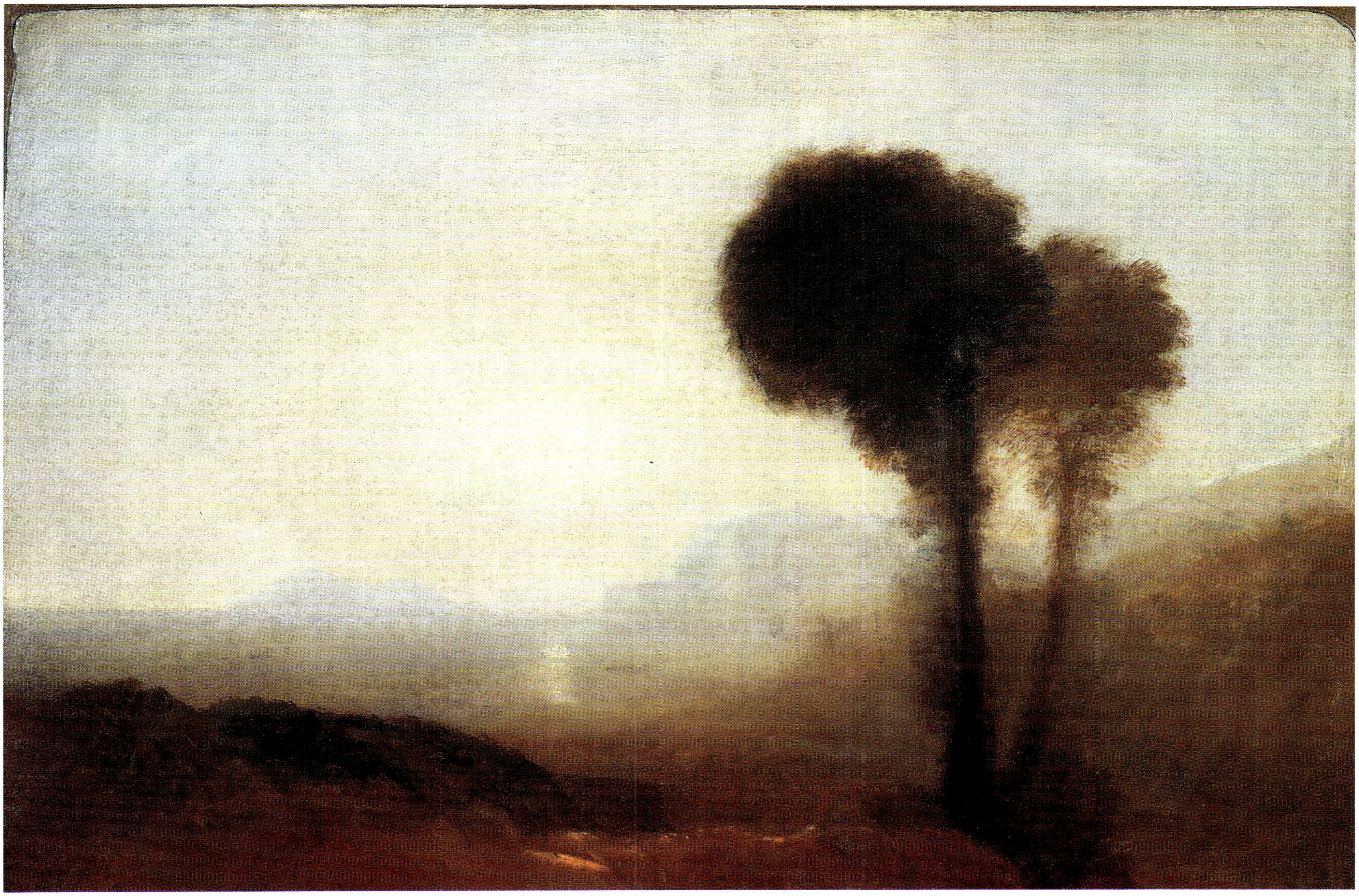

J.M.W. Turner, Seacoast with a Ruin.
Tate Gallery, London, Turner Bequest.

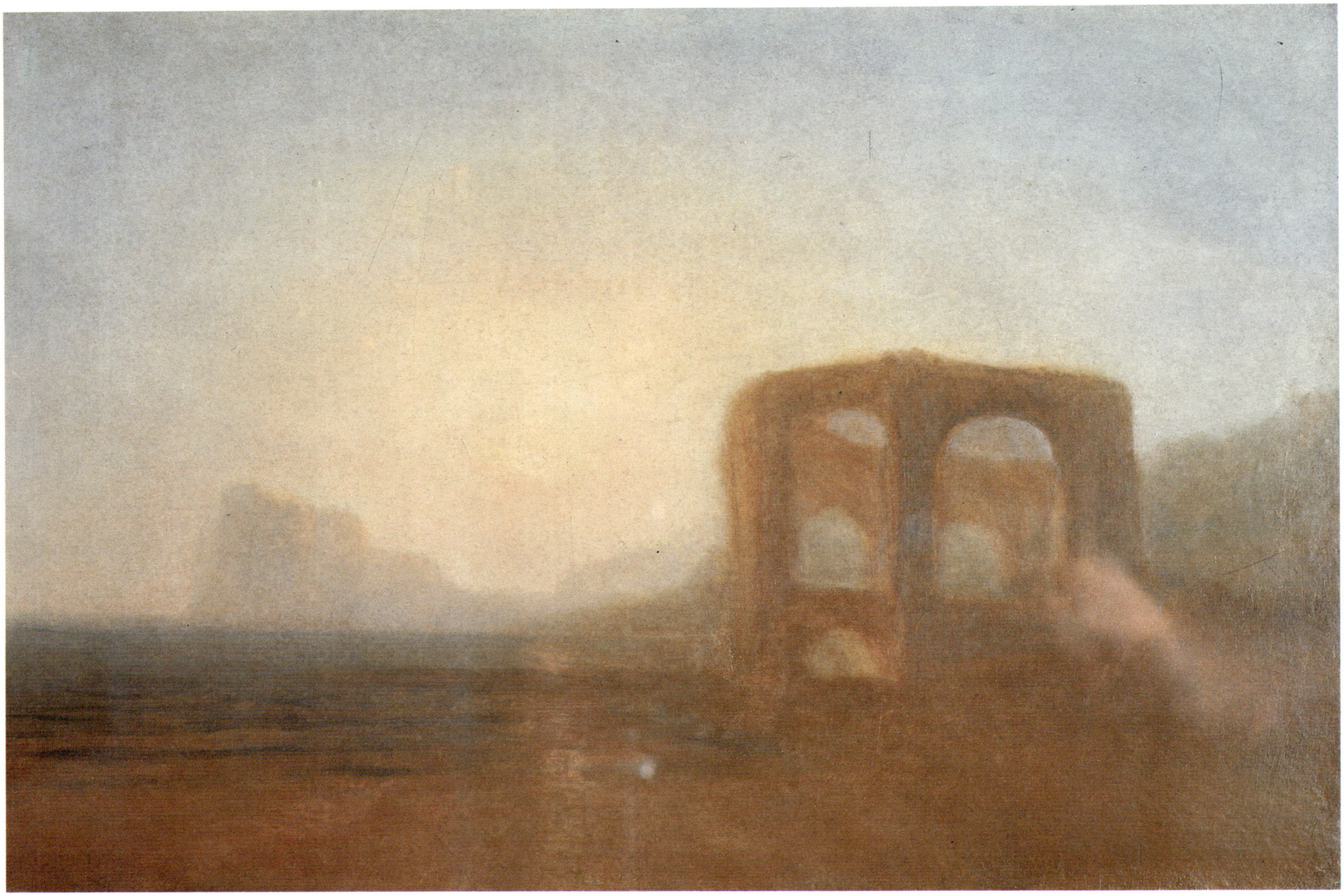

S.F. Schedrin, Seascape with Sorrento.
Naples, Museum of San Martino.

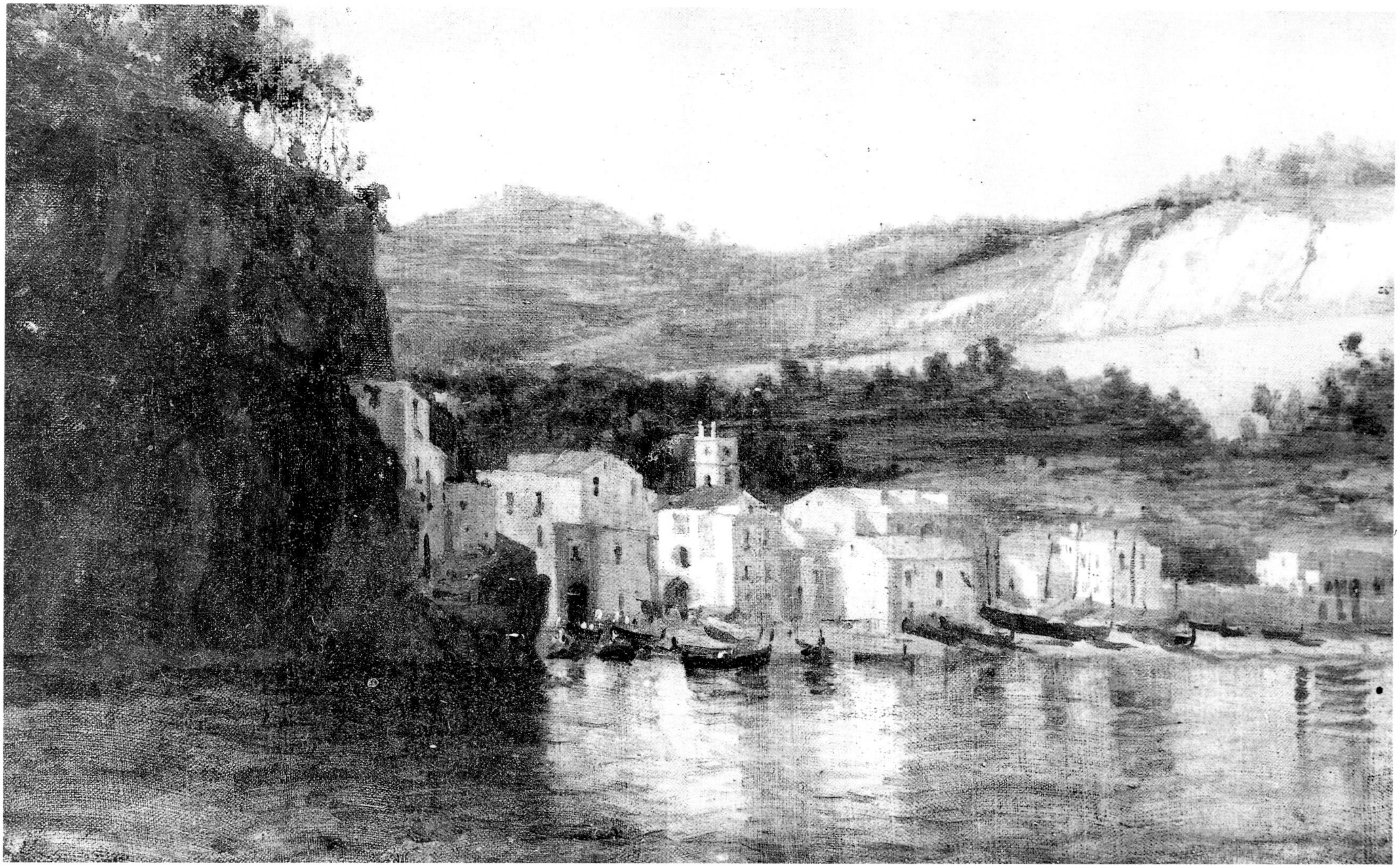

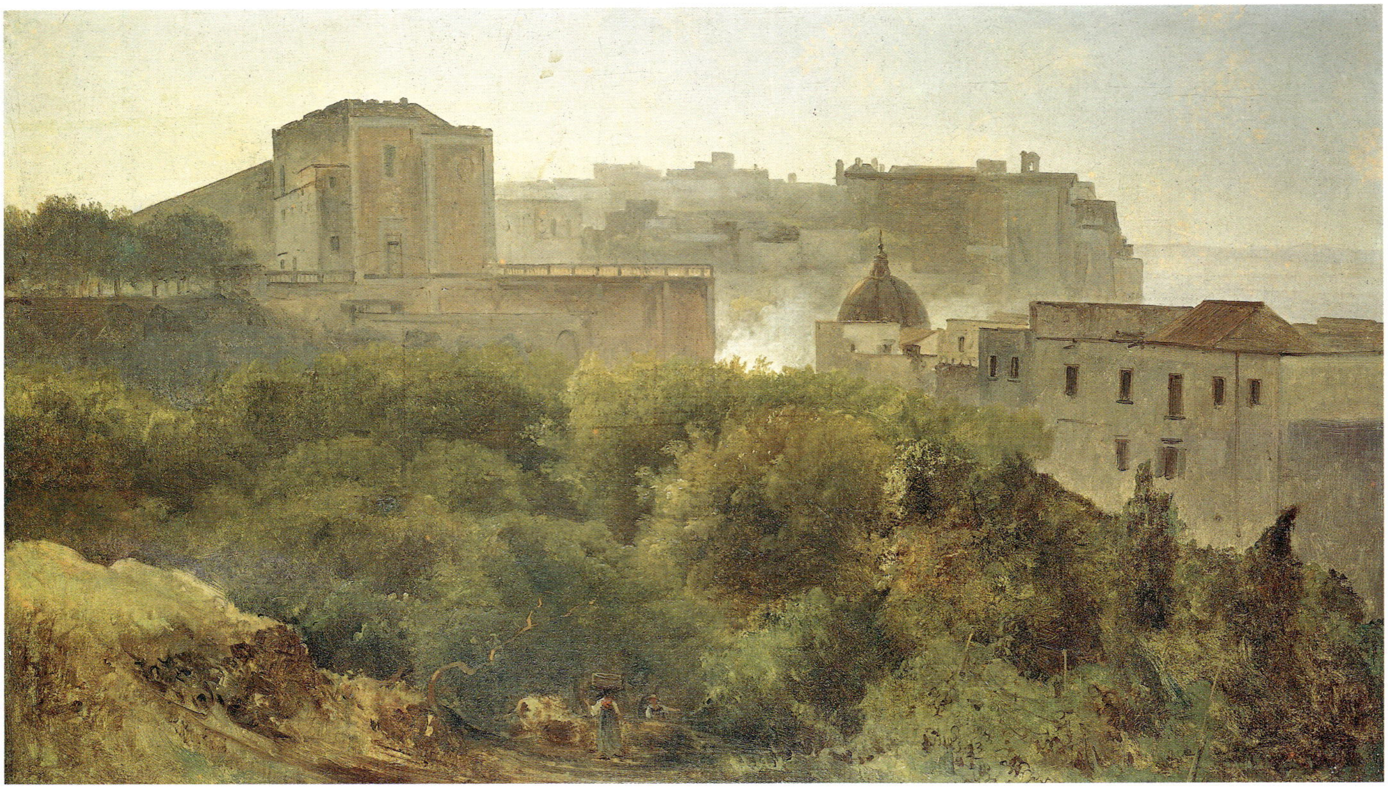

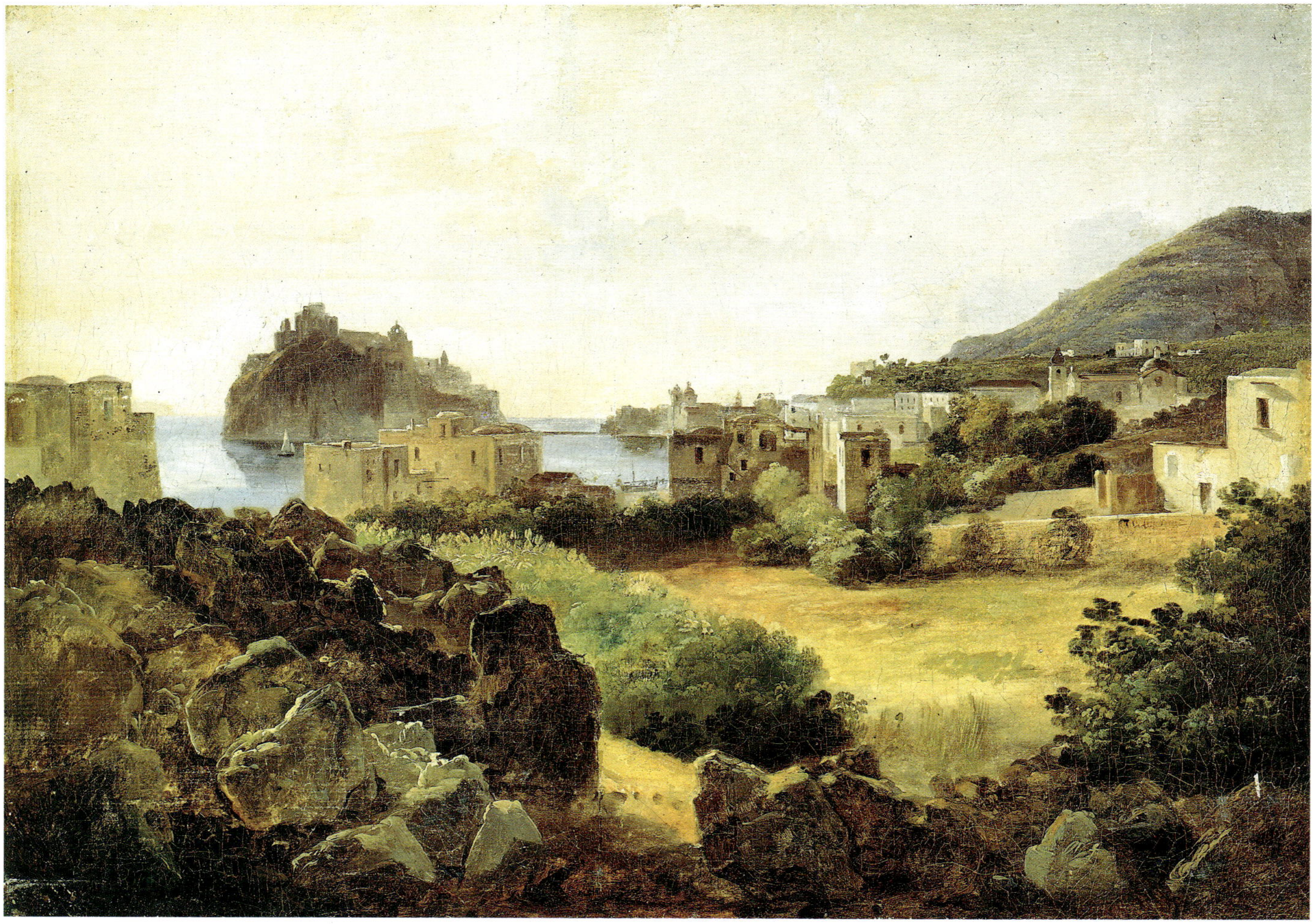

Anton Sminck Pitloo, Palazzo Francavilla with Pizzofalcone in the background. Naples, Banco di Napoli Gallery at Capodimonte Museum.

Anton Sminck Pitloo, View of Ischia. Galleria dell'Accademia di Belle Arti, Naples.

Anton Sminck Pitloo, The Mole Lighthouse. Museum of San Martino, Naples.

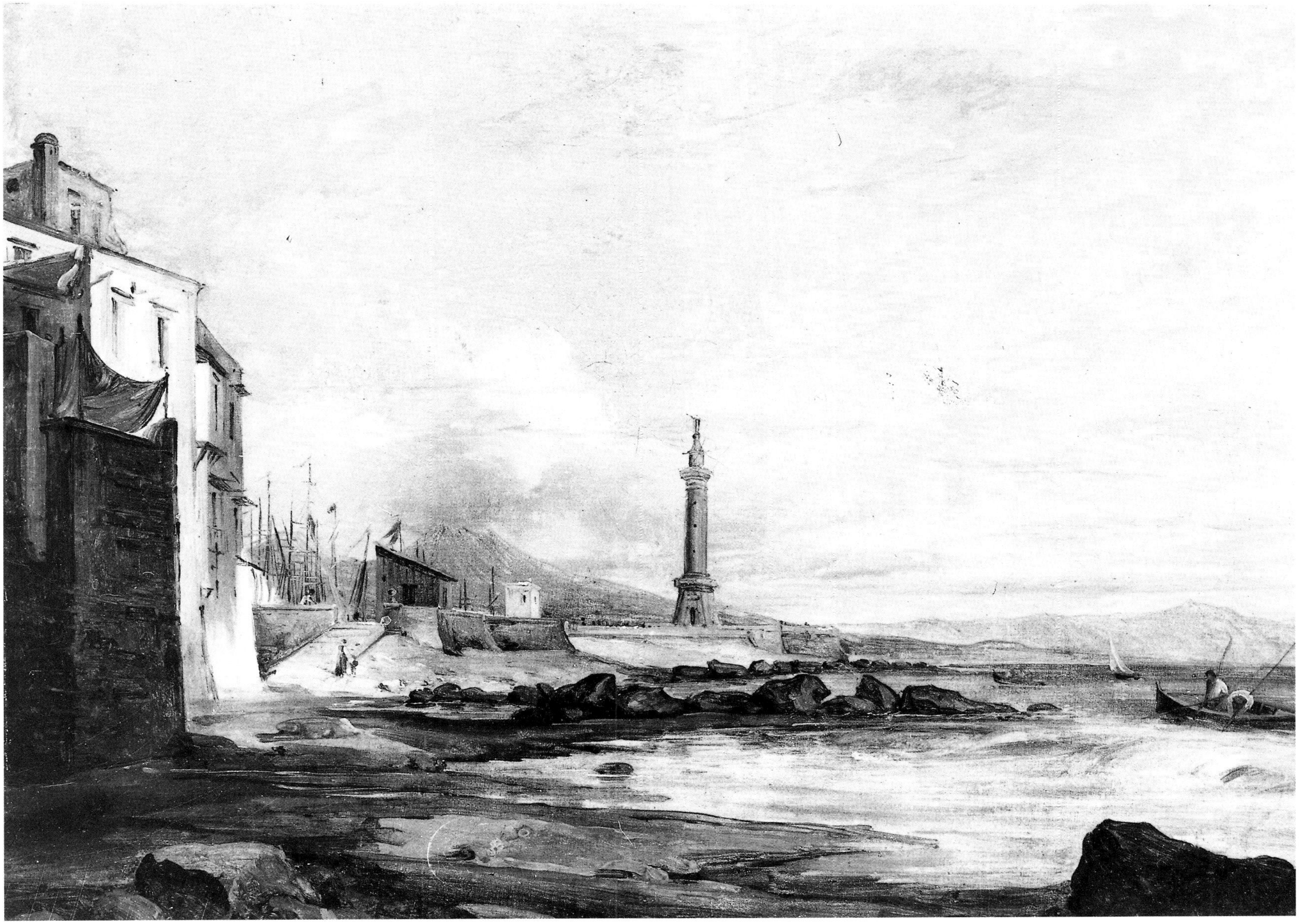

Giacinto Gigante, Sunset over Capri.
Naples, Museum of San Martino.

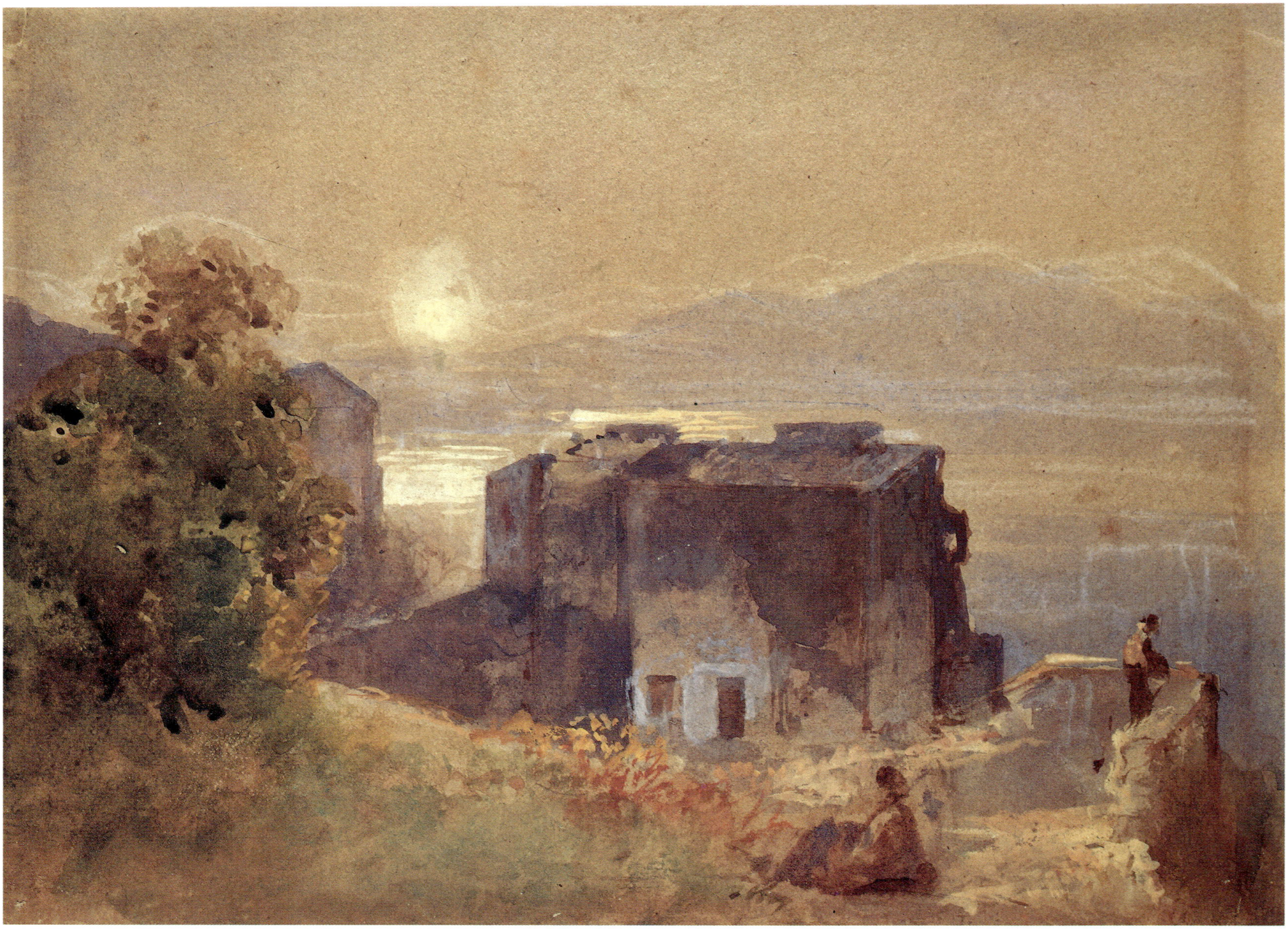

Giacinto Gigante, The Bay of Naples from the Arenella. Naples, Museum of Capodimonte.

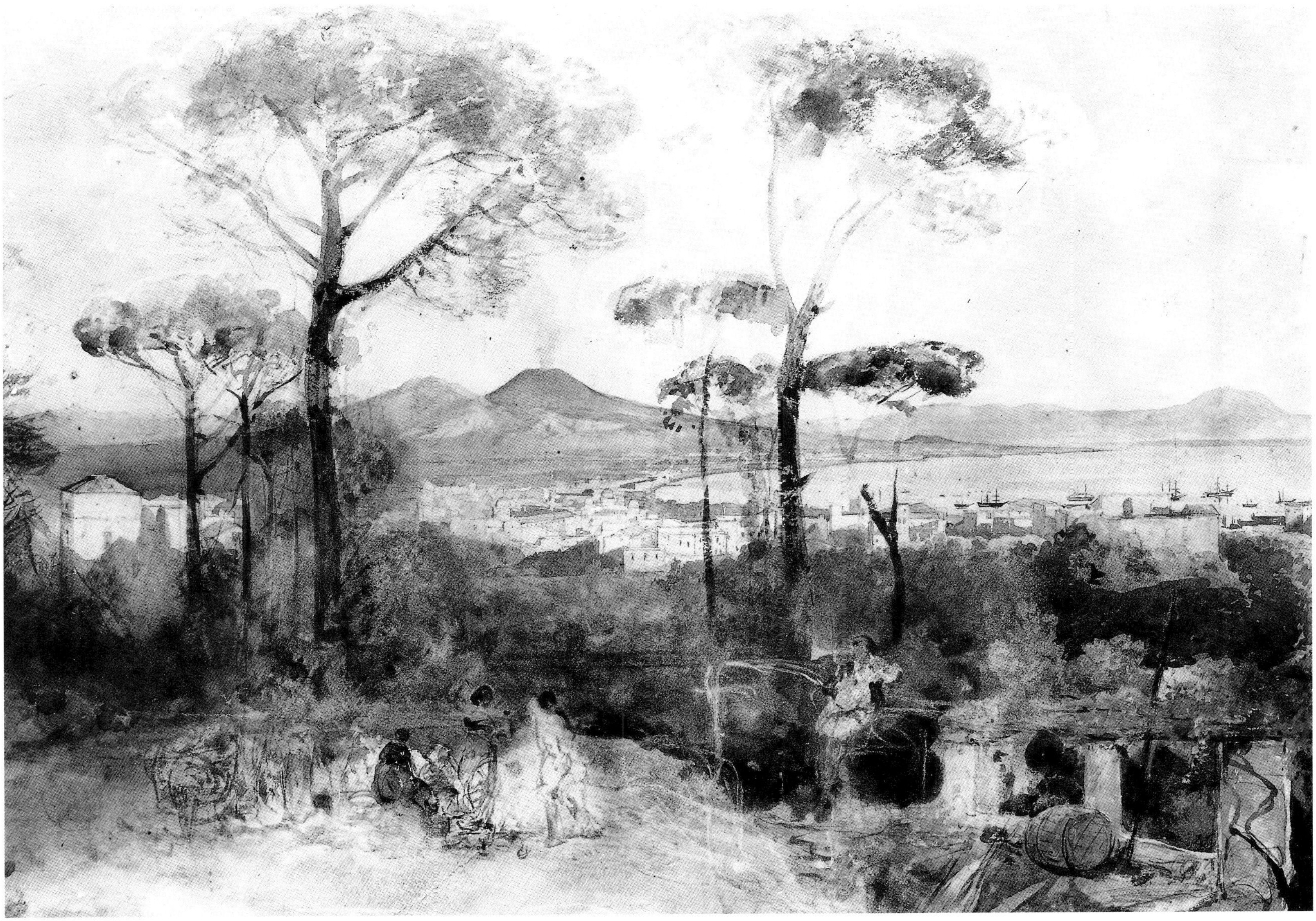

Giacinto Gigante, The Via dei Sepolcri at Pompeii. Naples, Museum of San Martino.

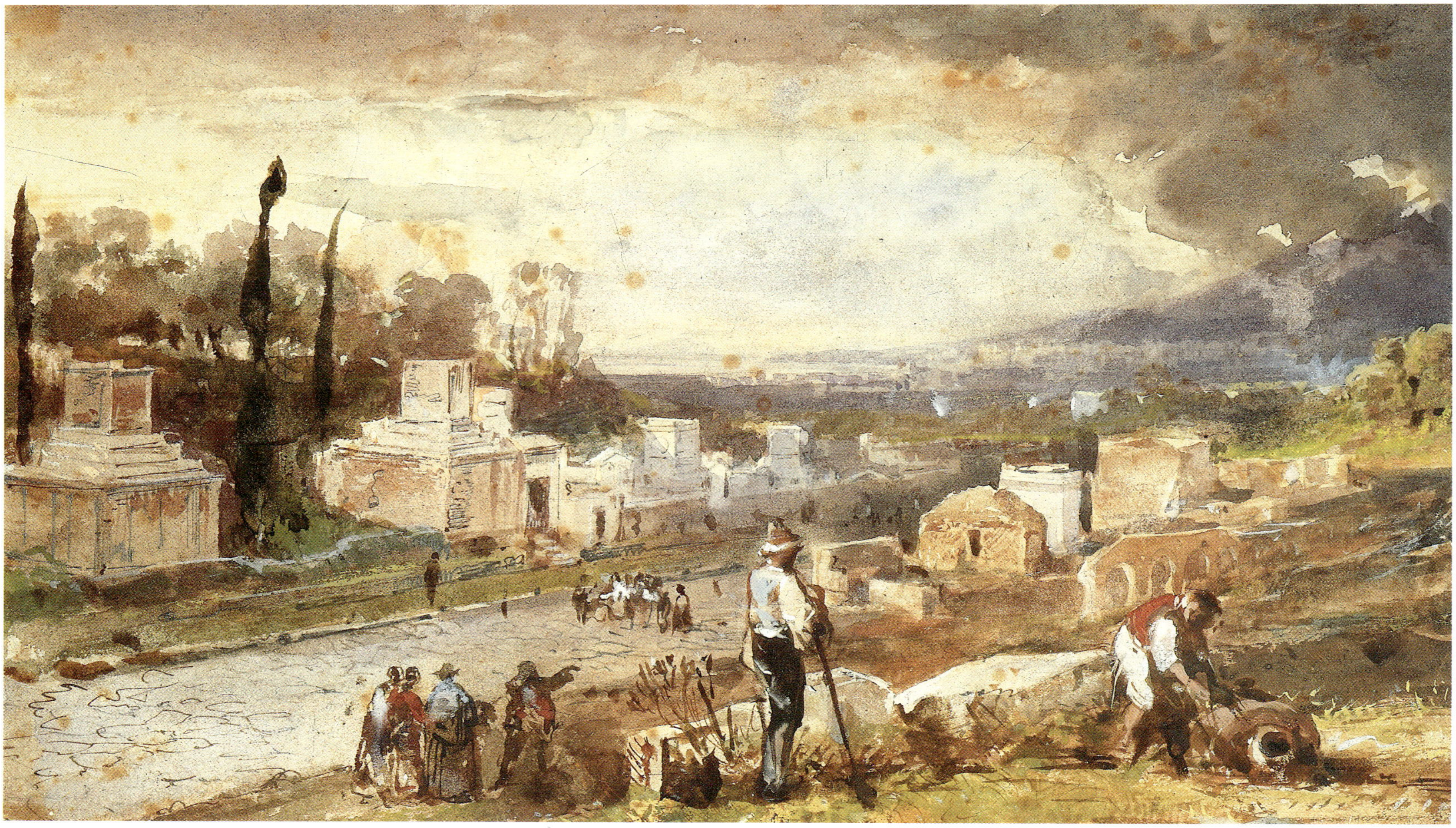

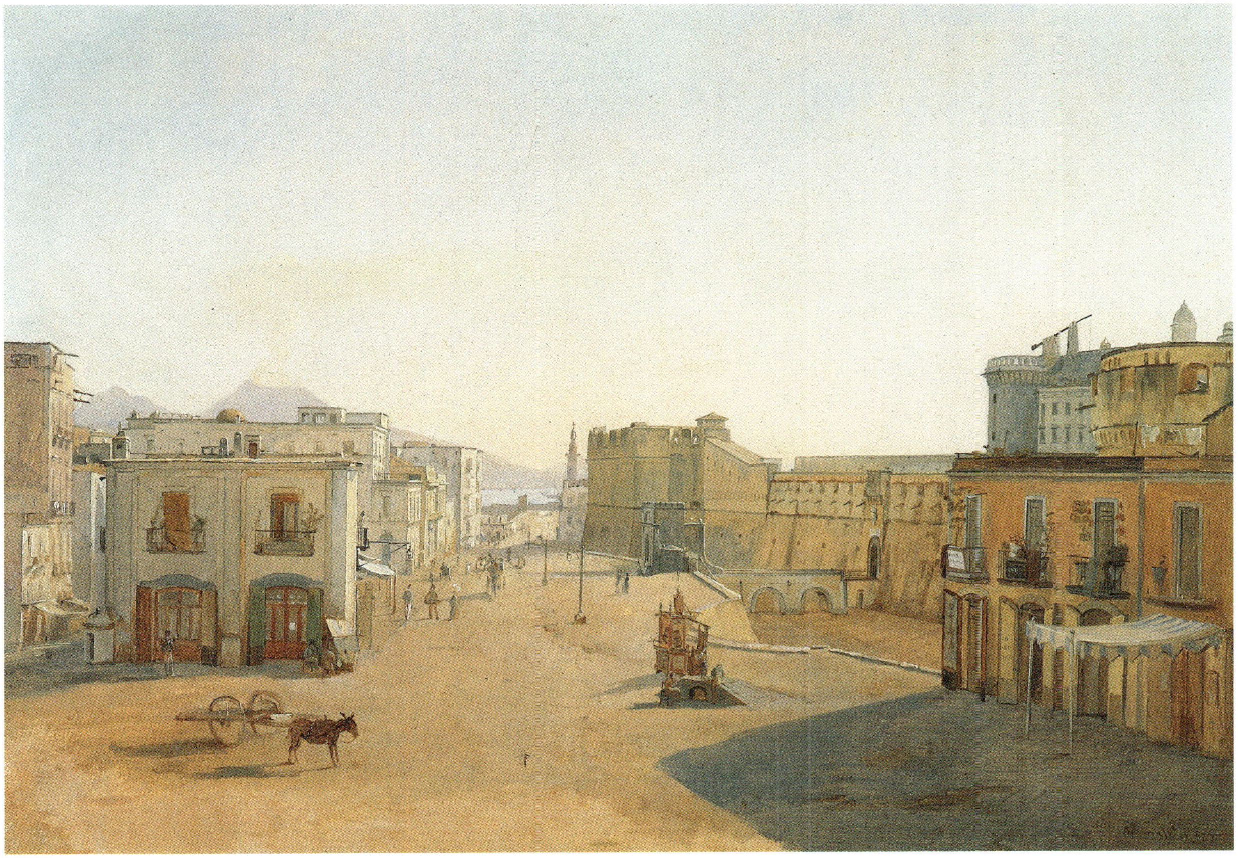

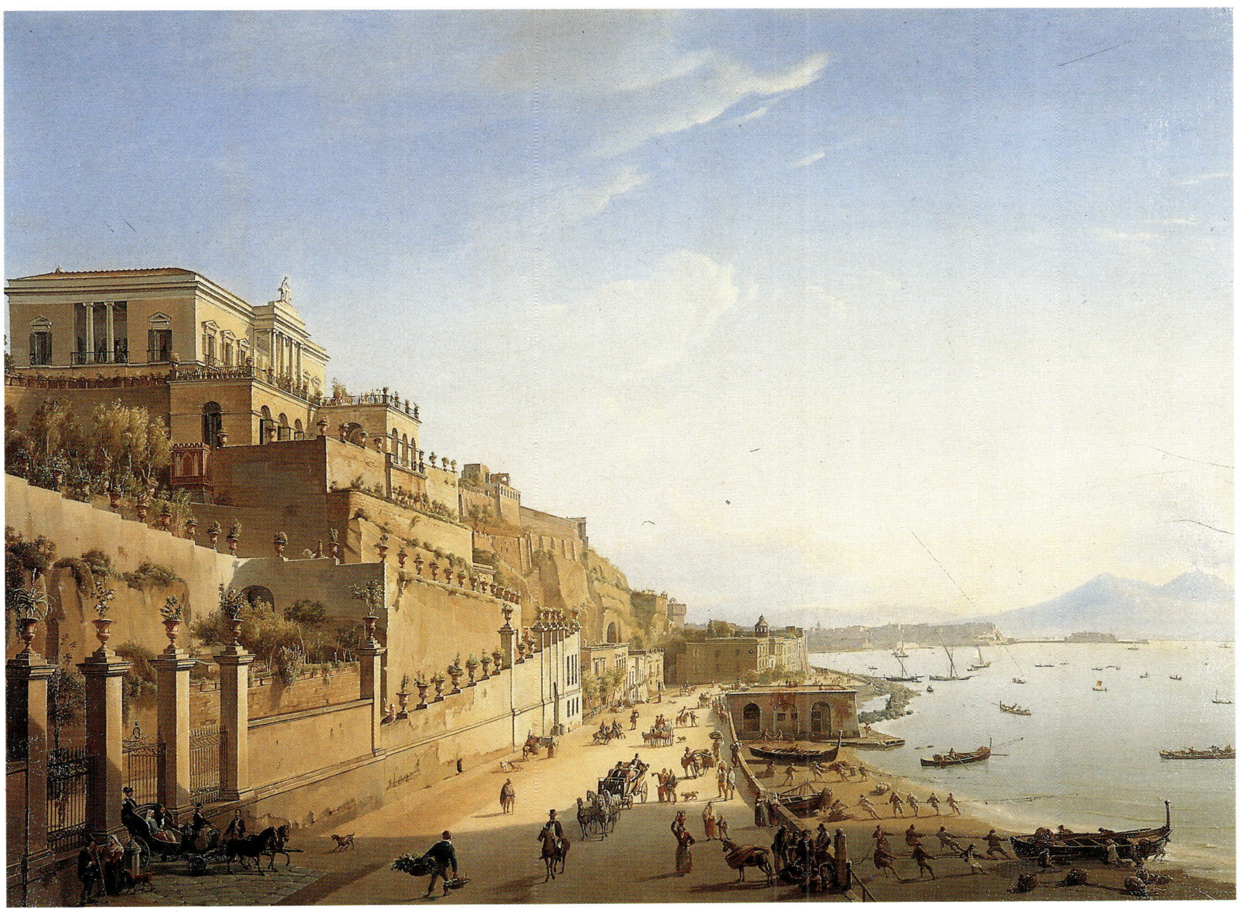

Frans Vervloet, Largo di Castello with the Lighthouse on the Mole. Naples, Museum of San Martino.

Frans Vervloet, Villa Doria d'Angri at Posillipo. Naples, private collection.

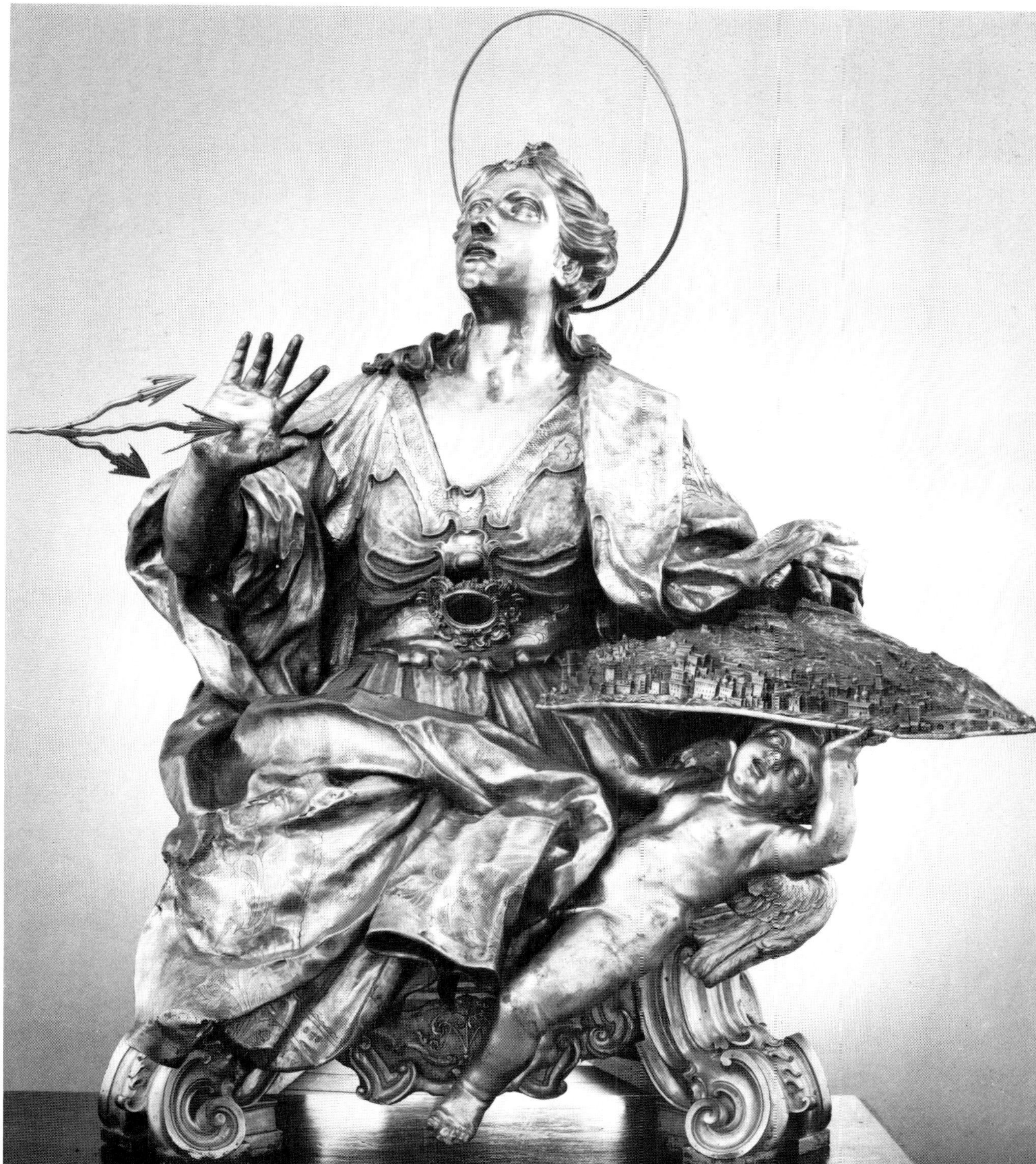

Carlo Schisano, Saint Irene.
Naples, Chapel
of the Treasure of San Gennaro.

Royal Porcelain Factory of Naples (Real Fabbrica), Known as the Oca Service or Service with Neapolitan Views.
Glass cooler. Naples, Museum of Capodimonte.

Royal Porcelain Factory of Naples (Real Fabbrica), Known as the Oca Service or Service with Neapolitan Views.
Bottle cooler. Naples, Museum of Capodimonte.

Royal Porcelain Factory of Naples (Real Fabbrica), Known as the Oca Service or Service with Neapolitan Views.
Oval Soup Tureen. Naples, Museum of Capodimonte.

Royal Porcelain Factory of Naples (Real Fabbrica), Known as the Oca Service or Service with Neapolitan Views.
Ice-box. Naples, Museum of Capodimonte.

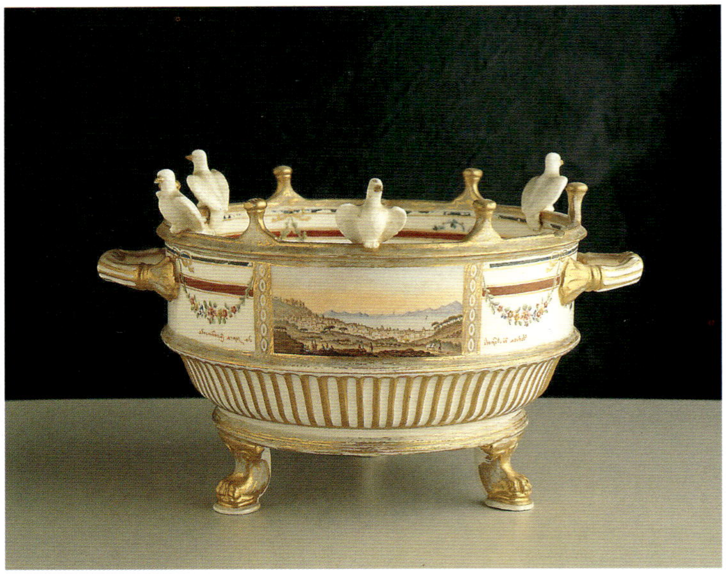

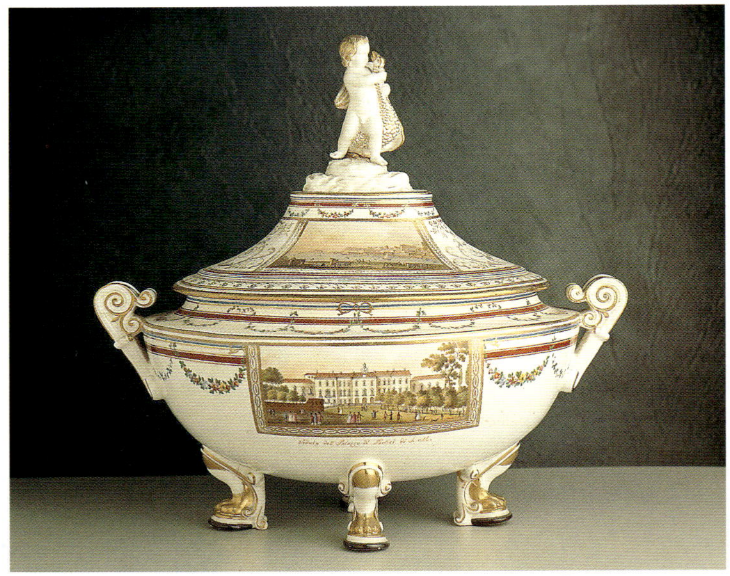

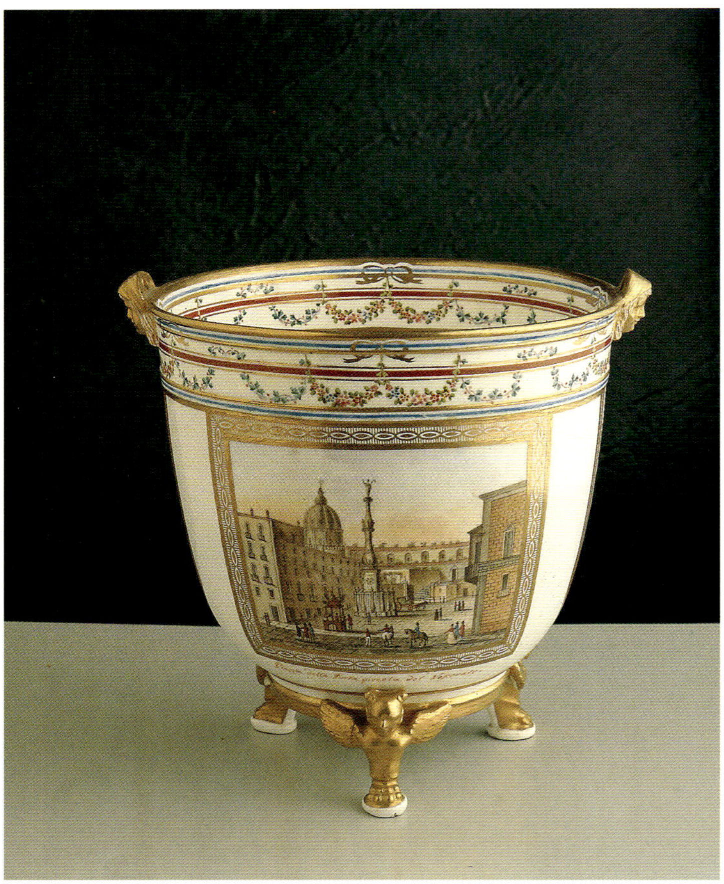

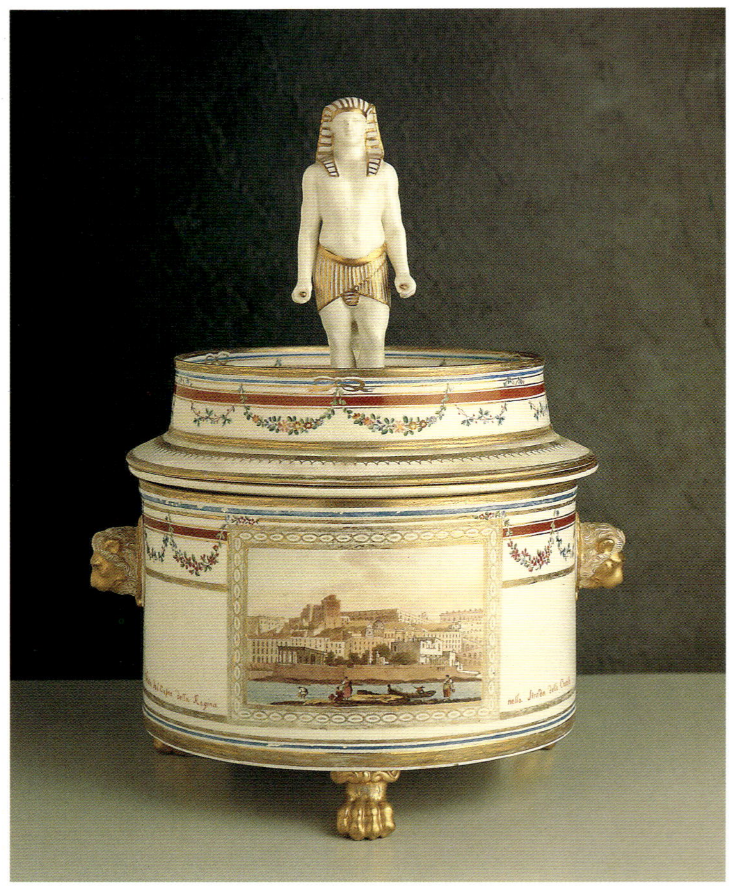

Royal Porcelain Factory of Naples (Real Fabbrica), Known as the Oca Service or Service with Neapolitan Views.
Round Plate. Naples, Museum of Capodimonte.

Royal Porcelain Factory of Naples (Real Fabbrica), Known as the Oca Service or Service with Neapolitan Views.
Square Plate. Naples, Museum of Capodimonte.

Royal Porcelain Factory of Naples (Real Fabbrica), Known as the Oca Service or Service with Neapolitan Views.
Triangular Plate. Naples, Museum of Capodimonte.

Royal Porcelain Factory of Naples (Real Fabbrica), Known as the Oca Service or Service with Neapolitan Views.
Large Oval Plate. Naples, Museum of Capodimonte.

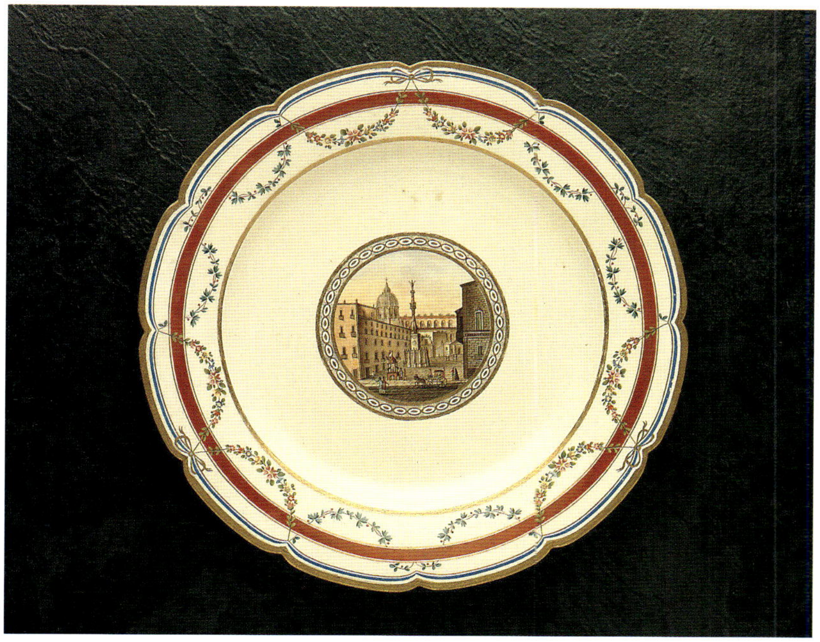

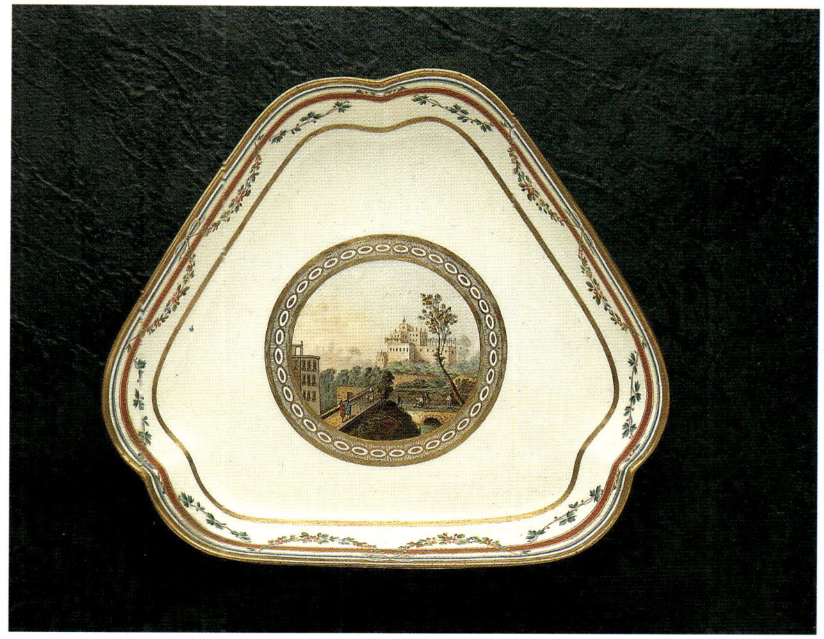

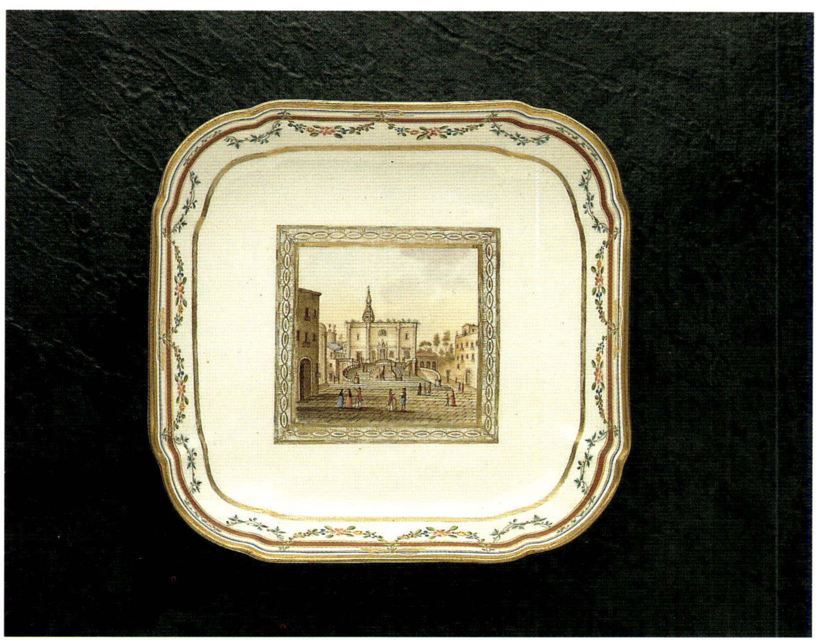

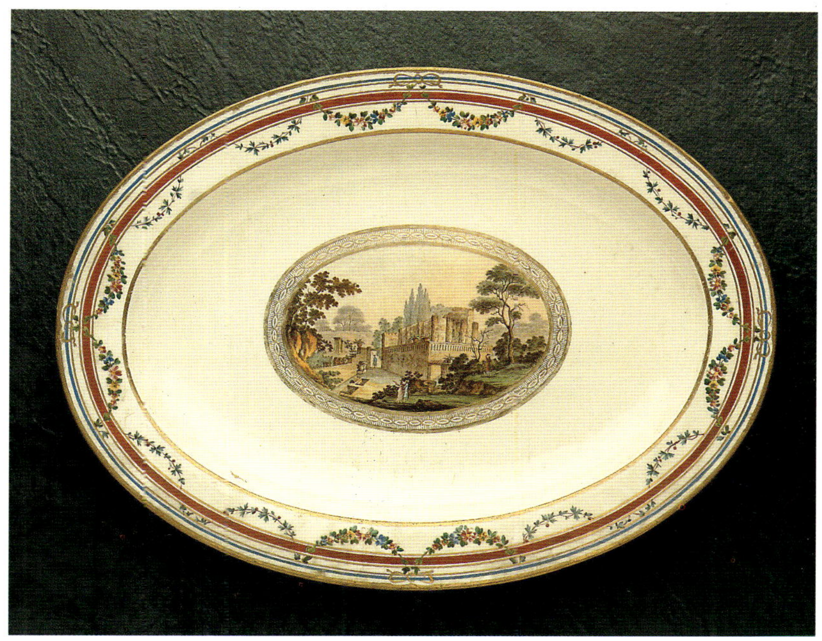

Royal Porcelain Factory of Naples (Real Fabbrica), Solitaire set with scenes of the ports and bays of the Kingdom. Naples, Museum of Capodimonte.

Giovanni Gramont and French porcelain, Library Set. Naples, Museum of Capodimonte.

Giovanni Gramont and French porcelain, Library Set, details. Naples, Museum of Capodimonte.

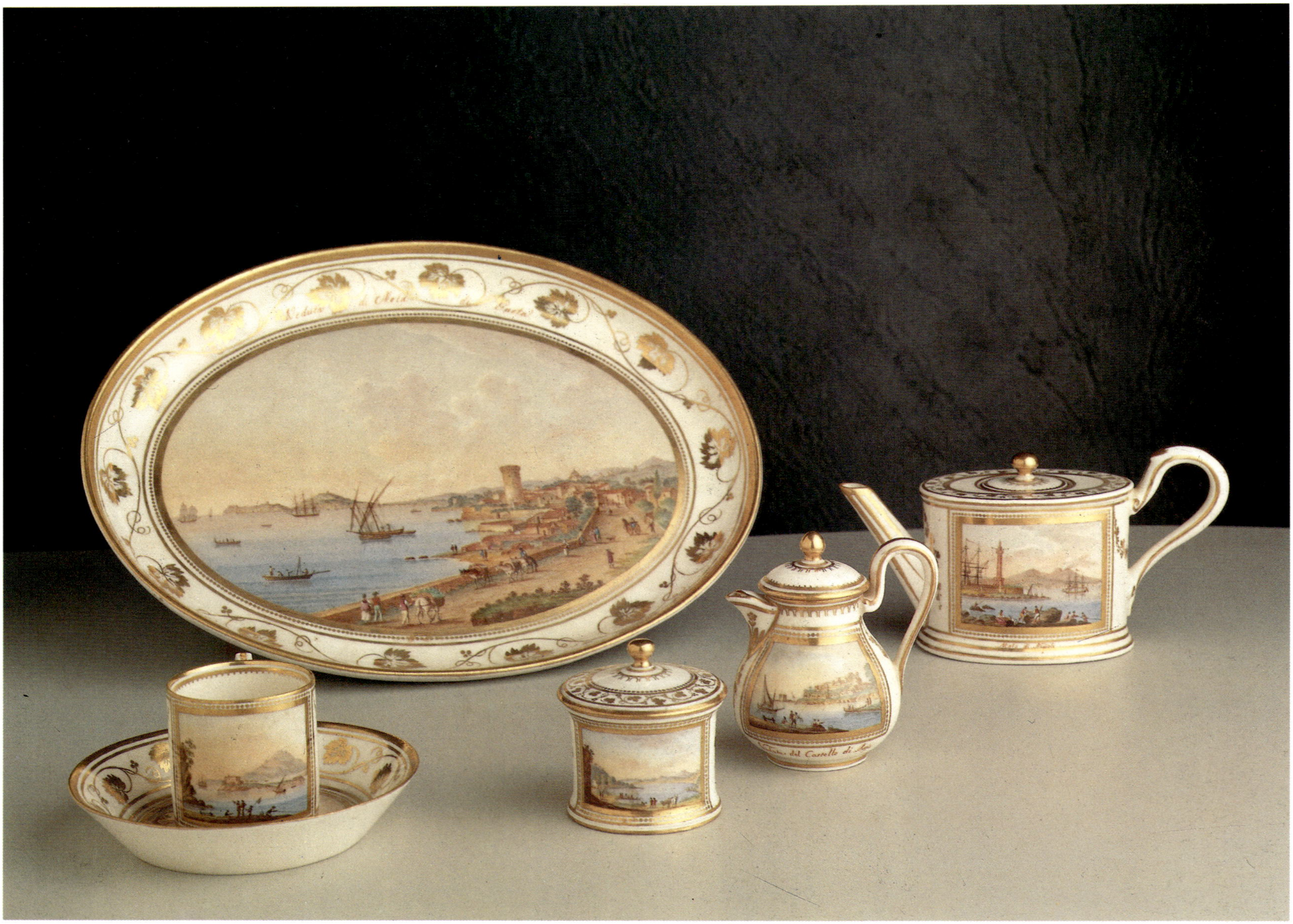

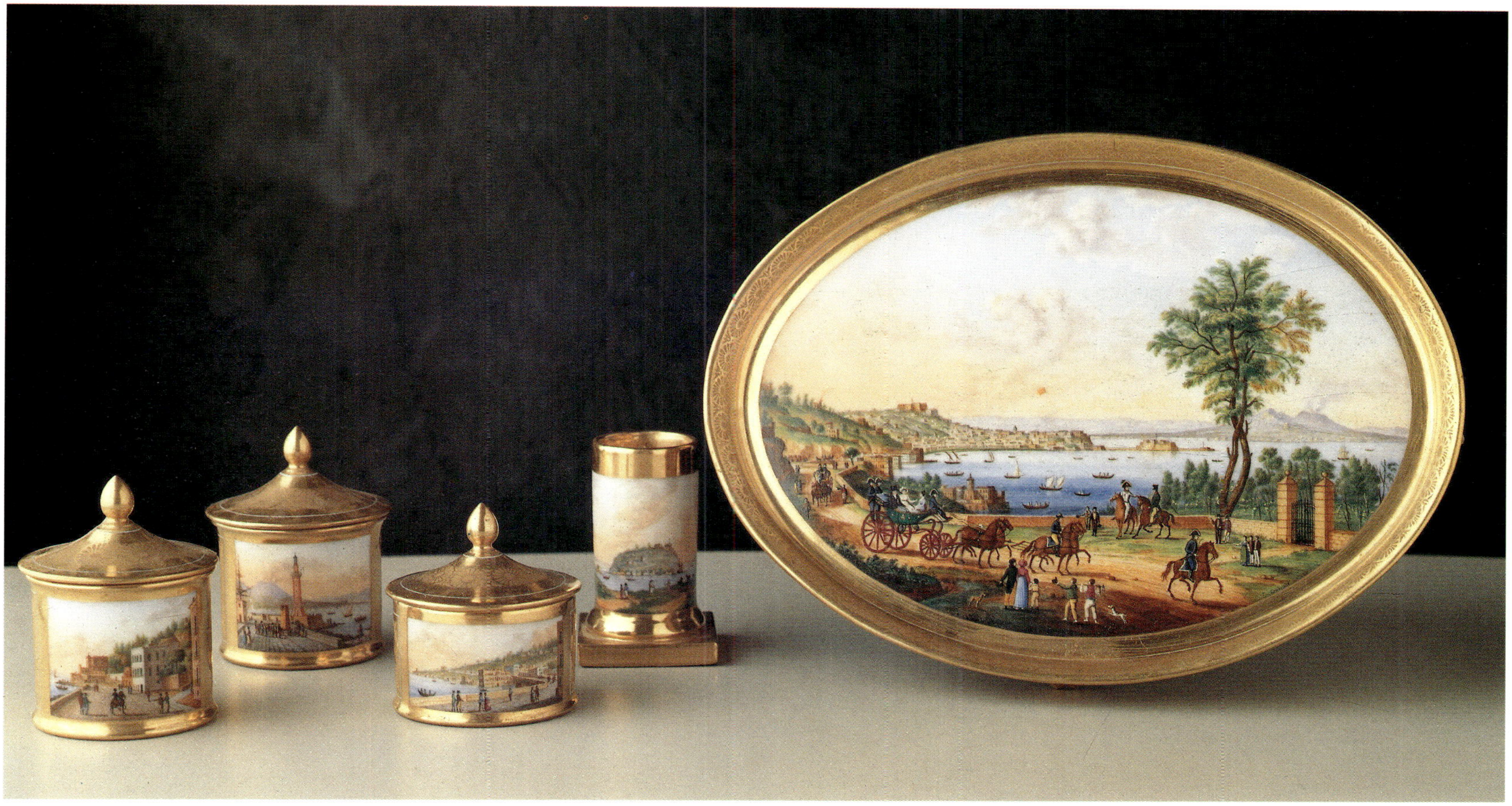

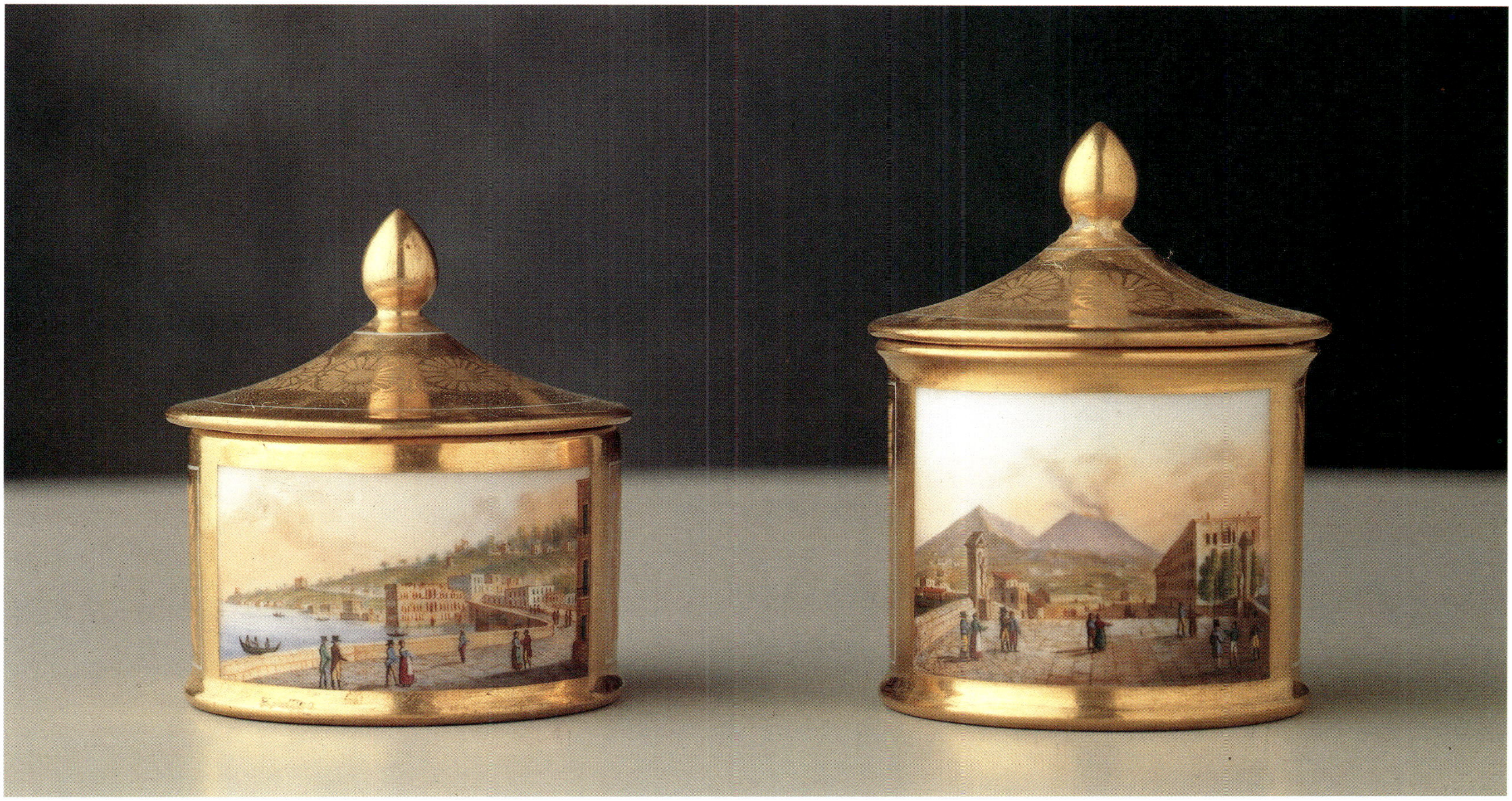

Doccia Porcelain, Dinner Service. Naples, Museum of Capodimonte.

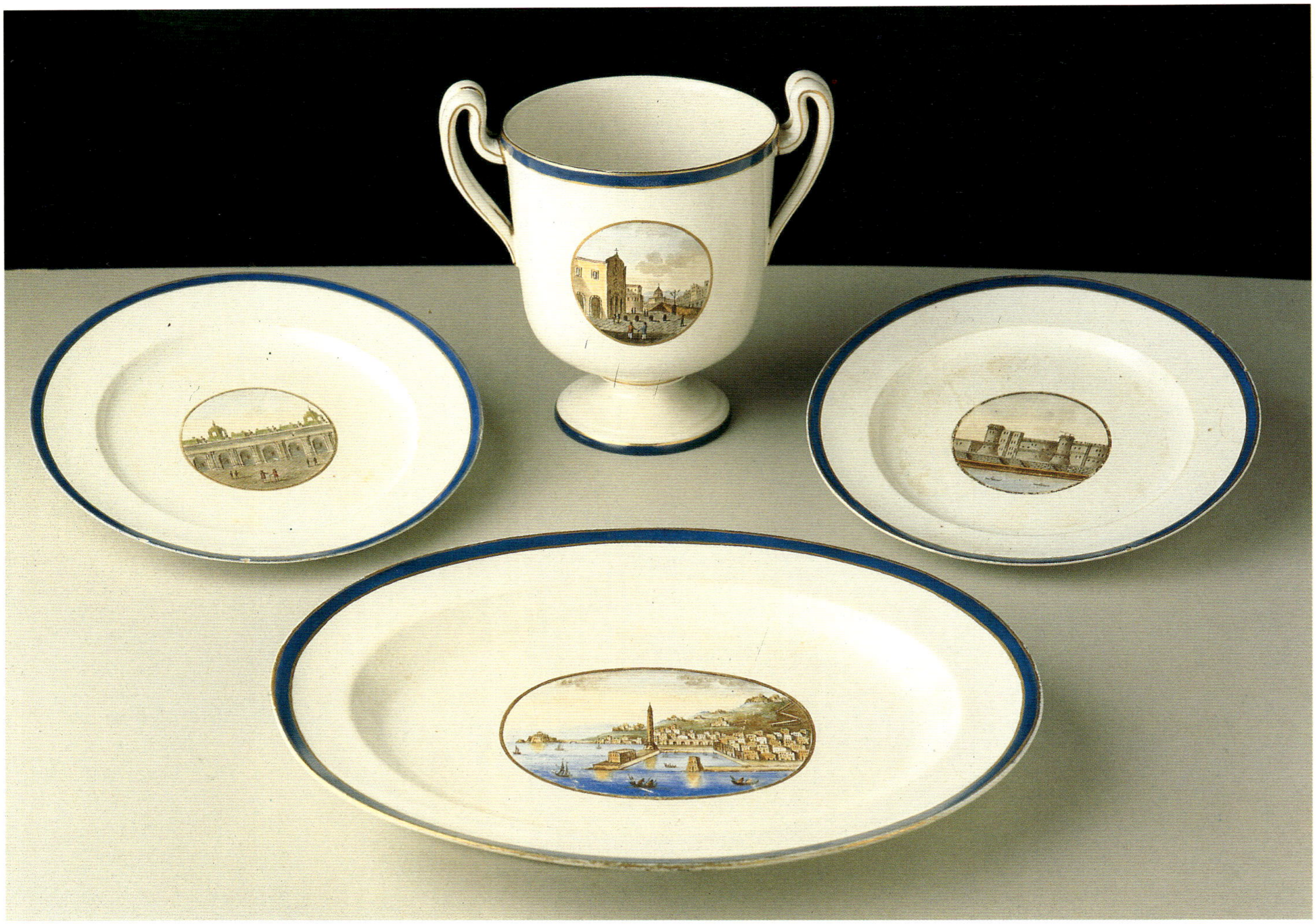

Clock, after 1827. Naples, Museum of Capodimonte.

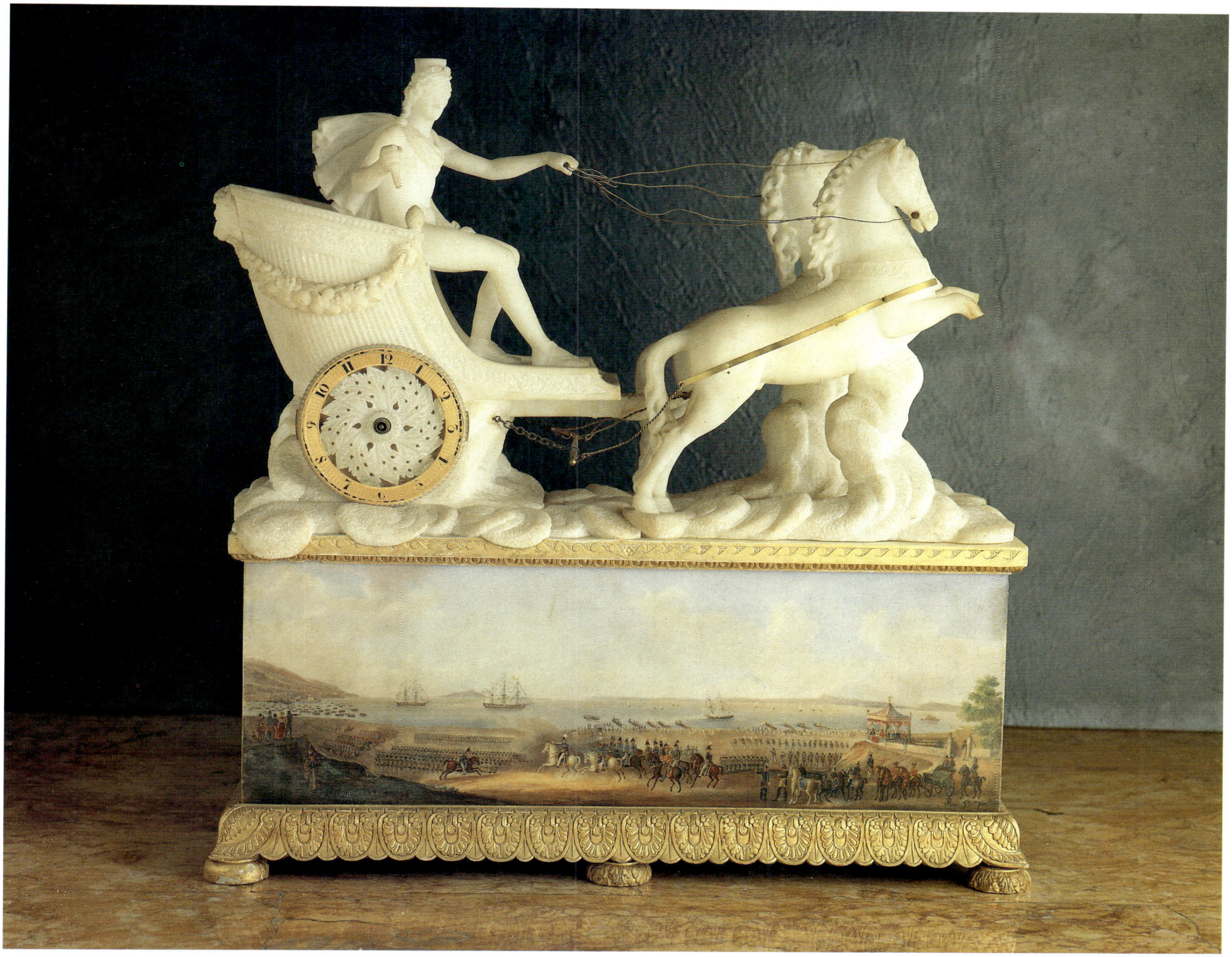

Table 1830-32. Naples, Museum of Capodimonte.

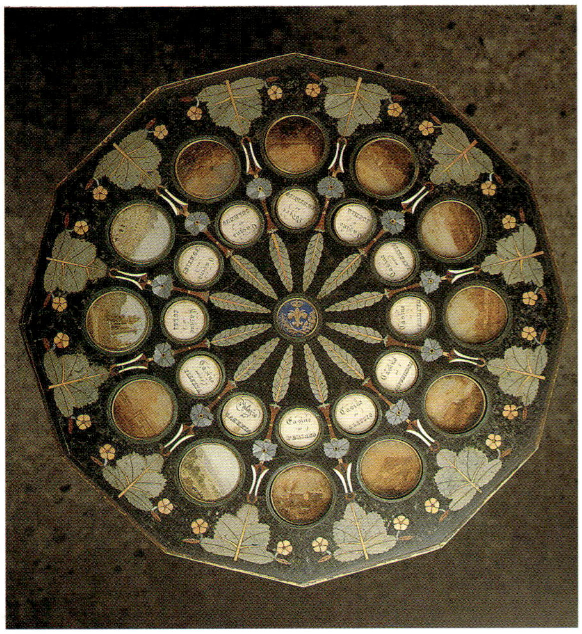

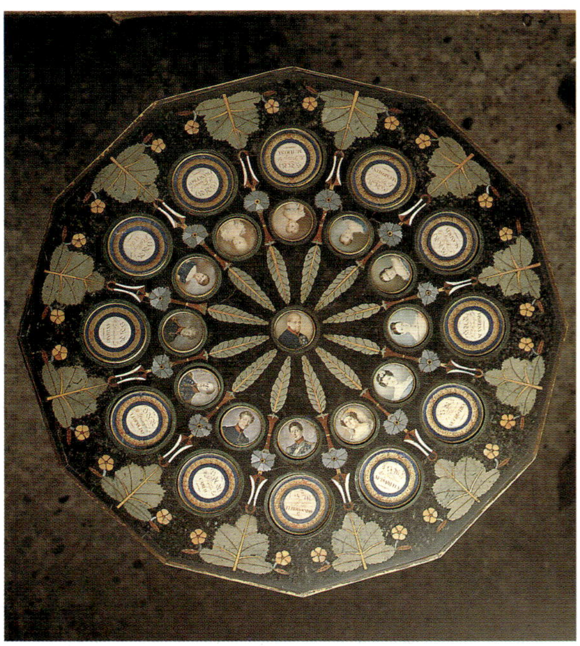

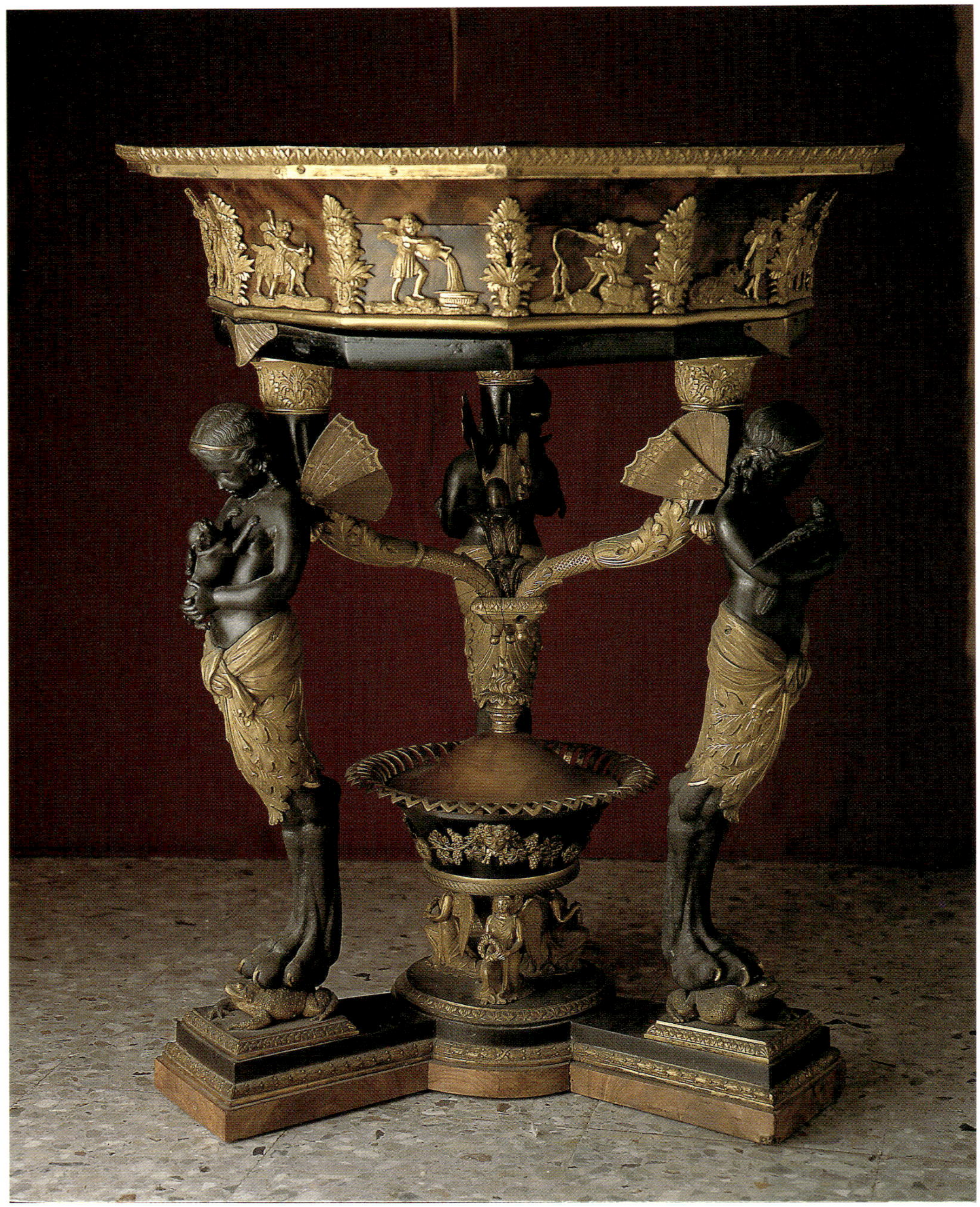

Biographical Notes and Entries

Biographical Notes and Entries

Pietro Antoniani
Milan c. 1740/50 - 1805

The only available information about this artist can be found in a few words entered in the *Enciclopedia Metodica... delle Belle Arti* (1817-24) edited by Pietro Zani, who describes Antoniani as a painter of landscapes and seascapes from Milan, active around 1775 who produced work of good quality. On the basis of this information Alberto Martini conducted wider research into this artist in 1965, and came up with 1750-60 as the decade when he was born. He felt that Zani's date of 1775 probably represented the half-way point of Antoniani's career. The few works that are dated are the only evidence that can be used to attempt a reconstruction of the artist's activity, which all dated between 1770-80.
Nothing is known about his stay in Naples, nor his journeys abroad, to England for example. These journeys are only guesswork though, based on the fact that many works are owned by British collectors and stately homes. He certainly interested Sir William Hamilton, who personally commissioned two views – *Naples from Mergellina* (1771) and the *Eruption of Vesuvius of 1767* (1776), now in British collections. He also received commissions from Charles Towney (a famous collector of marble) and Sir Henry Brudenell who bought four paintings by the artist between 1775-76 (Russell 1985, p. 1538) which could be the *Views from Il Carmine, Posillipo, the Riviera di Chiaia and the Hill of Posillipo and Santa Lucia,* signed and dated in those years and kept at Lulworth Manor. At Houingham Hall there is another painting by Antoniani of Naples seen from the sea.
In the 1780's and 1790's, of the foreign travellers and artists who flocked to the Bourbons' capital with its truly international environment many were working on the large-scale projects which were to be published around that time. In this setting Antoniani produced his most successful work – pleasant views of the city from angles which were particularly cherished by his patrons and now established as a thriving local tradition, with a whole series of conventional topographical references which had become stereotypes in the wake of Joli's and Ricciardelli's clear-cut transparent renderings. Compared to these two painters, and Joli in particular, with his faithful representations of views in the manner of Van Wittel interpreted by Joli with expressive limpidity, Antoniani, who was a generation younger was more inclined to a rather repetitive descriptiveness; his colours were pleasant enough but his mannerism produced contrived perspectives. These were rather attractive in themselves, but obviously dictated by the need to please his clients and this explained the taste for decorative painting with scenographic expedients. Often we find ourselves looking at works where the view itself – reiterated time and time again – ends up by being merely a pretty framework for a commemorative event at court or in aristocratic circles, a photo album of everyday life of the period, described with a wealth of details and genre figures (now also part of the repertoire). All this was in keeping with the image of Neapolitan life and people which was beginning to take shape in the imagination of collectors of this kind of work. In effect, it was the first step in the direction of the Neapolitan stereotype which was to become so popular later on. [M.U.]

Eruptions of Vesuvius in 1767
Oil on canvas, 64.5 x 30.5, pl. p. 58
Inscribed on the verso:
Eruzzione Ultima Celebre
del Vesuvio del 1767
Petrus Antoniani delint. ed fect. 1776
London, William Mostyn-Owen

As is well known, Antoniani received many commissions from British patrons. This painting, with a view of *Naples from Mergellina* exhibited in 1771 (Spinosa in Spinosa-Di Mauro 1989, p. 195, no. 95, fig. 93) was actually part of Sir William Hamilton's collection, and both were sold as part of the Hamilton sale by Christies on 17th April 1801. They later became part of the Earl of Wharfcliffe's collection, where they remained until the late 1950's.
Other eruptions of Vesuvius by Antoniani are known, some of which were attributed to Volaire, but none of them were painted from this viewpoint which was called the Atrio del Cavallo. They were usually painted from high up or from the Miglio d'Oro area to the south-east, rather than from Naples itself. Another painting which depicts the eruption of 1767 from the viewpoint in this picture was sold by Christies on 24th May 1985 in Lot 5 (Spinosa in Spinosa-Di Mauro 1989, p. 195, no. 101, fig. 99). [M.U.]

Bibl.: Martini 1965, p. 85, fig. 64; Causa-Picone 1978, p. 38; Russell 1985, II, p. 1538, fig. 6).

View of Naples with the Eruption of Vesuvius
Oil on canvas, 20.5 x 41, pl. p. 58
Naples, D'Amodio Collection

This is a previously unknown work which shows the subtle quality of Antoniani's depiction of urban landscapes of Naples. This view of Naples with Vesuvius erupting in the background and the port in the foreground is reminiscent of earlier popular subjects by Bonavia and Joli. Antoniani's brushstroke is more vigorous, almost like a naive painter, which distinguishes him from the sophisticated commemorative works painted by his two illustrious predecessors. [N.S.]

Didier Barra
Metz c. 1590 - ?

Didier Barra was born in Metz (Lorraine) in the last decade of the 16th century, as records tell us discovered by Tribout de Morembert from the same town. Barra left Metz at a very early age, perhaps around 1608, and this is all that was known about his life. He was certainly active in Naples for quite a long time, presumably from c. 1630 to the late 1650's.
Only recently has more information emerged about him. According to the traditional sources of Neapolitan history (De Dominici 1742, II, Celano-Chiarini 1856-60, IV, Galante 1872) there were two foreign artists working in Naples at about the same time under the name of Monsù Desiderio – Didier Barra and François de Nomé. Research carried out by Sluys (1954) and Causa (1961) finally solved the mystery: Barra was a brilliant landscapist, an acute recorder of the city, more like a cartographer because of his precise descriptions of places, but he was also an excellent painter and a master in the use of light. De Nomé, on the other hand, was only capable of producing bizarre architectural compositions, fantastic and tormented views.
The point of departure in the reconstruction of Barra's work is the *Bird's eye view of Naples* signed and dated: «Desiderius Barra ex Civitate Metensi in Lotharingia F. 1647» at the National Museum of San Martino in Naples. A copy of this view was found recently in a private Neapolitan collection, which is slightly larger than the one at San Martino. In 1643 Didier Barra was paid by the bank of San Giacomo in Naples for twelve landscapes of Naples commissioned by Giovan Battista Riario. Some more views of Naples are attributed to Barra which are part of panel paintings, like in the one by Onofrio Palumbo showing *San Gennaro praying for Naples*, datable around 1651-52 belonging to the Arciconfraternita dei Pellegrini in Naples; and another attractive landscape in a work by Giuseppe Marullo, originally in the church of San Gennaro dei Cavalcanti, subsequently moved when the church was destroyed and now stored in the church of San Pietro Martire.
From what is now recognised as Barra's work, quite a large number of paintings show views of Naples painted from the sea, consequently the whole of the city is visible. Others represent the better known and loved places in Neapolitan landscape painting – *Vesuvius* (from a private collection in Rome and in Lot 4, Mondolfo Sale at Christies in 1978), the *Port* (from a private collection in Naples and at the Wadsworth Atheneum in Hartford); *Naples from the East with Castel dell'Ovo and Posillipo* (from a private collection in Rome, the Dalla Vecchia collection in Naples and the National Museum of San Martino). These paintings prove just how specialised the artist was in this field. The point of departure for these views of the city were probably the topographical engravings by Alessandro Baratta, who made the *Bird's eye view of the City of Naples* (1627-70). Causa (1958, p. 46) suggested that Barra had originally trained as a cartographer, and De Seta, on the subject of landcape painting as a genre (1980, pp. 48-50) stressing the precise topographical nature of this painter sees Barra as one of the first real landscape painters. The *View of Naples from the Sea* attributed to Barra which was recently sold (Daverio, Silbernagl) shows certain similarities with works by François de Nomé, who painted a *View of Naples* (now in the Dalla Vecchia collection) and a *View of St. Mark's Square in Venice* (see the exhibition catalogue *Le Venezie possibili* Venice, 1985, p. 85, no. 26). Barra's

contacts with De Nomé can also be seen in the *Feast of the Redeemer in Venice* (at the Galleria Nazionale di Arte Antica in Rome) and the painting showing *Largo di Palazzo Reale in Naples* (Sluys 1961, p. 61). [B.D.]

View of Naples from the Sea
Oil on canvas, 114x175, pl. p. 33
Milan, private collection

This extraordinary view of Naples seen from the sea was attributed to Didier Barra because of the very clearly drawn urban fabric. The tail end of the curved flash of light which appears in the stormy sky could be interpreted as the artist's signature.
By «straightening» the natural curve of the Bay of Naples, Barra lines up Castel dell'Ovo with the hill of Pizzofalcone, Palazzo Carafa and Castel Nuovo as far as the eastern part of the city, and the effect is totally unrealistic. The ray of sunlight falling on Castel Sant'Elmo stresses its isolated and privileged position in the city.
The coat of arms which can be seen in the upper part of the picture could well be that of Juan Alfonso Enriquez, Admiral of Castille and Spanish viceroy in Naples from 1644 to 1646, as Nicola Spinosa suggests.
The painting was probably meant to record the admiral's arrival or departure, as some of the feluccas and sailing ships in the port are firing salvoes from their cannons.
The painting belongs to an aristocratic Neapolitan family. [B.D.]

Carlo Bonavia
Active in Naples between 1751 and 1788

The scarcity of biographical information and records regarding this artist (who was probably from Rome) is compensated for by a large number of paintings, and more are coming to light all the time. On the basis of signed or initialled paintings his work falls into the period starting 1751, the year he painted a view with *The Mole of Naples and the Lighthouse* and ending 1788, when he painted *Castel dell'Ovo* (now at the Academy of Arts, Honolulu). However, within this period it is difficult to clearly establish in what succession his identified works were produced, since the style appears pretty much the same, even when Bonavia repeats a theme years later. A hypothetical chronological survey of his work was proffered by Constable (1959-1960-1962) which still appears valid and can be completed with new findings – the *Mole of Naples* (already mentioned) which was sold by Christies in London in 1983 (Spinosa in Spinosa-Di Mauro 1989, p. 191, no. 57, fig. 56); the *Seascape in the Moonlight* of 1753 (op. cit. 1989, no. 58, PI, 24); the *Coast Scene* at the Metropolitan Museum of New York of 1754 (op. cit. 1989, no. 59, fig. 57); the *Landscape with Diana bathing* of 1758 (Zeri-Gonzalez Palacios 1978, p. 559, fig. 6); the *View of the Islands of Ischia and Procida* of 1758, recently sold by Christies in New York (10th January 1990, Lot 178) and the *Landscape with Diana and Actaeon* of 1761 (Zeri-González Palacios, op. cit. fig. 1). Bonavia was also an engraver, but few works are known – five sheets with Neapolitan landscapes at the Aschenbach Foundation for Graphic Arts of San Francisco (Constable 1959, pp. 36-41; Causa-Picone in Naples 1979-80, I, p. 400, no. 229; Causa-Picone in Detroit 1981, p. 251, no. 80) and one with Bonavia's complete signature with *Roman Ruins* in the F.J.B. Watson collection (Constable 1959, pp. 36-37, fig. 22).
The undisputed protagonist of his paintings is the Neapolitan landscape – creeks along the coast, rocky chasms, quiet bays, eruptions of Vesuvius and shipwreck scenes, in compositions which are sometimes faithful to life but more often a combination of architecture and landscape in a free interpretation of the real topography of the places, modified by scenographic devices, repeated at intervals.
His style of painting, which he learned in the old tradition of local landscape art after the manner of Salvator Rosa and Leonardo Coccorante shows traces of more recent influences, like Claude Joseph Vernet, who was in Naples twice, in 1737 and 1746, and suggests a meeting between the two artists. From Vernet's repertoire Bonavia borrows not only themes, perspectives and taste – often repeating them over and over which has caused many problems of attribution – but even the use of media. Consequently, we find a refined use of colour which is typically Rococo, and a genuine emotion in interpreting natural phenomena and the landscape, which is far removed from that lucid analytical technique adopted by other landscapists like Joli and Fabris. The strong influence of Vernet is clearly seen in paintings like the *Coast Scene* of 1754, the *Waterfall* at the Museum of Capodimonte of 1755 (Spinosa in Naples 1979-80, p. 286, no. 153), the *View of the Coast with Shipwreck* of 1757 on the London market, and the *Scene with Waterfall* of 1787 at Honolulu (Constable 1959, p. 42). Reminiscent of Vernet again are – *View of Villa Firmian at Posillipo* of 1756, and among others, *Coast Scene with Natural Arch* of the same year, which came to light at Agnews in 1953, and of which there is a variation at the Royal Palace in Naples (Causa-Picone 1988, p. 78, fig. 89), and finally the sophisticated composition entitled the *Italian Gondola*, so typical of Vernet's work, of which versions are extant at the Prado and the Hermitage though the original is now lost from which the engraving by P.J. Duret was taken (Paris 1977, p. 124, fig. 128).
What can only be considered imitations of Vernet's drawings, though only certain parts were chosen, are the *View of Castel Nuovo* and the *View of Castel dell'Ovo* (Spinosa in Spinosa-Di Mauro 1989, p. 192, no. 66, fig. 67 and no. 69, fig. 68). [R.M.]

Coast Scene
Oil on canvas, 88x144.8, pl. p. 52
Turin, private collection

This painting can probably be dated around 1755 owing to stylistic affinities with the *Coast Scene in the Moonlight* in a private Roman collection dated 1753 (though the last figure is indistinct) and the *Coast Scene* at the Metropolitan Museum in New York which bears the date 1754 (Spinosa 1989, p. 192, nos. 58-9, PI. 24, fig. 57). As in all his paintings, Bonavia was strongly influenced by Vernet's style and choice of subject; here too, Bonavia freely uses existing features of the Neapolitan coastal landscape putting them in an imaginary setting. The bastion recalls that of the Carmine church and is also a recurrent feature in Vernet's scenes. This detail also recalls the wings painted by Vernet, on the opposite side, in his *Port in the Evening* dated 1751 at Uppark (Paris 1977, p. 66, fig. 33). Bonavia does not attempt an exact depiction or even an identifiable one but rather a highly emotional vision, created by the harmony of the composition and above all by his extremely effective use of colour. Here he uses warm tones like pink and yellow, typical of a Neapolitan sunset which softens all the outlines in the scene. [R.M.]

Bibl.: Spinosa in Spinosa-Di Mauro 1989, p. 192, no. 61, fig. 58.

Lord Napier's Villa or Villa delle Cannonate *
Oil on canvas, 84x142, pl. p. 52
Rome, private collection

In comparison with the views where Bonavia freely and imaginatively blends pretty scenes from the Neapolitan coast, this villa called Lord Napier's or Villa delle Cannonate is faithfully painted from life and still stands today. A guess could be made at the date on the basis of records dated 1760 formerly in the possession of H. Bier (Constable 1959, p. 30, no. 13), but Bonavia often repeated his subjects and also used the same kind of style, thus it is difficult to establish an exact date for paintings by this prolific artist. Another version is in a private collection in Vienna. [R.M.]

Bibl.: Spinosa 1987, II, p. 277, fig. 373; Spinosa in Spinosa-Di Mauro 1989, pp. 191-92, no. 60, fig. 59. [R.M.]

Virgil's Tomb with Castel Sant'Elmo and the Charterhouse of San Martino in the background
Oil on canvas, 49.5x74, pl. p. 53
Naples, D'Amodio collection

This scene is also inspired by Vernet's work. Bonavia's is an imaginary interpretation in a clear-cut harmonious style including real landmarks, which are practically stock features by now. The pervasive luminosity with a refined use of pink shades suggests twilight. Another version of this painting is known with slight variations in the figures indicated by McCormick, when it came on to the market at the Mortimer Brandt sale at New York, formerly attributed to Clerissau (McCormick-Constable 1960, p. 371, fig. 3). In both paintings on the left in the foreground is Virgil's tomb – a columbarium from the Augustan period and a favourite place to visit for aristocratic travellers on the Grand Tour owing to the blend of ruins and nature. The inscription on the right imitates the one which appears on the edge of the tomb, added in 1544 by the Canonici Regolari Lateranensi from the nearby church of Santa Maria di Piedigrotta. The same angle can be found in 18th century work by Clerissau and Antonio Dominici; the latter signed and dated 1784 a small oil on copper now belonging to the Museum of San Martino (Spinosa in Naples 1979-80, I, p. 292, no. 159). Two more paintings of the same subject were identified by Constable as *Virgil's Sepulchre* in a private collection in New York (1960, p. 371, fig. 2) and *Tower in Ruins* at Hill Country, Stourhead House in Wiltshire (1962, p. 217, no. 8, fig. 8). The two scenes with Virgil's tomb are actually more similar to another Roman mausoleum called San Vito found on the Via Campana at Pozzuoli and painted several times by Giacinto Gigante (De Caro, Capri 1984, p. 24, no. 11). [R.M.]

Eruption of Vesuvius from the Mole Lighthouse in the Moonlight
Oil on canvas, 97.5 x 134, pl. p. 54
Signed and dated 1757
Beaulieu, National Motor Museum, Lord Montagu

Formerly part of the Marqis of Mortimer's collection, this painting was commissioned by Lord Brudenell (1734 - c. 1777) during his travels in Italy with stages recorded in Naples from 1755 onwards. This forms a pair with a painting in the Buccleuch collection at Queensbury and shows a *Coast Scene* after Vernet (Washington 1985, p. 256). A copy which is neither signed nor dated is in a private collection in Rome and was published by Spinosa (1989, p. 192, no. 63, fig. 60). The same theme with very slight variations in size and angle and with daylight which tends to change the appearance of the picture, is the *Mole Lighthouse with Vesuvius in the distance* signed and dated 1758 and sold at Christies in 1922 (Lot 58), one of a pair with *Castel dell'Ovo* dated the same year (Constable 1959, p. 29, no. 10, fig. 9). [R.M.]

Bibl.: Constable 1962, p. 123, fig. 1; Spinosa in Spinosa-Di Mauro 1989, p. 19, no. 63.
The painting has been restored with a contribution from the Galleria Voena in Turin.

Coast Scene near Naples at Sunset
Oil on canvas, 90 x 78, pl. p. 55
Naples, D'Amodio Collection

A pendant to *Coast Scene in the Moonlight*, this painting obviously differs in the treatment of light, which here is a warm and rosy setting sun. Both paintings recall Vernet, and combine true topographical features and imaginative ones in a clearly identifiable vision. The Roman mausoleum in the foreground is dedicated to San Vito, and was discovered on the Via Campana near Pozzuoli. Bonavia used the same subject in two paintings published by Constable in 1960 (p. 377, fig. 2) and 1962 (p. 217, no. 8, fig. 8). On the hill Castel Sant'Elmo is clearly silhouetted, a recurrent addition to scenes of the Phlegrean coast. (R.M.)

Coast Scene in the Moonlight
Oil on canvas, 90 x 78, pl. p. 56
Naples, D'Amodio Collection

This painting appeared as a pendant to *Coast Scene near Naples at Sunset* at an auction by Etude Couturier Nicolay in May-June 1990. This newly discovered painting, which is a rare vertical work, is a scene of the coast near Naples combining reality and fantasy. Features of the landscape and pieces of architecture are drawn from life though freely interpreted, taking on the appearance of stage-sets, which is typical of Bonavia's style. His greatest source of inspiration was Claude Joseph Vernet, and here the viewpoint, choice of landscape and pictorial quality are reminiscent of Vernet. Another version of the coast in the moonlight, smaller in size but vertical again and with slight variations is in a private Milanese collection. There is also a resemblance as regards the subject of this painting (noted by Utili) to another painting in the same collection, though the composition in the latter is larger, and it is horizontal (Utili 1987, p. 90, no. 56). Two similar subjects appear in a painting published by Constable in 1959 (p. 32, no. 21, fig. 15), sold on the London market, and in a painting published by Spinosa in 1989 (p. 192, no. 61, fig. 58) sold in London by Colnaghi (R.M.).

John Robert Cozens
London 1752-1797

The son and pupil of the landscape draughtsman, teacher and theoretician Alexander Cozens (1717-1786). He exhibited at the Society of Artists from 1767 to 1771, and showed an oil-painting *Hannibal in his March over the Alps, Showing to his Army the Fertile Plains of Italy* at the Royal Academy in 1776.
In that year he accompanied the antiquarian and collector Richard Payne Knight (1751-1824) through Switzerland to Rome, where he stayed until April 1779. He was a friend and sketching companion of Thomas Jones, in whose *Memoirs* he is frequently mentioned. On his return to England Cozens was taken up by his father's pupil and friend, the young millionaire William Beckford (1760-1844), collector, author and eccentric, and in 1782 was engaged as draughtsman on Beckford's third journey abroad. Beckford's letters and seven sketchbooks kept by Cozens during the tour record their progress through Germany and the Alps and then by way of Venice, Padua, Verona and Rome to Naples, where their retinue arrived early in July.
The entire party succumbed to malarial fever, from which Beckford's musician, John Burton, died and Cozens took several weeks to recover. Beckford was a difficult patron and Thomas Jones noted Cozens's sense of relief at his departure from Naples on 10 September. Until then he had stayed with Beckford at Sir William Hamilton's villas first at Posillipo and then at Portici, and his sketchbooks record views in those neighbourhoods as well as studies made on expeditions around the coastal areas of the Gulf of Salerno; by 11 December Cozens was back in Rome, where he again based himself for nine months. He left for England on 15 September 1783, met Beckford in Geneva in late October and was in London by 19 November when he met Jones, also newly-returned from Italy. Little is known of Cozens's later years; he continued to paint finished watercolours of Alpine and Italian subjects, but by early 1794 he was suffering from serious mental disorders and was placed in the care of Dr. Thomas Monro, a leading physician as well as a discerning collector: Monro was among Turner's earlierst patrons, encouraging both him and Thomas Girtin to copy works by Cozens in his collection. Prominent among those who organized a fund to support Cozens was his early patron Richard Payne Knight, but Beckford refused assistance, and in 1805 his collection of ninety-four watercolours of Italian subjects by Cozens was sold at auction. [L.S.]

Vesuvius
Watercolour over pencil,
368 x 528 mm, pl. p. 72
Trustees of the Victoria and
Albert Museum, London (D.715)

No preparatory drawing exists in Cozens's Grand Tour sketchbooks for this composition, but in the weeks following his arrival in Naples in July 1782 Cozens made numerous sketches in the area of Portici, where William Beckford and his entourage stayed at Sir William Hamilton's villa during August and early September. An old inscription on the frame of another version of this watercolour (Barlow Bequest, National Gallery of Scotland) identified the building shown here as the Convent or Hermitage of San Salvatore, at the western end of the Atrio del Cavallo between Vesuvius and Somma. [L.S.]

Vesuvius from the Myrtle Plantation at Sir William Hamilton's Villa, Portici
Watercolour, 250 x 333 mm, pl. p. 72
Trustees of the Victoria and
Albert Museum, London (D. 716)

Early in August 1782, William Beckford 'whose exquisitely delicate habit of body obliged him frequently to change his Situation and Air' (Thomas Jones, *Memoirs,* 3 August) and his entourage, including Cozens, moved from Sir William Hamilton's villa at Posillipo to his other villa near Portici, sketches of which by Cozens range in date from 9 August to 7 September. Like the rest of his party, Beckford had succumbed to malarial fever in July, and at the Villa Angelica he was able to recuperate, spending much of his time in the cool of the *pagliaro* shown here in the foreground (a more detailed close-up of the *pagliaro* was sketched by Cozens on 30 August). On 27 August he wrote to a friend: 'Your letter found me peacefully seated in a Straw Hut surrounded by myrtles, a pine rising just before the door, the Sun setting in a Sea of gold and Vesuvius flushed with purple' (Lewis Melville, *The Life and Letters of William Beckford of Fonthill,* London, 1910, p. 161). Beckford's sense of tranquillity was abruptly ended by the death of Lady Hamilton (Catherine, Sir William's first wife), to whom he was devoted, at the end of the month, which was followed by the death of his music master John Burton on 3 September. On 10 September Beckford sailed for Marseilles, leaving Cozens behind, 'once more a free Agent and loosed from the shackles of fantastic folly and Caprice' in the words of Thomas Jones (*Memoirs,* 3 September).
This watercolour is based on a drawing, dated 18 August, extending across

two pages of a sketchbook, in which a pine tree is shown immediately to the left of the *pagliaro* – just as Beckford described – somewhat obscuring the view of the slopes of Mount Vesuvius. In this, the second of two versions, Cozens has moved the tree to the far left of the picture, creating a stronger design in which Mount Somma and Vesuvius become the dominant elements. [L.S.]

A Shepherd's Hut between Naples and Portici
Watercolour, 261 x 365 mm, pl. p. 71
Trustees of the Victoria and Albert Museum, London (84-1894)

Although William Beckford was later to refer to Cozens as 'an ungrateful scoundrel' he seems, while they travelled together, to have valued his ability to express in visual form those sentiments of poetic melancholy that suffuse his letters and travel-journals. Cozens's watercolour of a shepherd seated dejectedly outside his hut, apparently oblivious to the shower of rain passing overhead, echoes Beckford's mood in a letter: 'A corroding melancholy preyed upon my vitals and darkened the bright sky of Italy. My steps... were guided to desert Hills that lift themselves up above vast wastes with here and there a shepherd's hut or neglected Sepulchre. In such scenes have I mused away whole hours by the evening light, and the moss has often drunk my tears. I never saw any human being in those wildernesses except one day a poor boy whose master had beaten him cruelly and who sat down amongst the broom to cry and call upon his Mother' (Lewis Melville, *The Life and Letters of William Beckford of Fonthill*, London, 1910, p. 158). Cozens's watercolour was based on a drawing in Volume IV of his sketchbooks, which is inscribed *Between Naples and Portici* and dated *Novr. 8*, the day after he had made a group of studies of the temples at Paestum. Although the watercolour follows the study closely, neither the stormy sky nor the shepherd and his flock are shown in the drawing. [L.S.]

Mare Morto, with the Islands of Procida and Ischia in the Distance
Watercolour, 184 x 425 mm, pl. p. 68
Trustees of the British Museum, London (1878-12-28-5)

According to inscriptions on several studies in volume V of the sketchbooks, Cozens was in the Bay of Baia area on 2 December 1782, making sketches of the view towards the Cape of Miseno and Ischia: this watercolour is probably based on a lost sketch of that date. Both this and *Near the Mouth of the Garigliano*, belonged to John Henderson (1764-1843), a collector and close friend and neighbour of Dr Thomas Monro, Cozens's physician and patron. According to his son, both watercolours, which are of an unusual format for Cozens, were acquired direct from the artist, and were among his last works. [L.S.]

Near the Mouth of the Garigliano
Watercolour, 184 x 425 mm, pl. p. 68
Trustees of the British Museum, London (1878-12-28-7)

Cozens based this watercolour on a study in pencil and grey wash dated 8 December 1782 in the last sketchbooks used by him in the Naples region; on 11 December a friend in Rome noted that he had just arrived from Naples. The sketch (volume V.22) is also inscribed with the classical name of the river (noted by Horace for its gentleness): *The Mouth of the Garigliano – The Liris – one post beyond Molo di Gaeta*. In its general style and dimensions, this watercolour is probably a pair to the *Mare Morto*, and also belonged to the artist's patron John Henderson. [L.S.]

The Bay of Naples
Watercolour over pencil, 430 x 577 mm, pl. p. 67
Signed: *J. Cozens*
Trustees of the British Museum, London (1878-12-28-8)

Although no preliminary study for this subject is known, Cozens's sketchbooks show that he was drawing in the heights above the city in November 1782, not far from where his friend Thomas Jones was living and working in an apartment in the Vicolo del Canale. This panoramic view of the Bay is taken from a *vantage point* favoured by several other British landscape painters, including Thomas Jones and Francis Towne, although only Cozens chose to omit one of the most striking features, Vesuvius itself. Three versions of this composition by Cozens are known: one is in the National Gallery of Ireland and another, dated 1790, is in the Yale Center for British Art, New Haven. This is the largest and perhaps the earliest, and was presented to the British Museum by the son of the artist's patron John Henderson. Here Cozens has heightened the promontory on which the Castel S. Elmo stands, giving it greater emphasis. The design is typical of Cozens's reticence, which is apparent both in the organization of the composition and in the delicate tones of grey-green and pale blue with which he evokes the scene and which emphasize the quiet, meditative mood of the watercolour. [L.S.]

Castel S. Elmo
Watercolour over pencil, 305 x 450 mm, pl. p. 66
Signed and dated: *J. Cozens* 1790 and inscribed on the verso *Castel of St Elmo at Naples* and indistinctly *Mrs Mo...ters*
The Trustees of the British Museum, London (1981-3-28-1)

This watercolour of the Castel S. Elmo, one of Cozens's most dramatic designs, is based on a drawing in pencil and grey wash dated 10 November 1782, on p.22 of volume IV of the artist's Grand Tour sketchbooks. As so often in Cozens's work, rapid sketches made while he was in Italy provided the basis for finished watercolours often made years after his return to England. In the case of the more popular subjects, more than one version exists, sometimes as many as eight or nine.
However, this watercolour is the only known finished version of this subject, and was not among those painted for William Beckford; *Mrs Mo...ters*, presumably the person who commissioned this, has not been identified. One must assume that the stark, haunting and sublime quality of this work, which makes no concessions to conventional eighteenth century notions of landscape composition, had little appeal for contemporary collectors. In its almost abstract treatment of forms and spatial relationships it suggests a parallel with Thomas Jones's oil sketches of walls and rooftops in Naples made in 1782, which Cozens may well have seen while he was in the city that year. Here Cozens has allowed nothing to distract attention from the cliff-like wall of the Castle, which he treats as if it were an Alpine precipice, its towering scale emphasised by the introduction of the diminutive shepherd in the foreground. [L.S.]

Coast Scene between Vietri and Salerno: Storm Effect
Watercolour over pencil, 265 x 375 mm, pl. p. 70
Trustees of the Victoria and Albert Museum, London (D.714)

The basis for this watercolour was a drawing in pencil and grey wash in volume III of Cozens's sketchbooks made on 23 September, the same day as the study for *Evening at Vietri with Raito beyond*. In the preparatory drawing, however, there is no indication of the dramatic storm that Cozens depicts in the finished composition. It is possible that William Beckford, for whom the watercolour was painted, asked Cozens to heighten the drama of the rocky coastline scene by including a storm, perhaps as a conscious contrast with the tranquil mood of V & A D.707, rather as Claude-Joseph Vernet had painted contrasting but complementary seapieces. John «Warwick» Smith also painted a storm in the Gulf of Salerno, but, by comparison with Cozens's atmospheric and convincing interpretation, Smith's is melodramatic in effect. [L.S.]

Coast Scene between Vietri and Salerno
Watercolour, 261 x 374 mm, pl. p. 69
Trustees of the Victoria and Albert Museum, London (D. 707)

This watercolour is based on a study in pencil and grey wash, squared for transfer, inscribed *Near Vietri* and dated 27 September in Volume III of Cozens's Grand Tour sketchbooks.
Anthony Blunt suggested (Sotheby's sale catalogue 29 November 1973) that the sketch shows the Torre di Mano d'Albore, in which case Cozens's view is taken looking south-westwards from a point on the coast near Marina di Vietri. The soft evening light, suggested by the delicate use of colour, enhances the mood of tranquillity, contrasting with the dramatic storm effect of *Coast Scene between Vietri and Salerno: Storm Effect* (V & A D. 714). [L.S.]

Evening at Raito with Vietri Beyond
Watercolour over pencil, 368 x 533 mm, pl. p. 69
Private collection, London

After Beckford's departure from Naples on 10 September 1782, Cozens began to make various expeditions beyond the immediate environs of the city. The third volume of his sketchbooks shows that between 18 September and 1 October he based himself in the area around Vietri and Salerno. The combination of the rugged, wooded coastline, punctuated by fishing villages, and the sea was, to judge from the number of sketches he made, particularly attractive to him. This watercolour, a view looking over Marina di Vietri towards Raito and Monte Pertuso in the soft light of evening, is the most beautiful of several versions: it was based on a study in pencil and grey wash dated 23 September. [L.S.]

The Two great Temples at Paestum
Watercolour, 245 x 368 mm, pl. p. 70
Trustees of the Victoria and
Albert Museum, London (p. 2 - 1973)

The fourth volume of Cozens's sketchbooks records his travels between 18 October and 14 November 1782. The first few drawings are of places in the immediate coastal environs of Naples, including Posillipo and the Island of Nisida. He then travelled northwards, making sketches around Capua Vecchia, before turning south to Paestum. Here he drew four views of the great Doric temples, one of which, the study for this watercolour, is dated 7 November. Three other finished watercolours were later derived from these sketches, all four of which belonged to Beckford.
The rediscovery of the Greek temples at Paestum in the middle of the eighteenth century aroused considerable archaeological and architectural interest. At first dismissed as no more than primitive curiosities, by the late 1770s they were widely admired for their monumental qualities. This shift of opinion was due largely to the series of etchings by Piranesi, *Differentes vues... de Pesto,* published almost immediately after his death in 1778. Beckford was a great admirer of Piranesi, and it is probable that Cozens, who certainly owned a number of prints by him, also knew his etchings of Paestum. Their restrained, almost melancholy mood is echoed in Cozens's watercolours, while the figures in the foreground here recall those in many of Piranesi's compositions. [L.S.]

Saverio Della Gatta
Recorded in Naples between 1777 and 1827

With Alessandro D'Anna, Della Gatta was one of the greatest masters of the gouache technique, which was to take root in the late 18th. and continue for the whole of the 19th. century in Naples. The gouache was particularly popular with foreign travellers, but due to such demand this kind of work often fell into trite, stereotyped images.
Little is known about Della Gatta, who often signed himself Xavier. He studied with Jacopo Cestaro, and according to records of 1777 (« Napoli Nobilissima », IX, no. VII) in 1779 he signed the drawing to be used for the engraving *View of Vesuvius during the Eruption of 1779* which with other drawings by Pietro Fabris and Alessandro D'Anna were included in the *Historical considerations regarding the Eruption of Vesuvius which began on 29th. July 1779 and continued until 15th. of August* by Gaetano De Bottis, published in the same year by the Royal Printers.
The first view using gouache with the *Beach of the Marinella* in a private collection in Naples (most of his works are privately owned and consequently are not often seen in museums) shows one of the most attractive scenes of the urban landscape, which includes some lively groups of figures (Alisio, Naples 1985, p. 73). During these years Della Gatta became well known for his illustration of Neapolitan folklore and costumes - the *Woman from the Maone district* bears the date 1781 and was found with other pictures, perhaps originally part of the same folio at Christie's in London on 2nd. July 1985. For this particular aspect of his work, Della Gatta received a commission from the royal family to paint with D'Anna the various costumes of the Kingdom of Naples, which would be used for the decoration of the china manufactured by the Real Fabbrica (Carola Perrotti 1978, p. 225).
His activity in landscape painting is in general similar to Pietro Fabris in style, and he even copied some of Fabris' work, like the *Plain of Paestum*, for example, signed and dated 1783 - the copy of a painting sold by Christie's in London in December 1983; or the *View of Naples from the Rock of Posillipo* signed and dated 1785, copied from a work by Fabris of 1778 and sold at Sotheby's London salesroom (Spinosa in Spinosa-Di Mauro 1989, p. 201, no. 165, fig. 143). This tendency is also true of his illustration of costumes. One good example is the sheet with two *Calabrian Musicians* which interprets an idea by Fabris illustrated in the *Collection of Costumes* of 1773, painted in gouache together with the *Costumes of the Province of Basilicata* (Mancini, Naples 1985, pp. 192 and 197).
Further references can be seen in the *View of Posillipo from the beach at Marinella* of 1784, and a sheet bearing the same date of *Naples from Posillipo* or again in other works without a date like *Lord Napier's Villa or Villa delle Cannonate* (Naples 1985, fig. on p. 58) and the *Temple of Apollo on the Lake of Aversus* (*ibidem*, p. 141).
In 1794 he may have been in Rome, as a tempera would seem to indicate, perhaps from life, of *Countryfolk and Animals near the Tomb of Cecilia Metella* (Fabiani-Fino 1985, pp. 67-75).
However, Della Gatta also used other sources of inspiration for his scenes of the Neapolitan countryside. He was familiar with the English landscapists, but above all he probably knew Giovan Battista Lusieri and it was this artist who inspired the subtly lyrical atmosphere of his landscapes. This is confirmed by works like the *Bay of Naples from Portici* more or less copied from Lusieri, (the Lusieri is in a private collection in Rome while Della Gatta's work illustrating the same subject and dated 1787 was sold by Hazlitt of London), and the *View of Rione Terra at Pozzuoli* signed and dated the same year, and also in a private Roman collection.
It is probable that these contacts with English landscapists and Lusieri were encouraged by Sir William Hamilton, who possessed « a superb picture of the frightening eruption of Vesuvius » (Knight 1985, p. 54). Other gouaches by Della Gatta belonged to Lord Cawdor who was in Naples in 1786 (William 1987, p. 459). After 1790 it was principally Philipp Hackert who influenced the rest of his works in gouache, as can be seen in the *Farewell of Aeneas and Anchises* of 1791 (Naples 1985, fig. on p. 144), *Pozzuoli and Nisida* of 1802 (*ibidem*, p. 208, no. 3.13) and the two sheets with the *Repression of 1799* dated the same year in the Praz collection (Stefano Susinno, Naples 1988, pp. 108-09, 117, figs. 2a, 2b) to which can be added two more historical subjects of 1800 - the *Battle between English and Bourbon ships against the revolutionaries in the Channel of Procida* at the Musum of San Martino (Naples 1985, figs. on pp. 54-5).
After the manner of Hackert once again and with strongly commemorative intentions are the two gouaches with the *Return of Ferdinand from Sicily welcomed at the Bridge of the Maddalena* and the *Return of Maria Carolina seen from the Molo Grande*, both dated 1802 (Spinosa in Spinosa-Di Mauro 1989, p. 202, no. 175, Pl. 99). The theme of the *Eruption of Vesuvius* and the particularly spectacular one of 1794 appears in three sheets at the Museum of San Martino and two private Neapolitan collections (Tecce, Naples 1985, p. 93 and 202). The artist's late works were never such good quality as his earlier ones and became increasingly trite and repetitive, also because they were commissioned by less educated and refined clients. Some rare exceptions (only because they record with renewed visual intensity unknown places in the Naples area or places which were later altered of which disappeared) are the *Barracks of the gladiators in Pompeii* and the *Temple of Isis*, dated 1824 (Spinosa in Spinosa-Di Mauro 1989, p. 202, nos. 176-77, Pl. 100-101-102) and the large set of sheets with paintings of folk traditions and costumes, like the *Tarantella* of 1820. [R.M.]

Naples from Portici
Gouache, 41.4 x 65.2, pl. p. 87
Signed and dated: *Xav. s. Gatta p. 1787*
Rome, private collection

This is one of the views that Della Gatta took from Giovan Battista Lusieri. There are only very slight variations - the perspective chosen, the landscape in the foreground on the right-hand side and the poses of the figures. These figures of local people, captured while they were improvising a tarantella in the street, are borrowed from Pietro Fabris. The illustrative and pictorial techniques used are typical of most of Della Gatta's work, which always closely adheres to the taste for landscapes and the style of the English painters who had settled in Naples. [R.M.]

François De Nomé
Metz 1593 - c. 1640

From a marriage certificate found by Causa (1956, p. 33) it appears that De Nomé was born in Metz (Lorraine) in 1953. In 1602 he went to Rome and stayed there for eight years to complete his training, subsequently moving on to Naples. Causa (1956) and

Sluys (1961) made extensive research into the life and art of this painter, who was often confused with another artist from Lorraine, Didier Barra. De Nomé was an eccentric artist, known for his architectural fantasies and imaginary scenes, full of mystery, which have given rise to interesting psychoanalytical interpretations. The discovery of signed and dated works and records, like the marriage certificate mentioned above of 1613 and a receipt for the payment of twelve paintings representing events from the life of the Pharaohs from 1618, has provided precious information about this artist.
De Nomé left his home town too early to assimilate the artistic trends of that area and trained in Rome in the circle of Northern European artists. Among these was Balthasar Lauwers, a Fleming who painted wall perspectives and landscapes, studying with Paul Bril and influenced by Agostino Tassi. It was probably Lauwers who taught De Nomé perspective and draughtsmanship, though the strongest influence seems to have been the Frenchman Jean Androuet Du Cerceau, active in Paris between 1550-1600, who specialized in engravings of Roman ruins and often combined topography with imaginary architecture. Du Cerceau's engravings were known both in France and in Rome, and were very popular among collectors. According to research by M.R. Nappi in 1986, De Nomé learnt this mannerist style from Hans Vredemann de Vries, a painter of architectural subjects active in Rome between 1610-20. These influences can be recognized in De Nomé's early work, for example the interiors of cathedrals in the Harrach Collection at Schloss Rohrau, the *Marriage of the Virgin Mary* dated 1621, formerly in a private collection in Naples (Causa 1956, fig. 22), the *Circumcision*, signed and dated 1623 at the Yale University Art Gallery at New Haven and the *Presentation in the Temple*, belonging to a private collection, also dated 1623. The architectural setting of these scenes also reveals a close relationship between the scenery painting of late Florentine mannerism and a group of engravers working at the court of the Medici's at the turn of the century. Among these were Jacques Callot and Cantagallina, the latter being the engraver of sets painted by Giulio Parigi, who according to Causa (1956, p. 42) was one of the main exponents of that love for depicting ruins, also characteristic of De Nomé's work.
De Nomé's painting technique – patches of paint applied with a thick brush and highlighting with white, and the dramatic effects obtained by the use of dark shades enlivened by intense blobs of light make this artist's work quite distinctive. Good examples are *Christ driving the Merchants from the Temple* (Giovanetti Collection, Naples), and *Christ entering Jerusalem* (Dalla Vecchia Collection, Naples). Two more paintings belonging to this group and attributed to De Nomé are the *View of Naples seen from the Sea* and *Bird's-eye-view of the Phlegrean Fields, Procida, Vivara and Ischia.* While the first one is very similar in composition to the views painted at a later date by Didier Barra, the second seems more like an imaginary place, even if the area is recorded in exact detail. Recently two views of *St. Mark's Square* in Venice have appeared on the market, attributed to De Nomé (cf. exhibition catalogue of *Le Venezie Possibili*, Venice 1985, p. 85, no. 26, and Chaucer Fine Arts, July 1989, no. 12).
Nothing certain is known about the artist after 1634, the date which appears on the painting entitled *Ruins and Arches* formerly in the Alomello Collection in Rome (B.D.).

View of Naples
Oil on canvas, 66 x 97, pl. p. 33
Naples, Dalla Vecchia Collection

This painting was published on the occasion of the «17th. century in Naples» exhibition (Naples 1984-5), attributed to De Nomé and dated after 1647. Comparing this view with other similar ones which had made their way on to the market in the meantime or were in private collections (*Bird's-eye-view of the Phlegrean Fields, Procida Vivara and Ischia* from the same collection and *Naples seen from Sea* from the Silbernagl Collection, attributed to either Barra or De Nomé) it is evident that De Nomé was particularly skilful in the painting of landscapes, probably influenced by his fellow countryman Didier Barra, a painter of bird's-eye-views of Naples and environs and active in Naples in the same period.
However, the date of 1647 would seem rather late and Nappi (1988, p. 173, note 27) sets it in the early 1630's. [B.D.]

Bibl.: Nappi, Naples 1984, p. 250, no. 2.63; Nappi 1988, p. 173, note 27; Spinosa-Di Mauro 1989, pp. 15, 149, 158, note 74 & 187, no. 4.

Abraham-Louis-Rodolphe Ducros
Maudon 1747 – Lausanne 1810

From Vaud in Switzerland, Ducros studied at the Academy of Chevalier de Fassion (1769) and travelled with his tutor in Flanders. In 1776 he went to Rome where he frequented the artists of the Académie de France, directed at the time by Vien, also meeting Swiss artists like Jacques Sablet. In 1778 he went as far as Southern Italy, staying in Naples where he was well received by Sir William Hamilton before moving on to Sicily. While in Naples he painted some watercolours including a view of the port of Pozzuoli (Manchester, Whitworth Art Gallery).
During his long stay in Rome, Ducros made a series of engravings painted over in watercolour in which he was helped by Volpato and these were very popular with the foreign travellers. However, the French Revolution caused a decline in the number of foreign clients. Ducros was expelled from the Papal State in 1793 after the murder of the French diplomat Bassville, because he was suspected of being too «democratic». After a short stay in the Abruzzo he settled in Naples, a protégé and provider of work for Hamilton and Acton. Most of the watercolours painted in Naples and the surrounding area are now at the Musée Cantonal de Beaux-Arts in Lausanne. During the French occupation in 1799, Ducros tried in vain to claim damages from the republican government, but when the Bourbons were reinstated he had to flee to Malta. Before going back to France for good in 1807, he stayed in Naples again. On his return to France at first he had a very hard time, but then managed to open a school of painting in Lausanne, where he died in 1810. In the last decade much interest has been aroused by the views in watercolour which have been exhibited in British, Swiss and Italian exhibitions of this typical illustrator of the Grand Tour. [P.B.]

Nisida from Posillipo
Mixed media on paper glued
to canvas, 107 x 78, pl. p. 88
Naples, private collection

On his exploration of the coast round Posillipo Ducros found new and original views. He was attracted not only by the famous places with their vestiges of ancient and modern buildings like the *Temple of Fortune* at Marechiaro or the *Harbour of Marechiaro* (Lausanne, Musée Cantonal des Beaux-Arts) but like Wright of Derby he was fascinated by the rocky caves and chasms as in the famous view of *Posillipo seen from Donn'Anna* at the Museum of San Martino or the *Grotto of Thunder* at Lausanne.
Ducros was also interested in the loneliest and wildest parts of the coast – the *Beach of the Gaiola* at Lausanne and the *Cola di Trentaremi* both published recently by Spinosa (Spinosa-Di Mauro 1989, nos. 187-88, Pl. 122-26) offer two excellent examples of this search for hidden nature – the great walls of stone and rocks could only be reached from the sea, and here were the signs of a new sensitivity of the romantic kind, which was to culminate in the gloomy and apocalyptic view of the *Eruption of Vesuvius with Shipwreck* (Kenwood-Manchester-Lausanne 1985-86, no. 37). Here though, it is early morning. The fishing scenes at sea and on the shore provide the poetic realism which pervades this view of the tip of Posillipo, with Nisida and Pozzuoli emerging from the blue sea with the green shades of the tuff rocks reflected in the quiet waters, stressing the calm atmosphere of unspoiled nature, caressed by the soft light of a virtually cloudless sky. All this is beautifully transmitted by watercolour and gouache used together. [P.B.]

Bibl.: Spinosa-Di Mauro 1989, nos. 187, Pl. 122, 126.

View of Villa Acton at Castellammare
Mixed media on paper glued
to canvas, 81.5 x 161.5, pl. p. 90
Signed and dated: *ducros fecit anno MDCCXCIV* with handwritten note on the stones on the left-hand side: *Vue de casia de...General Hacton a Castellammare dessiné d'après nature par Louis Ducros L'an 1794.*
London, Hazlitt, Gooden & Fox Ltd.

Despite being a Swiss citizen, Ducros was expelled from the Papal State after the murder of Bassville in 1793. During the French Revolution he sought refuge in Naples and was given protection by Sir William Hamilton and Lord Acton (1736-1811) who were also his patrons and had much influence with the King of Naples. Ducros painted a commemorative work of the fleet under Acton's command in four large watercolours which show different views of the shipyards at Castel-

lammare when the ships were being certified as seaworthy – a subject inspired by an oil of Philipp Hackert's after Vernet's famous *Ports of France* (cf. catalogue of the Kenwood, Manchester and Lausanne exhibition *Images of the Grand Tour*, Geneva 1985-86, nos. 38 and 77).
The artist also painted a watercolour in 1794 for Acton which was unusual and very decorative representing the *Pavillon chinois dans la fôret près du Cazin de S.E Monsieur le Général Acton à Castellammare* (*ibidem* no. 79). This picture of Castellammare, which is on display for the first time, shows the «cazin» or villa which is certainly not in the Neapolitan style but rather an English version of Louis XVI architecture, which Acton had built near Castellammare di Stabia. This large building occupies the centre of the composition with the gates of the drive peeping through the thick vegetation of the garden, while on the right is the «forest» in the park with Vesuvius silhouetted in the distance. There are several groups of figures standing round the fountain and the drinking-trough and they give the picture its liveliness. This is a typical view of Ducros' with its limited perspectives on the various planes, giving the impression of disorderly and fertile nature which romantically overhwelms buildings and ruins. [P.B.]

Posillipo seen from Palazzo Donn'Anna
Watercolour on paper glued to canvas, 67 x 105, pl. p. 89
Naples, Museum of San Martino

This painting is particularly interesting because it is one of the very few watercolours on paper from this period which clearly shows the Villa Emma, Sir William Hamilton's residence at Posillipo, with its distinctive semicircular terrace (N.S.).

Bibl.: Ferrari, Naples 1962, p. 48, no. 33; Chessex, Lausanne 1986, pp. 104-5, no. 76.

Pietro Fabris
Active in Naples from 1754 to 1804

It is still difficult today to draw up a reliable biography of this artist. He often calls himself «English» (for example, in the preface to his *Raccolta di varii Vestimenti ed Arti del Regno* of 1773, in the painting the *Departure of Charles from the Port* of 1761 and on the sheet belonging to the San Martino Museum *La Luciana*) and even Sir William Hamilton called him «English» in his introduction to the *Campi Phlegraei*, which was illustrated and edited by Fabris. It was in London, in fact, that he exhibited his drawings and views of Naples at the Free Society in 1768 and in 1772 at the Society of Artists. He also made some drawings for the engravers Paul and Thomas Sandby for the volume *Twenty views of Naples and its environs*. However, it is well known that Fabris worked prevalently in Naples, as is recorded in a large number of oil paintings, gouaches, drawings and engravings of costumes which are part of a great many public and private collections, some also belonging to antique dealers. And it was in Naples that Fabris received commissions from refined and educated aristocrats who were travelling on the Grand Tour round Italy and the Southern Mediterranean to widen their culture.
On the basis of dated works, his career started between 1756-57 (the year he painted the *Scenes of Popular Life*) and 1804 when he signed and dated the drawing in the San Martino Museum of the *Game of Leapfrog*. In 1804 again, the Neapolitan printers Gervasi published five engravings with scenes from the life of the local people (Fino 1989, p. 61, note 5).
The influence of his early studies in the moderately classicist style of the mid-18th. century can be clearly seen in two religious subjects, which are signed and can be dated around the 1760's due to similarities with Fischetti and Celebrano (Spinosa 1987, no. 231, figs. 314-15).
Early on though, his inclination was towards landscapes and refined illustrations of events at court and from everyday life, enlivened by tarantellas, picnics on the sea-shore and folk entertainment, where the Neapolitans are always observed with the gentle irony of painters like Rossi, Bonito and Falciatore. His early work in fact is all genre painting, where a clear analogy can be traced with the Neapolitan «presepe» (Christmas crib figures) tradition, as Nicola Spinosa acutely remarks (1989, p. 32).
A strictly orthodox approach to landscape painting can be seen in the first works he is known to have painted of this kind, which are strongly influenced by Joli, like the commemorative paintings of scenes from court life such as the *Cuccagna al Largo del Castello* formerly belonging to Agnew, where the urban context with its ephemeral scenery, shortly to be raided by a tumultuous crowd of Neapolitans, is merely a pretext for the small figures in the foreground which include members of the royal family (Spinosa 1987, II, P. 162, no. 304, fig. 402; Spinosa in Spinosa-Di Mauro 1989, p. 200, no. 154) or the *Departure of Charles from the Port* of 1761, or again the *Procession of royal ships at Posillipo* of which there are several known versions depicting the various stages of the ceremony. The *Ball Game* of 1768 at the Marylebone Cricket Club in London is also reminiscent of Joli in its choice of subject.
In addition to Joli, Fabris was influenced by Bonavia's style who in his turn was inspired by views after the style of Vernet. To this period belong the *Coast Scene with Temple*, both signed and dated 1763, formerly part of the collection of the Marquis of Breadalbane, then passing on to Agnew (illustrated in «The Connoisseur», CXXXIV, 1956, no. 541, PI. XI). Other works of the same period are the *Views of Pozzuoli* of 1772 (Spinosa in Spinosa-Di Mauro 1989, p. 200, no. 155, fig. 139, the *View of Naples* of 1778 which is very similar to the *View of Naples from Mergellina* formerly the property of the Earl of Betty (Zeri-González Palacios 1978, V, p. 59, figs. 3-4-5).
In 1773 he engraved the plates of the famous *Raccolta di varii Vestimenti ad Arti del Regno* (an album of costumes of the Kingdom of Naples), which required transferring on to copper plates all the characters in their realistic everyday poses which make his scenes so lively, in oil or gouache, and which are to be Fabris' stock-in-trade from now onwards (Mancini 1985).
The dedication in this volume is to Sir William Hamilton, the Envoy Extraordinary of His Britannic Majesty, sent to the court of the King of the Two Sicilies in November 1764 – a lover of science, a collector and patron of the arts from the early years of his tour in Naples.
In 1768 Fabris and Hamilton undertook a journey to Sicily, and Hamilton (who already possessed 32 works by Fabris) ordered from him all the illustrations for his celebrated *Campi Phlegraei* published in Naples in 1776 and followed three years later by the *Supplement*.
In the same style as the 59 plates engraved for the *Campi Phlegraei* where the influence of Philipp Hackert can be clearly recognised is the gouache signed and dated 1776 of a *View of Pozzuoli*, sold at auction by the Hotel Drouot in Paris on 23rd. November 1929, and another showing a *Tuff Quarry at Casalnuovo* in a private Neapolitan collection (Spinosa in Spinosa-Di Mauro 1989, p. 201, no. 164, PI. 91). Furthermore, the plates of the *Eruption of Vesuvius of 1760* drawn from life, are similar in subject to two paintings in a private Milanese collection (Spinosa in Spinosa-Di Mauro 1989, p. 201, 162, figs. 145-46).
In 1777, Fabris signed and dated a *View of Fishermen in a Grotto by night* (from a private Roman collection) and in 1778 a *Scene of Popular Life on the Frisio Beach at Posillipo*, which Della Gatta later copied (Spinosa 1987, II, p. 163, no. 309).
The latest painting to be identified as Fabris' work is dated 1792 and shows the *Preparations for the Pilgrimage to the Sanctuary of the Madonna dell'Arco*, which was to be a model for much 19th. century work (Spinosa 1987, II, p. 163, no. 310, fig. 410).
Fabris, like Bonavia, remained faithful to his chosen style and used stock compositions all through his work. Unlike Bonavia though, his interpretation of the landscape was a careful observation of reality and detailed analysis of country scenes and depiction of social life. His best work does not fall into the trend of folklore and picturesque renderings so typical of some of the more hurriedly painted views with their repetition of stock scenes and characters, painted singly or in groups. [R.M]

Sellers of Victuals along the Via della Marinella
Signed on the recto

A Tarantella with Posillipo in the background
Signed on the recto
Oil on canvas, 70.8 x 98.9 each, pl. p. 79
Naples, private collection

These paintings by Fabris, sold in London in 1984, are the oldest ones known (Spinosa 1987, II, p. 162, no. 302). The four canvasses making up the set (including *Scenes of Popular Life in a Grotto in Posillipo* (1756) and *Water-melon Sellers near the Port* (1757) which are not part of this exhibition) are large in size and show the whole range of Fabris' style and choice of

subject-matter in his depiction of urban landscapes, priority being given to scenes of everyday life.
These scenes were mostly painted from life and were his favourite subjects. The characters over time became stock figures, usually taken from low-class Neapolitan life – peddlers, fishermen selling their wares, urchins, acrobats, serving girls, arranged by the artist in the urban scene (which are real places along the coast of Posillipo and towards the eastern part of the city) like groups from the famous «presepe» (the Neapolitan Christmas crib, see Spinosa in Spinosa-Di Mauro 1989, p. 32). However, he managed to preserve the visual immediacy of the genre scenes and removed the erudite and ceremonial nuances which still characterised the compositions, a mixture of sacred and profane typical of the 18th. century «presepe».
In this sense, a clear reference can be seen in Fabris' work to the painted or carved figures by Francesco Celebrano, in particular in two paintings in the church of Santa Chiara in Bari. Contact between Fabris and Celebrano is confirmed by the similarity between *Hunting Scene with Ferdinand IV of Bourbon*, signed by Fabris in 1773 and now at the Royal Palace of Caserta and the painting by Celebrano at the Prado and San Martino (Spinosa 1987, II, p. 93; no. 71, fig. 85). As regards the landscape part, Fabris is clearly influenced by Bonavia and Ricciardelli, and at times even Joli in those works after 1760.
Some groups of figures in paintings on display are copied (a typical technique of Fabris') in later pictures like *Folk Festival at Posillipo* in the Alisio collection in Naples (Spinosa in Spinosa-Di Mauro 1989, p. 251, no. 158), in the pair belonging to the Royal Family's Holyroodhouse collection (Spinosa 1987, II, pp. 162-63, no. 306) and again, with variations, in the last painting dated 1792 showing the *Preparations for the Pilgrimage to the Sanctuary of the Madonna dell'Arco* in London (Spinosa 1987, II, p. 163, no. 310, fig. 410). Of the painting with *Sellers of Victuals* two preparatory sketches are known – one at the Museum of San Martino, the other sold by Sotheby's London salesroom on 11th. December 1980. [R.M.]

Bibl.: London 1984, pp. 66-71; Spinosa 1987, II, p. 162, no. 302, Pi. 66-69 and p. 465, no. 328, fog. 429; idem in Spinosa-Di Mauro 1989, p. 200, no. 152.

Picnic at Posillipo
Oil on canvas, 56 x 102

Minuet at Baiae
Oil on canvas, 56 x 102, pl. p. 78
Caserta, Royal Palace

Part of a set belonging to the royal collection of Caserta, which includes a *Country Outing* this pair is probably attributable to Fabris' early work, inspired by Bonavia's landscapes but attentive to colourful characterisations of events from folk life. The Caserta painting, however, can be distinguished from the numerous other versions on the same theme at the Museum of San Martino, in various private Neapolitan collections and in two paintings belonging to the Marquis of Exeter's collection at Burghley House, one dated 1770 (Spinosa in Spinosa-Di Mauro 1989, p. 209, no. 159, fig. 14) due to its more refined and delicate brushwork.
These paintings were obviously for a cultivated «jet-set» of foreign travellers and aristocrats in Naples during the Grand Tour. They could well be the «two views of Posillipo and Bambocciate» by Fabris which have been recorded in the inventories of the Royal Palace of Caserta since 1817 and were hung «in the apartments of His Highness, the heir to Francis of Bourbon». [R.M.]

Bibl.: Micdione-Daprà, Paris-Lyons-Capri 1987, pp. 78-84.

The Procession of Royal Ships at Palazzo Donn'Anna
Oil on canvas, 56 x 97, pl. p. 79
Naples, private collection

This was formerly attributed to Joli (Utili, Venice-Milan 1987, pp. 92-3) then recognised as being Fabris' work due to a more brilliant and transparent use of colour, and a more subtly analytical interpretation of the little scenes in the foreground in front of Palazzo Donn'Anna.
The attribution to Fabris can be confirmed by the fact that the painting is quite obviously similar to a pair of other works by Fabris because they depict the same subject – the procession of royal ships at Posillipo during the traditional folk festival called «Posillicata», which was also painted by Joli (now at the Kunsthistorisches Museum in Vienna). The two paintings by Fabris are at Aranjuez and the Palace of the Zarzuela in Spain, the second signed and dated (Urrea, Madrid 1988, p. 148; Martinez, Madrid 1989, no. 32). A copy exists of the second which is neither signed nor dated at the Museum of San Martino (cf. previous entry). [R.M.]

Bibl.: Spinosa in Spinosa-Di Mauro 1989, p. 200, no. 156, fig. 138).

The Ball Game
Oil on canvas, 73.6 x 128.3, pl. p. 80
Signed and dated 1768
London, Marylebone Cricket Club

Signed and dated 1768, this painting comes from the rather rare works by Fabris illustrating various episodes from the ceremonial side of court life. The depiction of this old-fashioned ball game which was taking place in the presence of the royal family and the most important dignitaries of the court was being played in the dry moat at the bottom of the Aragonese walls near the monastery of San Giovanni a Carbonara (now the Garibaldi Barracks at Foria). At this time the same subject was painted by Antonio Joli, although from different angles, three versions of which exist at the Kunsthistorisches Museum of Vienna, the Museum of San Martino and a private Neapolitan collection (cf. biography). In Fabris' picture the vanishing points are the Tower of San Michele and the Ponte Nuovo, which was knocked down in the 19th. century. As for other similar subjects, Fabris puts more into his work than mere illustration, bringing out the folk theme and descriptive technique rather than the commemorative, official aspects. This can be noticed in this unique blend of popular spectacle, which relates the event but in a picturesque way, with characters and costumes from the aristocracy and figures taken from low-class Neapolitan life. [R.M.]

Bibl.: Mancini 1968 p. 296, fig. 59; Spinosa-Di Mauro 1989, p. 200, no. 157, fig 140.

Drawing-room in the Apartment in Naples of Lord Fortrose with a Group of Musicians.
Drawing-room in the Apartment in Naples of Lord Fortrose with a Group of Fencers.
Oil on canvas, 33.5 x 47.6 each, pl. p. 81
Edinburgh, Scottish National Portrait Gallery

These were formerly attributed to Pyne, then correctly recognised as being Fabris' work by Spinosa (who picked out the self-portrait of the artist from the group of musicians owing to a likeness in *Scene of Ferdinand IV hunting Wild Boar*, signed and dated 1773 at the Royal Palace of Caserta). These two interiors, formerly thought to be the Neapolitan residence of Sir William Hamilton – Palazzo Sessa – were carefully studied by Powell-Jones, who was able to identify Lord Fortrose as the client who ordered the pictures, who later became Lord Seaforth and was in Naples between 1769-70. Acton (1964, p. 182) also mentioned that Fortrose was a patron of the arts and music in particular. Powell-Jones also realized that the interiors were actually one drawing-room divided by the artist into two. On the basis of a label on the back of the paintings Powell-Jones also managed to accurately identify the people portrayed: William Hamilton sitting playing the piano, Gaetano Pugnani playing a violin in front of him in the scene with the musicians, and Lord Fortrose in his elegant costume with one hand resting on his foil in the centre of the scene with the fencers. In this scene is also a rather portly figure which seems to be that of the composer Niccolò Jommelli. In support of the identification of the drawing-room are the collections of weapons, Greek vases, a crucifix, paintings and drawings on the walls, which are in keeping with the taste of Lord Fortrose. The date on the labels on the back of the two paintings is 1770, which would seem to bear out the identification. In the same year Fabris painted a *View of the Duomo of Palermo and the Square* one of a pair with another view of Palermo dated 1770, which testifies to the presence of Lord Seaforth in that city with the painter (Christie's London, March-April 1990).
These paintings also contain interesting information about music in the 18th century. Recitals were usually held in the drawing-rooms of private houses and palaces, like those of Lord Fortrose and Sir William Hamilton. From recent research by Harrison James Wignall (shortly to be published by the Univesity of Brundeis in the U.S.A. as we are told by Annalisa Porzio) we learn that in May 1770 Leopold Mozart and his son visited the English envoy in Naples.
Although the figure in the corner seated at the harpsichord has been identi-

fied by Powell-Jones as Lord Fortrose's music master Paolo Orgitano (c. 1740-1796), it would be fascinating to think that this group was honoured by the presence of no less a personage than the 14-year-old Wolfgang Amadeus at the spinet with Leopold Mozart (without his violin). The two paintings from Edinburgh are also interesting because they show the taste in decor and furnishings of the second half of the 18th century and the objects which were part of contemporary collections. Furthermore, here Fabris is seen in a different light – this is, in fact, very much like the interiors which were popular in the early 19th century in the Biedermeier style. [A.M.]

Bibl.: Thornton 1984, figs. 176-177; Powell-Jones 1985, pp. 104-107; Spinosa 1987, II, p. 163, no. 307, Pl. 72-73; Hawcroft, Manchester 1988, pp. 81-2, no. 88.

Giacinto Gigante
Naples 1806-1876

Giacinto Francesco Paolo Gigante was born on 11th. July 1806 in a house on the slope leading up to Sant'Antonio a Posillipo. His parents were Annamaria Fatati and Gaetano Gigante, a painter of frescoes and genre scenes who had studied with Diano.
Giacinto's career in 19th. century landscape painting which expresses with Pitloo and Vervloet «the greatest skill in perception of the Italian landscape» according to Zeri (1976) and «interpretation with sentiment» (Causa 1967) started with studies outside the usual academic environment, which were pleasingly eclectic.
Essential to his vision of realism was the outlining he used in his drawing, which he learned as one of the first engraving techniques at the Royal Printing Office where he worked in the 1820's, and his rational way of depicting reality, called «camera lucida» in the private lessons he followed with J.W. Hüber and another pupil, Vianelli, in the afternoons. His drawings were made on tracing paper (using the «camera optica»), painted in watercolour and were then ready to be sold. To this period and genre belongs a drawing in pen with touches of watercolour – *Naples seen from the Grotto of Posillipo* (1820, part of the Astarita Donation at the Museum of Capodimonte) with the autobiographical note «etched by myself and then published». Other works of the same period are the set of drawings of *Ischia* and *Capri* of 1822-23, reminiscent again of his work at the Royal Printers, but more loosely connected. In fact, these were probably the result of «surveys» carried out in those years while the maps were being drawn up of the island («Cartografia topografica ed idrografica di Napoli e dintorni», see Fusco 1989, p. 388).
From 1821 onwards, after Hüber left Naples, Gigante and Vianelli studied with Anton Sminck Pitloo at Vico del Vasto in the Chiaia area. Gigante continued to explore the Neapolitan and Campanian countryside through drawings from life and his first oils, like the *Lake of Lucrino* (1824) at the Museum of San Martino, which shows traces of Pitloo's influence. Pitloo's vibrant use of colour, similar to that of Dahl, Rebell, Turner, Wilson, Bonington and the pictorial synthesis of Corot enabled him to «transfer to a modern form the old erudite leitmotiv» (Causa 1966) in a freely expressed style of landscape painting, where the descriptive aspect is turned into «an area for pictorial research» and romantic feeling. These were the results he obtained in various stages, by revisiting 17th. century Neapolitan landscape painting and assimilating the features of Pompeian frescoes. These features can be seen in works like *Variations*, which was a deliberate copy of a painting by Micco Spadaro at the Correale Museum in Sorrento and in what he learned from the excursions he made to the excavations of Pompeii. This progress in his style can be dated after 1835, and above all between 1844-50, when he was particularly influenced by Turner.
In 1824 he was awarded a prize in the second class of landscapes by the Royal Institute of Fine Arts, according to an autobiographical note recorded by Limoncelli. However, he was not officially on any regular course and in 1826 he «was obliged to register as a student again» (as we are told by Maria Zenon in 1922) so as to avoid military service. Between April and May 1826 he worked in Rome for the painter Johann Jacob Wolfenberger, an entrepreneur and dealer in popular views. In the same year he took part in the Exhibition of Fine Arts at the Bourbon Museum with four watercolours, now lost. His marriage to Eloisa Vianelli (1831) coincided with the beginning of his career as a successful landscape painter, and in 1829-30 he illustrated the *Viaggio Pittorico nel Regno delle Due Sicilie* (a journey through pictures of the Kingdom of Naples) published by Cuciniello and Bianchi, working with Vianelli, Carelli, Fergola and Marinoni. In 1832 he illustrated *Esquisses pittoresques et descriptives de la ville et environs de Naples* (picturesque sketches of Naples and the area), furnishing a hundred lithographed drawings after Wenzel, many of which were of the excavations of Pompeii. From 1835 (according to Ortolani in 1928) he received commissions from some Russian aristocrats in Naples, which are kept at the Museum of Capodimonte and include: a watercolour of *The Villa of Chiaia from Palazzo Esterhazy* «while the Count De Maistre was in residence there» (part of the Astarita collection) and *San Martino, the Charterhouse and Bay of Naples from Villa Graeven*, a sketch for the Emperor of Russia.
At the Hermitage in Leningrad there is a *Landscape* of 1839, *Sorrento* (1842), a *View of Naples* (1845), *Bay of Naples* (on paper dated 1849), *Monastery in the mountains* (1862) and *Baiae* (on paper).
With his friends from the Russian Embassy, where he had been introduced by Schedrin in the 1820's, he visited Rome several times to paint landscapes, and in 1846 he accompanied the Tsarina on a journey to Palermo, compiling an *Album of Sicily* and painting the oil *The Amphitheatre at Taormina* (formerly in the Polisiero collection). He alternated the more commercial and sophisticated «maniera rosa» of those years (as in *Palermo, Piazza della Zeza*) with more striking works, almost of photographic intensity (*Naples from the Vomero*, A.F.S.G. 3028, Polisiero collection).
With the fruits of years of frenetic activity, Gigante bought an estate on the slopes of the Vomero which he called Villa Salute, where he lived surrounded by an enormous family, which had grown in size owing to the marriages of his eight daughters with other families of painters – including Fergola, Zezon, Witting and Pasquale De Luca. It was not until 1850 that he was called by the Bourbon court and commissioned to make drawings of Gaeta to be sent to Vienna to the Archduchess Maria Teresa. In 1851 he was required to give drawing lessons to the young princes and in 1852 he accompanied the royal family to their residences in Caserta, Ischia and Gaeta. Ortolani dates the watercolours of *Hanging Gardens at the Royal Palace* and *View of the Bay* around this time, which were sold at auction by Giosi in 1932. After 1860 «in a gloomy and discontented frame of mind» he moved away from these subjects, turning to interiors of churches and studies of figures, like the monastic views of Donnaregina, and favouring episodes of romantic painting like the sketch of *Garibaldi entering Naples* (Museum of San Martino).
In 1860 he was requested to paint the Interior of the Duomo of Naples by Victor Emanuel II, completed in 1863 (Museum of Capodimonte) which he showed at the Exposition Universale in 1867, making the journey to Paris personally. Gigante was to return to Paris in 1869, seven years before his death [A.P.].

The Bay of Naples from the Arenella
Oil on canvas, 47.3 x 64, , pl. p. 101
Naples, Museum of Capodimonte
Angelo Astarita Bequest, inv. no. 5223

The fact that this work is from the Astarita family collection, who were on friendly terms with Gigante's heirs, makes it likely that this is from one of the artist's folios from his house in the Arenella district.
This *Bay of Naples* is generally considered to belong to the early 1840's and to a set of studies seen from the same viewpoint, which include a drawing painted over in watercolour of 1838 in the Astarita Collection at Capodimonte (inv. no. 5239), the Ferrara Dentice watercolour at San Martino (inv. no. 23135) and the «pink period» oil painting dated 1844 in a private Neapolitan collection (*Landscape Painting in Naples* catalogue 1990, p. 159).
The repetition of this kind of landscape theme, subsequently to become a convention (the same subject was painted by the Russian Ivanov between 1843-48, cf. Bologna 1990, no. 33) shows how important Gigante was to be in creating a romantic stereotype of the city and a prototype for postcard views (cf. Fusco 1983). However, the relaxed quality of the painting and the «unfinished» appearance of the foreground remove Gigante's work from any formal category.

Bibl.: Ortolani 190, Pl. VIII; Causa 192, Pl. 303; Spinosa 192, p. 24; Fusco, Naples 1983, cat. 48, p. 35.

The Via dei Sepolcri at Pompeii
Watercolour, 21.5 x 32, pl. p. 102
Signed and dated (bottom left): *Pompei maggio 1862 G. Gigante*
Naples, Museum of San Martino
Ferrara Dentice Collection, inv. no. 23105

Between 1829-32 Gigante contributed to the *Viaggio Pittorico nel Regno delle Due Sicilie*, written by Raffaele Liberatore for which Gigante supplied a set of illustrations of the archeological excavations at Pompeii, since the 18th. century a compulsory stop on the Grand Tour. Later Gigante also painted this subject more romantically (see *Supper at Pompeii* at the Correale Museum in Sorrento).
In the 1861-62 period Gigante returned to painting archeological scenes, now with a greater insistence on «atmospherics» and a more poignant spirit, though his depiction was faithful to life, as this viewpoint and ruins have subsequently been identified by archeologists (De Caro, Naples 1983).
The same subject, with a stronger topographical intention, appears in the drawing dated 12th. October 1861 in the Astarita Collection at Capodimonte Museum (cf. Spinosa 192, no. 155).

Bibl.: Causa 1967, PI. XXXVI; Ortolani 190, fig. 2, p. 212; Essen 1973, P. 246, no. 369; De Caro-Fusco, Naples 1983, P. 49, cat. 95.

Sunset over Capri
Watercolour, tempera and white lead on cardboard, 23.5 x 30.5, pl. p. 100
Naples, Museum of San Martino

The setting sun in the distance behind the island of Ischia and the cottage with the parapet – from where the view is taken – are the only topographical features which could be used to give this late work of Gigante's a title. His vision of the landscape from the 1850's onwards (a good example is *Countryside around Caserta*, dated 1857 and a useful reference for developments in Gigante's work during this period, see Fusco, Naples 1983) dissolved into pure atmosphere and emotion. «Turner has taught us that light can be broken down into the thousand reflections which make up an image, and be the sole protagonist of that adventure which is painting ...» (Causa 1972). In his *Sunset over Capri*, (datable around 1860) Gigante shows that he has assimilated Turner's treatment of light, combining it with his own imaginative substratum and very personal relaxed technique, as in *Avellino*, from the Zezon Salvago Collection, where the presence of figures gives greater concreteness to the emotion of a landscape.

Bibl.: Ortolani 1930, PI. 16; Ortolani 1942, PI. 113; Causa 1967, PI. XXXVII; Causa 1972, P. 804; Susinno 1974, no. 38; Fusco, Naples 1983, cat. 9, p. 45.

Philipp Hackert
Prenzlau 1737 – San Pietro di Careggi 1807

The most important source of information about the life and works of Hackert is the biography written by Goethe. Hackert was a painter at the court of Naples and this is where he met Goethe in 1787. They met several times after this, and their relationship was mutually beneficial – Goethe held Hackert in very high esteem, otherwise he would not have written his biography, although he wrote it and published it after Hackert's death, in accordance with both of their wishes. It was published by Cotta in Tübingen in 1811.
The life of the landscape painter Philipp Hackert (who was born in Prenzlau in 1737 in the Brandenburg area and died in Florence in 1807) shows remarkable tenacity and coherence. He began to study in Berlin and soon was successful – two views of the Berlin zoo of 1761 were purchased for King Frederick II's collection. From this moment on, the painting which is most characteristic of all Hackert's work began to take root – the landscape painted «from life», which was a novelty at the time and made a great impression, despite the fact that in this part of the 18th century a landscape was only really considered a work of art if it was in the «ideal» tradition. After having spent some time in Pomerania and Sweden, and three highly successful years in Paris (1765-68) Hackert and his brother Johann Gottlieb (Prenzlau 1744 - Bath 1773) travelled to Rome in December 1768. Hackert was never to leave Italy again.
The main quality of Hackert's work is always finding new beauty spots to paint. For this reason he travelled constantly so as to sketch and paint surrounded by nature. Thus, in 1769, he spent four months at Tivoli and in 1770 several months in the Naples area. Naples was considered the most beautiful city in Italy at that time, and Hackert was provided with a letter of presentation when he arrived there for Sir William Hamilton, the famous English Ambassador for whom he was to paint many pictures He also received commissions from Catherine the Great – large paintings celebrating the Russian naval victory over the Turkish fleet, which are a historical record. In the following years, Hackert often returned to Naples and the surrounding area. In 1777 he undertook a journey to Sicily and made drawings and watercolours of ancient cities and Greek temples, which can be considered particularly interesting as they opened up a new trend in landscape painting.
Among the first orders of work he received from King Ferdinand IV were four small landscapes painted in gouache in 1782, for the royal study at the Palace of Caserta (to which three more were added in 1792). These were followed by four paintings showing the four seasons for the royal lodge on Lake Fusaro (1783-85). As orders from the king increased, Hackert was given the post of court painter in 1786 and settled in Naples. Another brother Georg (Prenzlau 1755 - Florence 1805) came to Rome and worked as an engraver on copper, obtaining the equally prestigious position of «graveur du Roi», responsible for all the engravings of Philipp's work. In the official position he now held, Philipp received special commissions – like the excessively large pictures of hunting scenes and military manoeuvres. These paintings merely recorded events, and although Hackert actually enjoyed this kind of work it tended to condition and restrict his horizons, inevitably leading to a decline in quality.
He much preferred the large set of paintings of the *Ports of the Kingdom* which initially included six large views of Naples and Campania in 1787, and other works necessitating journeys to Apulia in 1788 and Sicily and Calabria in 1790. Here the influence of his friend Vernet could be felt, who had been commissioned to paint a cycle of large-sized paintings entitled *Ports of France*. Hackert's scenes of Southern Italian ports are particularly interesting, as no record of these ports existed before them. They were subsequently split up and are now in different states of conservation (some very poor) and deserve to be examined and studied in their original condition.
In 1799 Hackert left Naples. He had to flee due to uprisings which had caused the whole court to remove to Sicily, and the entry of the French put an end to an intense period of creativity in the city.
With his brother Georg he reached Leghorn by ship in May 1800 and finally settled in Florence after staying for a year in Pisa. He bought a piece of land at San Pietro di Careggi just outside the gates of Florence, not far from Villa dei Medici and here he spent most of the time working until his death in 1807.
In his Neapolitan period Hackert undoubtedly produced his best work, and in particular his best landscapes. By 1770 he had already started painting landscapes of the surroundings of Naples, the city which was to become his home from home. These views, so true to life, were in great demand with many foreign visitors who had come to Italy from all over Europe, often important personages who wanted to take home with them a souvenir of the places and beauty spots they had visited. The extraordinary success which Hackert had during his lifetime is easily understandable if one considers the milieu and taste of the period.
Between 1750-1800 the countryside and gardens, which had previously been ignored, became quite the fashion. A new way of seeing nature encouraged the birth of landscape gardening in England, and the success which English gardens had all over Europe was one of the decisive factors for the rise of landscape painting. Hackert's realistic views, based on subjective perceptions, fitted in well with this change in taste and the need to see the beauty of the countryside as it really was.
Trees were one of Hackert's leitmotivs – in many of his large pictures his trees are powerfully expressive and herald the romantic ideal of nature. The essence of his landscapes is their faithfulness to reality, a synthesis between objectivity and figurative composition. Historically speaking, his extremely rational approach has much of the predominating philosophy of the Enlightenment. It is the «view» in the modern sense of the word, that is, the image which faithfully refers back a city or a landscape which Hackert sought to recreate in his «view from life», and to elevate it to the status of art, a status which was not yet acknowledged.

His way of seeing and interpreting places, the clarity and orderliness of the natural phenomena he painted are the great qualities of Hackert's art, which certainly found favour with Goethe – in particular, two views of Vesuvius erupting in 1774 and 1779. Although Hackert was essentially interested in depicting realistically, it would not be altogether fair to describe his style as repetitive. The rational and at times chilly atmospheres of his work were not only typical of this artist but of the spirit of the times. His realism is tempered by elements of the Classical tradition with romantic undertones, and in form and content reflects a whole era. [W.K.]

The Bay of Pozzuoli at Dawn
The Bay of Pozzuoli at Dusk
Oil on canvas, 65 x 96.5 each,
pl. p. 74
Signed and dated 1802
Naples, private collection

These are part of a set of paintings (one is not present in this exhibition) whose theme is the Bay of Pozzuoli seen at dawn and dusk from the Solfatara looking towards Ischia or Vesuvius (Cleveland Museum of Art; Sotheby's 23rd March 1966, Lot 104). It is likely that each painting dates back to a different year, even after Hackert left Naples in 1799, and that they are taken from the same set of sketches made from life – which was typical of Hackert's method of work. The whole set can be said to represent his best work, an Arcadian Neoclassical interpretation of these views of Pozzuoli.
The landscape at the National Gallery of Modern Art in Rome is from the Mario Praz collection at Palazzo Premoli and appears in the inventory with the improbable date of 1798. It was bought from Sestieri in Rome in 1951.
The two views in private collections can be considered complementary, both in the viewpoints chosen and the dawn/dusk theme. [N.S.]

Bibl.: Kroenig 1986, pp. 14-23; Susinno, Rome-Naples-Milan 1987-88, p. 117, no. 1; Spinosa-Di Mauro 1989; no. 149, Pl. 77, 79-80.

The English Garden at Caserta
Tempera on paper, 46.5 x 96.5,
pl. p. 76-77
Signed and dated 1792
Caserta, Royal Palace

Ferryboat on the Sele River
Tempera on paper, 46.5 x 69.5,
pl. p. 75
Caserta, Royal Palace

These are part of a well-known set of seven temperas «a guazzo» with scenes of the «royal residences» – two from 1782 and the others from 1792 – commissioned by Queen Maria Carolina to decorate the study of King Ferdinand IV at the Royal Palace at Caserta. The other scenes which are not on display show *San Leucio* (1782), *Ischia, Persano, Capri* and *Cava de' Tirreni*.

Bibl.: Scavizzi, Naples 1962, p. 56; Causa, Naples 1979-80, I, pp. 336 & 346, nos. 118a-b; Arbace, Ischia 1984, p. 32, no. 2; Muzii, Naples 1985, p. 81; Spinosa 1987, p. 166, no. 136.

Antonio Joli
Modena c. 1700 – Naples 1777

Joli can be considered the most representativie Italian artist in Naples during the course of 18th. century landscape painting, and the heir of Gaspar Van Wittel's clear, realistic views dating back to the beginning of the century. Joli absorbed Van Wittel's typical characteristics and assimilated them into his own personal vision, an original language of art which was to be integrated into the fertile tradition of painters working in Naples, whether Neapolitans or not, on the theme of local landscapes from the mid-18th. century onwards.
Joli's training was ecletic, as he studied and became famous in an international environment, in contact with the most interesting artists in the history of landscape painting.
He was born in Modena right at the beginning of the century and was trained in the studio of Raffaello Menia Rinaldi. By 1720 he had moved to Rome where he was working in the entourage of Giovanni Paolo Pannini, whose style of painting and culture can be seen in Joli's scenographic inclinations. It was in this field, in fact, that Joli produced his early work in Modena and Perugia for Palazzo Donnini. Between 1732 and 1742 he worked for the Venetian theatres of San Samuele, San Cassiano and San Giovanni Crisostomo, and here he first came into contact with Canaletto and Bellotto. It was probably during these years that Joli began to paint landscapes, learning from the work of these two great masters. All his life, Joli was to paint both scenographic and landscape subjects, without any overlap between the two genres or contrived effects, as if the artist was conscious of the different characteristics of both kinds of work, of the different places they were to decorate and the different clientèle (Mancini 1964).
In these years he began to make a series of long journeys round Europe, which brought him into contact with particularly stimulating environments and cultural circles. From Germany, he went to London in 1744 to paint the scenery for *Rosalina* at the King's Theatre, Haymarket; in following years he painted more scenery for London theatres and for the director of the King's Theatre – John James Heidegger (with the important title of *Surintendent des Plaisirs d'Angleterre*) and decorated the hall at Heidegger's Richmond mansion with a set of views painted on panels in oils of various European cities, Chinese style landscapes, and Vesuvius erupting seen from the bridge of the Maddalena in the style of Sandrart's prototype of engraving of the 1631 eruption (Croft Murray 1941).
He also painted a set of views of London and the surrounding area and works for Chesterfield House. These were the years when Canaletto was in London too, and Joli – who was often called «the Neapolitan Canaletto» – probably benefited enormously from the direct influence of the most famous of Venetian masters. In 1750 he was present at the court in Madrid where he received the commission through the good offices of the opera singer Carlo Broschi Farinelli to paint scenery for the Buen Retiro Theatre, and for the Palace of Aranjuez, for which he was very highly paid, receiving great honours. He also continued to paint landscapes, as we know from a view of Rome formerly in an English collection signed and dated in Madrid (Urrea Fernandez 1977, p. 151). In 1754 he obtained permission from the king to return to Italy, and probably to Naples, though the following year he was in Venice to help found the Academy of Painting and Sculpture.
His best known landscapes date back to this period. In fact the fame that he had acquired abroad, both at the courts and in aristocratic circles soon made him the favourite artist with the many foreign travellers who came to Italy in those years. The most popular of his paintings – the famous views of various well-known spots in Naples (now partly at Beaulieu and partly at Bowhill) belong to a vast collection of canvasses with views of different Southern Italian cities commissioned in various stages by Lord John Brudenell, later the Marquis of Monthermer, a young heir with illustrious forebears. After a traditionally aristocratic education – Eton and Paris – Brudenell came to Italy in 1754 with his tutor to complete his education, staying in Naples between 1756 and 1758. He is one example of Joli's noble clients, who also included, needless to say, Sir William Hamilton – the English Envoy Extraordinary at the Kingdom of Naples.
A letter from Luigi Vanvitelli to his brother in April 1759 talks of Joli being in Naples. To this period belongs a set of paintings, all signed and dated, of the temples of Paestum – the oldest illustrated record of the temples in existence, and from only slightly later are the various versions of the *Departure of Charles of Bourbon from Naples*, seen from the sea and the land now kept in Naples, Vienna and Madrid. In 1762 he officially became head scenographer at the San Carlo theatre as a replacement for Vincenzo Re on Charles of Bourbon's orders. Joli was now considered «very skilful at painting, especially detailed work, perspective, views of the countryside and seascapes... recommended by designers working for the theatre, stage, and scenery for court entertainment like Bibiena, who speaks well of him in Vienna and in Italy, in addition to his ability to paint excellent frescoes for halls and rooms» (Spinosa 1979, p. 389). This is how the Prince of Nicandro described Joli to the King and it gives a good idea of the kind of work Joli would be doing for the next fifteen years.
Records of all kinds, including payments and of course his paintings themselves, enable a reconstruction of these years to be attempted. He was highly praised for his works at the San Carlo theatre and the court theatre at the Palace of Caserta, as G. Tiraboschi (1781) writes: «(He was) extremely inventive and very natural in his style» but above all «wonderful at illustrating the words of the poets». This is an interesting comment because it points to a new kind of sensitivity, which was not common those days, regarding the

relationship between the stage space and the content of the works being staged. In additions to the stage-sets were his projects for festival «machines» for special ceremonies at court or for fairs, like the great Fiera of 1763 set up on the Largo di Palazzo in front of the Royal Palace. He also received professional recognition, in fact he was given the title of Professor at the Academy of Design, for which Luigi Vanvitelli envisaged a series of reforms. Although Joli was not in very good health (Vanvitelli did not call him to help in the decoration of the Palace of Caserta despite his ability, as the work was considered too tiring for him) he did decorate the antechamber at Palazzo Gravina (1773-75) though this work is now lost, and the Queen's boudoir at the Royal Palace (1776), also lost. He continued to produce a large amount of landscapes of Naples and surroundings, often commissioned by the royal family and sent as presents to foreign courts as records of some special event. With his lucid and rational precision Joli puts to good use what he learned from Vanvitelli, creating his own personal blend of art combining faithfulness with reality and interest in human nature (but not folklore) in his landscapes. Alongside the «official» views of the city, seen through the most famous places, there are views which penetrate far deeper below the surface, something which «had not happened for a good many years, since Viviano Codazzi and more recently (though only partially) Gaspar Van Wittel» (Spinosa in Spinosa-Di Mauro 1989, p. 30).
To what extent this was a result of demands made on him by clients is unknown at present. However, what is certain is that by the 1760-70's the art market was well stocked with pictures sold as souvenirs of the Grand Tour. Joli's attentiveness to detail at every level of his work, from architecture to nature and humanity really had little in common with pictures being turned out for souvenirs. He is undoubtedly one of the greatest landscape painters at European level that Southern Italy has ever had. [M.U.]

The Royal Palace and Castelnuovo
The street in front of the Royal Theatre of San Carlo
Oil on canvas, 61.4 x 59.5 each
The Gate of Spirito Santo
The Street of Santa Maria di Costantinopoli
Naples from the Port
Largo San Gaetano
The Marketplace
«Cuccagna» in front of the Royal Palace
Oil on canvas, 48.5 x 77.5 each,
pl. p. 39-46
Beaulieu, Lord Montagu of Beaulieu

Carnival in front of Castel Nuovo
Largo San Ferdinando with Royal Carnival Procession
Oil on canvas 49 x 75 each, pl. p. 47-49
Plain of Paestum with the Temples
Oil on canvas, 78 x 126
Selkirk, Bowhill, Duke of Buccleuch K.T.

This group of paintings includes much of the work commissioned from Joli by Lord Brudenell, a young aristocrat on his tour of Italy during the 1755-80 period. Brudenell was in Naples between 1756 and 1758 and to this period belong a large number of landscapes of Southern Italy painted by Joli, such as Agrigento, Messina and Palermo, now divided among the Beaulieu and Bowhill collections, and private ones.
Of the Bowhill group there are also three pictures of Naples – two showing the famous *Royal Procession at Piedigrotta,* of which there are other versions at the San Martino Museum and the Kunsthistorisches Museum in Vienna, and a *View from Santa Lucia,* another popular theme.
Two versions are known of the *Plain of Paestum with the Temples,* seen from the same angle though smaller in size – one belongs to a private Neapolitan collection, the other was sold by Sotheby's on 19th. April 1986 (lot 61) – in addition to a more interesting version seen from high up (at the Norton Simon Museum of Pasadena) and some foreshortened views at Caserta (signed 1759) and belonging to Colnaghi. These are the first pictures of history being rediscovered and they became prototypes for a whole series of later pictures on this theme. These ones were drawn from life by Joli, and six engravings by Filippo Morghen of these views of 1776 state them as being after Joli's work. Two years later Thomas Major also made two engravings of Paestum from views by Joli purchased by Sir Thomas Gray, Envoy Extraordinary of His Britannic Majesty, who was to be followed by Sir William Hamilton, and who also possessed two paintings by Joli with the ruins of Paestum (Knight 1985, p. 55).
Joli's paintings for Lord Brudenell are the first views of Naples seen from inside the city in a new style, and they are interesting because they show us how the city was built at the time and what Neapolitan society was like. In the painting identified by Gino Doria in 1962 as Calata Trinità Maggiore (the street running past the old San Carlo theatre before Nicolini refurbished it) there is the only image we have today of this part of the city at the time (Di Mauro in Spinosa-Di Mauro 1989, pp. 164-66). Finally, of great interest too are the two Bowhill paintings crowded with figures painted during carnival time, especially Largo San Ferdinando with the royal processions coming from Via Toledo and the allegorical float similar to a drawing by an anonymous artist at the San Martino Museum (Naples 1979-80, II, p. 335, no. 580a). [M.U.]

Bibl.: Bologna-Doria-Pannain 1962, pp. 18-20; Briganti 1969, p. 74, figs. 27-28; Washington 1985, p. 256, no 275; Spinosa in Spinosa-Di Mauro 1989, p. 193, no. 71, Pl. 31-38).
The restoration of the paintings in Lord Montagu's Collection was paid for by the Voena Gallery of Turin.

The Bay of Naples from the Slopes of Vesuvius
Oil on canvas, 127 x 162, pl. p. 50
Naples, Museum of San Martino

This painting is extremely spectacular in its composition, with the great pinetrees in the foreground and the sweeping view of all of the Bay of Naples as far round as Procida and Ischia. This was made possible by the angle chosen from the slopes of Vesuvius, probably from a spot near San Giorgio a Cremano. The same viewpoint was used during this period owing to its vast sweep by the Duke of Noja for his view of the city in his famous map. Later on Lusieri (1783), Della Gatta and Ducros also painted views of the Bay of Naples from similar viewpoints (Spinosa-Di Mauro 1989, pp. 202-203, nos. 174, 182, 185). Four other versions are known of the original view, in different sizes and with slight variations – one is in the collection of the Banca Commerciale Italiana in Rome (Bacchi, Rome 1909, p. 71, nos 11 & 27); two more belong to a private Florentine collection and to the dealer Sestieri of Rome (Bacchi, op. cit. p. 74); the fourth was sold by Sotheby's of New York on 4th. January 1988, lot 145 (Spinosa in Spinosa-Di Mauro 1989, p. 193, no. 74, fig. 78). In all the versions excepting the Sestieri one, the king can be seen in the foreground with a Capuchin friar paying homage to him. [M.U.]

Bibl.: Spinosa in Spinosa-Di Mauro 1989, 193, no. 74, Pl. 39.

The Royal Procession at Piedigrotta
Oil on canvas, 55.3 x 97.3, pl. p. 51
Naples, Museum of San Martino

Formerly attributed to Fabris and Ricciardelli, this painting was finally identified as Joli's work by Nicola Spinosa, who suggested that it was probably a preparatory study or a smaller version of two large-sized canvasses of the same subject which depict the royal procession on its way to the church of Piedigrotta. There are copies of these paintings at the Kunsthistorisches Museum in Vienna and in the Duke of Buccleuch's collection at Bowhill, which were among other works commissioned by Lord Brudenell between 1757-58. Finally, also at the San Martino Museum in Naples are copies of both pictures, in a poor state of conservation and with no attribution.
The same subject was used by Pietro Fabris in a painting now in store at the Uffizi in Florence (Spinosa 1987, p. 159, no. 285) and by Antoniani in a work belonging to a private Neapolitan collection (Utili, Venice-Milan 1987, p. 95, no. 67). [M.U.]

Bibl.: Spinosa in Spinosa-Di Mauro 1989, p. 193, no. 77, Pl. 43).

Ferdinand IV on Horseback with the Court at Capodimonte
Oil on canvas, 72 x 126, pl. p. 50
Naples, Museum of San Martino

This picture of Ferdinand IV as a young man, which appears almost a commemorative and allegorical «scene», symbolizing the ideal and institutional link between the Palace of Capodimonte which was being built and the capital city of the Bourbon kingdom seen in the background, must have been painted after Joli settled in Naples in 1762. Another version signed by Joli with virtually no variations is at the Kunsthistorisches Museum in Vienna (80 x 179). [N.S.]

Thomas Jones
Radnorshire, Wales, 1742-1803

The younger son of a Welsh landowner, Jones was intended by his family to become a clergyman, and was studying at Oxford when his great-uncle, who was financing his education, died. He therefore left in 1761 without completing his degree, and decided to follow his own inclination to become an artist. He became a pupil of Henry and William Pars at Shipley's School and also studied at the St. Martin's Lane Academy. From 1763 to 1765 he was a pupil of Richard Wilson, an experience which coloured his initial approach to the landscape of Italy. In 1766 he became a member of the Society of Artists and began to exhibit landscapes in the style of Wilson. However as early as 1770/1 he was making oil-sketches from nature that hint at his later achievements in this medium. In 1776, with assistance from his father, he was able to travel to Italy, a project planned for some years, where he remained until 1783, the most significant part of his artistic life. The journal he kept is an invaluable source of information on the daily lives of visiting artists, their relationships with patrons and their views on the customs of the Italians. Jones based himself in Rome, hoping to attract patronage from visiting grandees and making sketching expeditions in the Campagna with fellow artists. In September 1778 he went to Naples, his first expedition being the ascent of Vesuvius, which had recently erupted and which was to be the subject of several of his pictures. His *Memoirs* record numerous trips into the countryside around Naples as well as by boat to Posillipo and Sorrento. In December Jones and John «Warwick» Smith took lodgings together at «Gennaro di Napoli», where Jones stayed until his return to Rome on 23 January 1779. In Rome he took an apartment in the same house as William Pars – reputedly once Salvator Rosa's – in the Via Gregoriana, near the Trinità dei Monti. According to his *Memoirs*, «having no prospect of any more Commissions at Rome, & those I was engaged in, being all of them Views in the Environs of Naples», Jones decided to return to Naples in May 1780. Until his final departure for England on 3 August 1783 Jones lived in a succession of apartments in the city. He acted as guide to various friends who were visiting the city, notably Francis Towne, William Pars and John Robert Cozens and mixed with other artists including Giuseppe Bonito, Giovanni Battista Lusieri, Pierre Jacques Volaire and Jacob Philipp Hackert. Although he largely failed to attract the commissions he longed for, it was in Naples that he painted his masterpieces, the series of oil sketches of buildings that are among the most remarkable of the century. After his return to England, he continued to paint classicising landscapes in the style of Wilson, exhibiting a *Bay of Naples* at the Royal Academy in 1784. In 1787 his elder brother died and Jones inherited the family property in Wales, moving there with his wife and family in 1789. He gave up his professional career, but continued to paint for pleasure, his last known work being dated 1796. Jones's *Memoirs* were published in 1951, but his rediscovery as one of the most original artists of the eighteenth century was further delayed until 1954, when some fifty oil sketches were sold at auction by one of his descendants. [L.S.]

In the Bay of Salerno
Watercolour over pencil,
284 x 435 mm, pl. p. 64
Signed, dated and inscribed: *Sirenusa The Scopuli Sirenum of the Antients 16 Novr. 1778 T.J./in the Bay of Salerno – commonly calld the Galli Islands;* and with a key to the main landmarks
Trustees of the British Museum, London 1960-12-5-1

The artist's *Memoirs* record an expedition he made in November 1778 during his first visit to Naples. Accompanied by a friend, Jones took a boat to Sorrento on 16 November and spent the next three days exploring the surrounding coastline. On 17 November they hired mules to cross the promontory and arriving at «the top of the Precipices which hang over the Bay of Salerno... alighted and scrambled down the Rocks along a narrow winding path hewn into rude irregular Steps – dined at a lone house belonging to a poor fisherman and situated on a rock over the Sea – hired a boat and visited the Galli Islands». This carefully drawn view looks westwards to Li Galli Islands off the southern shore of the Sorrentine Peninsula, which had been known to Virgil as the islands of the Sirens, the name inscribed by Jones across the top of the drawing. His key identifies the principal landmarks, including the Faraglioni island off Capri (3), the Punta Campanella, then called *Minerva* (2), the village of Nerano (4) and high in the hills the town of S. Agata (5). [L.S.]

The Bay of Naples and the Mole Lighthouse
Oil on paper, 244 x 397 mm, pl. p. 63
Signed: *T.J.* and inscribed on the verso: *Naples March 1782*
Private Collection, England

Thomas Jones lived in an apartment near the Mole for part of his first visit to Naples in 1778, and from May 1780 until May 1782 in «a large new built house or Palace» near the Dogana del Sale and close to the east side of the Castel Nuovo. The Mole was a centre of much social activity. Jones noted in his *Memoirs* that it was a favourite place for walking in the evening and meeting friends; on his first day in Naples, 15 September 1778, he went out after dinner and met his fellow artist John «Warwick» Smith, who had been in the city for six months. Together they saw across the Bay «a large stream of redhot Melted Lava running down the Side of the Mountain», Vesuvius having erupted a few days earlier. Here, Jones's viewpoint is looking towards the hills of the Sorrentine peninsula.
This oil sketch, painted in March 1782, is different in character both from his sharply defined analytical studies of buildings in Naples and from his carefully annotated topographical watercolours. The delicate, subtle colouring and sensitivity to atmosphere reveals another aspect of Jones's artistic personality. [L.S.]

Bibl.: Naples 1962, p. 59, no. 51; Causa 1981; Spinosa 1987, p. 161, no. 297; Hawcroft 1988, p. 94, n. 110; Spinosa-Di Mauro 1989, p. 198, no. 131.

Houses in Naples
Oil on paper, 254 x 381 mm, pl. p. 62
Signed and dated on the verso: *Naples August 1782 TJ*
Trustees of the British Museum 1954-10-9-12

By mid June 1782 Jones had moved into an apartment on the third floor, «reckoned the genteelest and consequently the dearest... with the exclusive use of the Lastrica» of a house in the Vicolo del Canale below Capodimonte, opposite a church which he called S. Maria della Segola (S. Maria Antesecula, destroyed by bombing in 1943). «From this *Lastrica*... you Commanded a view over great part of the City, with the Bay, Mountains of Sorrento & Island of Capraea – on the other side, the Rocks, Buildings & Vineyards about Capo de Monte – and where I spent many a happy hour in painting from Nature... It was in this house I may say, that I spent by far the most agreeable part of my Time during my Sojourn in Naples». Jones and his family stayed in this apartment until 4 May 1783, although in December 1782 he took a more centrally placed room for painting and exhibition in the Vicolo del Mariscallo de' Svizzeri.
The viewpoint from which this study was made suggests that Jones was painting either at a window or, as his *Memoirs* suggest, from the roof terrace of the house. [L.S.]

Bibl.: Gere 1959, pp. 93-4; Causa 1981; London 1985, p. 30; n. 131; Hawcroft 1988, p. 91, n. 104; Spinosa-Di Mauro 1989, p. 198, n. 130.

Rooftops in Naples
Oil on paper, 143 x 350 mm, pl. p. 63
Signed, dated and inscribed on the verso: *T.J. Naples Aprile 1782*
Visitors of the Ashmolean Museum, Oxford

Shortly after his arrival in Naples towards the end of May 1780, Jones found a second floor apartment «Just by Mrs Sherry's Hotel» in «a large new built house or palace» near the Dogana del Sale and close to the east side of Castel Nuovo. Although it was not until after he had left these lodgings on 3 May 1782 that he referred in his *Memoirs* to «making finished Studies in oil on primed paper» of buildings which he could see from his window or *lastrica*, the dates on several oil sketches show that he had already begun this practice. These studies are Jones's most original and beautiful works. His viewpoints are uncompromising, as in this and other sketches of walls and rooftops which are placed parallel with the picture plane and without any of the conventional compositional devices. Jones's feeling for architectural form is shown in the carefully placed patterns of rectangular shapes and the use of dark recesses contrasting with the brighter areas of crumbling stuccoed façades. [L.S.]

Bibl.: Naples 1962, p. 60, n. 54; Detroit and Chicago 1981, pp. 200-201, n. 72b; Gowing 1985, pp. 44, 63; Hawcroft 1988, p. 90, n. 100.

Gaiola
Watercolour over pencil,
197 x 502 mm, pl. p. 64
Signed, dated and inscribed:
Gajola on the Coast of Pusilipo near Naples 1778 and 1796 TJ
National Museum of Wales, Cardiff

Thomas Jones made his first visit to Naples between 15 September 1778 and 23 January 1779. He and his travelling companion from Rome, the sculptor Giuseppe Plura (d. 1753), took rooms in a house on the Mole kept by «Sormanj a Swiss» and his English wife, who, much to Jones's delight, supplied them with English beer and food. Towards the end of the month, friends arrived from Rome – the painter Jacob More (1740-1813), and the architects Thomas Hardwick (1752-1829), Robert Brettingham (c. 1750-1820) and John Henderson (d. 1786) – to see the eruption of Vesuvius, which Jones notes was particularly dramatic. On 29 September, Jones's *Memoirs* record that the party took a boat for Baia, but high winds and a rough sea made it impossible for them to go any further than Gaiola, where they went ashore and walked to Pozzuoli, hiring a man to carry their provisions, and visiting the Solfatara and Lake Agnano before returning to Naples: this watercolour must have been based on a drawing made on this occasion.
The date *1796* inscribed near the top of the sheet suggests that at this later date – probably the time at which Jones was writing his autobiographical *Memoirs*, based chiefly on the journal he had kept in Italy – he was also sorting through and annotating his sketches. [L.S.]

Bibl.: Spinosa-Di Mauro 1989, p. 198, no. 125.

Landscape with a Dome
Oil on paper, 140 x 215 mm, pl. p. 65
Inscribed on the verso:
Naples 1782 T.J.
Birmingham City Museum
and Art Gallery

At the beginning of May 1782 the lease on Jones's apartment near Castel Nuovo, where he had lived for the preceding two years, expired. He found another painting room in the Convent of S. Maria a Cappella Vecchia where he worked for a few weeks, «situated in the Borgo of the Chiaja & very near Sir Wm Hamilton's palace», which had views from its single window «into a small Garden, and over a part of the Suburbs, particularly the *Capella Nuova*, another Convent, the *Porta di Chiaja*, Palace of Villa Franca, and part of the Hill of Pusilippo... all of which objects, I did not omit making finished studies of in Oil upon primed paper» (*Memoirs*, 3 and 12 May 1782). Although not inscribed with the exact date on which it was painted, this oil sketch accords well with Jones's description of the view from the convent window. [L.S.]

Bibl.: London and Cardiff 1970, p. 25, no. 63; Cambridge and London 1981, p. 22, no. 23; Gowing 1985, p. 47.

Giovan Battista Lusieri
Rome ? c. 1755 – Athens 1821

Giovan Battista Lusieri – also known as Titta and Don Tito – was probably born in Rome and was from a Roman family, according to records found recently. Early works which can certainly be attributed to him with views of cities show that even at the beginning of his career he used great precision in his landscapes and worked in a very personal style, sensitive to the romantic and aesthetic emotions evoked by the landscape, but attentive to an exact interpretation of reality with that typically transparent effect given by clear bright watercolour. Some good examples are *View of Rome from the Aventine* (Hawcroft, Manchester 1988, p. 20, fig. on p. 35) and *View of Rome from Monte Mario* at the Academy Gallery in Vienna, dated 1783 (Eigenberger 1927, p. 236; Williams 1982, pp. 492-96, fig. 22). Lusieri reads the landscape with vibrant sentiment and lyricism, a result which could only be achieved by being familiar with contemporary English landscape painters – Jones, 'Warwick' Smith and Cozens, but also – and above all – Vernet. His studies contributed enormously to his «sentimental» style, which however remains absolutely faithful to reality and to an objective, detached interpretation of topography. Lusieri was already in Naples by 1782, and had been introduced into the circle of wealthy patrons of the arts, German and Russian ambassadors and educated foreigners on the Grand Tour, especially English travellers, as Thomas Jones tells us in his *Memoirs*, often speaking of Lusieri as friendly and supportive. This was the year he painted *View of Naples from Capodimonte* (Spinosa 1987, II, p. 336, no. 242) sold by Sotheby's London salesroom on 30th. June 1986 with another 19 watercolours, all from Lord Elgin's collection. Thomas Bruce, Lord Elgin and Kincardine, was famous for having bought the marble statues by Phidias from the Parthenon of which he had engravings made, printed in 1818. Elgin bought a large number of watercolours and studies from the artist's family after his death. The group, which was broken up at the London sale comprised views of Naples, including two covering sheets according to recent research by Spinosa (in Spinosa-Di Mauro 1989, p. 202, no. 182). There were also *Posillipo from Portici*, *View of the Plain of Caserta* and *View of the Bay from Posillipo* (Spinosa in Spinosa-Di Mauro 1989, pp. 202-03, nos. 182-83), and a *View of Palermo and the Conca d'Oro* which with other paintings in the English collection is a record of the artist's journey to Sicily.
These works tell us much about Lusieri's style, but also about the way he worked. As Thomas Jones mentions, Lusieri sketched from life, first lightly drawing the whole view in pencil, even the smallest details. After that he would paint the view in watercolour and then give more tone to the shaded areas. And even where his work is unfinished his precise pencil drawing shows the landscape to perfection (Spinosa in Spinosa-Di Mauro 1989, p. 28).
In 1783 Lusieri was called to the court of the Bourbons to paint for the Queen. It has recently been discovered from records that in 1786 he personally asked the King and Queen, to whom he took the unusual initiative of writing personally, for permission to print twelve views of Naples and surroundings.
These views had been ordered by Maria Carolina for the Governor of Flanders, and Lusieri asked for, and was granted, copyright for a twelve-year period. In 1787 though, Lusieri requested the Camera Reale di Santa Chiara to see to the matter with some urgency (Italian Foreign Ministry, file 4624, see register).
In 1784 Lusieri signed and dated another *View of Portici* which is in a private Neapolitan collection. The watercolour of *Naples from Pizzofalcone* (1791) at the Paul Getty Museum at Malibu is spectacular not only for the size of the sheet on which it is painted, but also for the precision of the scene and the clear-cut vision, which would suggest an important commission – the place Lusieri was painting from was Palazzo Sessa, Sir William Hamilton's residence. Also dated 1791 is the *View of Naples from the Fort of Vigliena*, enlivened with colourful episodes of everyday life in the foreground (Spinosa in Spinosa-Di Mauro 1989, p. 203, no. 185).
In 1793 Lusieri signed and dated an *Eruption of Vesuvius*, now in a private Neapolitan collection. On the same theme is a watercolour dated 1797 which was sold at Christie's on 5th. July 1983 (Hawcroft, Manchester 1988, p. 84). In 1799 he was employed by Lord Elgin on Sir William Hamilton's recommendation to accompany Elgin on his journey as ambassador to Constantinople, with a break in the journey in Athens. The contract was signed in Messina and provided that Lusieri should hand over to Elgin all the works painted during this period. Lusieri spent the last 22 years of his life in Athens. Unfortunately all the drawings with views of the places he visited (some unfinished, according to records) were lost in a shipwreck in 1828 when these works were being taken to England. Only one is left in the Elgin collection and shows the *Temple of Philopappos*. In the Elgin collection at Broomhall there are about a hundred drawings bought in 1824 from the artist's family. Besides watercolours with studies of animals, boats and figures there is a sketchbook with preparatory studies for his largests compositions. Two identical watercolours with traditional costumes, delicately painted but with a strong sense of mass, were purchased by the J.B. Speed Art Museum (J.B. Speed Art Museum Bulletin, 25, 1966, p. 7). [R.M.]

Posillipo from Portici
Watercolour, 57.2 x 93.7, pl. p. 84
Signed and dated: *Titta Lusier f. 1783*
United Kingdom, private collection

Naples from Portici
Watercolour, 57 x 93.6, pl. p. 85
United Kingdom, private collection

The two sheets were sold separately at Sotheby's London salesroom on 30th. June 1986, and only recently have been shown to be a single view of the whole of the Bay of Naples seen from Portici. The view was painted from Villa Sarlo, adjoining the property of the Caravita family and still in existence (no. 16 Via Marittima). On the

extreme left is the Fortino del Granatello, on the right the new quay which was being built, the old brick factory and the façade of Villa Elboeuf on the coast; after these landmarks the bay sweeps round as far as Posillipo and the islands. As Lusieri liked to paint large-scale scenes in great detail at wide angles he needed big sheets of paper. Evidence of this can be seen in *Naples from Pizzofalcone* at the Paul Getty Museum; in fact Lusieri while in Athens repeatedly requested paper 10' by 18' from Lord Elgin and his secretary W. Richard Hamilton. Lusieri himself records the views of Athens and Costantinople of 1877 as being this size. However, these works were unfortunately lost when the ship travelling from Greece to England went down during a storm, carrying all the drawings made during the years he had worked for Elgin.
In these two paintings Lusieri uses a method of work which was typical of Northern European painters – drawing from life, complete with topographical details, painted in his studio then touched up in the shaded areas. The result is a meticulous, clearly defined interpretation of reality, achieved by brillant draughtsmanship, which is reminiscent in its precision of Hackert's work. But while Hackert is detached and clinical, Lusieri is sensitive to atmosphere and uses light, luminous tones more typical of the English landscapists he certainly knew, who were working in Naples at the time.
The two watercolours are from the large collection of Lusieri's work bought by Lord Elgin when the artist died through the mediation of W. Richard Hamilton. At the Sotheby's sale 21 works were sold, mostly with views of Naples and these are now scattered. The same subject was painted by Saverio Della Gatta in two different versions in gouache. [R.M.]

Bibl.: Williams 1982, pp. 492-96; Spinosa in Spinosa-Di Mauro 1989, pp. 202-03, nos. 182-83, Pl. 106-07.

Naples from Mergellina
Unfinished watercolour, 62.3 x 93, pl. p. 82
United Kingdom, private collection

Naples from Mergellina
Unfinished watercolour, 54.5 x 96.9, pl. p. 83
New York, the Woodner Family Collection

Another two sheets sold separately at the Sotheby's sale of June 1986 from the Elgin collection have been put back together (Spinosa-Di Mauro 1989, p. 202, nos. 182-83, Pl. 108-09) and show in one single view the Bay of Naples from the Casino del Pignatelli to Mergellina, Castel dell'Ovo and Vesuvius at the far end of the scene. As usual, Lusieri's work is extremely precise in all the topographical details from the great palace on the ridge of Posillipo to the rows of fishermen's dwellings at Chiaia, the houses on the slopes and the Vesuvian area in the background, where important landmarks can still be picked out. Lusieri wanted to show as clearly as possible the places people visited, and for this reason he chose a viewpoint situated high up, which was varied to focus in the best possible way on the features of the landscape.
The virtuosity of this technique was much admired by his contemporaries and is clearly visible in this watercolour. He uses a pencil (an English brand of graphite called Middleton) to outline the landscape drawn from life, with a meticulous eye for detail and with plenty of «local colour», as can be seen from his many sketches of figures, animals and boats, some from his sketchbook, which are still kept in the Elgin collection at Broomhall. After the drawing stage, he adds the skilful brushwork, carefully choosing luminous tones, from the lightest to the darkest. Sometimes Lusieri leaves certain details unfinished – boats or trees, for example. In this watercolour only the outlines have been drawn of the shore of Mergellina, so full of life, and which was to give still greater depth to the scene. [R.M.].

Bibl.: Spinosa 1987, II, p. 166, no. 342, Pl. 74-5; Spinosa-Di Mauro 1989, p. 203, no. 138, Pl. 108-9 and pp. 161-62.

Vesuvius erupting at Night
Watercolour, 43 x 55, pl. p. 86
Signed and dated 1793
Naples, private collection

Although the style is as usual a meticulously realistic view, very reminiscent of Hackert's particular attention to detail, the scene as a whole is a revisitation of the landscape due to the position of Vesuvius, which looms up behind the hill of Pizzofalcone and Castel dell'Ovo and the imaginary wings which give greater depth to the view. This watercolour is similar in subject-matter to the one dated 1793 (64 x 97) belonging to the Duke of Wellington's collection (Williams 1982, fig. 23) and another identical view dated 1797 showing Vesuvius during the eruption which took place ten years earlier, according to an inscription on the verso. This version is in a private collection in the United Kingdom (Hawcroft, Manchester 1988, pp. 84-6, no. 93). [R.M.].

Bibl.: Spinosa in Spinosa-Di Mauro 1989, p. 203, no. 186.

William Pars
London 1742 – Rome 1782

Pars studied in London at the St. Martin's Lane Academy and at Shipley's School until 1761, when his brother Henry took over its management and he became an assistant; it was here that he met Thomas Jones, a pupil at Shipley's in 1761, who was to become his closest friend. He established himself as a portraitist and had ambitions to be a history painter, but in 1764 he was commissioned as draughtsman to accompany Richard Chandler and Nicholas Revett on an expedition to Greece and Asia Minor, sponsored by the Society of Dilettanti. After his return to England in 1766, a number of the watercolours he had made on the tour (now in the British Museum) and a set of drawings of the Parthenon marbles were engraved in *Ionian Antiquities* (vol. I, 1769; vol. II, 1797) and *Antiquities of Athens* (vol. II, 1789; vol. III, 1795). In 1770, the year in which he was elected an Associate of the Royal Academy, Pars accompanied the 2nd Viscount Palmerston on a tour through the Alps and the north Italian lakes, exhibiting seven Swiss views at the Academy in 1771 which anticipated the Alpine watercolours of J.R. Cozens and Francis Towne. Subsequently Pars was employed by Palmerston on tours to Ireland and the Lake District, and in 1775 he returned to Italy, again sponsored by the Society of Dilettanti. As Jones noted in his *Memoirs,* Pars also had personal reasons for going to Italy; he had become involved with the wife of a fellow artist, and «finding [they] could not remain long in England» they decided to go abroad. In June 1778 Jones recorded the death from consumption of «Mrs Pars», who was buried in the Protestant Cemetry in Rome. Pars was to live in Italy until his own sudden death in 1782, eking out his allowance by making copies after the Old Masters and receiving commissions for a few portraits. In 1779 he shared lodgings with Jones in Salvator Rosa's house, in the Strada Gregoriana: Jones describes the death in June 1779 of Anton Mengs who also had rooms in the same house. Pars was commissioned to copy Guido Reni's *Aurora* in the Palazzo Rospigliosi in 1779 and in October 1780 Jones records that he went briefly to Naples to paint a copy of Titian's *Danae* in the Gallery at Capodimonte, returning to Rome in mid-November. It is possible however that Pars visited Naples earlier on, to produce the drawings of Baia and the Bay of Naples that were aquatinted by Paul Sandby in 1776, although there is no other evidence for this visit. His next documented visit to Naples took place at the end of May 1781, when he stayed until 12 August. For most of the time he lived with Thomas Jones and his family, and the two of them enjoyed sketching expeditions, including the ascent of Vesuvius. While in Naples, Pars also finished a portrait of the *Marchesa S'a Marco*, a commission that he had brought with him from Rome. In January 1782 Jones noted that he had Pars's copy of the *Danae* (which had been left at his house since 1780) packed up and sent to Rome by sea. His *Memoirs* include no further reference to Pars until 2 November, when he records the death of his friend. Pars had been at Tivoli, and «making a Drawing at... the Grotto of Neptune, he imprudently sat the whole time with his feet in the water – Being taken with a fit of Shivering, he was wrapt up in a blanket and sent off immediately to Rome in a Calass, where He the next day expired». [L.S.]

The Temple of Venus, Bay of Baia
Watercolour with pen and ink,
405 x 563 mm (image);
468 x 628 mm (sheet), pl. p. 66
Inscribed below the image:
A Ruin on the Coast of Baia
Birmingham City Museum
and Art Gallery

An expedition to see the imposing ruins of the so-called temples at Baia (ancient thermal establishments) was an essential item on visitors' Neapolitan itineraries. Thomas Jones records many visits, including one when he and his friends dined in the Temple of Venus, and another with William Pars on 6 June 1781. The party left Naples at 4 in the morning, «and arrived about 10 at Vaccula (the antient Bauli). This place which consists only of a few paltry houses, is famous for its wine, & which, after a hearty meal of broiled mullets, we thought exquisite – we coasted it afterwards to the Temples at Baja, where we stop'd to make Sketches, in despite of the neighbouring Soldiery, and so round to Pozzuoli – landed and refreshed on the little Island of Nisida and got home a little after Sun Set». This watercolour by Pars would have been based on a sketch made during a visit to Baia, almost certainly on one drawn in Jones's company on this occasion. Pars shows the ruined octagonal Temple from the North West, from an almost identical viewpoint to that chosen by Francis Towne in a sketch made on a visit with Jones on 20 March 1781 (Sheffield City Art Galleries). [L.S.]

Bibl.: Birmingham 1980, pp. 39-40, no. 48; Hawcroft 1988, p. 113, no. 137; Spinosa-Di Mauro 1989, p. 199, no. 141.

Anton Sminck Pitloo
Arnhem 1791 – Naples 1837

Considered to all effects «Neapolitan», Pitloo settled in Naples in 1815 and was to remain there till his death. This artist is usually regarded as the master and initiator of the School of Posillipo, due to having given a new lease of life to Neapolitan landscape painting by blending local colour with the fervid emotions of the English and French landscapists from the 1820-30's. As Causa so aptly remarks: «He removed all the stereotyped precision of detail from the landscape and made it ripe for experimentation with different modes of painting» (and expression) (Causa 1983, p. 13). Pitloo was born at Arnhem in Holland and studied at art school from 1803 to 1808 with H.J. Von Ameron. He received a grant from Louis Napoleon and was in Paris from 1808-11, studying with Victor Bertin according to his biographer Mattei (1860) though Dutch historical sources say he worked with Jean-Joseph Xavier Bildaud. This was the environment which had produced Valenciennes and the classical landscapes of Achille Michallon, and which was to form the talent of Corot ten years later. These experiences were assimilated by Pitloo (cf the drawings at the Società Napoletana di Storia Patria, the Museum of San Martino and the Piazza collection in Naples) in addition to influences of Claude visible in certain finished works, like *Cava dei Tirreni* from the Praz collection.
From 1812-15 Pitloo continued his training in Rome, with another pupil Abraham Terlink working for the Dutch group of artists Voogt, Verstappen and Van der Berg. Causa (1956) and Ortolani (1970) stress the importance of some of François Granet's lesser known works from the 1802-24 period in Rome, for example some small panels at the Museum of Aix-en-Provence. Granet was instrumental in introducing an intensely lyrical landscape, small in size and intimate in tone, based on the «resurgence of the «macchia» and the airy luminosity of Dutch painting» (Ortolani, p. 243) which bears similarities both to Corot's and Pitloo's work.
After the fall of Napoleon and the suspension of his grant, Pitloo moved to Naples in search of fortune, invited there by a Russian diplomat who was a great conoisseur of art – Gregory Vladimir Orloff.
Pitloo continued to alternate life in Naples with journeys to the lakes of Lombardy and to Palermo. Drawings of these subjects, dated 1819, are kept at the Gabinetto Nazionale Disegni e Stampe in Rome. He also spent some time in Rome, and in 1820 married Giulia Mori, sister of the engraver Ferdinando. At his house at 15 Vico del Vasto in Naples Pitloo opened a private school of painting, the core of the School of Posillipo, frequented from 1821 by Giacinto Gigante and Achille Vianelli, and from 1819 by Silvester Schedrin, Smargiassi, Duclère, Franceschini, De Francesco and Pasquale Mattei (according to recent discoveries made by Lossky, 1989, p. 31). By 1822 Pitloo was already so famous as to be awarded the honorary chair of landscape painting at the academy, and the chair in 1824, for which he presented his references in the form of a *List of Works and Clients* updated to that year (Lorenzetti 1935, p. 406) and the painting of the *Palazzo Francavilla with Pizzofalcone in the background* (Banco di Napoli collection at the Museum of Capodimonte).
Earlier works which are influenced by trends already mentioned, like Claude and the Dutch school, are the *Ponte Lucano* and the *Marmore Waterfall* (Sorrento, Correale Museum), the *Temple of Minerva Medica* and the *Foro Triangolare at Pompeii* (Amsterdam, whereabouts unknown), *Ruins of Temples at Tivoli* (formerly in a private collection at Torre del Greco), the *Church of St. George at Velabro*, painted in 1820 for the King of Holland, *Castel dell'Ovo at Sunrise* (Rome, National Gallery of Modern Art, and the already mentioned *Cava dei Tirreni*, painted for La Bouchère probably in the early 1820's (cf. Di Mayo 1985, p. 12 and Susinno 1988, p. 114). *Ferdinand I hunting in the Astroni Park* (Correale Museum of Sorrento) and *Temples at Paestum* (Capodimonte, shown at the exhibition of 1826) are all chronologically part of this group. *Palazzo Francavilla with Pizzofalcone in the background* (1824), displayed at the 1826 Exhibition at the Bourbon Museum with a *View of Ischia* (Academy Gallery) mark the turning-point towards greater autonomy of style, of «exploration into formal reality, through vigorous vibrant brushwork which reveals a strong aspiration to a new concept of light and atmosphere» (Causa 1983, p. 13). Raffaello Causa sees the reaching of this turning-point as a link with the romantic landscape of the English school, from Thomas Jones to Constable and Bonington. According to Causa (1972, p. 795) an important influence was Turner, in Naples in 1819, who exhibited his paintings in 1828 in Rome; another artist who contributed to this change in Pitloo's style was the Dane Christian Dahl, in Naples between 1820-21, and who «gives less importance to drawing and more to a strongly expressionist medium ... succeeding in bathing the outlines of the view in such bright light that they are unrecognizable» (Causa 1983). The style of works like *Santa Lucia* (c. 1824, in a private Neapolitan collection) is clearly inspired by the presence of Bonington in Naples the same year. From Camille Corot (in Rome in 1825 and Naples in 1828) Pitloo learned how to free the landscape «from all the narrative and documentary paraphernalia», reducing it to the essentials.
Works where the blend of 17th. century Dutch art and Corot's «sentiment du lieu» can be felt are those painted between 1824 and 1828, like *The Mole Lighthouse* at the Museum of San Martino, the *Country Cottage* (D'Angelo collection), and *Houses in the Sunlight* (Solothurn collection). A group of works dating back to the early 1830's – *Torregaveta* (1833), *Bacoli* (1834) and the *Castle of Baiae* at the Correale Museum in Sorrento – are characterized by intense atmosphere and light, achieved by «a range of silvery and pearly hues ... and lightened, transparent shadow effects ... a constant living emotion» (Causa 1972, p. 796). Later, his views were simplified even further in composition, perhaps owing to the second visit of Corot to Rome in 1834. A group of paintings from this period are: *Coroglio* and *La Riviera di Chiaia* (in the Correale and Cesareo colections), *Castel dell'Ovo* (formerly in the Rebuffat collection), while later works such as *Cava dei Tirreni from Monte Crocelle*, the *Mill on the Gragnano* and *Sunset over the Bay of Naples* (almost an «impression», a «soleil couchant» according to Causa) are more closely connected with Turner and even Gigante.
In his last works his pictorial synthesis tends to a rapid distortion of form in an almost expressionist style, as in *Return from the Sanctuary of the Madonna dell'Arco*, a drawing at the San Martino Museum.
Pitloo's work as academy professor left its traces in the commitment to revisit the places and style of the landscape from life («during his autumn holidays he went out on sketching expeditions so as to prepare all his work for the winter», Pasquale Mattei tells us) and he handed on his experience to his students by giving them his own paintings to work from. He also took part in several Bourbon Exhibitions (1826, 1830 and 1837). By 1836 though, he was suffering from serious physical and psychological disorders, worsened by financial problems due to a crisis in the art market, caused by the cholera epidemic.
In 1837 Pitloo also succumbed to cholera. His paintings were offered to the Academy for sale by Sofia Pitloo, Duclère's wife, and later on most of them were bought by the Count of Correale (now in the Correale Museum of Sorrento). These works include 27 oil paintings on paper glued to canvas, small in size and ranging from studies or copies of well-known works and examples of refreshingly innovative landscapes, like the *Phlegrean Shore* (Causa Picone-Di Mayo 1985, no. 16) which in 1985 were added to a number of works by Pitloo belonging to the Banco di Napoli collection at the Virgilio Gallery in Rome.
B. Lossky proposed that no. 14 – *Neapolitan Couple in Folk Costumes* – should be removed, as it was a preparatory sketch for Schedrin's *Terrace at*

Sorrento and other studies of figures by this Russian artist. This exhibition may well be able to throw some light on the issue: in fact, this aspect of Pitloo's work requires further study, both in works which are difficult to attribute to Pitloo, like the *Landscape of Cava dei Tirreni with Figures of Peasants* (London, Sotheby's), of an unusually large size (125 x 175) but also in paintings which are certainly his work, like *Piazza Sant'Antonio in Sorrento*, signed and dated 1827 and illustrated in Causa 1984, p. 28 (A.P.).

The Mole Lighthouse
Oil on canvas, 24 x 32, pl. p. 99
Museum of San Martino, Naples
Purchased from the Ochsembein Collection in 1951

Published by Causa in 1956, this painting of which there is no record and which is not dated is attributed by Causa to the 1824-28 period, and clearly influenced by 17th. century traditional Dutch painting and Corot's «sentiment du lieu». According to criticism in the catalogue of the exhibition on *Smargiassi and his time* (Naples 1987) in this painting a strong link can also be seen with «the typical Flemish themes of Thomas Wijck and Lingelbach», revisited with a more concise and vigorous handling.
This *Mole Lightouse* was the product of a trend developing in Naples and Rome around 1810-20 which could be defined as a new, realistic style of landscape painting. In fact this painting bears a certain resemblance to Rebell's Neapolitan works, for example *Mergellina* (1815, Österreichische Galerie) where the treatment is relatively unsophisticated and the paint is loosely applied, or to *Palazzo Donn'Anna* of 1821, with its intense reflections of light on water.

Bibl.: Causa 1956, PI. 21; Lavagnino 1956, I, p. 458, fig. 417; Picone, Naples 1962, cat. 72, fig. 37; Causa 1967, PI. 1; Martorelli, Naples 1987, p. 147, PI. 32.

Palazzo Francavilla with Pizzofalcone in the background
Oil on canvas, 44 x 75, pl. p. 98
Naples, Banco di Napoli Gallery at Capodimonte Museum
From the G. Casciaro Collection, purchased in 1942

Urban development around Mount Echia at the turn of the century makes it impossible to clearly identify the viewpoint in this work, which would appear to include the dome of Santa Maria della Vittoria and the pinkish silhouette of Palazzo Cellammare. Though there are no other landmarks which can contribute to the exact identification of this work and a critical appraisal of it, it is known to be one of his mature works and can be safely dated around 1824-26.
During this period Pitloo painted a similar subject on two occasions, once as a diploma piece for the Chair of Landscape which was «an oil painting on canvas from life of a group of trees in a large garden at Chiatamone, called the Francavilla Wood» (cf. Ortolani 1970, p. 66) and one for the Bourbon Exhibition of 1826 – *Scene with the Garden of Chiatamone*, cat. no. 85. When Serge Ortolani gave the title *Pizzafalcone from Palazzo Cellammare* to the Casciaro canvas he rejected the idea that this could be the 1824 diploma piece, considering it a more conventional treatment though it did contain some more easily recognizable features – a wood with a marble group of Ferdinand IV revered by Neptune and Parthenope which skirted a small lake formed by the waters from the Chiatamone source, (cf. Lorenzetti 1936, PI. 22 and Martorelli 1984, p. 134). Both Lorenzetti and Causa in later writings stated that this was actually the 1824 painting, concluding that this new position as Professor of Landscape coincided with an innovative scene with a stronger sense of atmosphere.

Bibl.: Pfister 1925, p. 168; Napoli 1936, p. 37; Molajoli 1953, p. 47, no. 74; Causa 1956, PI. 22, pp. 69, 73, 115; Causa 1967, p. 28, PI. II; Martorelli et al edited by N. Spinosa 1984, pp. 134-36; Martorelli, Naples 1989, pp. 74-5.

View of Ischia
Oil on canvas, 33 x 46, pl. p. 98
Galleria dell'Accademia di Belle Arti, Naples
Inv. no. 612, in store at Capodimonte Museum

Part of a collection of works belonging to the Accademia used «to show the students of this Institute works of art produced by their teachers» (Caputi 1971), the *View of Ischia* is generally believed by the critics to be later than the *Palazzo Francavilla with Pizzofalcone in the background* and datable around 1824-5, thus belonging to the mature period of Pitloo's *oeuvre*. Luisa Martorelli has identified the viewpoint from which the Castle is depicted as being the Campo dell'Arso, described by a «Romantic» traveller as «the arena of a vast amphitheatre» which appears beyond some gardens «covered on both sides of the road by a layer of lava ... the greenery of these heights is a beautiful contrast to the black lava below and the blue of the sea which it borders on». (De Ferrari 1826, p. 575).
Ortolani though, attributed this work to Gigante and datable twenty years later (cf. 1970, P. 207). The subject was also depicted by Vianelli in a painting on paper in sepia and white lead at the Museum of Capodimonte, but with the addition of figures and the choice of a different composition (cf. Ischia 1984, p. 65).

Bibl.: Naples 1936, p. 57; Causa 1956, PI. 23; Causa 1967, PI. III; Causa-Mormone-Caputi 1971, no. 567, p. 121, XX, Martorelli, Ischia 1984, pp. 62-63; Daprà et al 1988, p. 158.

Gabriele Ricciardelli
Active between the 1740's and 1780's

Recent studies about Neapolitan landscape painting (Spinosa-Di Mauro 1989) and new discoveries of dated works in private collections have provided greater information about the life and work of Gabriele Ricciardelli and interesting details about his position in the context of landscape painting in the Naples area in the 18th. century. Traditionally linked to Joli's method of landscape drawing and Fabris' and Antoniani's use of colour on the basis of his known works, today Ricciardelli can be better assessed in the light of this new information which shows him to be quite independent in his choice of style.
Son of the landscape painter Giuseppe, he was probably a pupil of Nicola Bonito, and Jan van Bloemen in Rome. In 1741 he was working for the Bourbon court with the scene painter from Parma Pietro Righini, decorating some of the ornamental panels over the doors at the Royal Palace, which are now lost. His training in landscape painting (almost certainly encouraged by Righini) inspired his early work, an example of which are the idealized landscapes of varying sizes signed and dated 1741, once part of a sumptuously decorated aristocratic villa near Benevento and now in a private Neapolitan collection.
In the late 1740's he was given the important task of painting some rooms at the royal villa of Portici (as De Dominici records) «of varying sizes» and once again no longer in existence. A new and significant date in his biography is 1747, which appears on the back of four signed paintings kept in the Breakfast Room at the Elizabethan Calke Abbey, in the heart of England, recently reopened by the National Trust. These consist of a *View of the Bay of Naples from the Hill of San Martino, Naples from Il Carmine*, a *View of Mergellina* and a *View of Pozzuoli and the Bay of Baiae* with elegant figures of noblemen in the foreground. These paintings of such an early date are a preview of what Ricciardelli's work was to be like much later on, rather than bearing direct resemblance to Joli, who did not work in Naples before 1754; in fact most of Joli's work can be dated at least three years later. Thus, Ricciardelli's style can be considered totally independent of Joli, and of course of Fabris and Antoniani for chronological reasons (Spinosa in Spinosa-Di Mauro 1989, p. 30).
It is not yet known whether the Calke Abbey paintings were taken to England by a traveller on the Grand Tour or commissioned from the painter on the spot. The rare historical sources in the United Kingdom speak of him as being in Dublin from 1753-60, working under the patronage of Lord Allen. During this period he painted portraits in addition to Irish landscapes, and even decorated important buildings (like the ceiling of the Rotunda Hospital Chapel – Strickland 1913; op. cit., 1969, p. 276).
His absence from Naples is also confirmed by record of a payment dated January 1754, which Gabriele's brother Carlo received from a certain Teodoro Davel for a painting sent by the artist from Dublin (Rizzo 1989, p. 49). In 1758 and 1759 he was still in Dublin and later in London – his *View of Chiaia* at Castle Howard is dated 1768, and he exhibited in London in 1777. Quite probably he returned to Naples at least once between these dates, because Cardon made his four engravings from Ricciardelli's views of Naples in 1765, of which several more versions were to follow later. These engravings bear dedications by important foreign visitors accredited at the Bourbon court. The four viewpoints

chosen by Ricciardelli on this occasion – with the addition of the Ponte Nuovo and the Riviera di Chiaia, together with the English views of 1747 show a progressive evolution of the need (already felt by early 18th. century landscape painters) to give greater details of the new urban development, which could no longer be shown by the traditional bird's eye view of the previous century, or by the more modern though totally inadequate east and west viewpoints.
However, Ricciardelli showed no interest (as far as is known) in the «inner city» a theme which Joli was to develop so skilfully later on. Ricciardelli's long stay abroad could also be the reason for the numerous versions of his most famous views of Naples, as if while away he was working from memory or from sketches taken from life, varying each painting with local colour, which was to be characteristic of his style in later years. Even the light in his pictures – the «delicate pink, blue and turquoise transparencies» and the «more detailed and meticulous drawing» (Spinosa in Spinosa-Di Mauro 1989, p. 31) would seem to indicate the subtle tastes of foreign clients. [M.U.].

The Bay of Pozzuoli
Oil on canvas, 42x99.5, pl. p. 57
Rome, private collection

This is one of the most celebrated scenes on the Phlegrean coast in Italian and foreign landscape painting, due to the area's natural beauty and the picturesque old town of Pozzuoli. Ricciardelli paints this subject in another work (belonging to the Calke Abbey collection) in a rather more «Arcadian» version. The painting exhibited here seems later than the English one (probably painted around 1747) because of the care used in the composition. It was first thought to be by Joli, though when it was sold at auction by Christies on 29th. June 1979, lot 59, it was attributed to Fabris and sold as one of a pair with a pretty view of Agrigento. Nicola Spinosa has recently come up with evidence that this is Ricciardelli's work, on the basis of an engraving by Francesco La Marra published in the *Collection of Antiquities of Pozzuoli, Baiae and Cumae* by Paolo Antonio Joli in 1768 and another one by Etienne Giraud around the same time (Di Mauro in Spinosa-Di Mauro 1989, p. 185, note 97). [M.U.]

Bibl.: Spinosa in Spinosa-Di Mauro 1989, p. 195, no. 92, fig. 92.

Sylvester Feodosievitch Schedrin
St. Petersburg 1761 – Sorrento 1830

Written Schtschedrin in German and Chtchedrine in French, this artist signed himself Schedrin. A little known artist, due to the difficulty of consulting records in Russian and absence of his most significant paintings from museums (until the Louvre purchased *Terrace at Sorrento* in 1986, see Lossky 1989) Schedrin appears to be closely connected to the «artistic revolution» of the Posillipo School with its images of Naples and environs during the 19th. century.
Naples can be considered his mature period, between 1825 and 1830, when he died suddenly at Sorrento, where he is buried. A student at the Academy of Fine Arts at St. Petersburg from 1800-12, Schedrin trained with the landscape painter Fedor Alexeyev (1753-1824) who brought together the styles of Canaletto (learnt in Venice) and the French school (Leprince through Mikhail Ivanov) producing a rather conventional image common over the Continent in the late 18th. century. His father – Fedosy Schedrin – was also instrumental in his training, as he was a sculptor and director of the Academy. So was his uncle Semyon, who held the chair of landscape painting and was employed as an easel-painter by the Grand-Duke Paul. Both were influenced by the French and Russian cultural climates, Semyon in particular who had studied with Casanova in Paris and was an imitator of Vernet.
Although he obtained a grant for a journey to Rome in 1812, Schedrin did not manage to get there until 1818, due to the difficulties of travelling during the Napoleonic Wars. In 1819 he was sent to Naples to paint two views of the city for the Imperial court and by 1820 he was a fixture among the Russians in that city who were part of the diplomatic corps. He was the guest of the poet Batjushkov and knew many of the German artists who were painting and experimenting in Naples at the time, Pitloo in particular, whom he praised in his letters. In March 1821 he was obliged to leave Naples on the orders of the Russian ambassador because of uprisings and was sent back to Rome.
His earliest known works belong to the academic landscape genre, though between 1822-25 Schedrin started to modify his vision and tended towards a more realistic and luministic interpretation. His meeting with Pitloo was instrumental in bringing about this change – the *View of the Colosseum* of 1822 at the State Museum of Leningrad (displayed at the Soviet Exhibition in 1989, cat. 31) shows that Schedrin's conventional approach is enlivened by an intense use of light on the openings of the monument, a typical feature of Pitloo's. His works from 1824 onwards, for example the *Scene with the Lake of Albano* (in the same museum) prove that by now Schedrin was throwing off the conventional style of landscape painting (see Lossky) and around 1826 had achieved this turning-point, in fact even before Pitloo. The study of light is systematically carried forward in the repetition of subjects at different times of the day, his favourite source of light being directly overhead. Figures are no longer only accessories and are now protagonists on the *scene*, carefully observed in their gestures and costumes but not given excessive importance like the «peasants» in Leopold Robert's work. In *Mergellina* of 1826 and even more so in *Terrace at Sorrento* (versions of which are in Paris and Moscow) the scene is no longer simply topographical, now it reaches a climax of atmosphere – light, coolness, human figures, costumes. Other Neapolitan subjects are – the *Riviera di Chiaia* of 1826 (belonging to the Tretiakov Gallery, at present on display at the Soviet Exhibition, cat. 105), *Santa Lucia* from the State Museum of Leningrad (cf. Madrid 1981, no. 8), *Castel dell'Ovo from Mergellina*, a nocturne of 1828 at the Pushkin Museum in Moscow (cf. Causa 1972, Pl. 283). Subjects of the surrounding area, which he explored during the summer months in search of places «never encountered by landscape painters» are *Marina Grande at Capri* (Tretiakov Gallery, cf. Utili 1988, Pl. 89), the *Small Creek at Sorrento* (Leningrad), the *Amalfi Coast* in a private Neapolitan collection, published by I. Bociarov and J. Glusciova (196, p. 53), *Meta* of 1830 at the San Martino Museum and a group of scenes of rocky coastlines with fishermen, including *Fishermen on the Shore* of 1826, at the Tretiakov Gallery which has enabled the identification of a variation of *Landscape with a Tower* at San Martino; and again the *House by the Sea with Fishermen* at the gallery of the Royal Palace of Naples.
In Naples Schedrin also met Giacinto Gigante and became his friend. It is known that Schedrin recommended Gigante to his compatriots in Rome in 1825 and that in 1855 he authenticated one of his paintings (Ortolani 1970, p. 193). Gigante is also mentioned in letters by Schedrin to Raffaele Carelli, who more than any other Neapolitan painter was influenced by the Russian. In 1828-9, on the basis of stylistic features of the later work *Terrace at Sorrento*, now at Leningrad (according to Lossky), a meeting is presumed to have taken place with Corot. The last summer of his life – 1829 – Schedrin spent travelling through Northern Italy and Switzerland, visiting Pisa, Genoa, Milan and Geneva en route and staying in Rome the following winter. Now a sick man, Schedrin returned to Naples and died in Sorrento on 8th. November 1830.
The increase in the number of paintings attributed to Schedrin over the years have enabled a clear picture to be made of his art, even if it is not certain whether he was really the driving force behind Neapolitan Realism in the 19th. century (Paolo Ricci 1981, p. 16). Though on the basis of this, Boris Lossky suggests that the *Studies of Figures, Animals and Landscapes* (displayed at the Carlo Virgilio Gallery in 1985 and purchased by the Banco di Napoli) usually attributed to Pitloo should actually be considered Schedrin's work, as Pitloo had little interest in folk themes, and there is a resemblance to other works by Schedrin, for example the *Guitar-player* (cat. 1985, no. 14) which could be a study for the group of figures in *Terrace at Sorrento* in the Louvre.
Lossky mentions that other Russian critics are doubtful about the attribution of the *Castel dell'Ovo at Dawn* at the Gallery of Modern Art in Rome, which is similar to an oil painting of the same subject at the Tretiakov Gallery and proves that Pitloo and Schedrin painted in a very similar style at times (A. P.).

Seascape with Sorrento
Oil on canvas, 25 x 40, pl. p. 97
Naples, Museum of San Martino

Purchased by the Museum for the topographical section and attributed to Pitloo, this work which has the name of the painter written in Latin characters was recognized by Raffaello Causa as being a study for an oil of the same

subject at the Pushkin Museum in Moscow (Picone, Naples 1962).
In a book by Serge Ortolani, not yet published in 1962, the author attributed this work to Schedrin, pointing out the presence of a similar view in the Bianchi Collection, and dating both around 1830.
In the better known works painted by Schedrin of the Sorrento coast there is resemblance in the shape, colour and treatment of the rocks – «he spreads impasto about in a softly luminous manner» says Ortolani of the *Scene of Vico* exhibited in Bologna and Naples (Bologna 1990, cat. 43) datable around 1825-30.
The view of the coast seen from the sea with the reflection of the fishermen's dwellings on the water was to be a leitmotiv in romantic painting in Naples right up until this century.

Bibl.: Picone, Naples 1962, cat. 8, fig. 39; Ortolani 19 O, p. 193; Causa 1972, pp. 800 & 82, fig. 284; Ricci 1981, p. 16.

John «Warwick» Smith
Irthington 1794 – London 1831

A leading topographical draughtsman and occasional painter in oils, Smith was known in his own day not only as «Warwick» Smith – a sobriquet derived from his patron, the 2nd Earl of Warwick, who financed his stay in Italy – but also as «Italian» Smith on account of the material he collected between 1776 and 1781. He figures frequently in Thomas Jones's *Memoirs*, which contain several references to sketching with «my friend Smith the Landscape painter». According to the *Memoirs*, Smith left Rome for Naples on 22 March 1778; when Jones arrived in the city on 15 September 1778 the first fellow-countryman he encountered was Smith. In December and January the two artists shared lodgings at «Gennaro di Napoli» near the Arsenal, until Jones returned to Rome towards the end of the month. Smith stayed in Naples until July, when he rejoined his friends in Rome; he travelled back to England via Switzerland with Francis Towne in 1781. Probably under the influence of Francis Towne and William Pars the watercolours painted by Smith in Italy began to have a greater intensity and richness of colour. While he seems to have been less innovative than his associates in Italy, he was the one to gain public notice since he alone of the group had his work regularly exhibited in London in subsequent years, and attracted the patronage of leading connoisseurs. After his return to England he travelled extensively in Wales and the Lake District, which provided the material for several publications including *Select Views in Great Britain*, 1784-5. *Select Views in Italy*, published in parts between 1792 and 1796, was among the most popular collections of topographical engravings, and before he set out for his first visit to Italy in 1819 Turner copied every plate in a small sketchbook as part of his preparations. Smith became a leading member of the Society of Painters in Watercolours (founded in 1804), serving as its President in 1814, 1817 and 1818. He last exhibited there in 1823. [L.S.]

Naples from Capodimonte
Watercolour over pencil,
165 x 243 mm, pl. p. 73
The Trustees of the British Museum, London (1879-7-12-194)

This is from a small group of watercolours painted by «Warwick» Smith in and around Naples, now in the British Museum, several of which are dated 1778 (later versions are also known); this was probably painted in the same year. Smith's view here is taken from Capodimonte, looking towards the Castel S. Elmo, with the Monastery of S. Martino perched slightly below it. The wooded heights above the city near Capodimonte were much favoured by British artists: William Pars, Thomas Jones, Francis Towne and J.R. Cozens, as well as Smith, all sketched in this area. [L.S.]

Bibl.: Binyon 1907, p. 108, no. 11.

Naples from Sir William Hamilton's Villa at Portici
Pencil and watercolour, 200 x 315 mm, pl. p. 73
Birmingham City Museum
and Art Gallery

This watercolour, which originally belonged to the artist's patron Lord Warwick, was probably painted in connexion with the engraving by William Byrne and William Lowry, dated 1798, which was published as plate 58 in Smith's *Select Views in Italy*, to which it is close both in size and in details of topography. A larger version, dated 1781, was formerly in the Newall Collection (Christies's 13 December 1979, no. 69). The text accompanying the plate noted that «The royal palace of Portici is spacious and well situated, open on one side to the sea, on the other to a large garden and wilderness of evergreen oaks, planted by the late King on the ashes of Vesuvius, which forms the background, and seems to rise out of the grove itself. Behind this wilderness, higher up the mountain, stands a most delightful villa, belonging to Sir William Hamilton, the English Ambassador. From a balcony in front of this house was the present view taken: it commands a prospect of the whole of the city and bay of Naples, which is justly considered as one of the most interesting and beautiful scenes in the world». [L.S.]

Bibl.: Lockett 1980, p. 31, no. 21

Francis Towne
Exeter ? 1739/40 – London 1816

Towne's exact date and place of birth are uncertain, but he was probably born in Exeter, Devonshire. By the mid 1750s he was a student at Shipley's School in London, where he came to know William Pars and where he may first have met Thomas Jones, who was a student in 1761. His early works, chiefly oil-paintings, were exhibited at the Society of Artists and at the Free Society; he exhibited intermittently at the Royal Academy between 1775 and 1810 and at the British Institution between 1808 and 1815. Until he went to Italy in 1780 he worked chiefly in the neighbourhood of Exeter, making topographical drawings and paintings and teaching well-to-do amateurs. His distinctive style developed in the 1770s, and is apparent in the watercolours he made during a tour of Wales in 1777. His finest work however was inspired by his visit to Italy, which he made at the age of about forty in 1780-1781. He arrived in Rome in October 1780, and although he did not keep a written journal as Thomas Jones did, his carefully annotated and dated watercolours form a visual account of his movements. In Rome he went on sketching trips with fellow artists including John «Warwick» Smith and there exist in the British Museum several examples of watercolours made on the same occasion by each artist. On 8 March 1781 Towne arrived in Naples for a short visit, leaving for Rome on 3 April; Jones had been living in the city since May 1780 and the two friends had therefore not seen one another since Jones left England in 1776. The *Memoirs* show that Jones acted as Towne's guide in and around Naples, and also reveal differences in their temperaments. Threatened on one occasion by ill-tempered soldiers at an inn at Baia and frightened on another by a group of Sbirri di Campagna, whom they mistook for Banditti, Towne's nervous disposition contrasts with Jones's jaunty accounts of these incidents. Towne returned to Rome until July, when he left for England in the company of John «Warwick» Smith, travelling via Florence and the Lakes to Switzerland, where they spent part of September in the Alps, an experience which inspired a small group of watercolours justly considered his masterpieces.
On his return to England, Towne spent more of his time in London, although he continued to visit Devonshire and in 1786 sketched in the Lake District; most of his exhibited works were based on his Italian and Swiss studies. In 1807, at the age of sixty-seven or so, he married a ballet dancer, who died in the following year at the age of twenty-seven. An unsuccessful candidate for election as an Associate of the Royal Academy on four occasions, the lack of recognition and the appelation of a provincial drawing master left him embittered. It was perhaps this sense of disappointment with the establishment that led him, in 1805, to organize his own one-man exhibition in London. When he died in July 1816, he bequeathed a group of seventy-five watercolours he had painted in Italy to the British Museum. Largely unappreciated in his own lifetime, Towne's concentration on pattern and bold effects led to a reawakening of interest in his work in the present century. [L.S.]

The Descent from Capodimonte
Watercolour with pen and black ink over pencil, 322 x 466 mm,
pl. p. 92
Signed and dated: *No. 7. F. Towne delt., 1781* and inscribed on the verso *Naples. No. 7. Coming down from Capa de Monta drawn on the spot by Francis Towne, March, No. 7, 1781.*
The Trustees of the British Museum, London (1972. U. 640)

On 8 March 1781 Thomas Jones noted Towne's arrival in Naples: «I was glad to see him... and as his stay in

Naples was not proposed to be long, I gladly offered my Services to be his Cicerone... I was able to conduct him to many picturesque Scenes of my Own discovery, entirely out of the common road of Occasional Visitors, either Cavaliers or Artists». Jones and Towne shared similar tastes in landscape, both liking such «picturesque Scenes» as well as more celebrated locations. Capodimonte, with its fine views over the city and bay of Naples, must have been among the first places visited by Towne; as his note on the verso indicates, this watercolour shows a cluster of buildings on the rocky descent to the city.

The watercolours made by Towne in Italy form a visual journal. He meticulously annotated and numbered each one, often giving the date and the time it took him to make the drawing, and on occasion the weather conditions: this was the seventh in his Neapolitan series. Unfinished watercolours in the British Museum suggest that his method was usually to draw the subject on the spot, and perhaps to put in some grey wash, adding the colour and pen outlines later on. Like J.R Cozens and «Warwick» Smith, he used the drawings he made in Italy as the basis for later watercolours and for a few oil paintings, although his work was not greatly appreciated in his lifetime and he received few commissions. [L.S.]

Bibl.: Bury 1962, p. 126.

Near Naples
Watercolour with pen and black ink over pencil, 320 x 468 mm, pl. p. 92
Signed and dated: *F. Towne delt., 1781. No. 11* and inscribed on the verso: *No. 11. Naples. Drawn on the spot by Francis Towne, March 1781.*
The Trustees of the British Museum, London (1972, U. 735)

In the company of Thomas Jones, Towne explored the countryside around Naples – but not without incident, as Jones recalled in his *Memoirs.* On one occasion, while sketching in the Bay of Baiae, they went to an inn where a soldier took offence at their behaviour and threatened Jones with a knife: «"Birbone che sei, sai tu che cosa sia d'affrontare un Signore Soldato?" – Towne was almost frightened to death – The old woman screamed and beg'd of them for the holy Virgin's sake not to kill the poor foreigners». A few days later, Jones took Towne sketching near S. Maria de' Monti, a monastery on a ridge beyond Ponti Rossi between Capodimonte and Capodichino. «This sequestered place was environed on all sides with Hanging rocks... a variety of wild Shrubs, and overshadowed by branching Trees – Here, says I, Mr Towne, is Salvator Rosa in perfection we only want *Banditti* to compleat the picture – I had scarcely uttered the words, when turning round a Projection of the Rocks, we all at once pop'd upon three ugly-looking fellows dressed in the fantastic garb of the *Sbirri di campagna,* with long knives, cutting up a dead jack Ass. ... Towne started back as if struck by an electric Shock... "I'll go no farther" says he... however he might admire such Scenes in a Picture – he did not relish them in nature». This watercolour, although not inscribed with the exact location, shows a view very similar to that described by Jones and may even have been drawn on this occasion, since the buildings in the distance may be the Castel Sant'Elmo; beyond, there is a glimpse of the Bay. [L.S.]

Bibl.: Bury 1962, pp. 79, 127.

The Palazzo Donn'Anna
Watercolour with pen and black ink over pencil on two pieces of paper, 253 x 469 mm, pl. p. 91
Signed: *No. 19 Francis Towne delt* and inscribed on the verso: *No. 19 Bay of Naples Francis Towne delt 1781*
The Trustees of the British Museum, London (1972.U.645)

Towne's spare, linear style, which was dependent on bold pen outlines and flat washes of colour, is apparent here. The Palazzo Donn'Anna would have been seen by Towne on his way out of Naples going towards Posillipo, Pozzuoli and Baia. It was begun by Cosimo Fanzago for Donn'Anna Carafa, wife of the Spanish Viceroy, the Duke of Medina, c. 1642; it was left incomplete in 1644, and according to a contemporary guidebook was used as a glass factory in the 1870s. [L.S.]

Bibl.: Bury 1962, p. 127.

Joseph Mallord William Turner
London 1775-1851

Turner was arguably the greatest landscape painter of the Romantic era. He was born the son of a London barber and spent his adolescent years as a humble assistant to printsellers and architectural draughtsmen. In 1789 he entered the Royal Academy Schools, exhibiting his first watercolour in 1790. From about 1794 to 1796 he attended the informal academy organized by Dr. Monro, copying drawings by J.R. Cozens and others. Although he began by painting views of country houses and the fashionable «picturesque» ruins of abbeys and castles, he aspired to the representation of grander aspects of landscape, and in 1796 exhibited a night scene, *Fishermen at Sea,* the first of many ambitious oil paintings influenced by great masters of the past, both British and Continental.

Throughout the 1790s he toured England and Wales, and visited Scotland in 1801. He was elected an Associate member of the Royal Academy in 1799 and, at an exceptionally young age, Royal Academician in 1802. In that year, during the brief Peace of Amiens, he travelled abroad for the first time, visiting France and Switzerland. Besides exhibiting at the Academy, where he was appointed Professor of Perspective in 1807, Turner opened his own private gallery in 1804. His paintings included classical and heroic subjects, as well as lyrical and pastoral scenes of English life; he publicized his work in a series of engravings entitled *Liber Studiorum* issued under his close supervision between 1807 and 1819. Although he continued to make tours in England, especially in the North where he stayed with his long-standing friend and patron Walter Fawkes in Yorkshire, he was not able to return to the Continent until the end of the Napoleonic Wars. In 1817 he toured the Rhine Valley, and in 1819 fulfilled a long delayed ambition to visit Italy. He left London on 31 July and after travelling through France and the Alps arrived in Venice on 8 or 9 September, leaving four or five days later for Rome, where he based himself until early October. Sir Thomas Lawrence noted on 6 October that Turner «is going immediately to Naples», a plan confirmed by «12 Oct.» scribbled on a sketch of Terracina. By 9 November he was near Albano on his way back to Rome, and at the end of the month, at the proposal of Canova, he was elected an honorary member of the Accademia di S. Luca. Reclusive by nature, we know few personal details of Turner's stay in Naples, although his presence was recorded by several contemporaries. He made the ascent of Vesuvius, and dined once with the British Minister. However, it is possible to follow his movements from his sketchbooks, which show that he visited many of the most celebrated beauty spots and classical sites of the region, including the Bay of Baiae, Pozzuoli, Lake Avernus, Pompeii, Amalfi, Sorrento and Paestum, as well as exploring Naples itself. This was to be Turner's only visit to Naples. On his return to England he painted several finished watercolours of Neapolitan subjects, but it was not until 1823 that he exhibited *The Bay of Baiae, with Apollo and the Sibyl,* his most important painting to have been influenced by the landscape and classical associations of the area. He returned to Italy in 1828, when he exhibited a number of his paintings in Rome, but did not travel further southwards. In the early 1830s he toured almost annually in France, and he returned in 1834 to Germany, becoming increasingly involved in designing plates for books of «Picturesque Tours», and in making illustrations for such authors as Lord Byron and Sir Walter Scott. A further visit to Italy in 1840 gave rise to a fine series of watercolours of Venice, which had already provided the subject matter for a number of oil paintings.

Throughout the 1830s and early 1840s he spent much time in Switzerland, which inspired his last great watercolours in the years 1842-46. Although he tried to attract clients for these, few people responded to the breadth and subtlety of his late style. He visited Germany in 1844 and France in 1845, but for the remainder of his life lived in retirement, his health failing, although he continued to work, exhibiting at the Royal Academy for the last time in 1850. He died on 19 December 1851, and was buried in St. Paul's Cathedral. The contents of his studio were bequeathed by Turner to the nation, and since 1987 have been housed in the Clore Gallery at the Tate Gallery, London. [L.S.]

The Bay of Naples and Vesuvius
Pencil and watercolour, 253 x 401 mm, pl. p. 93
Tate Gallery, London, Turner Bequest CLXXXVII-13

Turner left Rome for Naples shortly after 6 October 1819, and a dated sketch (TB CLXXXIV-22a) shows that

he was at Terracina on 12 October; he had returned to Rome by mid-November. His presence in Naples was recorded by several contemporaries, including the son of the architect John Soane who wrote to his father: «Turner is in the neighbourhood of Naples making rough pencil sketches to the astonishment of the Fashionables, who wonder of what use these rough draughts can be – simple souls!». As Turner reportedly told someone in Rome «it would take up too much time to colour in the open-air, he could make 15 or 16 pencil sketches to one coloured». This, in fact, seems almost certainly to have been his practice in Rome and Naples in 1819. Although it can be difficult when looking at a watercolour such as the present work to determine whether it was coloured on the spot, so fresh and spontaneous does it seem, Turner's comments noted above seem to suggest that he added the colour later (see TB CLXXXVII-18) or, as here perhaps, based a watercolour on a rapid pencil sketch of much the same view (TB CLXXXIV-53v, 54r). Unlike most of the studies made in Rome, which were drawn on carefully prepared opaque grey grounds, these Neapolitan watercolours show Turner's concern with capturing some elusive phenomenon of light: the translucent washes of colour are applied directly to the white paper.
As a young artist in the 1790s Turner had copied some of the Neapolitan views made by J.R. Cozens, which in their exquisite, almost melancholy mood are among the most evocative depictions of the city and its setting. Turner's approach was very different, more direct and perhaps more accurate in the way he recorded the brilliant Mediterranean sunshine, the busy city shimmering below the heights of the Castel S. Elmo, and the beautiful panorama admired by the poet Shelley a year earlier, in November 1818: «the blue water of the bay, forever changing, yet forever the same». In the following year, 1820, Turner painted a considerably more finished watercolour based on this study for his friend and patron Walter Fawkes, but it is in this work that we are most keenly aware of the immediate impact that Naples made on him in 1819. [L.S.]

Bibl.: London 1974, p. 91, no. 235; Wilton 1982, pp. 41-2, no. 31; Powell 1987, p. 80.

Vesuvius
Pencil, partly finished in watercolour, 254 x 405 mm, pl. p. 94
Inscribed by the artist:
(?) *Tuffa Rock yellow*
Tate Gallery, London, Turner Bequest CLXXXVII-18

One of Turner's reason for going to Naples was in the hope of seeing an eruption of Vesuvius, which was passing through a phase of volcanic activity during 1817-1819. While in Naples, Turner made the ascent of Vesuvius with two other travellers, one of whom was a young architect, Thomas Leverton Donalds (1795-1885), whose party he asked to join; and he acquired a round snuff-box made from lava from Vesuvius which he reputedly used as a palette in Italy. However, the main eruption did not occur until late in November, when Turner was back in Rome. Although several of his sketches show plumes of smoke emerging from the crater, none record any spectacular signs of eruption. In this study, Turner concentrates his attention on Vesuvius, serenely poised between sea and sky, every fissure clearly defined by light and shade. Turner's working process on this occasion seems to have been to make a pencil sketch on the spot, which he subsequently worked up with watercolour. Here we are made vividly aware of how he could transform a rough pencil sketch into an exquisite piece of painting. He has ignored the foreground, but has brought the central features of composition to life with washes of colour. The little touches of pigment on the left-hand side of the paper are where he has tried out his colours. [L.S.]

Capri from Naples, with the Castel dell'Ovo
Pencil and watercolour, 258 x 405 mm, pl. p. 93
Tate Gallery, London, Turner Bequest CLXXXVII-21

While in Naples, Turner made a number of views looking out to sea from the same vantage point, but under differing weather conditions and at various times of day. Here his interest has been captured chiefly by the relationship of the sky and the sea: topographical considerations are of secondary importance, the Castel dell'Ovo being shown as an isolated feature, almost like a great ship at anchor. In other studies, variations on the same view are shown under more serene conditions (TB CLXXXVII-2, 6 and 20). [L.S.]

Bibl.: London 1974, p. 91 no. 233

Coast Scene near Naples
Oil on millboard, 41 x 59.5, pl. p. 95
Tate Gallery, London, Turner Bequest (05527)

Both this and no. 05330 belong to a group of ten oil sketches, all of similar dimensions, some of which are painted on muslin stretched over millboard, others directly on board. A number of these sketches seem to show landscapes in the vicinity of Naples and Rome. Although very different in character and technique from earlier sketches from nature painted by Turner in England c. 1807 and 1813 they have a freshness and directness suggesting that they may have been painted in front of the motif, but with formal compositions in mind from the outset. Although Turner visited Naples only once, in 1819, they have usually been associated with his second visit to Italy in 1828. However, there are arguments in favour of each dating. Against the date of 1819 is the fact that Turner seems to have preferred the use of pencil and watercolour during this stay, rather than oils, although in 1828 he painted at least three large scale pictures (which he exhibited in Rome) and began work on another eight to ten. The style and mood of these sketches have much in common with the *View of Orvieto, painted in Rome* (1828) and clear reminiscences of Claude, perhaps more characteristic of the 1828 visit. But in favour of 1819 is that the ruin in no. 05330, the Temple of Venus, appears in *The Bay of Baiae, with Apollo and the Sibyl* exhibited in 1823; it is more probable that Turner referred back to a study made in 1819 rather than that he subsequently painted a sketch of this type. To conclude: the argument in favour of dating these sketches to 1819 is sufficiently strong to suggest that the question is still far from being resolved. [L.S.]

Bibl.: Paris 1983, p. 111, no. 48; Butlin and Joll 1984, p. 180, no. 320; Powell 1987, p. 159.

Seacoast with a Ruin
Oil on muslin mounted on millboard, 41 x 60, pl. p. 96
Tate Gallery, London, Turner Bequest (05530)

The ruin appears to be the Temple of Venus at Baiae seen from the northwest, the same viewpoint as in William Pars's watercolour. The dating of this sketch is uncertain, and is discussed more fully in the preceding entry. Turner's sketchbooks show that he made pencil drawings both of the general vista of the Bay of Baiae and also of the Temple of Venus (T.B. CLXXXIV) in 1819, which he subsequently used in the preparation of his painting *The Bay of Baiae, with Apollo and the Sibyl*, exhibited at the Royal Academy in 1823. This small oil may date from 1819 and could also have been part of the artist's preparations for the final picture. However, it could equally well be a later recollection, perhaps based on pencil drawings. Turner's working processes are not always easy to determine and an element of uncertainty must remain. [L.S.]

Claude-Joseph Vernet
Avignon 1714 – Paris 1789

Son of a modest carriage painter of Avignon, Vernet was the pupil of P. Sauvan, a painter of historical subjects, then of Jacques Viali in Aix-en-Provence, where his early works are recorded in 1731. With the help of some French patrons Vernet left for Rome in 1734, where he stayed for almost twenty years. Encouraged by the Director of the Academy although he was not a «pensionnaire» he followed the lessons of Pannini and Locatelli, and met the painter of seascapes from Lyons Adrien Manglard, who had been living in Rome since 1715. He was also able to observe works by Claude and Salvator Rosa, who particularly influenced his picturesque portrayal of rocky landscapes.
Vernet's fame spread rapidly thanks to an international clientèle – artists like Solimena, Conca, Costanzi and Slodtz; important Frenchmen like the ambassador Saint-Aignan, the Abbé de Canillac, the Marquis de l'Hôpital, and above all English visitors – relations being facilitated by his marriage in Rome to an Irish girl.
Although he painted some magnificent views from life of Rome – the *Ponte Rotto, Villa Ludovisi, Ponte e Castel Sant'Angelo* and of Naples (where he went for the first time in 1737) Vernet was more inclined towards imaginary picturesque scenes. After his experiences in Rome and Naples his favourite subjects became

sunrises and sunsets, mist, moonlight, storms, painting his works in pairs or in sets like the *Four Parts of the Day* of 1750 (Russborough, Eire). Nominated a Member of the Academy in 1745, Vernet regularly sent his seascapes to the various exhibitions from 1746 onwards, where they were received enthusiastically. In 1750 he met Vandières, the future Marquis of Marigny who was travelling in Italy with Cochin and Soufflot. His fame as a topographer and painter of seascapes was so widespread that he was entrusted with one of the most important works of Louis XV's reign – the set of paintings showing the military and commercial ports of France.

Returning to France in 1753, Vernet began to tour the ports one by one managing to finish fifteen views of *Ports of France* in just ten years (at the Louvre and Maritime Museum).

In 1762 he had to give up this laborious task and settle in Paris, where he continued to receive commissions from all over Europe and to be highly praised by the critics, in particular by Diderot, who had a *Storm* painted by him, and like his contemporaries was extremely moved by the dramatic effect of the group of figures exhausted and terrified by the storm: «Je voyais toutes ces scènes touchantes et j'en versais des larmes réelles» he wrote in 1767.

From this year onwards his creativeness and capacity for innovation began to fail and Vernet tended to exploit the same themes that had made him famous twenty years earlier, even if the quality of his work was still very fine. Moreover, the enormous number of pupils, followers and imitators of his style affected his own work. In the last year of his life he painted the historical landscape entitled the *Death of Virginia* (at the Hermitage in Leningrad) adapting his favourite subject – the storm – to the literary atmosphere of work by his friend Bernardin de Saint-Pierre [P.B.]

Charles of Bourbon hunting Coots on the Lake at Licola
Oil on canvas, 75 x 155, pl. p. 38
Signed
Caserta, Royal Palace

Part of the collections of the Royal Palace of Naples ever since it was painted, in 1938 it was transferred to the Royal Palace of Caserta. This picture is published by A. Gonzalez-Palacios and F. Zeri (*Un appunto su Vernet a Napoli* in «Antologia di Belle Arti», 7, 1978, p. 12-23) as «the original painting commissioned by the King, as the artist himself states, and the prototype for a second version painted in Rome for the French Ambassador to Naples, the Marquis de l'Hôpital».

The «French» version is slightly larger (92 x 183) and was confiscated from the possessions of the émigrés during the revolution. It was hung in Versailles in the late 19th. century and displayed at the London and Paris exhibitions on Vernet of 1976-77.

The «Neapolitan» version, which has no date, was probably painted before 1746, when the Marquis de l'Hôpital commissioned from Vernet (according to his own records) «une copie du tableau de la chasse du Lac de Patria que j'ai fait pour le Roi des Deux Siciles», for which he received 150 «écus».

It seems likely as Conisbee suggests (Paris 1976-77, nos. 16, 18) that in the boat with Charles of Bourbon (who was to become King Charles III of Spain) the person standing up with the red sash of the Order of San Gennaro is Paul-François de Galluccio, the Marquis de l'Hôpital and French Ambassador to Naples from 1740 to 1752. Raffaello Causa (Naples 1979-80, no. 183) remarks that «in the Caserta painting there is a strong sense of atmosphere, with the dark heavy raincloud fending the sky and as it passes rapidly casting a shadow over the waters of the lake, which are clear and calm in the distance. The title of this work should be *Storm over Lake Patria*, which is unexpectedly pervaded by pre-Romantic sentiment, despite the theme which is academic and commemorative. In fact it is the first of a long series of royal hunting and fishing scenes which were to become popular later on with many a great artist, like Fabris, Hackert, Pitloo, Fergola and so on».

Some doubts have been expressed about where this fascinating and lively hunt was actually taking place. The Acropolis of Cumae and the island of Ischia can be clearly seen behind the royal boats, though after mentioning the unlikely idea that this could be the Lake of Fusaro, Causa quotes R.T. Giaminelli, and his words would seem to prove that this is «the Lake of Licola, which no longer exists» which «around the 15th. century was called Lake of Coots», and until the late 19th. century was still part of «the royal hunting grounds».

Further information on the topography suggests that «if it is in fact Lake Fusaro, when looking towards Cumae one should not be able to see the outline of the island of Ischia because it should be behind the observer, and the hill of Cumae should be on the right-hand side. If it is Lake Patria, Cumae and Ischia should be much further away from the observer. Moreover, the hill of Cumae cannot be seen from Lake Patria because it is obscured by the hill of Sanseverino, which lies between Licola and Varcaturo. What is more, in Vernet's picture the lake reaches the foot of the Cumaen acropolis». These details are perfectly correct, but one wonders why Vernet spoke about the «tableau de la chasse du lac de Patria», when asked to copy one of his most significant works from his Italian period [P.B.].

Bibl.: Paris 1976-77, nos. 16, 18; González-Palacios, Zeri 1978, pp. 12-23; Naples 1979-80, no. 183; Spinosa-Di Mauro 1989, no. 55, Pl. 23.

Naples from La Marinella *
Naples from Mergellina *
Oil on canvas, 767 x 155, pl. p. 19
Alwhick, Duke of Northumberland's Collection

Though these works are similar in composition to two paintings of the same subjects at the Louvre, there are variations in the positioning of the figures and the paintings are different in size.

The pair on display originally belonged to the Boulogne (1787) and Dubois (1788) collections in France and they were reproduced and published in Saint-Non's *Voyage Pittoresque*. According to Conisbee they can be dated around the beginning of the 1740's, and therefore they were painted a few years before the Louvre pair, which was commissioned in Rome by the Abbé de Canillac in 1742 but not finished until 1748, according to an inscription on the Marinella canvas. [N.S.]

Bibl.: Conisbee, London 1976, nos. 7-8; Conisbee, Paris 1976-77, pp. 49-50, nos. 8-9; Rosenberg, Naples 1979-80, I, p. 338, nos. 182a & 182b.

Frans Vervloet
Malines 1975 – Venice 1872

Born in the Belgian town of Malines into a family of artists, Vervloet learnt the trade from his father Frans Vervloet I, professor at the Academy of Fine Arts. His brother Johann Joseph and his wife Augustine were also painters, and some of their works of architectural subjects are kept at the Royal Palace in Naples (Napier 1855, p. 95). After having shown his ability with a painting in the local church of St. Rombault (according to Ortolani painted expressly for this church) Frans was sent to Rome with a grant in 1822. Napier, a 19th. century source, dates Vervloet's meeting with Camuccini around this time. Camuccini was very impressed by the «precision and patience» shown by Vervloet in the *Interior of St. Peter's* bought by the King of Holland (now at the Rijksmuseum in Amsterdam), and pleased by the Neoclassical style of the composition. However, during Vervloet's stay in Rome it was his meeting with François Granet that was to be all important, because of his expressive use of light typical of the early 19th. century French landscapists (Causa 1956, p. 74). From 1825 onwards he settled in Naples (some of his drawings of Naples and Apulia date back to 1823), and in this period he produced his first set of paintings of the area – *Views of Largo di Castello*, looking towards and away from the mole, and a *Hill of San Martino* (Museum of San Martino). The limpid simplicity of these works «show, at so early a stage, the highly poetic atmosphere that Vervloet was capable of creating, which unfortuantely was to yield to the more stylized and fashionable painting of the times», as Causa tells us (*op. cit.* p. 74).

According to this critic, Vervloet was afflicted by the same problem as Pitloo – how to blend colour with atmosphere in a personal style «using clear, transparent tones» with the Northern European perception of Mediterranean light seen «through the unusual filters of softened hues» (Causa 1972, p. 798). During his long stay in Naples he lived at Largo Ascensione in the Chiaia area, where his children were born, and was in contact with Carelli, Gigante, Abbati, Maldarelli, Mancinelli, Franceschini and Palizzi, as is recorded by De Rinaldis (1922, pp. 81-82). This critic found an autobiography signed by Vervloet which had never come to light as it was still in his family. This was later bought by the Correr Museum in Venice (G. Lorenzetti 1947, p. 288). From 1826 onwards he took part in the Bourbon

Exhibitions, and is mentioned in 1830 as an honorary professor at the Academy, where he specialized in scenes of interiors, and was instrumental in making this genre popular in Naples (see Biancale, quoted in Ortolani 1970, p. 186).
Now famous at an international level, Vervloet developed his own version of the Canáletto style veduta, revisiting this tradition with a methodical approach and great optical awareness (cf Lorenzetti, op. cit.) and opened a studio in Venice during the period 1832-39, spending most of his time between Naples and Venice, though he also visited Florence, Siena and Dalmatia.
Ferdinand II commissioned from him a *View of St. Mark's Square* (Royal Palace of Naples), signed and dated 1837, a *Cathedral of Palermo* (moved from the Royal Palace to Villa Rosebery in Naples) and an *Interior of the Palatine Chapel of Palazzo dei Normanni*, exhibited in 1841.
His intention to paint the interior of St. Sophia took him to Istanbul in 1844, however he received no help from the embassy and he was not granted permission from the Turkish authorities. In 1845-46 the Tsar ordered two *Views of Villa Floridiana in Naples* from him (the studies of these are at the Museum of San Martino) which show the artist's great love for beautiful buildings and their surroundings, rather than the urban landscape in general, and this trend can also be seen in the *House of the Doria Family at Posillipo* (1848), in a private Neapolitan collection.
His finished works are in good condition due to his lengthy preparation and method of work, as we know from records. It took him two years to complete *St. Mark's Square*, and Napier is right when he talks about Vervloet's methodical «perseverance» and the accuracy of the image – for «not only are there arches, statues, friezes, lattice-work, capitals, cornices and all the elements of Classical architecture, described with the greatest precision, but every window of every house in the background has a proper pane of glass; every creeper on the wall, chimney and stone caught in his gaze is a portrait in its own right (*op. cit.* 1956, p. 99). And as Picone adds: «He had two hundred years of Flemish painting behind him... which he neither forgot nor wanted to forget» (1954, p. 12).
During the 1848 rebellion he took shelter in Gaeta, which is the setting for *Pius IX blessing the Artillery* (Museum of San Martino).
He continued to work in Venice, Naples and Leghorn until the fall of the Kingdom of the Two Sicilies, and in 1861 exhibited an *Interior of the Charterhouse of San Martino* in Florence at the Prima Nazionale. He finally settled in Venice and died there in 1872.
There are few paintings which can be definitely attributed to Vervloet, though there are a great many drawings known to be his work – in Naples at the San Martino Museum, in the Lucchesi Palli Collection at the National Library in Naples, at the Società Napoletana di Storia Patria, in Venice at the Correr Museum and in Turin in private collections. [A. P.]

Largo di Castello with the Lighthouse on the Mole
Oil on canvas, 42 x 58, pl. p. 103
Black gilt-edged frame
Signed and dated (bottom right-hand corner): *V. Naples 1825*
Inscription on the wooden frame: *F. Vervloet / Piazza Castello / Naples 1825*
Naples, Museum of San Martino (inv. 13543, purchased on 28-2-1915).

This is one of the three views looking towards and away from the Mole purchased by the Museum of San Martino and part of the collection of paintings. There is a variation of this subject in the Dalla Vecchia Collection, with the addition of many figures and a ship burning at anchor in the port, which is also attributed to Vervloet. [A. P.]

Bibl.: Naples 1936; Naples 1945, cat. 87; Ortolani in Thieme-Backer, Vol. XXXIV, 1940, p. 306; Picone 1954, p. 6; Lavagnino 1956, I, p. 416; Causa 1956, p. 89; Naples 1962, cat. 96; Causa 1967, Pl. XXII, 1972, p. 798.

Villa Doria d'Angri at Posillipo
Oil on canvas, 80 x 100, pl. p. 103, in a gilded wooden frame
Signed and dated (on the left-hand side of the wall)
1848/Naples Vervloet
Naples, private collection

In the manuscript of Frans Vervloet's *Diary*, kept at the library in the Correr Museum of Venice there is an appendix with a list of paintings datable to the 1815-52 period, with details of the client and sale price (see Pittaluga 1970). On the subject of the «six paintings» of 1848 on the back of sheet 12 of the 3rd. folio, Volume I appear the words: «no. 274 for the same client (H.M. the Emperor of Russia) *Vue de Naples prise de Pausillipon avec le palais d'Angri*; 5,000 francs».
From the date and the title of the subject it is evident that this painting of Naples was commissioned by the Tsar, Nicholas I, and it is one of the few works which were actually finished and preserved.
The features on the right-hand side of a drawing entitled *Naples, a View of the Bay*, especially the view of Chiatamone and Castel dell'Ovo and fishermen pulling in their nets (in a private collection in Turin published by Griseri in 1952-53, p. 8, fig. 8) would seem to indicate that it is a preparatory sketch for this painting.

Pierre-Jacques Volaire
(also called Le Chevalier Volaire)
Toulon 1729 – Lerici ? 1792 ?

From a family of painters in Toulon, Volaire was educated locally and began to work when Vernet came to Toulon in 1754, sent by Louis XV to paint the main ports of France. As assistant to Vernet he toured France with him for eight years, from one port to another. His relationship with Vernet influenced his work enormously, though it is not known when exactly he actually began to paint. In 1763 Volaire was still in Toulon, but the following year he is recorded in Italy, where he settled. First of all he visited Rome and was admitted to the Academy of San Luca in 1764. 5 years later he went to Naples and settled there. His first known Neapolitan work (not counting the *Waterfall* at the Museum of Toulon) is *Dance around the Fire*, a preparatory study for *Compiègne by Night*, dated 1770. Some other works also probably date back to this period, like the beautiful veduta by daylight of the *Gajola*, at the Paul Getty Museum. Soon Volaire began to distinguish himself from the many other foreign artists in Naples; mainly because he chose a subject which only one other of Vernet's followers had painted, Lacroix de Marseille. This subject was eruptions of Vesuvius seen at night, in full activity. He specialized in pictures of Vesuvius in the moonlight, exploiting the contrast between the reddish tones of the lava and the cold shades of the night, with reflections of the moon on the waters of the Bay of Naples. This theme, which became immensely popular with travellers on the Grand Tour, was used in many versions – over a dozen for the 1771 eruption observed on the spot and at least six for each of the various «groups» of eruptions he painted: in one case from the Bridge of the Maddalena, and in another seen from Naples.
Volaire exhibited in 1779, 1783 and 1786 at the *Salon de la Correspondance* in Paris, and in 1784 he became a member of the Academy of Marseilles. His last dated works are the *Seascape by Night* at the Royal Palace of Naples (1784) and the *Eruption of Vesuvius* in Toulon (1785). In 1786 he tried in vain to get Louis XVI to purchase his works through the mediation of the Count of Angivillier. He is usually believed to have died in Naples before 1802, but it has been suggested (by J. Foucard, Paris, 1974-75, pp. 666-67) that the *Voler peintre* who died in Lerici around 1790 after being manhandled by Neapolitan guards (cf. *Correspondance des Directeurs,* XVI, 1907, p. 89, & note 2 p. 90) was really Volaire, the specialist in volcanoes. A portrait of «Citoyen Volaire» was etched by Vivant-Denon, who also engraved one of his seascapes by night, while some plates of Saint-Non's *Voyage Pittoresque* are reproductions of Volaire's paintings of the Solfatara and Vesuvius. [P.B.]

Eruption of Vesuvius with the Bridge of the Maddalena
Oil on canvas, 129 x 260, pl. p. 59
Signed and dated *1782*
Naples, Capodimonte Museum

The largest group of works by Volaire of the crater of Vesuvius are painted *sur le lieu,* from the Atrio del Cavallo, and mainly refer to the eruption of 14th. May 1771.
Another set of views show the eruption of 8th. August 1779, clearly identifiable and seen from Naples (Naples, private collection; Paris, Cailleux collection). The viewpoint of another group with the bridge of the Maddalena in the foreground has not yet been identified (to which this particular painting belongs with five copies at the Sannio Museum in Benevento, the Avellino Museum, the Musée des Beaux-Arts of Nantes, Lulworth Manor, and the North Carolina Museum of Art, Raleigh). The Raleigh version, commissioned in 1777 by Henry Blundell, which «is as far as we know the model for the other views» (Spi-

nosa-Di Mauro, no. 108) should not be dated 1769, because there was no eruption that year. Furthermore, the Nantes version ordered or bought by Cacault when he was *chargé d'affaires* in Naples after 1788 is given the improbable date of 1737 by the museum. There is no reason why Volaire, who continually observed the activity of Vesuvius and took it down from life should reconstruct an event which only his master Vernet could have seen. This eruption could be the 1767 one, which severely damaged Portici and forced the king and his court to flee to Naples. William Hamilton writes copiously on this subject in a report to Morton, the Chairman of the Royal Society in London, later published in Hamilton's *Campi Phlegraei* (Naples, 1776, pp. 22-32).
One feature of the view is particularly interesting: over the bridge – where men, women, children, horses and carriages are rushing in all directions, stands only one of the two statues by Francesco Celebrano. It is known that the «miracle-working» statue of San Gennaro (as it was called in contemporary guides to the city) «was erected during the terrible eruption of 1767, which threatened to burn down the city. However, it ceased as soon as the Sacred Head of the Saint was brought there» (Hamilton's words). Thus, this is likely to be a record of that year. What is certain, is that the Capodimonte painting (signed 1782) is later than the «model» and even though the sizes vary slightly of the various versions, there are very few real differences (except for the unsigned version at Avellino) and they must be considered copies.
The scene of the eruption is grandiose and spectacular, with the long red lava flow working its way across the dark slope of the volcano and threatening the inhabitants of Portici, where the buildings are illuminated by the light of the flames. The Bridge of the Maddalena is crowded with people trying to escape from the villages on the slopes of Vesuvius, portrayed with a wealth of carefully drawn details. The odd explorer or figure consumed by curiosity who was daring enough to follow the eruption from the top of the volcano present in other paintings by Volaire has no place in this scene, which is pervaded by a general state of panic.
Similar scenes of people fleeing for shelter towards Naples can be seen in other artists, for example in Desprez. This artist made a set of large engravings with Francesco Piranesi, painted in watercolour and representing the 1779 eruption, where two small altars can be clearly seen over the bridge with statues of San Gennaro and San Giovanni Nepomuceno by Francesco Celebrano.
Volaire's fascinating use of colour is based on the play between dark tones of the night, the hot ones of lava and fires caused by the eruption and the cold shades of ethereal moonlight which are strikingly reflected on the clouds and the waves.
Connected with the Capodimonte painting and the set belonging to it is a small *Eruption* in the D'Angelo collection in Naples with Castel dell'Ovo in the centre and a procession of foundlings called in to pray for the eruption to stop, an example of local colour on a kind of bridge, which provides a contrast with the people fleeing in the opposite direction (Marina Causa Picone, *Volaire,* in «Antologia di Belle Arti», 5, 1978, p. 39 & fig. 22). [P.B.]

Bibl.: Spinosa-Di Mauro 1989, p. 196; no. 108.

Neapolitan Seascape by Night
Oil on canvas, 131.5 x 235, pl. p. 59
Signed and dated: *Peint par le chevalier Volaire 1784*
Naples, Royal Palace (inv. 4192)

After being deposited with the Avvocatura dello Stato in 1952, this large view subsequently became part of the Royal Palace's art collections and was published by Marina Causa Picone in her essay on Volaire (see «Antologia di Belle Arti», 5, 1978, pp. 24-48) and displayed in the 18th. century in Naples exhibition (cf. catalogue no. 81). This is a large copy of a painting which is one of a pair showing an imaginary landscape by day at the Castle of Compiègne, signed and dated 1770, for which a preparatory study survives in the Louvre. As Raffaello Causa observed, analyzing the differences between the two works, when fourteen years later Volaire decided to add some new details to the figures of local people dancing round the bonfire to the sound of the *tricheballacche* – «the setting of the painting, typically theatrical, was copied wholesale». Here there are elements clearly drawn from real life and from Volaires's imagination in this charming genre scene painted by night down by the seashore in Naples. However, from a topographical point of view it should be pointed out that the ridge rising behind the lighthouse on the mole and the rather strange-looking «square building with the statue of San Gennaro on the top» actually face the other way, and this view of Coroglio in other works by Volaire appears further back. This is one of the last works definitely known to be by Volaire, in fact only one later one survives dated 1785, an *Eruption of Vesuvius* at the Museum of Toulon. [P.B.]

Richard Wilson
Penegoes 1713 – Colomendy 1782

Born in Wales, he was the son of an Anglican clergyman who gave him a classical education and encouraged his interest in art. From 1729 until about 1735 Wilson was apprenticed to a minor portrait painter in London, Thomas Wright. By 1737 he had begun to paint landscapes, but practised chiefly as a portraitist. In 1750 Wilson travelled to Italy, where he stayed until 1756 or 7. According to an early biographer, Wilson left England «more with a view to improvement in that branch of art which he had hitherto professed [i.e. portraiture], than with any intention of devoting himself to another», but during a year-long stay in Venice his earlier interest in landscape painting was rekindled, and encouraged by Zuccarelli and subsequently by Claude Joseph Vernet in Rome, where he had arrived by the end of 1751, largely abandoning portraiture.
The influence of Claude, Gaspard Dughet and their followers was to be critical in the development of his style. He also profited from the practice of sketching from nature, and by the time he returned to England he had succeeded in combining his experience as a landscape draughtsman with the knowledge gained from close study of the classical tradition of landscape painting. Italy formed him as a painter in the Grand Style, committing him to the notion of ideal beauty, but also developed in him a sensibility and vision new in British painting. In Rome his chief patrons were British noblemen on the Grand Tour, notably the young Earl of Dartmouth, who in 1753 commissioned two large paintings of Rome and in the following year a series of around seventy finished drawings of the city and its surroundings. There is little documentary evidence of Wilson's movements outside Rome, but a sketchbook used by him in 1752 (Victoria and Albert Museum, London) includes four views of Vesuvius and shows also that he visited Herculaneum.
Wilson returned to Naples at least once in 1753-4 and perhaps again in 1756, to judge from two signed and dated sketches of a smoking crater, almost certainly Vesuvius (Royal Academy, London). On one of these visits he must have spent some time in the neighbourhood of Pozzuoli and Baiae, as well as Lake Avernus and Agnano and the islands of Ischia and Capri, all of which were later to provide him with the subjects of several paintings. On his return to England, probably in 1757, Wilson established a busy studio in London, painting many views based on drawings made in Italy, as well as English and Welsh landscapes. He elevated the country house portrait, long popular in England, to a new art form in which atmosphere and mood was as important as precise description. Historical landscapes were another aspect of his oeuvre, and in paintings such as *The Destruction of the Children of Niobe*, exhibited in 1760, inspired by Vernet and Gaspard Dughet, Wilson set out to show that a British-born artist could rival the Continental masters of Grand Style landscape art. Active in efforts to improve the status of painting and painters in England, Wilson took a leading part in the affairs of the Incorporated Society of Artists from its founding in 1759, one of the country's earliest exhibiting bodies, and in 1768 he was a founder member of the Royal Academy. Wilson was important as a teacher; among his pupils was Thomas Jones who studied with him between 1763 and 1765. Jones's first exhibited paintings were historical landscapes in the style of his master, and it was probably Wilson who inspired him with the idea of going to Italy. As he later recalled, «I had copied so many Studies of that great Man, & my Old Master, Richard Wilson, which he had made... in Italy, that I insensibly became familiarized with Italian scenes, and enamoured of Italian forms». By the mid-1770s, there was a decline in Wilson's health and fortunes, and he was given the post of Librarian of the Royal Academy in 1776 to ease his straitened circumstances at a time when he had almost ceased to paint. However, his posthumous influence on the generation of Constable and Turner ensures

his position as a key figure in the development of British landscape art. [L.S.]

Lake Avernus
Oil on canvas, 47 x 72.4, pl. p. 60
Tate Gallery, London

Wilson's view is taken from the north shore of Lake Avernus, looking southeast beyond the so-called Temple of Apollo and Monte Nuovo on the left, over the Gulf of Pozzuoli towards Capri in the distance; part of the peninsula of Baiae juts out into the sea in the far right distance. Lake Avernus, the abode of the Cumaean Sibyl, the site of Aeneas's descent into the underworld, was celebrated in Classical literature and thus became in the eighteenth century an almost mandatory excursion from Naples for any traveller on the Grand Tour. This painting, which can be dated on stylistic grounds c. 1760, was almost certainly based on a drawing (British Museum, London) made c. 1754-6, when the artist was living in Italy.
Wilson's chief achievement in his paintings of Italian scenes, however, lay in avoiding both the banality of simple topographical description and the over-obvious devices of pastiche. His subtle interpretation of the seventeenth century landscape tradition – he later said he admired Claude for «air» and Gaspard Dughet for «composition» – fused with his sensitivity to place and association to evoke a heightened sense of emotion and recollection in the spectator. [L.S.]

Bibl.: London 1982, pp. 203-204, no. 90.

Gaspar Van Wittel
Amersfoort 1652/53 – Rome 1736

Considered unanimously by the critics to be the founder of the new 18th. century conception of the veduta, Gaspar Van Wittel revolutionized the conceptual and objective premises of this genre and opened the way for the various schools which were to become famous in landscape painting in the most important Italian cities.
In fact Luigi Lanzi, a well-known historian writing at the turn of the 19th. century defines him «the painter of modern Rome», comparing Van Wittel's novel interest in features of contemporary Rome and everyday life with the importance of archeology and the typical portrayal of ancient monuments, which until then had been the established theme of landscape painting.
His journey to Rome around 1674 was practically *de rigueur* for an artist of the times, especially from Northern Europe. He had studied art in Utrecht, one of the most important centres working in the Italian style in the Dutch provinces with Mathias Withoos, painter of landscapes and still-lifes, who had visited Italy in the 1650's.
As soon as Van Wittel reached Rome he came into contact with the circle of Northern European artists already working there, called the *Schildersbent* – a group which was opposed to the official academic circles. Soon after he was employed as a draughtsman and topographer by a Dutch engineer Cornelis Meyer, who had come to Rome for the jubilee and owing to his knowledge of navigation had been asked by Pope Clement X to give his views as a consultant regarding the possibility of re-opening part of the Tiber between Perugia and Rome. To this period belongs the group of fifty drawings in which Van Wittel illustrates Meyer's project, presented to the Pope in 1676, probably all of the same date and drawn on his return to Rome from notes taken during his survey of the river.
Van Wittel's approach to composition varied very little and he was to use this *modus operandi* all through his career – first he made a simple sketch from life, then made a more complete drawing later usually in pencil and larger in size, highlighting in ink and at times in light-coloured washes which he then used as the basis either for oil paintings, a group of temperas much smaller in size or miniatures on vellum. The recurrent accent on the horizontal in his paintings is deliberate and is dictated by the sweeping vistas he liked, which are so lifelike and clearly-cut.
His preparatory drawings for most of his views of Rome date back to the 1680's and the viewpoints are totally new, later used over and over again but with very slight variations with a new focus on the scene that in no way alters the viewpoint. Of course, this method of work meant filling up sheets and sheets of paper.
To these years also belong the first temperas and oils of views of Rome. This large group of works with their transparent tones are based on the Tiber theme and show particular interest in everyday life taking place along the river-bank, which is decidedly an innovation for the times.
In the 1690's Van Wittel was in Northern Italy, as we know from his paintings of Lake Maggiore (seen from the Borromeo islands), Vaprio d'Adda, Verona, Venice, Bologna and Florence. His visit to Venice probably took place in 1695 and was extremely significant, as it inspired the local school of landscape painting. It was Van Wittel, in fact, whose novel angles and unusual compositions helped to found that great tradition that was to come to its climax with Canaletto and Bellotto.
Now Van Wittel was gaining fame all the time and was becoming more expert in landscape painting. In 1700 he was invited to Naples by the viceroy Don Luis de Cerda, Duke of Medinaceli, who must have met the artist and liked his work when he was in Rome as the King of Spain's ambassador to Pope Innocent XII. The viceroy had an ambitious plan – the recording of all the most important features of Naples and in particular new urban development which he had planned. However, political upheavals in the kingdom caused by the conspiracy of the Prince of Marchia, which the Austrians were behind, made Van Wittel leave the city fast, though he did return there later from time to time. Of 1700 there are records of the christening of the artist's first born, Luigi – later to become a great architect, with Don Luis acting as godfather.
The warm sunny Mediterranean light of Naples and the variety of nature and local colour gave Van Wittel many of his most successful ideas. A large number of his views of Naples were later finished in Rome, using material which he had collected from life. He was particularly skilful in portraying with great precision and intelligence the better and lesser known features of the city, now immortalized in his compositions. The most famous of these are – *Largo di Palazzo* (the oldest version is dated 1701) painted on copper and canvas; *Galleys in the Port* (1702) also copied several times with very slight variations; and a view of the city seen from the sea with the imposing shape of Castel dell'Ovo flooded by sunlight. Paintings which show features which were less traditional, but which were beginning to become popular are – the newly landscaped Riviera di Chiaia with trees and fountains ordered by Medinaceli; the novel view of the hill of Pizzofalcone looking towards Mergellina (only recently identified); the city seen from Posillipo, a theme which was to have great success; and last but not least the Phlegrean countryside, painted with spontaneity and simplicity. Van Wittel's painting is not «commemorative» or academic – he takes down the facts, perceiving them «as an inseparable whole... containing a wide variety of scenes from everyday life and the different features of the urban landscape» (Spinosa in Spinosa-Di Mauro 1989, p. 17). It is this blend of reality and humanity that makes Van Wittel so innovative, compared to traditional landscapists.
In Naples and in Venice Van Wittel's presence was a decisive factor for new trends in the veduta, which although they were not to develop immediately, and were also due to the contribution of the foreign artists who flocked to these cities, paved the way for local schools specializing in landscape painting around mid-century. Van Wittel was well aware how much Naples had inspired his work, because when he was admitted to the Academy of San Luca in 1711 he chose for his diploma piece one of his Neapolitan landscapes – one of the many views of the port, probably the version now kept at the Pinacoteca in Turin and dated the same year (Briganti 1866, p. 137).
His official recognition and fortune were continuing to grow. Van Wittel started what could almost be described as an early attempt at «mass production» in this field (though with the help of his assistants). This was necessary to meet the demands of his many clients and explains why so many copies of one subject were made. His copies though were never cold and calculating, and were all perfectly complete in the minutest of details which was typical of Northern European painters, and the care he used in his work emerges from correspondence with his clients. This «fixed image» was the only real flaw in a long career, though it was more common in his later works, also due to bad sight.
On two views of 1712, next to his signature appear the words *degli occhiali* (with glasses) for the first time, which are to become a characteristic of his. In fact during the last years of his life he suffered from cataracts but they did not stop him from working altogether. His last work is dated 1730 and is a view of Villa Pamphili in Rome. He

died on 13th. Semptember 1736 and was buried at Santa Maria in Vallicella. By this time Italian landscape painting, inspired by his enormous contribution, had begun to bear its first fruits. Soon after Naples would become one of the centres of this genre, following in the footsteps of that distinctive blend of nature and local colour so typical of Van Wittel. [M.U.]

Largo di Palazzo
Oil on canvas, 75 x 125, pl. p. 34
Banca Commerciale Italiana

This scene and the *Galleys in the Port* are the ones used most frequently by Van Wittel because of the importance of these landmarks. At the Museum of San Martino a smaller version is kept of this scene, from which six known copies were made. These include the Banca Commerciale one on display here (the largest in size), one in a private Roman collection which is slightly smaller initialled and dated 1701 and thus one of the oldest known pieces of work by Van Wittel (Briganti 1966, p. 249, no. 199); another version also dated 1701 at the Cincinnati Art Museum; two more with a wider view in Naples in the Avallone collection (Spinosa 1987, p. 154, no. 263) and another one on copper which is much smaller (14 x 18.5), sold by Christies on 27th. June 1983, lot 146. [M.U.]

Bibl.: Causa Picone, Naples 1962, p. 87, Pl. IV; Doria 1964, pp. 16-18, Pl. IV-XIII; Briganti 1966, p. 249, no. 200; Causa 1966, pp. 175-81; Causa Picone, Naples 1979-80, I, p. 412; Utili, Venice-Milan 1987, p. 18, no. 7; Middione, Edinburgh 1988, p. 17, no. 10; Spinosa in Spinosa-Di Mauro 1989, p. 188, no. 26, Pl. 7; Bacchi, Rome 1989, pp. 66-67, no. 11.22. [M.U.]

The Port
Oil on canvas, 48 x 62, pl. p. 34
Initialled and dated: *G.V.W. 1702*
Naples, Museum of San Martino

This is the oldest version of the Port, the one which was most frequently copied by Van Wittel during his life. Compared to the others, which are more faithful to the preparatory sketch at San Martino (Briganti 1966, p. 301, no. 106; Vitzthum, Gaeta 1980, p. 168, no. 75, Pl. 75) this version is foreshortened, which makes the castle (Maschio Angioino) seem more imposing. The same technique is used in the version at Holkham Hall, initialled and dated 1711. This painting was purchased by the Italian State in 1915 from the dealer Simonetti. [M.U.]

Bibl.: Lorenzetti 1934, p. 49; Causa Picone, Naples 1962, p. 87, no. 104, Pl. 6; Briganti 1966, p. 246, no. 191; Spinosa in Spinosa-Di Mauro 1989, p. 189, no. 29, Pl. 10.

The Port
Oil on canvas, 58 x 119, pl. p. 35
Signed and dated: *Gaspar Van Wittel Parthenope 1711*
Turin, Galleria Sabauda

This version of the Port is probably the finest as regards the quality of the painting and the composition of all the eighteen other versions of this theme known today. The dates range from 1702 (the San Martino version) to 1718, which appears next to the initials on a canvas sold at Sothebys on 19th. April 1989 (Spinosa in Spinosa-Di Mauro 1989, p. 189, nos. 29-30). In addition to the eight versions mentioned by Briganti in 1966 (pp. 246-8), nos. 191-98) over the years three more versions have come to light in private Neapolitan collections. The versions include one signed with Greek letters; a smaller one at the Gemäldegalerie in Berlin; one on copper in Zürich at Iduna Inc.; one at Kedleston Hall; one at Petworth House in Sussex; one sold at the Johnston sale at Christies on 20th. February 1925; one belonging to Colnaghi recently auctioned by Semenzato (sale of 13-12-1989, no. 129), and finally one sold by Sothebys on 19th. April 1989, already mentioned because it is dated 1718.
The Turin version is signed on the fountain at the centre of the picture and on the bale next to it is the inscription Parthenope - the old Greek name of Naples. This painting was Van Wittel's diploma piece when his application to become a member of the Academy of San Luca had been accepted in 1711 (Briganti 1966, p. 137). [M.U.]

Bibl.: Lorenzetti 1934, p. 55; Causa Picone, Naples 1962, p. 87, no. 102; Briganti 1966, p. 247, no. 195.

Chiaia from Pizzofalcone *
Oil on canvas, 75 x 174, pl. p. 38
Milan, private collection

Identified by Nicola Spinosa as Van Wittel's work, and dating back to his first stay in Naples, this painting is the only known view of the Chiaia area from this viewpoint, with the sea lapping the Riviera in the foreground, the beautiful Palazzo Cellammare and its gardens, and the many buildings scattered over the hill in the background with San Martino and Castel Sant'Elmo.
This view is particularly original - in fact as so often happens there is no precedent in the history of Neapolitan landscape painting and this viewpoint was not used again; the only other painting which depicts Chiaia, but from behind and only partially, is by Leonardo Coccorante (1739), which is a view from Calascione sweeping round the hill as far as Posillipo. A later copy of Van Wittel's painting, definitely not by the artist himself, is at the San Martino Museum in Naples. [M.U.]

View of the Chiaia District towards Mergellina
Oil on canvas, 50.5 x 104, pl. p. 36
Signed: *Gas van Wittel*

Naples from the sea
Oil on canvas, 48.5 x 102.7, pl. p. 36
Initialled and dated: *G.V.W. 1719*
Florence, Palazzo Pitti, Galleria Palatina

These two paintings, with a view of Albano dated 1710 and one of Verona were purchased in 1954 by the Superintendency for Art of Florence. In the bottom right-hand corner of the two on display is the coat-of-arms of the Colonna family. These pictures were originally part of an old collection belonging to this family including many other works by Van Wittel.
Another version in oils of the Chiaia scene is also in the same collection (Briganti 1966, p. 250, no. 203) of which there is a copy in tempera on vellum (op. cit. no. 204); another version in tempera is at the Landesmuseum in Kassel. The preparatory sketch is kept at Chatsworth.
Naples from the Sea is a very original work because it breaks away from the traditional canon of landscape painting which had been the axis running from Castel dell'Ovo to Castel Sant'Elmo since the 15th. century and the *Tavola Strozzi* (Di Mauro in Spinosa-Di Mauro 1989, p. 159. The preparatory sketch, with a light wash in watercolour is at the San Martino Museum (Briganti 1966, p. 300, no. 102d; Vitzthum, Gaeta 1980, p. 170, no. 76). Another version from the same viewpoint with slight variations in the boats out at sea, once in the Dukes of Medinaceli collection, now belongs to the Duchess of Lerma, San Roque near Cadiz (Spinosa in Spinosa-Di Mauro 1989, p. 189, no. 31, fig. 27). This model was used several times by Van Lint. [M.U.]

Bibl.: Chiarelli 1954, p. 109; Briganti 1966, pp. 249-50, nos. 201 and 202; Zampetti, Venice 1967, p. 26, no. 11; Susinno 1974, p. 80, and Pl. 14; Spinosa in Spinosa-Di Mauro 1989, no. 28, Pl. 8 & 9.

The Hill of Pizzofalcone
Sorrento
Oil on canvas, 71 x 123 each, pl. p. 37
Toledo, Hospital de Tavera

A set composed of these two paintings, plus two more scenes showing *Posillipo with Palazzo Donn'Anna* and *Naples from the Sea with Castel dell'Ovo*, part of the collection of the Duchess of Lerma at San Roque, Cadiz (Spinosa in Spinosa-Di Mauro 1989, p. 189, no. 31, figs. 26 & 27) and another two paintings of *Nisida and Cape Miseno* and *Nisida* (Seville, Fundacion Casa Ducal de Medinaceli) all used to belong to the Dukes of Medinaceli's collection in Seville, until they were scattered among various heirs. When Spinosa published them for the first time he connected them with the works commissioned from Van Wittel by the Spanish Viceroy who requested his presence in Naples - Don Luis de la Cerda, Duke of Medinaceli.
However, it was not possible to locate all six of the paintings until very recently, on the occasion of the exhibition on landscape painting in Naples. A group of drawings is related to these paintings - *Nisida,* formerly in the Rausch collection and now in a private Roman collection and displayed in the Naples exhibition (Briganti 1966, p. 277, no. 33d); *Mount Echia, Chiatamone and Castel dell'Ovo* at the San Martino Museum, which is smaller than the Toledo painting (Briganti 1966, p. 305, no. 132d; Vitzhum, Gaeta 1980, p. 162, no. 72); and finally the drawing of *The Bay of Pozzuoli,* signed and dated 1701, also at San Martino (Briganti 1966, p. 305, no. 131d; Vitzhum, Gaeta 1980, p. 150, no. 66) which although it cannot be considered a preparatory sketch for either of the two Seville paintings does show the same places from a viewpoint near the one used in *Nisida and*

Cape Miseno. At the Hospital de Tavera in Toledo there are two more scenes by Van Wittel of *Piazza Navona* and *St. Mark's Square*. [M.U.]

Bibl.: Spinosa in Spinosa-Di Mauro 1989, p. 189, no. 31, figs. 26-29.

Joseph Wright of Derby
Derby 1734-1797

Unusually for an eighteenth century artist who achieved considerable contemporary recognition, Wright spent the greater part of his career not in London, but in his native town of Derby. The son of an attorney, Wright trained between 1751 and 1753 and 1756 to 1757 in the studio of the fashionable portrait painter Thomas Hudson, whose pupils had included Joshua Reynolds, the future president of the Royal Academy.
Wright's early portraits inevitably reflected the influence of his master, and it was this metropolitan style that he took back to Derby, where he established a successful practice by 1760. His patrons were drawn from the local gentry and from the newly emerging middle classes whose prosperity derived from innovatory manufacturing processes.
In the 1760s, inspired by Rembrandt, Honthorst, Terbruggen and Shalken – and thus, ultimately, by Caravaggio – Wright began to move away from straightforward portraiture, painting a series of subject pictures showing darkened interiors with figures illuminated by lamplight or candlelight. These he exhibited from 1765 at the Society of Artists in London, the chief public showplace until the Royal Academy's first exhibition in 1769. Then subject matter was entirely novel in British art, and included the representation of contemporary scientific and industrial activities. Many of Wright's local friends and patron (who included Erasmus Darwin, doctor and philospher; John Whitehurst, clockmaker and geologist; Peter Perez Burtlett, cartographer and early aquatinter; Richard Arkwright, textile industrialist; and Josiah Wedgwood, who revolutionised the manufacture of ceramics) were intimately concerned, either as proprietors of industrial concerns, or as scientists or inventors, with the latest technological development. In paintings such as *A Philosopher lecturing on the Orrery*, 1766, *An experiment on a Bird in the Air Pump*, 1768, *The Iron Forge*, 1772, and *An Iron Forge viewed from without*, 1773, Wright expressed much of this enthusiasm for progress.
In November 1773, an established artist aged thirty-nine, he left for a visit to Italy, accompanied by his bride of four months, a pupil, Richard Hurleston (1763-1780) and the portrait miniaturist John Downman (1750-1824). They travelled by sea, reaching Nice in early December, where they stayed until the end of the month, and arrived in Rome on 3 February 1774. Like many fellow artists, Wright lodged near the Trinità dei Monti, and devoted himself to the study of classical antiquity and the work of Michelangelo. From Wright's correspondance with his family we know that he visited Naples in early October 1774, returning to Rome by 11 November. Above all else, the sight of Vesuvius impressed him most deeply, and he made several high-detailed studies on the spot. Other careful drawings of grottoes along the coast between Naples and Salerno later served as the basis for paintings.
Wright left Rome in June 1775, returning to England by way of Florence, Bologna, Venice, Parma, Turin and France, arriving in London by the end of September.
The most important effect of his travels had been a broadering of his subject matter to include classical and literary subjects (he had attempted one or two themes from ancient history previously, but without great success), and most importantly, landscape, which was to become a major element in his work. Italian views, notably of Vesuvius, the Girandola in Rome, Virgil's Tomb by moonlight, and recollections of the Campagna, provided him with themes for the next two decades, and inspired him to paint his native Derbyshire in equally distinctive style.
For two years after his return to England, Wright lived in Bath, hoping to fill the place of Gainsborough who had moved to London in 1774. Lacking Gainsborough's fluent elegance, he returned once more to Derby, where he stayed until his death. He exhibited at the Royal Academy between 1778 and 1794, but although he was elected an Associate in 1781, he quarrelled with the Academy and never became a full member.

Vesuvius
Oil on canvas, 42.5 x 71, pl. p. 61
Great Britain, Private collection

Before visiting Italy, Wright had painted few landscapes. His experience of Italian scenery, however, was to have a profound influence on his work; almost until the year of his death, his rimembrance of Lake Nemi and Lake Albano, the grottoes of the coast near Salerno, and most of all, the natural spectacle of Vesuvius and the man-made spectacle of Roman firework displays, the Girandola, were to provide subjects for pictures.
Like his earlier paintings which showed figures illuminated by lamps of candlelight in darkened interiors, his landscapes are characterised by a distinctive taste for dramatic pictorial effects, most evident in the complementary themes of volcanic eruptions and fireworks displays, «the one of the greatest effects of Nature, the other of Art that I suppose can be», as he noted.
Although Wright spent only a few weeks in Naples, between early October and early November 1774, the sight of Vesuvius was to inspire around thirty views of the spectacle. According to Sir William Hamilton, there had been no major eruption between 1776 and 1777, but he noted «Vesuvius has never been free from smoke, nor ever many mouths without throwing up red hot scoriae... usually follow'd by a current of liquid lava» (Hamilton 1779, Supplement p. 2) and «at Naples, when a lava appears, and not till then, it is styled an eruption» (Hamilton 1772, p. 20). Wright himself, in a letter to his brother written on 11 November 1774, was certainly impressed by what he saw: «there was a very considerable eruption at that time, of which I am going to make a picture. 'Tis the most wonderful sight in nature'». A painstaking and meticulous pencil sketch of the sloped of Vesuvius (Derby Art Gallery) made on the spot, attests to Wright's careful observation of the volcano, and was later used by him for reference, though for the more dramatic aspects of his Vesuvian paintings, he may have been indebted to the works of other artists who specialised in the subject, notably Pierre-Jacques Volaire, Pietro Fabris and Michael Wutky. However, Wright's depictions of fire and cascades of molten lava lighting up the night sky expressed not only a powerful and original aesthetic sensibility but also a keen scientific interest in natural phenomena.
Among Wright's friends was John Whitehurst (1713-1788), who from the mid 1760s was engaged in writing a geological treatise, *An Inquiry into the original State and Formation of the Earth*, published in 1778. Whitehurst, who drew on Sir William Hamilton's *Observations on Mount Vesuvius*, 1772, believed that a vast subterranean sea of fire existed beneath the surface of the Earth, occasionally manifesting itself in volcanic activity. As Wright wrote to his brother, «Remember me with respect to all my friends; when you see Whitehurst, tell him I wished for his company when on Mount Vesuvius his thoughts would have center'd in the bowels of the mountain, mine skimmed over the surface only». Benedict Nicolson believed that this was one of the few oil paintings actually executed during Wright's stay in Italy, dating from shortly after his return to Rome in November 1774. In size, technique and general feeling it corresponds to a view of the *Girandola* in Birmingham City Art Gallery (Nicolson 249). Both share a quality of first hand observation and are less overtly dramatic than later interpretations. Neverthless, *Vesuvius* is a carefully composed and balanced panorama design, in which foregrounds elements – notably the lighthouse on the Mole – are contrasted against the more distant volcano. Here, as in several pictures painted before he visited Italy, Wright has introduced a secondary light source, the moon in a clearing of clouds, offsetting the brilliance of Vesuvius.

Bibl.: Hamilton 1772; Hamilton 1779; Nicolson 1968, I, pp. 10, 76-79, 280, no. 273; II, p. 167; Sudbury 1987, pp. 11-12, no. 31.

Carlo Schisano
Saint Irene
Silver and gilt copper; ht. 120, pl. p. 105
Marked: NAP 1733, C.S., G.B.C.
With the inscription: *A. D 1732*
Naples, Chapel of the Treasure of San Gennaro

Adorned with a magnificent cloak decorated with arabesques, her gaze bent heavenwards, Saint Irene stops the lightning from striking Naples, which is symbolized by a likeness of the city held by a cherub in gilt-copper. Attached to the waist of the statue are the reliquaries of the saint, fashioned in gilt-copper like the base, and at the sides are scrolls in silver bearing the date 1732. According to records, this statue was a gift from the city when Saint Irene was made one of the patron saints in 1719, which encouraged the growth of popular devotion. After casting, the silver was chased and modelled by Carlo Schisano, as we know from the assay mark and records. On the statue and likeness of the city are the consular stamps of Geronimo di Benedetto and Art. Saint Irene has only been in the San Gennaro Chapel since 1760.
The theme of an angel holding a city dates back to a mediaeval tradition. This particular model of Naples is simplistic, showing only the most important landmarks, chosen for reasons of perspective and visual impact. The city is seen from the east, from the sea and at the observer's eye level. This is a panoramic view of the city, embracing the Molo Grande with the lighthouse and the small fort of San Gennaro, the tower of San Vincenzo deceptively seeming to rise up behind, and the bridge of the Maddalena which marks the boundary with the Vesuvian area. Famous landmarks which can be recognized are: Castel Nuovo with its bastions, the campanile of the church of Il Carmine, the dome of the Treasure Chapel and higher up the remains of the walls marking the boundary of the Charterhouse, which can be seen next to Castel Sant'Elmo. In the background the hill of Camaldoli rises up with the Hermitage, usually chosen to represent the skyline in views from the east [M.I.C.].

Bibl.: Bellucci 1915, p. 97; E.e C. Catello 1972, pp. 73, 120, 238; E.e C. Catello 1973, pp. 98, 150, 195, 280; E.e C. Catello 1974, p. 36; E.e C. Catello 1977, p. 85; E.e C. Catello 1980, II, p. 221; A. Catello 1987, p. 32; Di Mauro in Spinosa-Di Mauro 1989, p. 147.

Royal Porcelain Factory of Naples (Real Fabbrica)
Known as the Oca Service or Service with Neapolitan Views

A considerable part of the service which usually goes by the name of Oca (or the service «with Neapolitan views» as Nivi calls it) is kept at Capodimonte and comprises over four hundred pieces, all made of soft paste. The service was probably made for the Bourbon court and manufacture can be dated around 1793-1795 on the basis of records referring to the continual pressure brought to bear by the Vedore del Real Ramaglietto aimed at getting hold of a complete dinner service with the help of the House Steward. The final request on record is dated 1792. This date is borne out by the decoration, which consists of a gilded border with an oval pattern framing the scenes, beautifully designed but not of superior technical quality. It was not until 1806 in fact, that the Real Fabbrica achieved its best decorations using gilding.
The name used to denote the service today – Oca – derives from the handles of some of the tureen covers which are small replicas of a sculpture of a *Child strangling a Goose*, a Roman copy of a Greek piece, now at the Capitoline Museum. Other pieces have handles after the fashion of another Classical prototype from the same museum – the *Child with a Mask of Silenus*.
The leitmotiv of the service is the decoration, which is defined as *vedute obligate*, meaning scenes within rectangular, oval and square panels in accordance with the shape of the piece and complete with decorations of floral festoons and red and gilt bands. This kind of decoration can be seen in the Farnesian Service made during the early years of Venuti's management of the factory and it became popular in later years, for example in the 1807 inventories a service for the Royal Palace of Caserta is cited comprising over fifty pieces and decorated with scenes (Strazzullo 1979, pp. 195-97).
These fine views of Naples and the Kingdom of the Two Sicilies were inspired by contemporany engravings in volumes by Cardon, Sir William Hamilton and the Abbé de Saint-Non, published between 1764 and 1786, though paintings by Antonio Joli and Philipp Hackert were also used as models. In fact, some views by Hackert of the *Ports of the Kingdom* were copied, commissioned by the King in 1787 (for example on the ice-box – inv.no. 5606 – the ports of Gaeta and Palermo appear). The *Voyage Pittoresque* was also widely used, as is proven by the inventory of sales of the Real Fabbrica dated 1807 which shows prints, drawings and also»... three volumes of the *Voyage Pittoresque* minus the engravings which have been removed to be used as models by the painters...».
The small scenes of the Oca service have been attributed to Giacomo Milani (who was a painter at the factory from 1775 onwards and in charge of decoration between 1790 and 1797) but on closer examination it appears evident that not all the scenes were painted by the same artist. What is more likely is that many of the scenes of Naples like the Piazza Vescovado and Trinità Maggiore were designed by Milani in 1783 in his spare time, as later on coast and hill scenes were more popular (Minieri Riccio 1878 c, pp. 46-51).
The design of the Oca service was used again in simpler forms, like the Fleur-de-lys Service and in some solitaires and cups belonging to many public and private collections. Other plates from the same series are at the Fondazione Cagnola at La Gazzada and the Filangieri Museum in Naples.

a) *Ice-box*
Polychrome porcelain with gilding
ht. 35 cm, pl. p. 106
Marked N with a blue crown
Naples, Museum of Capodimonte
(Inv. no. 5603)

The ice-box consists of three pieces – the base which contained ice, the bowl for the sorbet and the cover with a handle resembling the standing figure of an Egyptian idol or athlete now at the entrance to the Pio-Clementino Museum in the Vatican. The whole piece is derived from the *epichysis* which was a small cylindrical long-necked jug used to hold oil made by the Italic tribes around the IV century B.C. often found in tombs. This form was used for the Etruscan Service and others. It is known that in August 1804 one of the factory craftsmen, Antonio Sorrentino, was working on «two Egyptian figures for the covers of ice-boxes», and a «cherub and mask for the covers of jars» though the modellers often exchanged their work when moulding. The scenes bear the following inscriptions in red: *View of the Queen's Mansion in the Street called Crocelle* and *Partial View of the Portico of Pompeii*. The former is an unusual view of this mansion which originally belonged to the Prince of Francavilla (who died in 1782) and later purchased by Ferdinand IV. The building was believed to have been destroyed when work was carried out on Via Caracciolo (De Filippis 1952, pp. 97-99) but recently it has been discovered that the building still stands behind the Faculty of Economics and Commerce (Knight 1986; G. and A.M. Guerra 1989).

b) *Bottle cooler*
Polychrome porcelain with gilding
ht. 21 cm, diam. 18.5 cm, pl. p. 106
Marked N with a blue crown
Naples, Museum of Capodimonte
(Inv. no. 5610)

This bucket-shaped piece is identical to a bronze vessel found at Herculaneum and illustrated in Vol. II of Saint-Non's *Voyage Pittoresque* (p. 48). The gilded porcelain base is composed of a ring with three feet in the shape of griffins and is a perfect copy of the prototype from Herculaneum even in the workmanship.
The scenes bear the inscriptions: *Piazza e Chiesa della Trinità Maggiore* and *Piazza della Porta piccola del Vescovato*.

c) *Glass cooler*
Polychrome porcelain with gilding
ht. 18 cm, diam. 30 cm, pl. p. 106
Marked N with a blue crown
Naples, Museum of Capodimonte
(Inv. no. 921)

This piece was inspired, at least in part, by an object found during exacavations. The button-shaped pommels at the sides are a copy of the handles on an Italic plate with red figures dating back to the 4th. century B.C. and now kept at the National Museum of Naples.
This object was also the inspiration for the glass coolers belonging to the Etruscan Service. Here the pommels are alternated with small doves and mark where the base of the glass would stand. For the feet in the shape of lions' paws and the lower part with

strigliata and the handles, forms were chosen which are typical of metal working. This piece is composed of two parts – one is cylindrical and made on a potter's wheel, the other part which is placed underneath is moulded and they were luted before firing. It bears the following inscription in red: *Veduta di Napoli da sopra Capodimonte* and *Veduta di una parte del golfo di Napoli.*

d) *Triangular Plate*
Polychrome porcelain with gilding
ht. 25 cm, pl. p. 107
Marked N with a blue crown
Naples, Museum of Capodimonte
(Inv. no. 5152)

The inscription in red reads: *Salita di S. Efrem Vecchio*

e) *Square Plate*
Polychrome porcelain with gilding
27 x 27 cm, pl. p. 107
Unmarked
Naples, Museum of Capodimonte
(Inv. no. 5761)

The edges are slightly fluted so as to highlight the corners. The inscription reads: *Veduta del prospetto della chiesa di S. Giovanni a Carbonara.*

f) *Large Oval Plate*
Polychrome porcelain with gilding
18 x 24 cm, pl. p. 107
Unmarked
Naples, Museum of Capodimonte
(Inv. no. 5614)

On this plate is a copy of an engraving from Volume II (PI. 81) of the *Voyage Pittoresque*: *Vue du Tombeau dela Pretze.se Mamia a Pompei*, engraved by Pars and drawn by Desprez.

g) *Round Plate*
Polychrome porcelain with gilding
diam. 36.3 cm, pl. p. 107
Unmarked
Naples, Museum of Capodimonte
(Inv. no. 5630)

The scene is the *Piazza della porta del Vescovato*, according to the inscription.

h) *Oval Soup Tureen*
Polychrome procelain with gilding
ht. 39.5 cm, pl. p. 106
Marked N with a blue crown
Naples, Museum of Capodimonte
(Inv. no. 5594-5595)

The tureen stands on feet of a wild animal and the handles are copied from bronze prototypes. The cover is conical in shape and on it is the group *Child strangling a Goose*. Each single piece was moulded and this is evident from the fact that the thicknesses are all identical. The tureen bears the inscription in red: on one side *Veduta del Palazzo di Cardito di S.M.* and on the other *Veduta del Palazzo di Portici di S.M.* On the cover is the *Veduta delle Crocelle e Castel dell'Ovo* and the *Veduta della Darsena e Palazzo Reale* [S.M.G.].

Royal Porcelain Factory of Naples (Real Fabbrica)
Solitaire set with scenes of the ports and bays of the Kingdom
Polychrome porcelain with gilding;
platter: 33.5 x 25.5; teapot: ht. 11; coffeepot ht. 11; sugar basin ht. 7; cup: ht. 6; saucer: diam. 14, pl. p. 108
Unmarked
Naples, Museum of Capodimonte
(inv. nos. 5067, 5068, 5069, 5070, 5071, 5072)

Many solitaire sets were made at the Real Fabbrica, and all of them were of very fine quality, both in design and decoration. The set exhibited here consists of five pieces, each bearing an inscription in red at the bottom relating to the scene depicted. On the oval platter is *Veduta di Mola di Gaeta*, on the teapot the *Molo di Portici* and *Molo di Napoli*, on the coffeepot the *Castello del Granatello di Portici* and *Veduta del Castello di Baja*; on the sugar basin *Isola di Nisita* and *Lago d'Agnano*, and on the cup and saucer *Procida ed Isola d'Ischia* and *Veduta della città di Pozzuoli.*
The scenes are framed with gilded borders and there are also vine-leaf decorations in gilt. Although each of these objects reproposes motifs which had been extensively used (see the gilding used on a solitaire set with hunting scenes at the Duca di Martina Museum in Naples, inv. nos. 1696-1697 and the amphors from a private Neapolitan collection, Caròla Perrotti 1986, p. 431) the general effect is one of classical simplicity, with the exception of the coffeepot which is in an earlier style. The paste is very white and has no flaws, and the gilding is clearly defined and shiny. These features would seem to suggest a dating around 1782-1800, when from the hands of Giuseppe Bruschi and Nicola Pintucci «...great artists in the making of porcelain ...» came some of the finest wares ever made (Minieri Riccio 1878 d, p. 44).
The miniatures strongly resemble the set of *Ports of the Kingdom* by Philipp Hackert, painted between 1789 and 1792, in fact the *Veduta di Mola di Gaeta* (also used for the ice-box in the Oca Service) and the *Molo di Napoli*, on the platter and teapot respectively are a faithful copy of paintings of the same name by Hackert, now at the Royal Palace of Caserta and the Goethe Museum in Frankfurt [S.M.G.].

Bibl.: Caròla Perrotti, Naples 1986, p. 468.

Giovanni Gramont and French Porcelain
After 1823
Library Set
Porcelain with painted decorations and gilding
pl. p. 109

Tray: 12.8 x 21
signed: *G.ni Gramont*
M impressed; inv. no. 7036
Ink-stand: ht. 6-9;
with the initials FB in gilt;
Inscription:
V.ta di Mergellina a Posillipo
V.ta del Ponte della Maddalena
inv. no. 7037
Pounce-pot: ht. 6-9
with the initials FB in gilt;
Inscription:
V.ta del Molo di Napoli
V.ta del Castello dell'Ovo
inv. no. 7038
Wafer pot: ht. 4.3-8
With the initials FB in gilt;
Inscription:
Villa reale di Napoli
Strada nuova di Posillipo
inv. no. 7039
Quill holder: ht. 8.6
Inscription:
V.ta dell'Isola di Nisita
inv. no. 7040

This service in French porcelain consists of an oval tray resting on four lions' paw feet, a cylindrical quill holder with a square base and three pots with covers – one for ink, one for sand and one for wafers. The tray is decorated with a scene of Naples in the centre seen from Posillipo, containing the landmarks of Vesuvius with a plume of smoke in the background, Castel Sant'Elmo and Castel dell'Ovo, with in the foreground two carriages and some horsemen. The scene is correct in all the details and perspective. The tray is entirely covered by the scene while on the other objects the scenes are contained within vertical bands, decorated with the Bourbon fleur-de-lys.
Giovanni Gramont decorated this service and signed the tray. All we know about this artist is a reference to him by Novi who records him as one of the artists active in Giovanni Pattey's workshop. Pattey had directed the Poulard Prad factory until 1818 but when it was taken over by Tourné and Del Re he went to France. Here he bought white porcelain to decorate in Naples and set up his own workshop, bringing in the very best artists, like Raffaele Giovine and Francesco Landolfi (Novi 1880, Vol. XIII, p. 539).
The dating of this set can be put after 1823, seeing as one of the scenes on the wafer pot is the Strada Nuova di Posillipo, which was started in 1812 on Murat's orders and finished in 1823 [L.Am.].

Bibl.: Caròla Perrotti 1972, IX, p. 849.

Doccia Porcelain
1810-25

Dinner Service
Decorated and gilded porcelain
Marked with a six-pointed star in gilt and red, pl. p. 110
Naples, Museum of Capodimonte
(inv. nos. 880-1247)

These exhibits are part of a large dinner service consisting of 369 pieces including plates, bowls, serving platters, compotes, vegetable dishes, fruit dishes and bottle coolers. There is a great deal of difference in the paste as the thickness varies, the translucency and the colour, which in some pieces is milky white and in others greyish. The service is tin-glazed and therefore rather opaque, while there are many flaws and paint drips on the bases. This type of porcelain was called *masso bastardo* and made by the Doccia factory from 1765 onwards and was mostly used for tableware until c. 1830.
This particular service is decorated with scenes of the cities of Florence, Rome, Naples and of other localities in the Kingdom of the Two Sicilies, painted in polychrome enamel on

round panels and bordered in gilt with a blue band.
Some of the most famous places depicted, whose names are often marked on the back, are the Riviera di Chiaia, Santa Lucia, Castel Nuovo, Castel dell'Ovo, Posillipo, Queen Giovanna's Palace, the Royal Botanical Gardens (founded in 1807), Nisida, archeological sites in the Phlegrean Fields, and views of the bay from the west and east. The same views, with slight variations were repeated very frequently. The depiction of the cities is not particularly exact, especially in the details of the monuments, and it would appear that these decorations have been copied from sketches and notes rather than engravings.
Among the artists mentioned in the records of the Doccia factory was Ferdinando Ammannati, active after 1808, who had worked at the Royal Factory in Naples. Ginori Lisci remarks that this kind of decoration was «imported» from Naples and was probably inspired (at least as far as the scenes of the Kingdom of the two Sicilies are concerned) by the drawings, models and notes that the Royal Factory had given Doccia when it closed down. A service «with painted scenes and a blue band» is mentioned in a list of coffee services and tableware from the period 1810-24 (Ginori Lisci 1963, p. 106, note 133; p. 310, no. 23). Some pieces of the service on display here can be seen in the Museo Irpino at Avellino, a similarly decorated plate belongs to the Duca di Martina Museum in Naples (inv. no. 2037) and many other similar pieces are in public and private collections [L.Am.].

Clock, after 1827
Alabaster and porcelain, 54 x 51 x 18
pl. p. 111
Naples, Museum of Capodimonte
(Inv. no. 5974)

A group of Phoebus riding in a chariot driving two horses stands on a high rectangular plinth supported by flat round feet and a gilt frieze with anthemia and foliage. The dial with a pierced centre represents the wheel of the chariot. On the plinth is a porcelain plaque with a scene of a military parade with the Bay of Naples in the background. Round the sides runs the following inscription:
Nel gran dì del Tuo bel nome / Di Alabastro un dono accetta / L'alma candida e perfetta / L'Alalabastro esprimerà / Se del Sol qui miri il cocchio / Se vedrai segnarsi l'ore; / Dal Ciel brama il Genitore / a Te lunga e lieta età. (on the left): *Te di Stabia io vidi al lido / Nell immagin d'un periglio; / Di Luigi un degno figlio, / Di Fernando emulator. / Il Tuo brando, il senno, e l'arte / Mi mostrò, che questa terra / Sprezzerà del mar la gurra (sic), / Se il Ciel regge il Tuo valor.*

The miniature on the base represents «H.R.H. the Duke of Calabria after his appointment as Commander-in-Chief of the Army on 11th. June 1827 simulating a battle at Castellammare», as can be seen in a lithograph by Mariani which like this miniature is copied from Salvatore Fergola (the lithograph is at Capodimonte and the resemblance was noted by L. Arbace). Furthermore, during the Exhibition of Objects of Fine Art held in Naples in October 1826 Fergola displayed several paintings including a scene of a stone mill at Castellammare (no. 279), which shows that he was familiar with the place painted on the plinth. It is also known that Fergola was Francesco I's favourite painter. In 1826 Fergola is known to have spent two months at Castellammare and in 1827 he drew the army on manoeuvres and the launching of the frigate Isabella (Ortolani, *Giacinto Gigante e la pittura di paesaggio a Napoli*, Naples 1970, pp. 169-70).
At the time there were two factories which worked alabaster. In the *Catalogue of Works produced by National Industry presented at the Solemn Exhibition on 30th. May 1822*, there is mention of pieces by Felice Vacal, who exhibited busts of the Duke and Duchess of Calabria (later to become King Francesco I and Queen Isabella of Spain), a sculpture representing Maritime Trade, vases in the Etruscan style, *campana* vases, sugar-basins, and even a clock stand (p. 18). Six years later, in the catalogue of the same exhibition held in Naples in October 1828, a certain Giuseppe De Grandis is mentioned, who had a workshop at number 6 on the Strada di Chiaja. He exhibited alabaster vases with Etruscan decorations (also called *campana* vases) of a temple with eight columns and gilded capitals, with other details (p. 36).
In the following exhibition in October 1830, Giuseppe De Grandis presented «a tazza decorated with Bacchanalia and gilt metal which symbolize royal insignia, small very decorative tazzas, *campana* vases, two show-cases full of various objects in alabaster and a collection of pieces of alabaster from Sicily» (p. 25). On that occasion, as is mentioned in the catalogue of the 1832 Exhibition, (p. 11) De Grandis was awarded a silver medal «for progress made in the working of alabaster». Although it is not known who made the case for this clock, it could well have been either of these craftsmen, though it is more likely to have been De Grandis' work. Furthermore, in store at Capodimonte there are many alabaster vases and ornaments which would appear to have been made in Tuscany, judging from the style, and can be dated around 1825-50. However, on the basis of the above records it would seem more likely that these objects were made in Naples during the same period.
The Duke of Calabria, to whom the Fergola miniature is dedicated, is the future King Ferdinand II, son of Francesco I and Isabella of Spain born in 1810. Therefore it seems likely that this clock is a present from Francesco I (king after 1825) for the name-day of the 17-year-old prince, who was a descendant of Louis XIV and grandson of Ferdinand IV [A.G-P].

Naples
Table 1830-32
Mahogany and bronze
86 x 66, pl. p. 112
Naples, Museum of Capodimonte
(inv. no. I.C. 3784 b)

A tripod base supports three figures with butterfly wings and loin-cloths with three-clawed feet resting on toads and joined together by cornucopias. The animals which the three figures are holding symbolize tameness (the lamb), loyalty (the dog) and innocence (the dove). In the centre of the base is a mahogany bowl with a cover and bronze mounts supported by three kneeling Victories. The frieze of the dodecagonal table-top is composed of the signs of the zodiac in gilt bronze alternating with swags of foliage, on mahogany. The top is in Sicilian green marble with plant motif mosaics in contrasting colours. There are twenty-five holes fitted with medallions which can be turned round (by means of a mechanism which also starts up a musical-box with an aria by Rossini). On the outer ring are twelve scenes of royal residences on one side and on the other the names of the members of the royal family; on the inner ring are the names of the royal residences on one side and twelve miniatures of members of the royal family on the other; at the centre is a medallion with on one side the Bourbon fleur-de-lys with a crown and the date 1830, and on the other a portrait of Francesco I, who died that year.
None of the miniatures of royal residences (these include Capodimonte, San Leucio, Persano, Caserta, La Ficuzza, Colli, Portici, Solanto, Partinico, Ischia, La Favorita and Cardito) are signed; they would appear to be the work of at least two artists and include scenes of Sicily. The miniatures (in addition to the one of Francesco I, signed by Giovine) are of King Ferdinand II (signed Sacco Bros.), Queen Isabella (Giovine), Queen Maria Cristina (Morghen), Princess Antonia (Morghen), Princess Amelia (Landolfi), Princess Carolina (anon.), Princess Teresa (anon.), Prince Francesco (Giovine), Prince Luigi (anon.), Prince Antonio (Sacco Bros.), Prince Leopold (Sacco Bros.), and Prince Carlo (Sacco Bros. 1830).
Francesco I died on 8th. November 1830, and the table was presumably commissioned before his death seeing as his portrait is at the centre of the table. However, the portrait of his son Ferdinand bears the title of His Majesty, and is accompainied by that of his wife Maria Cristina of Savoy, who he married in November 1832. So the table was probably finished around that time.
The medallions contain portraits of ten of Francesco I's children: the Duchess of Berry, by his first wife Clementine of Austria was married and no longer in Naples, and his eldest son Ferdinand, born in 1800 had died a year later. The two eldest daughters by his second wife Isabella of Spain were also married and did not live in Naples: Luisa Carolina had a son – the Infante Francesco di Paola, and Maria Cristina also had a son – Ferdinand VII. Among the painters of miniatures listed the most famous is Raffaele Giovine, who displayed many works during the exhibitions of National Industry, held in Naples in this period. In 1830, «D. Raffaele Giovine who lives at no. 95 on the Riviera di Chiaja» exhibited «a flower-holder with portraits of the Royal Family on

a crimson ground, decorated in blue and gold in relief». Four years later, in the 1834 catalogue he was given the title of «His Majesty's Painter». He had begun to paint under Murat (producing six vases with portraits of Murat, his wife and children, signed, and now at the Residenz in Munich). In 1826 he was awarded a medal for his work, the first in a long series of awards. In 1854, the journal *L'Osservatore di Napoli* mentions Giovine as being a decorator of porcelain, then living at 86, on the Strada San Mattia. He continued to work until the fall of the Bourbons.
The Sacco Brothers, who signed some of the other portraits, displayed one of the Duke of Calabria (the future king Francesco I) at the *Exhibition of Fine Arts* in October 1830, perhaps similar to the one on this table.
The elder brother – Francesco Paolo (1797-1864) – is the lesser known; the younger – Giuseppe (1805-1889) had a brilliant career first as a painter of miniatures at the Court of Naples and later at Loius-Philippe's court in Paris, and finally in London. He displayed some miniatures in the 1837 exhibition in Naples, including two of the king. Little is known of the other miniaturists who signed the work on this table, though Landolfi could well be the same artist who decorated porcelain some years earlier. As no records exist about the miniatures of the royal residences, it is practically impossible to say who painted them, although Salvatore Fergola (1799-1874), Francesco I's favourite artist, had been Court Painter for many years, and had been well paid for his fine work. In 1819 he had been to Sicily on behalf of the Duke of Calabria to paint some views, and during the following decade he had travelled continually with the royal family (Ortolani 1970, pp. 169-170). After the death of the King his fame began to decline, though he was still called by the court occasionally. This decline must have been the reason why he turned to decorating furniture; in the 1834 catalogue of the *Exhibition of Products of the National Industry* he is mentioned as working with D. Filippo Cirelli on lithographs and wood-cuts in a workshop in Largo San Giovanni Maggiore, where a round marble table decorated with painted lithographs was made, and another one with scenes in oil of the Galli islands of Sorrento and the Castle of Ischia (p. 45). Fergola received a silver medal for this work. Two years later in the 1836 Exhibition he displayed other similar work, including a «round folding table with decorations in gilt on a black ground and twelve scenes of Naples and environs painted in oil» (p. 64), which sounds very similar to the table on display here.
The inspiration for this unusual table is partly a classical prototype – a pair of marble trapezophora with winged figures holding shells resting on feet of wild animals. It is obvious that this was already very popular by 1830, as it was restored by Angelo Solari in 1834, to support a table-top in petrified wood with a precious chess-set in pietre dure for the King (see Gonzalez Palacios, *Mosaici e Pietre Dure*, Milan 1981, Vol. I, p. 73). These one-footed figures, here modified by the addition of symbolic animals, and alterations to the wings and toads used as supports must have really pleased the royal family, as there is another table at the Royal Palace in Naples with the same design. The supports with figures holding a shell, as in the marble table, are an imitation of classical prototypes found during excavations.
The Royal Palace table is unfortunately damaged, though until about fifty years ago it was decorated with medallions containing scenes of Pompeii and the portraits of the family of Francesco I. On the brace there was probably a flower-holder, as there are holes visible (F. De Filippis, *La Reggia di Napoli*, Naples 1942, Pl. LXXXVIII and M. Causa Picone and A. Porzio *Il Palazzo Reale di Napoli* 1986, p. 85 and fig. 160).
Regarding this exhibit, the identity is still not known of the various craftsmen who were involved in its making – a sculptor, decorator, bronze worker and cabinet-maker with the collaboration of various miniaturists and even a musical instrument maker [A.G.-P].

Bibl.: Brosio 1962, p. 77; Baccheschi 1966, p. 117; London 1972, no. 1760 (entry compiled by A. González-Palacios); Mottola Molfino 1977, II, figs. 308-9.

Bibliography

Undated
Bordini, S., *Storia del panorama*, Rome.
Kris, E., *George Hoefnagel und der wissenschaftiche Naturalismus*, in *Festschrift fur Julius Schlosser*, Zurich-Leipzig-Vienna.
1534
Di Falco, B., *Descrittione dei luoghi antiqui di Napoli*, Naples 1534.
1560
De Stefano, P., *Descrittione dei luoghi sacri della città di Napoli...*, Naples 1560
1604
Van Mander, K., *Het Schilder-Boeck...*, Harlem 1604 (ed. *Le livre des peintres*, edited by H. Hymans, 2 voll., Paris 1884-1885).
1616
Barrionuevo, G., *Panegjricus ill.mo ecc.mo domino Petro Fernandez a Castro Lemensium et Andreae Comiti etc.*, Naples 1616.
1624
D'Engenio Caracciolo, C., *Napoli sacra...*, Naples 1624.
1630
Capaccio, G. C., *Il forastiero*, Naples 1630 (edited by O. Morisani, Naples 1958).
1681-1728
Baldinucci. F., *Notizie dei professori del Disegno da Cimabue in qua...*, 6 voll., Florence 1681-1728.
1692
Celano, C., *Notizie del bello, dell'antico e del curioso della città di Napoli...*, 10 voll., Naples 1962.
1704
Orlani, P. A., *Abecedario pittorico...*, Bologna 1704.
1718
Petrini, F., *Vedute di Pozzuoli, Baia e Cuma*, Naples 1718.
1724
Celano, C., *Notizie del bello dell'antico e del curioso della città di Napoli...*, edited by Giovan Francesco Pace, 10 voll., Naples 1724.
1729
Pio. N., *Le vie dei pittori, scultori e di architetti in compendio in numero di 225*, m.s. nel code 257 Biblioteca Vaticana, from Libreria Capponi.
1736
Notice sur Pierre Van Lint peintre flamand du XVII siècle et sur les artistes de sa famille en Italie. m.s., 1736.
1742-45
De Dominici, B., *Vite dei Pittori, Scultori ed Architetti Napoletani...*, 3 voll., Naples 1742-45.
1752
Mecatti, G. M., *Racconto storico filosofico del Vesuvio...*, Naples 1752.
1753
Deschamps, J. B., *La vie des peintres flamands, allemands et hollandais*, V, Paris 1753.
1756
Vanvitelli, L., *Dichiarazione dei disegni del R. Palazzo di Caserta*, Naples 1756.
1758
Celano, C., *Notizie del bello dell'antico del curioso della città di Napoli...*, edited by Domenico Pulli, 10 voll., Naples 1758.
1760
Giannone, O., *Ritratti e Giunte sulle vie de' Pittori Napoletani*, m.s., 1760 (Biblioteca del Museo civico G. Filangieri, Napoli) ed. Naples 1941, edited by O. Morisani.
1761
De Bottis, G., *Ragionamento istorico intorno ai nouvi vulcani..*, Naples 1761.
1765
Roisecco, N., *Roma antica e moderna...*, Rome 1765.
1768
Paoli. A. P., *Antichità di Pozzuoli. Avanzi delle antichità esistenti a Pozzuoli Cuma e Baja*, Naples-Florence 1768.
1771
Gori Gandellini, G., *Notizie sugli intagliatori*, Siena 1771.
1772
Hamilton W., *Observations on Mount Vesuvius*, 1772.
1775
Carafa, G., *Mappa topografica di Napoli e i suoi contorni*, Naples 1775.
1776
Carletti, N., *Topografia universale della città di Napoli in Campagna Felice e note enciclopediche storiografiche*, Naples 1776.
Hamilton, W., *Campi Phlegraei. Observations on the volcano of the two Sicilies...*, Naples 1776.
1777
Volkmann, D. J. J., *Historschkritische nachrichten von italien*, Leipzig 1777.
1779
Hackert, P., *Serie di quattro vedute del Regno di Napoli*, Rome 1779.
Hamilton, W., *Supplement to the Campi Phlegraei...*, Naples 1779.
1781
Tiraboschi, G.. *Notizie degli artefici modenesi*, Modena 1781.
1781-86
Richard, J. C. (Abbè de Saint Non), *Voyage pittoresque ou description des Royaumes de Naples et de Sicile*, 4 voll., Paris 1781-86.
1784-86
Napoli Signorelli, P., *Vicende della coltura nelle Due Sicilie*, 6 voll., Naples 1784-86.
1786
Carletti, N., *Topografia di Napoli*, Naples 1786.
1787
von Ramhhor, F. W. B., *Ueber malerei und bildhauerarbeit in Rom*, Leipzig 1787.
1788
Orlandi, P. A., *Abecedario pittorico... ora notabilmente accresciuto fino all'anno 1775*, Florence 1788.
Sarnelli, P., *Guida di Napoli e Pozzuoli*, Naples 1788.
1789
D'Onofrio, P., *Succinte notizie intorno alla facciata della chiesa cattedrale di Napoli...*, Naples 1789.
Lanzi, L., *Storia pittorica dell'Italia*, Bassano 1789.
1790
Hackert, P., *Principi di disegno dei paesi disegnati dal vero e incisi da Vincenzo Aloja*, Naples 1790.
Inghirami, F., *Dichiarazione delle pitture di un servizio da Tavola modellato in porcellana nella R. Fabbrica di Napoli per uso della R. Altezza la Duchessa di Parma*, Naples 1790.
Morelli, F., *Raccolta degli antichi monumenti esistenti fra Pozzuolo Cuma e Baja luoghi del Regno di Napoli*, Rome 1790.
1792
Celano, C., *Notizie del Bello, dell'antico e del curioso della città di Napoli...* edited by Salvatore Palermo, 11 vol., Naples 1792.
Galanti, G. M., *Breve descrizione della città di Napoli e del suo contorno*, Naples 1792.
Raccolta di tutte le vedute che esistevano nel gabinetto del Duca della Torre rappresentanti le eruzioni del Vesuvio accadute fino ad oggi, Naples 1792.
Vasi, M., *Itinéraire instructif de Rome à Naples...*, Rome 1792.
1795
Vinci, B., *Elogio storico del celebre pittore Antonio Cavallucci da Sermoneta*, Rome 1795.
1796
De Rossi, G. G., *Vita di Antonio Cavallucci da Sermoneta pittore* Venice 1796.
1799
De Bottis, G., *Ragionamento istorico intorno all'eruzione del Vesuvio...*, Naples 1799.
1811
Goethe, J. W., *Philipp Hackert*, Tubingen 1811.
1813-30
Biografia degli uomini illustri del Regno di Napoli..., edited by Domenico Martuscelli, 16 voll., Naples 1813-30.
1815
Romanelli, D., *Napoli antica e moderna*, Naples 1815.
1817
Mazzinghi, J., *A guide to the antiquities and curiosities in the city of Naples and its environs*, Naples 1817.
1818
Napoli: cat. mostra, *Catalogo dei saggi de' prodotti dell'industria nazionale presentati nella solenne esposizione del 30 maggio 1818...*, Naples 1818.
Panvini, P., *Il forestiere. Alle antichità e curiosità naturali di Pozzuoli Cuma Baia e Miseno*, Naples 1818.
Ticozzi, S., *Dizionario dei pittori del rinnovamento delle Belle Arti fino al 1800*, Milan 1818.
1819-24
Zani, P., *Enciclopedia metodica critico-ragionata delle Belle Arti...*, 19 voll., Parma 1819-24.
1820
Grossi, G., *Le Belle Arti a Napoli*, 2 voll., Naples 1820.
Williams, H. W., *Travels in Italy, Greece and the Ionians Islands*, Edinburgh 1820.
1821
Lady Morgan – Voyage en Italie, Bruxelles 1821.
1822
Lanzi, L., *Storia pittorica dell'Italia*, Florence 1822.
1827
Vigo, L., *Memorie storiche di P. Paolo Vasta pittore Acireale*, Palermo 1827.
1828
Di Iorio, A., in *Biografia degli uomini illustri del Reno di Napoli...*, edited by Domenico Martuscelli, XIII, Naples 1828.
1829
Galanti, G. M., *Guida storico monumentale della città di Napoli e contorni*, edited by L. Galanti, Naples 1829.
Viaggio pittorico nel Regno delle Due Sicilie, Naples 1829.
1830
Morghen, F., *Gabinetto di tutte le più antiche vedute esistenti negli antichi monumenti di Pozzuoli, Cuma e Baia*, Naples 1830.
Napoli[1]: exhibition catalogue, *Catalogo delle opere di Belle Arti esposte nel Palagio del Real Museo Borbonico il dì 4 ottobre 1830*, Naples 1830.
Napoli[2]: exhibition catalogue, *Catalogo di saggi de'produtti della industria nazionale presentati nella solenne esposizione de' 4 ottobre 1830...*, Naples 1830.
1831
Ticozzi, S.. *Dizionario degli architetti, scultori e pittori d'ogni età e di ogni nazione*, Milan 1831.
1833
Napoli: exhibition catalogue, *Catalogo delle opere di Belle Arti esposte nel Palagio del Real Museo Borbonico il 30 maggio 1833*, Naples 1833.
1834
D'Afflitto, L., *Guida per i curiosi e per i viaggiatori che vengono alla città di Napoli*, Naples 1834.
1835
Alvino, F., *La collina di Posillipo*, Naples 1835.
1835-1837
Vigeé Lebrun, E., *Souvenirs de Mme Vigeé Lebrun*, Paris 1835-1837.
1835-52
Nagler, G. K., *Neues Allgemeines Künstler Lexikon*, 8 voll., Munich 1835-52.
1837
Naples: exhibition catalogue, *Catalogo delle opere di Belle Arti esposte nel Real Museo Borbonico il 30 maggio 1837*, Naples 1837.
1840
Alvino, F., *Guida del Real Museo Borbonico*, Naples 1840.
De Boni, F., *Biografie degli artisti*, Venice 1840.
1842
Catalani, L., *Discorsi sui monumenti patrii*, Naples 1842.
1843
D'Aloe, S., *Guide pour la galerie des tableaux du Musée Bourbon*, Naples 1843.
1845
De Simone, G., *Le Chiese di Napoli, descritte ed illustrate...*, Naples 1845.
Quaranta, B., in *Napoli e i luoghi celebri delle sue vicinanze*, Naples 1845, II, pp. 109-206.
Pistolesi, E., *Guida metodica di Napoli e i suoi dintorni per vedere con nouvo metodo la città adorna di piante e vedute litografiche*, Naples 1845.

1848
Siret, A., *Dictionnaire historique des peintres de toutes les écoles...*, Bruxelles 1848.
1851-1860
Mairette, P.J., *Abecedario*, Paris 1851-1860.
1852
D'Aloe, S., *Naples, ses monuments et ses curiosités avec un catalogue detaillé du Musée Royal Bourbon*, Naples 1852.
1854
D'Aloe, S., *Nouveau guide du Musée Royal Bourbon*, Naples 1854.
1854-90
Le Blanc, M.Ch., *Manuel de l'amateur d'estampes*, 4 voll., Paris 1854-90.
1855
D'Ambra, R.-De Lauzieres, A., *Un mese a Napoli. Descrizione della città di Napoli e delle sue vicinanze divisa in XXX giornate*, edited by G. Nobile, 2 voll., Naples 1855.
Napier, F., *Notes on modern painting at Naples*, London 1855.
1856-60
Celano, C., *Notizie del Bello dell'Antico e del Curioso della città di Napoli...*, edited by G.B. Chiarini, 5 voll., Naples 1856-60.
1856-1891
von Wurzbach, C., *Biographisches Lexikon der Kaiserthums Österreich (1750-1850)*, 60 voll., Vienna 1856-1891.
1857
Ceva Grimaldi, F., *Della città di Napoli dal tempo della sua fondazione sino al presente. Memorie storiche*, Naples 1857.
1859
Calà Ulloa, P., *Pensés et souvenirs sur la littérature contemporaine du Royaume de Naples*, Geneva 1859.
Dalbono, C.T., *Storia della pittura in Napoli ed in Sicilia dalla fine del 1600 a noi*, Naples 1859.
1860
Mattei, P., *Cenni biografici del cav. Antonio Pitloo*, «Polioroma pittoresco», XIX, 1860, 27, pp. 209-211; 28, pp. 217-220; 238-240, 246-247.
1861
Tischbein, J.H.W., *Ausmeinem, Leben*, Braunschweig 1861.
1862-63
Dumas, A., *I Borboni di Napoli...*, 11 voll., Naples 1862-63.
1863
Parthey, G., *Deutscher Bildersaal. Verzeichnis der in Deutschland vorhandenden Oelbilder verstorbener Maler aller Schulen*, I, Berlin 1863.
1864
Lagrange, L., *Joseph Vernet et la peinture au XVIII siècle*, Paris 1864.
1868
Crivelli, G., *Giovanni Brueghel, pittor fiammingo e sue lettere e quadretti esistenti presso l'Ambrosiana*, Milan 1868.
1869
Pjilips, J., *Vesuvius*, Oxford 1869.
1870
Barbier De Montault, X., *Les musées et galeries de Rome*, Rome 1870.
1872
Galante, G.A., *Guida sacra della Città di Napoli*, Naples 1872.
Rombouts, Ph.-Lerius, Th., *De Liggeren, en audere historische Archieven ter Antwerpesche Sint Lucas Gilde*, Antwerp-La Haye 1872, vol. II, pp. 591-596.
1875
Minieri Riccio, C., *Cenno storico all'Accademia Alfonsina istituita nella città di Napoli nel 1442*, Naples 1875.
Smargiassi, G., *Cenno storico sul paesagio e sui paesisti napoletani*, «Atti della Reale Accademia di Archeologia, Lettere e belle arti», VII, 1875, pp. 139-147.
1876
Migliozzi, A., *Nuova guida generale del Museo Nazionale di Napoli...*, Naples 1876.
1877
Carelli, G., *La pinacoteca Reale di Capodimonte. G. Mancinelli e G. Gigante*, Naples 1877.
Naples: exhibition catalogue, *Esposizione dell'arte antica napoletana*, edited by G. Filangieri e D. Salazar, Naples 1877.
1878
Minieri Riccio[1], C., *La fabbrica della porcellana in Napoli e sue vicende*, Memoria Accademia Pontaniana 27 January 1878, Naples 1878.
Minieri Riccio[2], C., *Notizie intorno alle ricerche fatte dalla R. Fabbrica della Porcellana di Napoli per rinvenire materiali a migliorare e perfezionare sempre più la manifattura della pasta della porcellana, le sue dorature e le miniature*, Memoria Accademia Pontaniana 10 February 1878, Naples 1878.
Minieri Riccio[3], C., *Gli artefici ed i miniatori della Real Fabbrica della Porcellana in Napoli*, Memoria Accademia Pontaniana 3-17 March 1878, Naples 1878.
Minieri Riccio[4], C., *Delle porcellane della Real Fabbrica di Napoli, delle vendite fattene e delle loro tariffe*, Memoria Accademia Pontaniana 7 April 1878, Naples 1878.
1879
Novi, G., *La fabbricazione delle porcellane in Napoli e dei prodotti ceramici affini*, «Atti dell'Accademia Pontaniana», XIII, 1879, pp. 515-554.
1883
La Lumia, I., *Il marchese Caracciolo*, in *Storie Siciliane*, Palermo 1883, IV, pp. 565-613.
1883-91
Filangieri, G., *Documenti per la storia, le arti e le industrie delle province napoletane*, 6 voll., Naples 1883-91.
1884
Bindi, V., *L'arte del paesaggio a Napoli. Brevi ricordi artistici*, Rome 1884.
1885
Barone, N., *Le cedole di tesoreria dell'Archivio di Stato di Napoli dall'anno 1460 al 1504*, «Archivio Storico per le Province Napoletane», X, 1885, 1, pp. 5-47.
1890
Conte, C., *La civiltà di Napoli...*, 3 voll., Naples 1890.
1891
Lojacono, D., *L'opera inedita De Majestate di Giuniano Majo e il concetto di principe negli scrittori della corte aragonese di Napoli*, «Atti della Reale Accademia di Scienze morali e politiche», XXIV, 1891.
1892
Capasso, B., *Topografia della città di Napoli ai tempi del ducato*, Naples 1892.
Ceci, G., *Ricordi della vecchia Napoli*, Naples 1892.
Croce, B., *La villa di Chiaia*, «Napoli Nobilissima», I, 1892, pp. 3-10, 35-39, 51-53.
Faraglia, N.F., *Notizie di alcuni artisti che lavorano nella Chiesa di San Martino sopra Napoli*, «Archivio Storico per le Provincie Napoletane», XVII, 1892, pp. 657-678.
1893
Croce, B., *Wolfgango Goethe alla locanda del signor Moriconi*, «Napoli Nobilissima», II, 1893, pp. 92-94.
1894
Percopo, E., *Nuovi documenti sugli scrittori e gli artisti dei tempi aragonesi*, «Archivio Storico per le Provincie Napoletane», XIX, 1894, 4, pp. 740-756.
1895
Bergeret de Grandcourt, P.J.O.-Fragonard, J.H., *Journal inédit d'un voyage en Italie*, Paris 1895.
Capasso, B., *Topografia della città di Napoli nell'XI secolo*, Naples 1895.
De Criscio, G., *I campi flegrei illustrati*, Pozzuoli 1895.
1896
Parisi, R., *Quattro quadri del Museo di San Martino di proprietà del Municipio di Napoli*, Naples 1896.
1897
Croce, B., *Dalle memorie del Pittore Tischbein*, «Napoli Nobilissima», VI, 1897, pp. 97-103.
Katalog der Galerie Harrach, Vienna 1897.
La Ville Sur-Yllon, L., *Padre Rocco e l'illuminizazione della città di Napoli*, «Napoli Nobilissima», VI, 1897, pp. 81-87.
Mele, E., *Un pittore tedesco alla corte di Napoli. Hackert*, «Napoli Nobilissima», VI, 1897, pp. 33-36.
Schipa, M., *Un ministro napoletano del secolo XVIII*, Naples 1897.
1898
von Boetticher, F., *Malerwerke des 19. Jahrhunderts*, II, tomo I, Dresden 1898.
Colonna, F., *Scoperte di antichità dal 1876 al 1897 con notizie delle scoperte anteriori e ricordi storico-artistici-topografici*, Naples 1898.
D'Ayala, M., *Angelika Kaufmann a Napoli*, «Napoli Nobilissima», VII, 1898, pp. 100-107.
Dayot, A., *Les Vernet*, Paris 1898.
1899
La rivoluzione Napoletana del 1799 illustra con ritratti, vedute, autografi a altri documenti figurativi e grafici del tempo. Albo..., edited by B. Croce, G. Ceci, M. D'Ayala, S. Di Giacomo, Naples 1899 (ed. Naples 1969).
1900
Borzelli, A., *L'Accademia del disegno a Napoli nella seconda metà del secolo XVIII*, «Napoli Nobilissima », XI, 1900, pp. 110-111; pp. 125-126; pp. 141-143.
Morelli, M., *La pinacoteca del Museo Nazionale*, from «Napoli d'oggi», Naples 1900.
1901
Borzelli[1], A., *L'Accademia del disegno durante la prima restaurazione borbonica 1799-1805*, «Napoli Nobilissima», X, 1901, pp. 1-5.
Borzelli[2], A., *L'Accademia del disegno del decennio 1805-1815*, «Napoli Nobilissima», X, 1901, pp. 22-26; pp. 53-56.
Borzelli[3], A., *L'Accademia del disegno dal 1815 al 1860*, «Napoli Nobilissima», X, 1901, pp. 105-107; pp. 124-126; pp. 138-141.
Don Ferrante, *La quadreria dei Principi di Avellino*, «Napoli Nobilissima», X, 1901, pp. 158-160.
Sansone, A., *Gli avvenimenti del 1799 nelle Due Sicilie*, Palermo 1901.
1901-1912
Mireur, H., *Dictionnaire des ventes d'art...*, 7 voll., Paris 1901-1912.
1902
Ceci, G., *Domenico Gargiulo detto Micco Spadaro*, «Atti dell'Accademia Pontaniana», XXXII, 1902.
Don Ferrante, *La quadreria dei Principi di Avellino*, Napoli Nobilissima, XI, 1902, pp. 173-175.
Filangieri, G., *La galleria Nazionale di Napoli*, in *Le gallerie Nazionali Italiane*, Rome 1902, V, pp. 208-354.
1904
Croce, B., *Veduta della città di Napoli nel 1479 col trionfo navale per l'arrivo di Lorenzo de' Medici*, «Napoli Nobilissima», XIII, 1904, p. 56.
1905
Ceci, G., *Domenico Gargiulo detto Micco Spadaro*, «Napoli Nobilissima», XIV, 1905, pp. 65-68, 104-108.
Croce, B., *Veduta della città di Napoli nel secolo XV*, «Napoli Nobilissima», XIV, 1905, pp. 33-35.
Hamel, M., *Corot et son oeuvre*, 2 voll., Paris 1905.
Peltzer, A., *Christoph Heinrich Kniep*, «Goethe Jahrbuch», XXVI, 1905, pp. 225-228.
Robout, A.-Moreau Nelaton, E., *L'oeuvre de Corot*, 4 voll., Paris 1905.
1906
Ceci, G., *Il largo di San Domenico*, «Napoli Nobilissima», XV, 1906, pp. 161-162.
1907
Binyon, L., *Catalogue of drawings by British Artists and Artists of foreign origin working in Great Britain... in the British Museum*, IV, London 1907.
Frimmel, Th., *Zu A.M.C.*, «Blätter fur Gemäldekunde», III, 1907, p. 191.
1907-50
Thieme, U.-Becker, F., *Allgemeines Lexikon der Bildenden Künstler...*, 37 voll., Leipzig 1907-50.
1908
Ceci, G., *Il primo critico del De Dominici*, «Archivio Storico per le Province Napoletane», XXXIII, 1908, pp. 618-636.
Rolfs, W., *Il più antico dipinto figurativo della città di Napoli*, «Archivio Storico per le Province Napoletane», XXXIII, 1908, pp. 736-745.

1909
Bosurgi, D., *Cenni critici sulla storia generale delle belle arti*, Naples 1909.
Dimier, L., *Un mot sur l'Ecole napolitaine. La Gallerie de S. A. Le Comte Harrach*, «Les Arts», 1909, 87, pp. 19-32.
1910
Dvořák, M.,-Matějka, B., *Topogaphie der...kunst - Denkmäle Im Königreich Böhmen*, XXVII, Der politische Bezirk Raudnits, Prague 1910, II, pp. 86 sgg.
Rolfs, W., *Geschichte der Malerei Neapels* Leipzig 1910.
Spinazzola [1], V., *Di Napoli antica e della sua topografia in una tavola del XV secolo rappresentante il trionfo navale di Ferrante d'Aragona dopo la battaglia d'Ischia*, «Bolletino d'Arte», IV, 1910, pp. 125-143.
Spinazzola [2], V., *Guide du Musée et de la Chrtreuse de San Martino*, Naples 1910.
1911
Ceci, G., *Saggio di una bibliografia per la storia delle arti figurative dell'Italia meridionale*, Bari 1911.
De Rinaldis, A., *Guida illustrata del Museo Nazionale ; parte seconda; Pinacoteca*, Naples 1911.
Florence: exhibition catalogue, *Mostra del ritratto italiano della fine del secolo XVI all'anno 1861*, Florence 1911.
Hymans, H., *Jan Brueghel d. Ä.*, in Thieme, E.-Becker, F., *Allgemeinbes Lexikon der Bildenden Künstler*, Leipzig 1911, V, pp. 98-99.
Naples: exhibition catalogue, *Mostra di ricordi storici del Risorgimento nel Mezzogiorno d'Italia*, edited by Salvatore Di Giacomo, Naples 1911.
Suida, W., *Öesterreichische Kunstschätze*, Vienna 1911.
Tarchiani, N., *La mostra del ritratto italiano della fine del secolo XVI all'anno 1861in Palazzo Vecchio a Firenze*, «Rassegna d'arte», XI, 1911, 5, pp. 77-92.
1911-13
Benediz, E., *Dictionnaire critique et documentaire des peintres, sculptores...*, 3 voll., Paris 1911-13.
1912
Calabi, A., *La pittura di paesaggio in Italia nel secolo XIX*, «Emporium», XXXVI, 1912, pp. 340-349.
D'Addosio, G. B., *Documenti inediti di artisti napoletani del XVI e XVII secolo*, «Archivio Storico per le Province Napoletane», XXXVII, 1912, pp. 593-616.
De Rinaldis, A., *Note su la pittura napoletana del '600*, «Ausonia», XVII, 1912, pp. 221-250.
D'Espinchal, G. T., *Journal d'émigration*, Paris 1912.
1913
D'Adossio, G. B., *Documenti inediti di artisti napoletani del XVI e XVII secolo*, «Archivio Storico per le Province Napoletane», XXXVIII, 1913, pp. 36-72, 232-259, 483-524, 578-610.
Fogolari, G., *L'Accademia veneziana di pittura a scultura del Settecento*, «L'Arte», XVI, 1913, pp. 242-272.
Ozzola, L., *Le rovine romane nella pittura del XVII e XVIII secolo*, «L'Arte», XVI, 1913, pp. 112-130.
Srickland, W., *A dictionary of irish artists*, Dublin-London 1913 (ed. Dublin 1969).
1914
Comelli, G. B., *Piante e vedute della città di Bologna*, Bologna 1914.
1915
Bellucci, A., *Memorie storiche e artistiche del Tesoro nella Cattedrale dal sec. XVI al XVIII*, Naples 1915.
1918
Piccirilli, L. M., *Un pittore di Guardia Sanframondi: Michele Foschini*, «Rivista storica del Sannio», IV, 1918, pp. 3-4.
1919
Croce, B., *Vedute della città di Napoli nel Quattrocento*, Naples 1919, (reprint in Aneddoti di Varia letteratura, I, Bari 1954, pp. 267-271).
1920
De Rinaldis, A., *Ascanio Luciani*, «Napoli Nobilissima», I n s., 1920, pp. 101-102.
Gargiulo Domenico, in Thieme, U.-Becker, F., *Allegmeines Lexicon der Bildenden Kunstler*, Leipzig 1920, XIII, pp. 194-196.
1921
Croce, B., *La bottega di un antiquario a Napoli sulla fine del Settecento*, «Napoli Nobilissima», II, n. s. 1921, pp. 21-22.
1922
De Rinaldis, A., *note* Battelli, G., *Due disegni napoletani di un pittore tedesco amico di Goethe*, «Napoli Nobilissima», III, n. s., 1922, pp. 81-82.
Florence: exhibition catalogue, *Mostra della pittura italiana del Seicento e del Settecento*, edited by Nello Tarchiani, 1922.
Ricciardi, E., *Posa della prima pietra della Reggia di Caserta*, «Napoli Nobilissima», III. n. s., 1922, pp. 115-117.
1924
Baiére, G., *Catalogue des peintures exposés dans les Galeries-École française*, Paris 1924.
Ojetti, U.-Dami, L.,-Tarchiani, N., *La pittura italiana dal Seicento e del Settecento alla mostra di Palazzo Pitti*, Milan-Rome 1924.
1925
Baldass, L., *Romantische Landschaften in der Wiener Galarie des 19. Jahrhunderts*, «Belvedere», VII, 1925, pp. 44-47.
Cavallucci, C. I.-Dupré, E., *Manuale di storia dell'arte italiana*, Florence 1925.
Pfister, F., *La scuola di Posillipo*, «Bollettino d'arte» 1925, pp. 163-183.
1926
Ingersoll Smouse, F., *Joseph Vernet peintre de marine 1714-1789*, Paris 1926.
1927
Croce, B., *Uomini e cose della vecchia Italia*, II, Bari, 1927.
Eigenberger, R., *Katalog der Gemäldegalerie der Akademie der Bildenden Künste*, Vienna 1927.
1928
Bruxelles: cat. mostra, *Exposition de l'art russe*, Bruxelles 1928.
1929
De Blasio, A., *Michele Foschini*, «Samnium», II, 1929, 3, pp. 26-27.
Limoncelli, M., *Pasquale Mattei*, Naples 1929.
Naples: exhibition catalogue, *Esposizione permanente del Circolo artistico di Napoli*, Naples 1929.
1930
Corna, P. A., *Dizionario della storia dell'arte in Italia*, Piacenza 1930.
Nicolini, F., *L'abate Galiani e il marchese Caracciolo*, Pegaso, 1930, II, pp. 641-694.
Nugent, M., *Alla mostra della pittura italiana del '600 e '700. Note e impressioni*, 2 voll., San Casciano Val di Pesa 1930.
Ortolani, S., *Giacinto Gigante*, Bergamo 1930.
Pontieri, E., *Lettera del marchese Caracciolo vicerè di Sicilia al ministro Acton*, «Archivio Storico per le Province Napoletane», XV n. s., 1930, pp. 201-312.
Ricciardi, E., *Medaglie del Regno delle Due Sicilie 1735-1861*, Naples 1930
Wahl, H., *Goethe in Bildnis*, Leipzig 1930.
1931
Florence: exhibition catalogue, *Mostra del giardino italiano*, Florence 1931.
Iaverskaia, N. V., *Scedrin* Moscow 1931.
1932
Ceci, G., *Palumbo Onofrio*, in Thieme, U.-Becker, F., *Allgemeines Lexikon der Bildenden Künstler*, Leipzig 1932, XXVI, p. 187.
Franciosi, A., *Villa Rosebery*, from «La vie d'Italie», 1932, pp. 646-650.
Goethe, J. W., *Viaggio in Italia 1760*, I, italian edition by Arturo Farinelli, Rome 1932.
Mazzucchetti, L., *La vita di Goethe seguita nell'epistolario*, Milan 1932.
Parrino, V., *Vito d'Anna e i suoi affreschi nelle Chiese di Palermo*, Palermo 1932.
Pontieri, E., *Lettere del marchese Caracciolo vicerè di Sicilia al Ministro Acton*, «Archivio Storico per le Province Napoletane», XVII, 1932, pp. 251-296.
Tescione, G., *L'arte della seta a Napoli e la colonia di S. Leucio*, Naples 1932.
Wahl, H., *Dressing Handzeichnunger von Goethe*, Leipzig 1932.
1933
Norsk Malerkunst - I Nasjonalgalleriet, Oslo 1933.
1934
Bodkin, T., *Orazio and the other Grevenbroech*, «Proceeding of the Royal Irish Academa», Dublin-London 1934.
Filangieri, R., *Castel dell'Ovo nelle sue più antiche rappresentazioni (1352-1456)*, Rassegna storica napoletana, II, 1934, 2, pp. 142-156.
Lorenzetti[1], C., *Gaspar Vanvitelli*, Milan 1934.
Lorenzetti[2], C., *Napoli nelle vedute dei pittori neerlandesi*, «Napoli, Rivista del Comune di Napoli», LX, 1934, 11-12, pp. CCXXVII-CCXXXVIII.
Ortolani, S., *La scuola di Posillipo*, Rome 1934.
1935
Bell, C. F.-Girtin, Th., *The Drawings and sketches of John Robert Cozens*, «The Walpole Society», XXIII, 1935.
Buscaroli, R., *La pittura di paesaggio in Italia*, Bologna 1935.
Göttsche, G., *Wolfgang Heimbach. Ein norddeutscher Maler des 17 Jahrhunderts*, Berlin 1935.
Lorenzetti, C., *Precisazione critiche e documenti sul pittore A. Sminck Pitloo (1791-1837)*, «Archivio Storico per le Province Napoletane, XXI n. s., 1935, pp. 390-412.
Morazzoni, G., *Le porcellane italiane*, Milan 1935.
Reau, L., *L'énigme de Monsù Desiderio*, «Gazette des Beaux Arts», LXXVII, 1935, 13, pp. 242-255.
1936
Naples: exhibition catalogue, *Il paesaggio nella pittura napoletana dell'Ottocento*, Naples 1936.
1937
Ceci, G., *Bibliografia per la storia delle arti figurative nell'Italia meridionale*, Naples 1937.
Pane, R., *Architettura del Rinascimento in Napoli*, Naples 1937.
1938
Benesch, O., *Katalog der Stifilichen Kunstsamml., Die Gemäldesamml. des Stiftlichen Museums des Stiftes Klosternenburg*, Klosternenburg 1938.
Cutolo, A., *L'ambasciatore Caracciolo*, «Il Roma», Naples 2 aprile 1938.
Filangieri, R., *Rassegna critica delle fonti per la storia di Castelnouvo* - Estratto dall'Archivio storico per le province napoletane, XXII-XXIII n. s., 1935-1937, Naples 1938.
Lorenzetti, C., *La pittura napoletana del secolo XVIII*, in Naples: exhibition catalogue , *La mostra della pittura napoletana dei secoli XVII-XVIII-XIX*, Naples 1938, pp. 143-222.
Ortolani, S., *La pittura napoletana del secolo XVII*, in Naples: exhibition catalogue, *La mostra della pittura napoletana dei secoli XVII-XVIII-XIX*, Naples 1938, pp. 13-113.
1939
Tintelnot, H., *Barocktheater und Barocke Künst*, Berlin 1939.
1940
Briganti, G.,*Chiarimenti sul Vanvitelli*, «Critico d'Arte», V, 1940, pp. 129-134.
Ortolani[1], S., *Veronese Antonio*, in Thieme, U.-Becker, F., *Allgemeines Lexikon der Bildenden Künstler*, Leipzig 1940, XXXIV, p. 291.
Ortolani[2], S., *Vervloet Frans*, in Thieme, U.-Becker, F., *Allgemeines Lexikon der Bildenden Künstler*, Leipzig 1940, XXXIV, p. 306.
Santangelo, A., *Nuovi acquisti per i Musei di Stato*, «Le Arti», II, 1940, 2, pp. 67-74.
Sgadari di Lo Monaco, P., *Pittori e scultori siciliani dal '600 all'800*, Palermo 1940.
1941
Croft Murray, E., *The painted Hall in Heidegger's House at Richmond*, «The Burlington Magazine», LXXVIII, 1941, 957, pp. 105-112; 958, pp. 153-159.
Naples: exhibition catalogue, *Mostra di stampa e disegni napoletani dell'Ottocento*, edited by Augusto Cesareo, Naples 1941.
1942
A Signed work by Antonio Joli, «The Burlington Magazine», LXXX, 1942, 969, p. 101.
Combe, J.,*Brueghel de Velours*, Paris 1942.
Livan, L., *Notizie d'arte tratte dai notatori e dagli annali del Nh. Pietro Gradenigo*, Venice 1942.
Lorenzetti, G., *La pittura italiana del '700*, Novara 1942.
1943
Börenius, T., *Heidegger and Joli: another Link*,

The Burlington Magazine, LXXXII, 1943, 982, p. 124.
De Filippis, F.-Morisani, O., *Pittori tedeschi a Napoli nel '700*, Naples 1943.
Pontieri, E., *Il tramonto del baronaggio siciliano*, Florence 1943.
1944
Romdahl, A., *Notes on Monsù Desiderio*, Göteborg 1944.
1945
Comanducci, A. M., *Dizionario illustrato dei pittori, disegnatori e incisori italiani moderni e contemporanei*, II ed., 2 voll., Milan 1945.
Naples: exhibition catalogue, *La scuola di Posillipo*, Naples 1945.
Pontieri, E., *Il riformismo borbonico nella Sicilia del Sette e dell'Ottocento*, Rome 1945.
1946
Brancato, F., *Il Caracciolo e il suo tentativo di riforma in Sicilia*, Palermo 1946.
Causa, R., *Appunti sulla formazione di Micco Spadaro*, « Il Sagittario », I, 1946, p. 26 sgg.
Colloqui con il cancelliere Von Müller di Wolfango Goethe, trans. by G. Gabetti, Rome 1946.
1947
Jandolo, A., *Antiquaria*, Milan 1947.
Lorenzetti, G., *Vedute di Venezia – Disegni di Francis Vervloet pittore fiammingo, al Museo Correr*, « Arte Veneta », I, 1947, pp. 288-292.
Paris: exhibition catalogue, *Paysages d'Italie*, edited by J. L. Vaudojer, Paris 1947.
1947-1969
De Marinis, T., *La biblioteca napoletana dei re d'Aragona*, 6 voll., Milan-Verona 1947-1969.
1949-1950
Klauner, F., *Zur Landschaft Jan Brueghels d. A.*, « Nationalmuserei Arsbok », 1949-1950, pp. 5-28.
1950
Briganti, G., *Pieter van Laer e Michelangelo Cerquozzi*, « Proporzioni », III, 1950, pp. 185-198.
Causa, R., *Angiolillo Arcuccio*, « Proporzioni », III, 1950, pp. 99-100.
Landes Museum Hannover, Hannover 1950.
Longhi, R., *Velazquez 1630. La rissa all'ambasciata di Spagna*, « Paragone », I, 1950, 1, pp. 28-34, Paris: exhibition catalogue, *Tresors des bibliotheques d'Italie*, Paris 1950.
Rome[1]: exhibition catalogue, *I bamboccianti, pittori della vita popolare del Seicento*, edited by G. Briganti, Rome 1950.
Rome[2]: exhibition catalogue, *Monsù Desiderio*, edited by G. Urbani, Rome 1950.
Romeo, R., *Il Risorgimento in Sicilia*, Bari 1950.
Sarasota: exhibition catalogue, *The fantastic vision of Monsù Desiderio*, Sarasota 1950.
Scharf, A., *Francesco Desiderio*, « The Burlington Magazine », XCII, 1950, 562, pp. 18-22.
1950-51
Walls, W., *Leonardo Coccorante. Some « Roman Ruin » Paintings at Temple Newsam*, « Leeds Art Calendar », IV, 1950-51, pp. 29-32.
1951
Clau, C., *J. M. W. Turner his life and work*, London 1951.
Hoogewerff, G. J., *De Bent vueghels*, The Hague 1951.
1952
Canton Sanchez, F. J., *Itinerario del Museo del Prado*, Madrid 1952.
Constable, W. G., *Carlo Bonavia and some painters of vedute in Naples*, in *Essays in honor of George Swarzenscki*, Chicago 1952, pp. 198-204.
De Filippis, F., *Le reali delizie di una capitale*, Naples 1952.
Lorenzetti, C., *L'Accademia di Belle Arti di Napoli*, Florence 1952.
Museo del Prado. Catalogo del los quadros, Madrid 1952.
Oppè, A. P., *Alexander and John Robert Cozens*, London 1952.
Pariset, F. G., *M. Desiderio nel Museo di Arti decorative di Parigi*, « Commentari », III, 1952, pp. 261-264.
Prota-Giurleo, U., *Pittori montenurresi del '600, con addizioni di A. Ragona*, Naples 1952.
1952-53
Griseri, A., *Disegni di Francis Vervloet (1796-1872) in una collezione torinese*, « Bollettino della Società di Archeologia e di Belle Arti », VI-VII, 1952-52, pp. 204-209.
1953
Brion, M., *L'énigmatique Monsù Desiderio*, « Arts », January 8, 1953.
Caviggioli Aurè, L., *Paesisti del 700 facilmente confondibili*, « Arte figurativa antica e moderna », VI, 1953, pp. 18-23.
Fodorov-Davidov, A., *La pittura di paesaggio russa del XVIII e XIX secolo*, Moscow 1953.
Molajoli, B., *Opere d'arte del Banco di Napoli*, Naples 1952.
Naples: exhibition catalogue, *Stampe e « guazzi » napoletani dell'Ottocento*, edited by Augusto Cesareo, Naples 1953.
Nuovi acquisti dei musei e gallerie dello Stato-G. Ricciardelli « vedute di chiaia », « Bollettino d'arte », XXXVIII, 1953, 4, p. 381.
Prota Giurleo, U., *Pittori napoletani del Seicento*, Naples 1953.
Thiéry, Y., *Le paysage flammand au XVII siècle*, Bruxelles 1953.
1954
Benevento: exhibition catalogue, *Achille Vianelli*, a cura di M. Rotili, Naples 1954.
Brion, M., *Desiderio peintre napolitain...*, « Plaisir de France », XXI, 1954, 187 bis, pp. 2 f. « Emporium », LX, 1954, 3, pp. 104-112.
Croce, B., *Una raccoltina di autografi*, in *Aneddoti di varia letteratura*, Bari 1954, III, pp. 109-112.
Ferraro, O., *Leonardo Coccorante e la « veduta ideata » napoletana*, « Emporium », LX, 1954, 1, pp. 9-20.
Naples: exhibition catalogue, *Mostra del ritratto storico napoletano*, edited by G. Doria e F. Bologna, Naples 1954.
Österreichische Galarie des XIX. und XX. Jahrhunderts im Oberen Belvedere, Katalog der Neueaufstellung, Vienna 1954.
Picone, M., *Disegni inediti di Vervolet al Museo di S. Martino*, « Il Fuidoro », I, 1954, pp. 138-142.
Sluys, F., *Le Lorrain Didier Barra est identifié aujourd'hui ave l'énigmatique Monsù Desiderio, peintre des cataclysures*, « Journal des Beaux Arts », 1954, 655, pp. 1-4.
Vienna: exhibition catalogue, *Österreichische Landschaften des 19. Jahrunderts*, edited by L. Münz, Vienna 1954.
1955
Longhi, R., *Vivaio Codazzi e l'invenzione della veduta realistica*, « Paragone », VI, 1955, 71, pp. 40-47.
Maggiore, D., *Arte e artisti dell'Ottocento napoletano e scuola di Posillipo*, Naples 1955.
Naples: exhibition catalogue, *Acquerelli di Giacinto Gigante*, edited by Raffaello Causa, Naples 1955.
Salerno: exhibition catalogue, *Opere d'arte nel salernitano dal XII al XVIII secolo*, edited by Ferdinando Bologna, Naples 1955.
Strazzullo, F., *Documenti inediti per la storia dell'arte a Napoli*, estratto da « Il Fuidoro », Naples 1955.
1956
Acton, H., *The Bourbons of Naples (1734-1825)*, London 1956. (it. ed. Florence 1960).
Brunetti, E., *Situazione di Viviano Codazzi*, « Paragone », VII, 1956, 79, pp. 48-69.
Causa[1], R., *François De Nomé detto Monsù Desiderio*, « Paragone », VII, 1956, 75, pp. 30-46.
Causa[2], R., *L'eruzione del Vesuvio nel 1631. Un dipinto di Micco Spadaro ed un poemetto di Giovan Battista Bergazzano*, Naples 1956.
Causa[3], R., *Pitloo*, Naples 1956.
Greindl, E., *Les peintres flamands de nature morte au XVII e siècle*, Paris-Bruxelles 1956.
Lavagnino, E., *L'arte moderna dai neoclassici ai contemporanei*, Turin 1956.
Maio, I., *De Majestate, inedito del secolo XV*, edited by F. Gaeta, Bologna 1956.
Maltese, C., *Monsù Desiderio Architetto di rovine*, in *Scritti di storia dell'arte in onore di Lionello Venturi*, Rome 1956, II, pp. 65-80.
Morazzoni, G., *La terraglia italiana*, Milan 1956.
Neapolis in Italia ..., pref. by Gino Doria, Milan 1956.
Pane, R., *Ferdinando Fuga*, edited by Raffaele Mormone, Naples 1956.
Schettini, A., *Giacinto Gigante*, Naples 1956.
Una corona napoletana figurata del Quattrocento, edited by Riccardo Filangieri, Naples 1956.
Zurich: exhibition catalogue, *Unnbekannte Schönheit*, Zurich 1956.
1957
Causa, R., *Pittura napoletana dal XV al XIX secolo*, Bergamo 1957.
Colletta, P., *Storia del Reame di Napoli*, edited by Nino Cortese, 3 voll., Naples 1957.
De Brosses, C., *Viaggio in Italia*, 3 voll., Milan 1957.
Donzelli, C., *I pittori veneti del '700*, Florence 1957.
London: exhibition catalogue, *Loan exhibition of pictures from the city art gallery*, Birmingham 1957.
Longhi, R., *Una traccia per Filippo Napoletano*, « Paragone », VIII, 1957, 95, pp. 33-62.
Naples: exhibition catalogue, *Vedute napoletane della raccolta Lemmermenn*, edited by G. Doria e O. Ferrari, Naples 1957.
Warner, O., *Sir Hamilton and Fabris of Naples*, « Apollo », March 1957.
1958
Briganti, G., *22 dipinti di una raccolta privata*, Rome 1958.
Brunetti, E., *Some unpublished works by Codazzi, Salucci, Lemaire and Patel*, « The Burlington Magazine », C, 1958, 666, pp. 311-316.
Gentile, S., *A proposito dell'edizione del trattato « De Majestate » di Iuniano Majo*, « Filologia romanza », V, 1958, pp. 143-209.
Norwich: exhibition catalogue, *Eighteent Century Italy and the grand tour*, edited by Francis Hawcroft, Norwich 1958.
Paris: exhibition catalogue, *Monuments et sites d'Italie vus par les dessinateurs français de Callot à Degas*, Paris 1958.
Rome[1]: exhibition catalogue, *Michael Swaerts e i bamboccianti*, Rome 1958.
Rome[2]: exhibition catalogue, *Pittori napoletani dell'600 e dell'700*, edited by N. di Carpegna, Rome 1958.
Busiri Vici, A., *Fantasie romane di J. Lingelbach*, « Studi Romani », VII, 1959, 1, pp. 42-53.
Catalano, F., *Il vicerè Caracciolo e la Sicilia alla fine del sec. XVIII*, in *Illustri e giacobini del Settecento italiano*, Milan-Varese 1959, pp. 7-26.
Düsseldorf: exhibition catalogue, *Österreichische Malerei 1800'1930*, Düsseldorf 1959.
Fiocco, G., *Alessandro Greevoenbroeck a Padova*, « Bollettino del Museo Civico di Padova », 1959.
Garnier, J. P., *Murat roi de Naples*, Paris 1959.
Gere, J. A., *An oil Sketch by Thomas Jones*, « British Museum Quarterly », XXXI, 1959, pp. 93-94.
Molajoli, B., *Ritratti a Capodimonte*, Turin 1959.
Morassi, A., *Il gran tour degli inglesi nel Settecento*, « Emporium », LXV, 1959, 1, pp. 51-66.
Povoledo, E., *Joli Antonio*, in *Enciclopedia dello Spettacolo*, VI, Rome 1959.
Romano, E., *La porcellana di Capodimonte*, Naples 1959.
Schudt, L., *Italienreisen im 17. und 18 Jh.*, Vienna 1959.
Ville vesuviane del settecento, Naples 1959.
Wallraf Richartz Museum der Stadt Köln Verzeichnis der Gemälde, Cologne 1959.
1960
Blunt, A., *A « veduta » by Angelo Maria Costa*, « The Burlington Magazine », CII, 1960, 693, p. 529.
Essen: exhibition catalogue, *Unvergängliches Österreich, Ferdinand Georg Waldmüller Und seine Zeit*, Essen 1960.
Gerson, H.-Ter Kuile, E. H., *Art and Architecture in Belgium 1600 to 1800*, London 1960.
Geneva: sale catalogue, *N. Rauch*, Geneva 1960.
Golf von Neapel, preface by Elisabeth Dryander, Munich 1960.
Heinz, G., *Katalog der Graf Harrach' Schen Gemäldegalerie*, Vienna 1960.
Mc Cormick, T. J., *Notes on some further attributions to Bonavia*, « The Art Quarterly », XXIII, 1960, pp. 371-374.
Morazzoni, G.-Levy, S., *Le porcellane italiane*, Milan 1960.
Pallucchini, R., *La pittura veneziana del '700*, Venice 1960.

Russo, G., *La città di Napoli dalle origini al 1860*, Naples 1960.
Sievers, J., *Das vorbild des «Neuen Pavillons» von Karl Friedrich Schenkel im Schlosspark Charlottenburg*, «Zeitschrift fur Kunst Geschichte», 1960, 23, pp. 227-241.
Vienna: exhibition catalogue, *Katalog der XLVIII. Wechselausstellung der Österreichischen Galerie, Barbara Kraft (1764-1825) / Michael Wutky (1738-1822)*, edited by F. Novotny e H. Aurenhammer, Vienna 1960.
Wilenski, R.H., *Flemish Painters*, 1430-1830, London 1960.

1960-1985

Dizionario biografico degli italiani, 31 voll., (A-D), Rome 1960-1985.

1961

Doria, G., *Bambocciate napoletane - Ventisei disegni inediti di d'Anna*, Naples 1961.
London: exhibition catalogue, *The italian scene. Drawings by Vanvitelli*, London 1961.
Paris-Rome: exhibition catalogue, *I francesi a Roma. Residenti e viaggiatori nella città eterna dal Rinascimento all'inizio del Romanticismo*, Paris 1961.
Prota-Giurleo, U., *Notizie inedite su alcuni pittori napoletani del '700*, «Partenope», II, 1961, 4, pp. 43-45.
Rome: exhibition catalogue, *L'Italia vista dai pittori francesi del XVIII e XIX secolo*, Rome 1961.
Sluys, F., *Didier Barra et François De Nomé dits Monsù Desiderio*, Paris 1961.
Winner, M., *Zeichnungen des Alteren Jan Brueghels*, «Jahrbuch der Berlin Museen», III, 1961, pp. 190-241.

1962

Brosio, V., *Mobili italiani dell'Ottocento*, Milan 1962.
Bury, A., *Francis Towne: lone star of watercolour painting* London 1962.
Campi Phlegraei, edited by Gino Doria, Milan 1962.
Constable, W.G., *Carlo Bonavia: An addendum*, «Art Quarterly», XXV, 1962, pp. 123-127.
Doria, G., *Il largo di palazzo e un quadro di G. Vanvitelli*, Milan-Verona 1962.
Doria, G.,-Bologna, F.-Pannain, G., *Settecento napoletano*, Turin 1962.
Fritz, R., *Wolfgang Heimbach, Hofmaler Christoph Bernhards von Galen*, «Westfalen», XL, 1962, pp. 315 sgg.
de Mongolfier, B., *Quatre vues de Paris de Charles-Léopold Grevenbroeck*, «Bulletin du Musée Carnavalet», 1962, 2, pp. 9-18.
Naples: exhibition catalogue, *Il paesaggio napoletano nella pittura straniera*, Naples 1962.
Strazzullo, F., *La corporazione dei pittori napoletani*, Naples 1962.

1963

Bellefiore, G., *La civiltà artistica della Sicilia*, Florence 1963.
Ginori Lisci, L., *La porcellana di Doccia*, Milan 1963.
Greigenhagen, A., *Nacklange griechenscher Vasefunde im Klanizismus*, «Jahrbuch der Berliner Museen», 1962, 5, pp. 84-105.
Rothenstein, J., *The Tate Gallery*, London 1963.
Salmi, M., *Introduzione in G. Pampaloni, Palazzo Strozzi*, Rome 1963.

1964

Causa, R., *Doni ai Musei e gallerie dello Stato*, «Bollettino d'arte», XLIX, 1964, pp. 419-429.
Die *Gemäldesammlung des Historichen Museums der Stadt Wien*, edited by P. Pötschner, Vienna 1964.
Doria[1], G., *Il largo di Palazzo a Napoli e Gaspare degli occhiali*, Verona-Milan 1964.
Doria[2], G., *It Museo e la Certosa di S. Martino*, Naples 1964.
Eemans, M., *Brueghel de Velours*, Bruxelles 1964.
Filangieri, R., *Castelnuovo, Reggia Angioina ed Aragonese*, Naples 2 ed., Naples 1964.
Krönig, W., *Eine Italien-Landschaft des 18. Jahrhunderts im Deutschen Archäologischen Institut zu Berlin. Philipp Hacherts Ansicht der Solfatara bei Neapel*, Berlin 1964.
Mancini, F., *Scenografia napoletana dell'età barocca*, Naples 1964.
Molajoli, B., *Notizie su Capodimonte. Catalogo delle gallerie e del Museo*, 5 ed., Naples 1964.
Mozzillo, A., *Viaggiatori stranieri nel sud*, Milan 1964.
Naples: exhibition catalogue, *Museo di S. Martino. Mostra di oggetti d'arte e di documenti storici scelti dalle raccolte dei depositi*, a cura di Marina Causa Picone e Anna Maria Bonucci, Naples 1964.

1965

Hairs, M.L., *Les peintres flamands de fleurs au XVII e siècle* 2 ed., Bruxelles 1965.
Krönig, W., *Ein Agrigent-Bild von Philipp Hackert in der Universität zu Köln*, «Wallraf-Richartz-Jahrbuche», 1965, 27, pp. 417-422.
Martin, A., *Notizia su Pietro Antoniani milanese a Napoli*, «Paragone», XVI, 1965, 181, pp. 80-83.
Perez Sanchez, A.E., *Pintura italiana del siglo XVII en España*, Madrid 1965.
Utrecht: exhibition catalogue, *Nederlandse 17e eeuwse-italianiserende Land-schapschilders*, Utrecht 1965.
Zwollo, A., *Zeichnungen von Caspar von Wittel und Hendrick Frans van Lint in deer Staatliche Museen zu Berlin*, «Forschungen und Berichte», 1965, 7, pp. 34-42.

1966

A view of the Arno, Florence, by Antonio Joli, «The Burlington Magazine», CVIII, 1966, 765, entry n. XXVI.
Baccheschi, E., *Mobili Italiani del Meridione*, Milan 1966.
Briganti, G., *Van Wittel e l'origine della veduta settecentesca*, Rome 1966.
Causa[1], R., *Napoletani dell'Ottocento*, Naples 1966.
Causa[2], R., *Un nuovo libro su G. Van Wittel ed alcuni suoi inediti*, «Napoli Nobilissima», V, 1966, pp. 175-181.
Doria, G.-Causa, R., *I tesori - La Reggia di Capodimonte*, Florence 1966.
Ferrari, O., *Porcellane del Settecento*, Naples 1966.
Florence: exhibition catalogue, *Artisti olandesi e fiamminghi in Italia. Mostra di disegni del cinque e seicento della collezione Frits Lugt*, edited by Carlos van Hasselt e Albert Blankert, Florence 1966.
Grohn, H.W., *Wolfgang Heimbach*, in Kindlers Malerei-Lexikon, III, Zurich 1966.
Krönig, W., *Philipp Hackert und Russland. Mit einem Verzeichnis der in Russland befindlichen Gemälde Hackers*, «Wallraf-Richartz-Jahrbuch», 1966, 28, pp. 309-320.
Mancini, F., *Scenografia italiana dal Rinascimento all'età romantica*, Naples 1966.
Mariani, V., *Gaspare Van Wittel detto degli occhiali*, «Il giornale d'Italia», December 30-31, 1966.
Munich: exhibition catalogue, *Meissener Porzellan*, Munich 1966.
Pottino, F., *Il Museo diocesano di Palermo*, Palermo 1966.
Rome[1]: exhibition catalogue, *Vanvitelli ed altri vedutisti*, Rome 1966.
Rome[2]: exhibition catalogue, *La pittura inglese da Hogarth a Turner (1730-1850)*, Rome 1966.

1967

Causa, R., *La scuola di Posillipo*, Milan 1967.
Causa, Picone, M., *Vetri a S. Martino*, Naples 1967.
Coniglio, G., *I viceré spagnoli di Napoli*, Naples 1967.
Florence: exhibition catalogue, *Paesisti bambocciati e vedutisti nella Roma seicentesca*, a cura di Marco Chiarini, Florence 1967.
González-Palacios, A., *David e la pittura napoletana*, Milan 1967.
Guzzi, V., *Il ritratto nella pittura italiana dell'Ottocento*, Milan 1967.
Krönig, W., *Der königliche Jagd-Pavillon im Fusaro-See bei Neapel und Philipp Hackerts Jahreszeiten-Bilder*, «Wallraf-Richartz-Jahrbuch», 1967, 29, pp. 219-242.
Lebensztejn, J.C., *Une «vanité» de Monsù Desiderio*, L'Oeil, 1967, 156, pp. 2-9.
Murolo, M.G., *Una villa Napoletana del Seicento - Villa Belvedere*, Rome 1967.
Naples: exhibition catalogue, *Arte francese a Napoli*, Naples 1967.
Venice: exhibition catalogue, *I vedutisti veneziani del Settecento*, a cura di Pietro Zampetti, Venice 1967.
Wagner, W., *Die Geschichte der Akademie der Bildenden Künste in Wien*, Vienna 1967.

1967-71

Koeman, C., *Atlantes Neerlandici*, 5 voll., Amsterdam 1967-71.

1968

Bregenz-Vienna: exhibition catalogue, *Angelika Kauffmann und ihre zeitgenossen*, Bregenz 1968.
Briganti, G., *I vedutisti*, Milan 1968.
Ferrajoli, F., *Napoli monumentale*, Napoli 1968.
Franz, H.G., *das niederländische Waldbild und seine Entstehung im 16. Jahrundert*, «Bulletin des Musées Royaux des Beaux-Arts de Belgique», XVII, 1968, 1-2, pp. 15-38.
Krönig, W., *Il padiglione borbonico al Fusaro e le «Quattro Stagioni» di Filippo Hackert*, «Napoli Nobilissima», VII, 1968, pp. 3-16.
Krönig, W., *Kehrtwendung der Blickrichtung in Veduten-Paaren von Philipp Hackert*, Wallraf-Richartz-Jahrbuch, 1968, 30, pp. 253-274.
Krönig, W., *Vesuv-Ausbrüche von 1774 und 1779 gemalt von Philipp Hackert*, in *Medicinae et artibus. Festschrift für Wilhelm Katner* , Düsseldorf 1968, pp. 51-60.
Laxenburg: exhibition catalogue, *Romantik und Realismus in Österreich, Gemälde und Zeichnungen aus der Sammlung Georg Schäfer, Schweinfurt*, Laxenburg 1968.
Mancini, F., *Feste e apparati civili e religiosi in Napoli da viceregno alla capitale*, Naples 1968.
Marqués de Lozoja, *El embarque de Carlo III en Nápoles*, «Reales sitios», 1968, 17, pp. 33 sgg.
Nicolson, B., *Joseph Wright of Derby*, London 1968.
Strazzullo, F., *Edilizia e urbanistica a Napoli dal '500 al '700*, Naples 1968.
Winkelmann-Rhein, G., *Blumen Breughel*, Cologne 1968.

1969

Bruxelles: exhibition, *Bruegel, le peintre et son monde*, Bruxelles 1969.
Catello, E., *Francesco Celebrano e l'arte nel presepe napoletano del '700*, Naples 1969.
De Seta, C., *Cartografia della città di Napoli, lineamenti dell'evoluzione urbana*, 3 voll., Naples 1969.
Franz, H.G., *Niederländische Landschaftsmalerei im Zeitalter des Manierismus*, Graz 1969.
González-Palacios, A., *Il mobile nei secoli - Italia*, III, Milan 1969.
Morelli, G., *Appunti bio-bibliografici su Gaspare e Luigi Vanvitelli*, «Archivio della Società Romana di Storia patria», XXIII, 1969, 1-4, pp. 117-136.
New York: exhibition catalogue, *In the shadow of Vesuvius*, a cura di J. Scholz, New York 1969.
Pane, R., *Recensione a* De Seta, C., *La cartografia della città di Napoli ...*, «Napoli Nobilissima», VIII, n.s, 1969, pp. 36-40.

1970

Bodart, D., *Les peintres des Pays Bas méeridionaux et ae Principauté de lièges à Rome au XVII siècle*, 2 vol., Bruxelles-Rome 1970.
Celano, C., *Notizie del Bello e dell'Antico e del Curioso della città di Napoli ..., con aggiunzione di Giovan Battista Chiarini*, preface Gino Doria, Luigi De Rosa, edited by A. Mozzillo, A. Profeta and F.P. Macchia, 3 voll., Naples 1970.
Corbo, A.M., *L'esportazione delle opere d'arte dallo Stato Pontificio tra il 1814 e il 1823*, «L'Arte», LXXIII, 1970, 10, pp. 88-113.
Donatone, G., *Maioliche napoletane della spezieria Aragonese di Castelnuovo*, Naples 1970.
Fawcett Thompson, R., *David Allan and the Hamilton Portraits*, «The Connoisseur», 1970, pp. 250-253.
Figures by a coast with shipping and ruins by Leonardo Coccorante, «The Burlington Magazine», CXII, 1970, 813, entry n. XLV.
Galasso, G., *Napoli nel viceregno spagnolo dal 1648 al 1696*, in *Storia di Napoli*, Cava dei Tirreni 1970, VI, tomo II, pp. 3-534.
Lorente, M., *Prado-Madrid*, 2 voll., Novara 1970.
Milan: sale catalogue, *Asta dell'eredità Antonio*

Colombo a favore della Casa del Cieco Mons. Edoardo Gilardi di Civate, Finarte, Milan, October 20, 1970.
Ortolani, S., *Giacinto Gigante e la pittura di paesaggio a Napoli e in Italia dal '600 all'800*, Naples 1970.
Pane, G., *Napoli seicentesca nella veduta di A. Baratta (I)*, «Napoli Nobilissima», IX, 1970, pp. 118-159.
Pittaluga, M., *Note su Francis Vervloet e la sua «Vie»*, «Antichità Viva rassegna d'arte», IX, 1970, 1, pp. 26-39.
Twickenham-Cardiff: exhibition catalogue, *Thomas Jones (1782-1803)*, Twickenham-Cardiff, 1970.

1971

Borrelli, G., *Il Palazzo Corigliano in Piazza S. Domenico Maggiore in Napoli*, «Realtà del Mezzogiorno», XI, 1971, pp. 77-88, 209-219, 319-340, 1157-1186, 1285-1315.
Busiri Vici, A., *I Poniatowsky a Roma*, Florence 1971.
Caputi, A.,-Causa, R.-Mormone, R., *La Galleria dell'Accademia di Belle Arti in Napoli*, Naples 1971.
Carola Perrotti, A., *La porcellana delle fabbriche borboniche*, in *Storia di Napoli*, Cava dei Tirreni 1971, VIII, pp. 607-648.
Colkelberghs, D., *H.F. Van Lint (Anversa 1648 – Roma 1763) copiste et imitateur de Claude Lorrain*, «Revue des archologues et Historiens d'art de Louvain», IV, 1971, pp. 185-197.
De Seta, C., *Atlante della città di Napoli*, Naples undated (1971).
Garms, J., *Die Briefe des Luigi Vanvitelli an material*, «Romische Historische Mitteilungen», XIII, 1971, pp. 201-285.
Goethe, J.W., *Gedenkausgabe der Werke, Briefe und Gesprache*, hsgb, von Ernst Beutler, IX, *Italienische Reise*, XIII, *Schriften zur Kunst*, Zurich 1971.
Grossmann, F., *Bruegel. The paintings*, London 1971.
Krönig, W., *L'eruzione del Vesuvio del 1779 in Hackert, H. Robert, Desprez e F. Piranesi*, in *Studi in onore di Roberto Pane*, Naples 1971, pp. 423-442.
Krönig, W., *Sepia - Zeichnungen aus der Umgebung Neaples von Philipp Hackert*, «Wallraf-Richartz-Jahrbuch», 1971, 33, pp. 175-204.
London-Manchester: exhibition catalogue, *Watercolours by John Robert Cozen*, edited by Francis Hawcroft, London 1971.
Pacelli, V., *Contributo a Francesco Celebrano pittore*, in *Studi di Storia dell'arte in onore di Valerio Mariani*, Naples 1971, pp. 259-269.
Spinosa, N., *La pittura napoletana da Carlo a Ferdinando IV di Borbone*, in *Storia di Napoli*, Cava dei Tirreni 1971, VIII, pp. 451-547.
Stechow, F., *Pieter Bruegel*, Milan 1971.
Toschi, P.-Penna, R., *Le tavolette votive della Madonna dell'Arco*, Cava dei Tirreni 1971.

1972

Bouret, J., *L'école de Barbizon et le paysage française au XIX* siècle, Neuchâtel 1972.
Carola Perrotti, A., *Porcellane e terraglie napoletane dell'Ottocento*, in *Storia di Napoli*, Cava dei Tirreni 1972, IX, pp. 833-879.
Catello, E.-Catello, C., *Argenti napoletani dal XVI al XIX secolo*, Naples 1972.
Causa[1], R., *La pittura del Seicento a Napoli dal naturalismo al barocco*, in *Storia di Napoli*, Cava dei Tirreni 1972, V, voll. II, pp. 913-994.
Causa[2], R., *La scuola di Posillipo*, in *Storia di Napoli*, Cava dei Tirreni 1972, IX, pp. 738-832.
Chiarini[1], M., *Filippo Napoletano ... e nascita del paesaggio realistico in Italia*, «Paragone», XXIII, 1972, 269, pp. 18-34.
Chiarini[2], M., *I disegni italiani di paesaggio dal 1600 al 1750*, Treviso 1972.
Colapietra, R., *Il governo spagnolo nell'Italia meridionale (Napoli dal 1580 al 1648)*, in *Storia di Napoli*, Cava dei Tirreni 1972, V, voll. I, pp. 161-278.
Demoulin, L., *Luigi Vanvitelli et la pose de la première pierre de la «reggia» di Caserta*, «Bulletin de l'Istitut historique Belge de Rome», 1972, pp. 445-452.
London: exhibition catalogue, *The age of Neo-Classicism*, London 1972.
Méras, M., *Deux Tableaux retrouvés des collections Bergeret de Grand court au château de Negrepelisse*, «Gazette des Beaux arts», CXIV, 1972, pp. 331-334.
Naples: exhibition catalogue, *La collezione Angelo Astarita al Museo di Capodimonte. Giacinto Gigante e la Scuola di Posillipo*, edited by Nicola Spinosa, Naples 1972.
Rome-Vienna: exhibition catalogue, *Artisti austriaci a Roma dal Barocco alla Secessione*, edited by Jörg Garms, Rome 1972.
Spinosa, N., *Luigi Vanvitelli e i pittori attivi a Napoli nella seconda metà del Settecento: lettere e documenti inediti*, «Storia dell'arte», 1972, 14, pp. 193-214.
Talamo, G., *Napoli da Giuseppe Bonaparte a Ferdinando II*, in *Storia di Napoli*, Cava dei Tirreni 1972, IX, pp. 33-130.
Valsecchi, M., *Paesaggisti dell'800*, Milan 1972.
Winner, M., *Neubestimmtes und Unbestimmtes im zeichnerischen Werk von Jan Brueghel d. Ä.*, «Jahrbuch der Berliner Museen», XIV, 1972, pp. 122-160.

1972-1976

Dizionario enciclopedico Bolaffi dei pittori e degli incisori italiani dall'XI al XX secolo, 11 voll., Turin 1972-1976.

1973

Blunt[1], A., *Recorders of Vanished Naples. I: Thomas Jones*, «Country Life» August 1973.
Blunt[2], A., *Recorders of vanished Naples – II: John Robert Cozens*, «Country Life», August 1973, pp. 568-570.
Blunt[3], A., *Seven Sketchbooks by John Robert Cozens*, Sotheby's, London, November 29, 1973.
Catello, E.-Catello, C., *Argenti napoletani dal XVI al XIX secolo*, Naples 1973.
Causa, R., *L'arte nella Certosa di S. Martino*, Cava dei Tirreni 1973.
De Seta, C., *Storia della città di Napoli dalle origini al Settecento*, Bari 1973.
Ducret, S., *Keramik und Graphik des 18. Jahrhunderts*, Braunschweig 1973.
Essen-The Hague-Zurich: exhibition catalogue, *Leben und Kunst in den Vesuvstädten*, Essen 1973.
Florence: exhibition catalogue, *Mostra di disegni italiani di paesaggio del Seicento e del Settecento*, edited by Mauro Chiarini, Florence 1973.
Gombrich, E.H., *La teoria dell'arte nel Rinascimento e l'origine del paesaggio*, in *Norma e forma*, Turin 1973.
González-Palacios, A., *Storia del mobile dal '500 al '900*, Milan 1973.
Luigi Vanvitelli, Naples 1973.
Pane, G., *Napoli seicentesca nelle vedute di A. Baratta (II)*, «Napoli Nobilissima», XII, 1973, pp. 45-70.
Pavel, P., *«Monsù Desiderio», Francois De Nomé*, «Sbornik praci Filosofiké Faculty Breuske University», XVII, 1973, pp. 187-195.
Putaturo Murano, A., *Miniature napoletane del Rinascimento*, Naples 1973.
Röttgen, S., *Recensione alla mostra The age of Neoclassicism*, «Arte illustrata», VI, 1973, 54, pp. 84-105.
Schreiner, L., *Die Gemälde des 19 und 20. Jahrhunderts in der Nds. Landsgalerie Hannover*, Munich 1973.
Zwollo, A., *Hollandse en Vlaamse Veduschildens te Rome (1675/1725)*, Assen 1973.

1974

Borrelli, G., *Leonardo Coccorante o del realismo magico*, «Realtà del Mezzogiorno», XIV, 1974, 12, pp. 957-972.
Catello, E.-Catello C., *Statue d'argento a Napoli nel Sei e Settecento*, in *Strenna napoletana per il 1974*, Naples 1974.
Ford, B., *The Earl-Bishop. An Eccentric and Capricious Patron of the Arts*, «Apollo», 1974, pp. 426-434.
La pittura napoletana dell'Ottocento nella raccolta Biagio D'Angelo, a cura di Alfredo Schettini, Naples 1974.
London: exhibition catalogue, *Turner 1775-1851*, edited by Martin Butlin, John Gage e Andrew Wilton, London 1974.
Marini, M., *Pittori a Napoli 1610-1656. Contributi e schede*, Rome 1974.
Pane, R., *Architettura e urbanistica del Rinascimento*, in *Storia di Napoli*, Cava dei Tirreni 1974, IV, tomo I, pp. 332-336.
Paris[1]: exhibition catalogue, *De David à Delacroix. La peinture française de 1774 à 1830*, Paris 1974.
Paris[2]: exhibition catalogue, *Louis Jean Desprez: 1734-1804*, Paris 1974.
Paris[3]: *Musée du Louvre-Catalogue illustré des peintures. École française XVII et XVIII siècle*, edited by P. Rosenberg-N. Reynaud.-I. Compin, Paris 1974.
Picone, M., *Disegni della Società Napoletana di Storia Patria*, Naples 1974.
Roberts, H., *Sehnsucht nach Italien, Bilder deutscher Romantiker*, Munich 1974.
Strazzullo, F., *Pittori e scultori del '700 a Napoli nelle relazioni di Luigi Vanvitelli*, from «Atti dell'Accademia Pontaniana», Naples 1974.
Sussino, S., *La veduta nella pittura italiana*, Florence 1974.

1975

Milan: exhibition catalogue, *Pittura inglese 1660-1840 – Due secoli di cultura, storia e costume in Inghilterra*, Milan 1975.
Naples[1]: exhibition catalogue, *Acquisizione 1960-1975*, Naples 1975.
Naples[2]: exhibition catalogue, *Da palazzo degli Studi a Museo Archeologico*, Naples 1975.
Pane, R., *Il Rinascimento nell'Italia meridionale*, Milan 1975.
Rosenberg, P., *La donation Pereire*, «La Revue du Louvre et des Musées de France», 1975, pp. 258-267.

1975-1976

Rozman, K., *Der maler Josef Tominz*, «Mitteilungen der Österreichischen Galerie», XIX-XX, 1975-1976, pp. 111 sgg.
Toledo-Chicago-Ottawa: exhibition catalogue, *The age of Luigi XV*, edited by P. Rosenberg, Toledo-Chicago-Ottawa 1975-1976.

1976

Bociarov, J.-Glusciokova, J., *Silvester Scedrin e la «Scuola di Posillipo»*, from «Novosti», it. ed., in «Sputnik», II, 1976, 46 f.
Carughi, U., in *L'Arciconfraternita della SS. Trinità dei Pellegrini*, Naples 1976.
Gerszi, T., *Bruegels Nachwirkung auf die niederländischen Landschaftsmaler um 1600*, «Oud Holland», 1976, 4, pp. 201-229.
London: exhibition catalogue, *Claude Joseph Vernet*, a cura di Ph. Conisbee, London 1976.
Marini, M., *Viviano Codazzi - Il capriccio del vero*, «Ricerche di storia dell'arte», 1976, 3, pp. 121-128.
Napoli e dintorni. Guida d'Italia del T. C. I., 5 ed., Milan 1976.
Negro Spina, A., *L'incisione napoletana dell'Ottocento*, Naples 1976.
Paone, M., *Il costume popolare salentino*, 2 ed., Galatina 1976.
Paris[1]: exhibition catalogue, Claude Joseph Vernet, edited by Ph. Conisbee, Paris 1976.
Paris[2]: exhibition catalogue, *La peinture allamande à l'époque du Romanticisme*, Paris 1976.
Röttgen, S., *Antonio Cavallucci. Un pittore romano tra tradizione e innovazione*, «Bollettino d'arte», LXI, 1976, III-IV, pp. 193-212.
Scibilia, A., *Caracciolo Domenico in Dizionario biografico degli italiani*, Rome 1976, XIX, pp. 337-347.
Zeri. F., *La percezione visiva dell'Italia e degli italiani nella storia della pittura*, in *Storia d'Italia*, VI, *Atlante*, Turin 1976, pp. 53-214.

1976-1977

Machyka, L., *Angelo Maria Costa da Milano*, «Umeni», 32, 1976-77, pp. 252-254.
Mottola Molfino, A., *L'arte della porcellana in Italia*, 2 voll., Busto Arsizio 1976-77.
Strazzullo, F., *Le lettere di Luigi Vanvitelli della Bibliografia Palatina di Caserta*, 3 voll., Galatina 1976-1977.

1977

Bologna, F., *Napoli e le rotte mediterranee della pittura da Alfonso il Magnanimo a Ferdinando il Cattolico*, Naples 1977.
Bordeaux: exhibition catalogue, *La peinture britannique de Gainsborough à Bacon*, Paris 1977.

Catello, E.-Catello C., *La Cappella del Tesoro di San Gennaro*, Naples 1977.
De Seta, C., *Napoli nel Settecento e le vedute di Etienne Giraud*, Milan 1977.
Faldi, I.-Mantura, B., *La Galleria Nazionale d'arte moderna*, Milan 1977.
Gaeta: exhibition catalogue, *Vedute di Gaeta nell'800 napoletano*, Gaeta 1977.
González-Palacios, A., *The art of Mosaics*, Los Angeles 1977.
London: exhibition catalogue, *French Landscape Drawings and Sketches of the Eigtheenth Century*, London 1977.
Ottawa-Toronto: exhibition catalogue, *Drawings by Gaspar Van Wittel from neapolitan collections*, edited by W. Vitzthum, Ottawa 1977.
Urrea Fernandez, J., *La pintura italiana del siglo XVIII en España*, Valladolid 1977.
Vajro, M., *Vedute di Napoli*, Naples 1977.
Zucco, C., *Le ipotesi progettuali dell'edificio da Cavallerizza a Museo*, in Naples: exhibition catalogue, *Da Palazzo degli Studi a Museo Archeologico*, Naples 1977.
1977-78
Paris: exhibition catalogue, *Porcelaines de Vincennes*, Paris 1977-78.
1977-1980
Salerno, L., *Pittori di paesaggio del '600 a Roma*, 3 voll., Milan 1977-1980.
1978
Baumgart, F., *Blumen Bruegel*, Cologne 1978.
Boston: exhibition catalogue, *Visions of Vesuvius*, a cura di A. Murphy, Boston 1978.
Busiri Vici, A., *Portici, piazzette e casolari di Roma e dintorni di Tommaso Fiammingo*, L'Urbe, XLI, 1978, 4, pp. 9-14.
Carola Perrotti, A., *La porcellana della Real Fabbrica Ferdinandea (1771-1806)*, Naples 1978.
Causa Picone, M., *Volaire*, «Antologia di Belle Arti», II, 1978, 5, pp. 24-48.
Delli, S., *Le piazze d'Italia. Tradizioni popolari e storia, arte e urbanistica*, Milan 1978.
De Martini, V.-González-Palacios, A., *Notizie sulla R. Fabbrica della porcellana – Postilla sugli acciai*, «Antologia di Belle Arti», II, 1978, 5, pp. 77-87.
von Eimen, H., *Deutsche malerei des Klassizismus und der Romantik*, Munich 1978.
Garzya, C., *Interni neoclassici a Napoli*, Naples 1978.
Michel, O., *Recherches sur J. Lallermand à Rome*, in *Piranesi et les français – Atti del colloquio di Villa Medici*, edited by G. Brunel (May 12-14, 1976), Rome 1978.
Naples: exhibition catalogue, *Capolavori dell'arte catalana*, Naples 1978.
Øystein H., *Ekplosion i domkirken aller malariet sem litteraner metafor*, in *En bog an Kunst til else Kai Sass*, 1978, pp. 186-192.
Pötschner, P., *Wien und die Wiener Landschaft, Spätbarocke und biedermeierliche Landschaftskunst in Wien*, Salzburg 1978.
Roland-Michel, M., *De l'illusion à «l'inquietante étrangeté». Quelques remarques sur l'evolution du sentiment et de la rappresentation de la ruine chez des artistes français à partir de 1730*, in *Piranesi et les français. Atti del colloquio di Villa Medici*, edited by G. Brunel (May 12-14 1976), Rome 1978, pp. 475 f.
Rome: sale catalogue, *collezione Mondolfo*, Christie's , Rome January 26, 1978.
Romano, G., *Studi sul paesaggio*, Turin 1978.
Ruotolo, R., *S. Brigida*, Naples 1978.
Spinosa, N., *L'opera completa di Ribera*, Milan 1978.
The Origins of Italian Veduta, exhibition catalogue, Providence 1978.
Zeri, F.-González-Palacios, A., *Un appunto su Vernet a Napoli*, «Antologia di belle arti», II, 1978, 5, pp. 59-61.
1979
Bushart, B., *Ein «anderer» Heimbach*, «Pantheon», XXXVII, 1979, 1, pp. 54-58.
Catalano, D., *Indagine radiologica della Tavola Strozzi*, «Napoli Nobilissima», XVIII, 1979, pp. 10-12.
Catalano, L., *I Palazzi di Napoli*, Naples 1979.
Causa, R., *Vedutisti stranieri a Napoli*, in Naples: exhibition catalogue, *Civiltà del '700 a Napoli 1734-1799*, Florence 1979, I, pp. 330-337.
Ertz, K., *Jan Brueghel der ältere (1568-1625): Die gemälde*, Cologne 1979.
Gaeta: exhibition catalogue, *Pasquale Mattei (1813-1879)*, Gaeta 1979.
González-Palacios, A., *The furnishings of the Villa Favorita in Resina*, «The Burlington Magazine», 1979, 913, pp. 226-243.
Krönig, W., *Philipp Hackerts Ansichten griechischer Tempel in Sizilien (1777)*, in Berlin: exhibition catalogue, *Berlin und die antike. Ergänzungsband zum Katalog*, Berlin 1979, pp. 363-377.
Lady Blessington at Naples, edited by Edith Clay, London 1979.
Lloyd, C.-Pane, C., *Three views of Naples in Oxford and Cambridge*, «Napoli Nobilissima», XVIII, 1979, pp. 148-154.
London: exhibition catalogue, *Jan Brueghel the Elder*, edited by K. Ertz, London 1979.
Marandel, J. P., *Pittori stranieri a Napoli*, in Naples: exhibition catalogue,*Civiltà del '700 a Napoli (1734-1799)*, Florence 1979, I, pp. 308-339.
Pane, R., *La Tavola Strozzi tra Firenze e Napoli*, «Napoli Nobilissima», XVIII, 1979, pp. 3-10.
Spinosa[1], N., *Gli anni di Carlo e Ferdinando di Borbone (1734-1805): continuità e crisi di una tradizione*, in Naples: exhibition catalogue, *Civiltà del '700 a Napoli 1734-1799*, Florence 1979, I, pp. 135-147.
Spinosa[2], N., *Notizie su ... e su Antonio Joli* in *Le Arti Figurative a Napoli nel Settecento (Documenti e ricerche)*, edited by C. De Seta, Naples 1979, pp. 385-391.
Strazzullo, F.. *Le Manifatture d'Arte di Carlo di Borbone*, Naples 1979.
Walch, P., *Foreign Artists at Naples: 1750-1799*, «The Burlington Magazine», CXXI, 1979, 913, pp. 247-252.
1979-1980
Naples: exhibition catalogue, *Civiltà del '700 a Napoli 1734-1799*, 2 voll., Florence 1979-1980.
1980
Alisio, G., *Napoli e il risanamento. Recupero di una struttura*. Naples 1980.
Basel: exhibition catalogue, *Caspar Wolf (1735-1783) – Landschaft im Vorfeld der Romantik*, Basel 1980.
Berlin: exhibition catalogue, *Meissen*, Berlin 1980.
Birmingham[1]: exhibition catalogue, *English watercolours and drawings: the J. Leslie Wright bequest*, edited by Andrea Rose, Birmingham.
Birmingham[2]: exhibition catalogue, *British Watercolours 1760-1930 from the Birmingham Museum and Art Gallery*, edited by Richard Lockett, Birmingham 1980.
Bologna: exhibition catalogue, *L'arte del Settecento emiliano – Architettura, scenografia, pittura di paesaggio*, Bologna 1980.
Bruxelles: exhibition catalogue, *Brueghel: une dinastie des peintres*, edited by K. Ertz, Bruxelles 1980.
De Martini, V.-González-Palacios, A., *La vendita della Real Fabbrica della Porcellana di Napoli nel 1807*, «Antologia di Belle Arti» 1980, 15-16, pp. 214-245.
De Seta, C., *Topografia umana e vedutismo nel Seicento: a proposito di alcuni disegni di A. Baratta*, «Prospettiva», 1980, 22, pp. 45-60.
Gaeta: exhibition catalogue, *Gaspar Van Wittel – Disegni dalle collezioni napoletane*, edited by W. Vitzthum, Gaeta 1980.
González-Palacios[1], A., *La Real Fabbrica della Porcellana di Napoli*, in Naples: exhibition catalogue, *Civiltà del '700 a Napoli 1734-1799*, Florence 1980, II, pp. 126-160.
González-Palacios[2], A., *Le arti decorative e l'arredamento alla corte di Napoli: 1734-1805*, in Naples: exhibition catalogue, *Civiltà del '700 a Napoli 1734-1799*, Florence 1980, II, pp. 76-95.
Krönig, W., *Filippo Hackert. Disegni a seppia dei dintorni di Napoli*, «Napoli Nobilissima», XIX, 1980, pp. 99-116.
Kuhn, B., *Der Landschaftsmaler Michael Wutky (1739-1822)*, Innsbruck 1980.
Mauro Mori, G., *Medaglie*, in Naples: exhibition catalogue, *Civiltà del '700 a Napoli 1734-1799*, Florence 1980, II, pp. 234-240.
New Haven: exhibition catalogue, *The art of Alexander and John Robert Cozens*, edited by A. Wilton, New Haven 1980.
Ricci, G., *Bologna – Le città nella storia d'Italia*, Rome-Bari 1980.
Ruckert, R., *Wittelsbacher Porzellan*, «Kunst e Antiquitäten», 1980, III, p. 20 sgg.
1980-1981
Paris-Geneva: exhibition catalogue, *Des monts et des eaux*, edited by M. Michel, Paris-Geneva 1980-1981.
Saccone, M. R., *Gaetano Forte*, in «Annali della facoltà di lettere e filosofia dell'Università di Napoli», XI n. s., 1980-1981, pp. 191-212.
1981
Causa[1], R., *Un pittore inglese nella corte di Ferdinando IV*, «Campania-Stagioni», II, 1981, 1, pp. 2-5.
Causa[2], R., *Genesi del «Voyage»; Le circostanze e i modi dell'opera*, in *Sul Voyage pittoresque dell'Abbate di Saint-Non*, Naples 1981, pp. 7-19.
Chicago-Detroit: exhibition catalogue, *The Golden Age of Naples. Art and civilisation under the Borbons 1734-1805*, 2 voll., Chicago 1981.
De Seta, C., *Architettura ambiente e società a Napoli nel Settecento*, Turin 1981.
De Seta[1], C., *La tradizione del «Grand Tour» ed il Voyage pittoresque*, in *Sul Voyage pittoresque dell'Abate di Saint-Non*, Naples 1981, pp. 21-28.
De Seta[2], C., *Napoli. Le città nella storia d'Italia*, Rome-Bari 1981.
Farinelli, F.-Isenburg, T., *Le intenzioni del pittoresco: i viaggiatori stranieri in Italia meridionale tra Sette e Ottocento*, in Bologna: exhibition catalogue, *Paesaggio, immagine e realtà*, Milan 1981, pp. 159-165.
Ford, B., *The Grand Tour*, «Apollo», December 1981, pp 390-401.
González-Palacios, A., *Mosaici e pietre dure*, Milan 1981
Gregori, M.-Ruotolo, R.-Bandera Gregori, L., *Il mobile italiano dal Rinascimento agli anni '60*, Milan 1981.
Knight, C., *I luoghi di delizie di William Hamilton*, «Napoli Nobilissima», XX, 1981, pp. 180-190.
Madrid: exhibition catalogue, *Pintores Rusos del siglo XIX*, Madrid 1981.
Mancini, F., *Con l'Abbé de Saint-Non alla riscoperta del popolare*, in *Sul Voyage pittoresque dell'Abbate di Saint-Non*, Naples 1981, pp. 29-37.
Michel, O., *Adrien Manglard peintre et collectionneur*, «Melanges de l'école française de Rome, M. A.-Temps Moderns», 93, 1981, pp. 823-926.
Naples: exhibition catalogue, *Mostra di vedute di Napoli nella collezione di stampe della raccolta d'arte «Fagliara» di proprietà dell'Istituto Suor Orsola Benincasa*, Naples 1981.
Omodeo, A., *Grafica napoletana del '600. Fabbricatori di immagini*, Naples 1981.
Paris-Naples-Pompeii: exhibition catalogue, *Pompei e gli architetti francesi dell'Ottocento*, Naples 1981.
Ricci, P., *Arte e artisti a Napoli*, Naples 1981.
Seghers[1], P., *Monsù Desiderio ou le théâtre de la fin du monde*, Paris 1981.
Seghers[2], P., *L'imitation aux Enfers*, «Connaissance des arts», 1981, 354, pp. 41-46.
Vallet, C., *Le «Voyage pittoresque» et «l'antiquariat» du temps*, in *Sul voyage pittoresque dell'Abate di Saint-Non*, Naples 1981, pp. 39-50.
Viatte, F., *Wilhelm Baur: un alsacien dans la Rome du XVII e siècle*, in *Les fondations nationales dans la Rome pontificale*, Rome 1981, pp. 685-712.
1982
Bologna, F., *La coscienza storica dell'arte d'Italia*, Turin 1982.
Catalano. D., *Riparliamo della Tavola Strozzi*, «Napoli Nobilissima», XXI, 1982, p. 64.
Conoscere la Galleria Sabauda. Documenti sulla storia delle sue collezioni, Turin 1982.
De Seta, C., *L'Italia nello specchio del «Grand Tour»*, in *Storia d'Italia-Annali*, Turin 1982, V, pp. 125-263.
De Vito, G., *Aniello Falcone & Co.*, in *Ricerche sul '600 napoletano*, Motta Visconti (MI) 1982, pp. 7-35.

Di Mauro, L., *Significati e simboli nella decorazione della Mappa del Duca di Noja*, in *Arti e Civiltà del Settecento a Napoli*, edited by C. De Seta, Rome-Bari 1982.
Fusco, M. A., *Il « luogo comune » paesaggistico nelle immagini di massa*, in *Storia dell'Italia-Annali*, Turin 1982, V, pp. 753-801.
Horn-Oncken, A., *Viaggiatori stranieri del XVI e XVII sec. nei Campi Flegrei*, « Puteoli », VI, 1982, pp. 67-135.
Le collezioni del Museo di Capodimonte, edited by Raffaello Causa, Milan 1982.
London: exhibition catalogue, *Souvenir of the Grand Tour*, London 1982.
London-Washington: exhibition catalogue, *Painting in Naples 1606-1705 from Caravaggio to Giordano*, London 1982.
Maddalo, S., *Adrien Manglard (1695-1760)*, Rome 1982.
Naples: exhibition catalogue, *Immagini di devozione popolare*, Venice 1982.
Rome: exhibition catalogue, *Claude Lorrain e i pittori lorenesi in Italia nel XVII secolo*, Rome 1982.
Romano, G., *L'idea del paesaggio italiano*, in *Storia d'Italia - Annali*, Turin 1982, V, pp. 265-269.
Ruotolo, R., *Mercanti – Collezionisti fiamminghi a Napoli – Gaspare Roomer e i Vandeneyden*, Massalubrense 1982.
Spantigati, C., *Le collezioni di pittura fiamminga e olandese della Galleria Sabauda*, in *Pittura fiamminga e olandese in Galleria Sabauda ...*, Turin 1982, pp. 29-37.
Williams, C., *Lusieri's surviving works*, « The Burlington Magazine », CXXIV, 1982, 953, pp. 492-496.
Wilton, A., *Turner Abroad*, London 1982.

1982-83

London-Cardiff-New Haven: exhibition catalogue, *Richard Wilson: the landscape of Reaction*, London Cardiff-New Haven 1982-83.

1983

Bedoni, S., *Jan Bruegel in Italia e il collezionismo nel Seicento*, Florence-Milan 1983.
Briganti, G.-Trezzani, L.-Laureati, L., *I bamboccianti. I pittori della vita quotidiana a Roma nel Seicento*, Rome 1983.
Briganti, G., *Viviano Codazzi*, in *I pittori bergamaschi dal XII al XIX secolo. Il seicento*, I, Bergamo 1983.
Cartografia Napoletana dal 1781 al 1889, edited by G. Alisio e V. Valerio, Naples 1983.
Causa, R., *Sterminatore Vesevo*, « F. M. R. », II, 1983, 15, pp. 53-76.
Causa Picone, M., *Gli interlocutori di Goethe*, in Naples: exhibition catalogue, *Goethe e i suoi interlocutori*, a cura di Annalisa Porzio e Marina Causa Picone, Naples 1983, pp. 105-313.
Cautela, G.-Maietta, I., *Epigrafia e città: iscrizioni medioevali e moderne nel Museo di San Martino in Napoli*, Naples 1983.
De Maio, R., *Pittura e controriforma a Napoli*, Bari 1983.
Genoa: exhibition catalogue, *Maestri dell'acquerello inglese. Acquerelli del Victoria and Albert Museum*, Rome 1983.
Gilly, W., *Wolfgang Heimbach*, in Oldenburg: exhibition catalogue, *Anton Günther Graf von Oldenburg 1583-1667*, Oldenburg 1983, pp. 89 sgg.
Hoff, U., *Cross-Currents in dutch and flemish painting in the seventeenth century*, « Apollo », CXVIIII, 1983, pp. 58-63.
Knight, C., *Il contributo di P. Fabris ai « Campi Phegraei » di Hamilton*, « Napoli Nobilissima », XXIII, 1983, pp. 1000-110.
Knörig, W., *Philipp Hackert: Zehn Aussichten von dem Landhause des Horaz 1780*, Düsseldorf 1983.
Munich[1]: exhibition catalogue, *G. Van Wittel Zeichnungen und Aquerelle*, Munich 1983.
Munich[2]: exhibition catalogue, *Im Licht von Claude Lorrain*, edited by Marcel Roethlisberger, Munich 1983.
Naples[1]: exhibition catalogue, *Goethe e i suoi interlocutori*, edited by Annalisa Porzio e Marina Causa Picone, Naples 1983.
Naples[2]: exhibition catalogue, *Napoli e la Campania Felix. Acquerelli di Giacinto Gigante*, Naples 1983.
Origins of Italian Veduta, Providence (Rhode Island) 1983.
Paris: exhibition catalogue, *La peinture napolitaine de Caravage à Giordano*, Paris 1983.
La pittura del Settecento a Roma, edited by Stella Rudolph, Milan 1983.
Pompeii: exhibition catalogue, *Itinerario a Pompei nell'800*, edited by Luisa Martorelli and Stefano De Caro, Naples 1983.
Turin: exhibition catalogue, *La pittura napoletana da Caravaggio a Giordano*, Milan 1983.
Vaduz: exhibition catalogue, *Wiener Biedermeier, Gëmalde aus den Sammlungen des Regierenden Fürsten von Liechtenstein*, edited by R. Baumstark, Vaduz 1983.

1983-84

Naples: exhibition catalogue, *Luoghi virgiliani. Immagini nel Tempo*, edited by Luciana Arbace, Naples 1983-84.

1984

Martorelli, L., in *Il patrimonio artistico del Banco di Napoli, catalogo delle opere*, edited by Nicola Spinosa, Naples 1984.
Adamo Muscettola, S., *Napoli e l'immaginario antico tra '600 e '800*, « Prospettiva », 39, 1984, pp. 2-10.
Alisio, G., *Napoli nel Seicento. Le vedute di Francesco Cassiano de Silva*, Naples 1984.
Bonito Oliva A., *Catastrofe di Desiderio*, in *Studi in onore di Giulio Carlo Argan*, Rome 1984, I, pp. 239-250.
Borrelli, G., *Costa Angelo Maria*, in *Dizionario biografico degli italiani*, Rome 1984, XXX, pp. 162-164.
Butlin, M.-Joll, E., *The paintings of J. M. W. Turner*, 2 voll., London-New Haven 1984.
Catalogo dell'arte italiana dell'ottocento, 13, Milan 1984.
Causa, R., *La pittura napoletana dell'Ottocento*, in *Catalogo dell'arte italiana dell'ottocento*, 13, Milan 198, pp. 99-114.
Chassex P., *Ducros' Italian Landscapes. The perception of landscape by a Swiss Painter at the end of 18th. century*, « Daidalos », 1984, 12, pp. 70-78.
Cologne: exhibition catalogue, *Heroismus und Idylle. Former der Landschaft um 1800 bei J. Ph. Hackert, J. A. Koch und J. C. Reinhart*, edited by Wolfgang Krönig, Cologne 1984.
Costamagna, A., *L'antico negli apparati borbonici*, in *Studi in onore di Giulio Carlo Argan*, Rome 1984, II, pp. 111-130.
Doria, G., *Viaggiatori stranieri a Napoli*, Naples 1984.
González-Palacios, A., *Il tempio del gusto*, Milan 1984.
Ischia: exhibition catalogue, *Immagini di Ischia tra XVIII e XIX secolo*, a cura di L. Arbace e L. Martorelli, Bologna 1984.
Krönig[1], W., *Die toskanische Pariode des Maleers Philipp Hackert (1799-1807)*, in *Scritti di storia dell'arte in onore di Roberto Salvini*, Florence 1984, pp. 551-563.
Krönig[2], W., *Philipp Hackert (1737-1807). Ein Werk-und Lebensbild*, in Cologne: exhibition catalogue, *Heroismus und Idylle. Formen der Landschaft um 1800 bei J. Ph. Hackert, J. A. Koch und J. C. Reinhart*, Cologne 1984, p. 16 note 4.
Krönig[3], W., *Museen: Düsseldorf: Philipp Hackerts « Aussichten von dem Landhause des Horaz » 1870 im Goethe-Museum »*, « Pantheon », 1984, 42, pp. 86-89.
Naples: exhibition catalogue, *Civiltà del Seicento a Napoli*, 2 voll., Naples 1984.
Pacelli, V., *Francesco Celebrano pittore: inediti e precisazioni*, in *Studi di storia dell'arte in memoria di Mario Rotili*, Naples 1984, I, pp. 503-519.
Paris: exhibition catalogue, *Dix siècles d'enluminure italienne (VIe-XVIe siècles)* edited by F. Avril, Paris 1984.
Salerno, L., *Inediti di Filippo Angeli e di Scipione Compagno*, in *Scritti di storia dell'arte in onore di Federico Zeri*, Milan 1984, II, pp. 553-560.
Santoro, L., *Le mura di Napoli*, Rome 1984.
Seicento napoletano: arte, costume, ambiente, edited by Roberto Pane, Milan 1984.
Spinosa, N., *La pittura napoletana del '600*, Milan 1984.

1985

Attanasio, S., *La villa Carafa di Belvedere al Vomero*, Naples 1985.
Budapest: exhibition catalogue, *A Nàpoli festézet aranykova XVII-XVIII szádad*, edited by Roberto Middione e Fausta Navarro, Naples 1985.
Catalogo dell'arte italiana dell'Ottocento, 14, Milan 1985.
De Seta, C., *Significati e simboli della rappresentazione topografica negli Atlanti dal XVI al XVIII secolo*, in *Le città capitali*, edited by Cesare De Seta, Rome-Bari 1985.
Fabiani, M.-Fino, L., *Scene di vita popolare a Napoli nell'età romantica*, Naples 1985.
Fabris, P., *Raccolta di vari Vestimenti ed Arti del Regno di Napoli*, edited by Franco Mancini, Naples 1985.
Gowing, L., *The originality of Thomas Jones*, London 1985.
Knight[1], C., *Albori, fortuna e declino delle « gouaches napolitaine »*, in Naples: exhibition catalogue, *Gouaches napoletane del settecento e dell'ottocento*, Naples 1985, pp. 53-68.
Knight[2], C., *La quadreria di Sir William Hamilton a Palazzo Serra*, « Napoli Nobilissima », XXIV, 1985, pp. 45-49.
Koeman, C., *Atlantes Neerlandici*, VI, *Alphean Aan den Rijn*, Amsterdam 1985.
Krönig, W., *Zu « Vedute » und « Panorama » im Werk von Philipp Hackert (1737-1807)*, « Zeitschrift für Schweizerische Archäologie und Kunstgeschichte », 1985, 42, pp. 269-273.
London: exhibition catalogue, *British Landscape Watercolours 1600-1860*, edited by Lindsay Stainton, London 1985.
Madrid: exhibition catalogue, *Pintura napolitana de Caravaggio a Giordano*, Madrid 1985.
Maggioni, C., *Due vedute di Urbino di G. Van Wittel*, « Notizie da Palazzo Albani », XIV, 1985, 1, pp. 93-97.
Marin, B., *Les miroirsde la ville. Représentations textuelles et représentations figurées Naples: 1550-1740*, in « Bollettino del C. I. R. V. I. », nn. 11-12, 1985, pp. 1-30.
Muzii, R., *Città e natura nelle gouaches tra sette e ottocento*, in Naples: exhibition catalogue, *Gouaches napoletane del settecento e dell'Ottocento*, Naples 1985, pp. 77-88.
Naples[1]: exhibition catalogue, *Gouaches napoletane del Settecento e dell'ottocento*, Naples 1985.
Naples[2]: exhibition catalogue, *Napoli antica*, Naples 1985.
New York: exhibition catalogue, *Landscape painting in Rome 1595-1675*, edited by Ann Sutherland Harris, New York 1985.
Richter, D., *Viaggiatori stranieri nel sud: L'immagine della Costa di Amalfi nella cultura europea tra mito e realtà*, Amalfi 1985.
Rome: exhibition catalogue, *Anton Sminck Pitloo 1791-1837. Un paesaggista olandese a Napoli: ventisette opere ritrovate*, edited by Elena di Majo, pref. Marina Causa Picone, Rome 1985.
Rossini, R., *Scrittori e pittoristranieri a Napoli nel XVIII e XIX secolo*, Cuneo 1985.
Russel, F., *Under Vesuvius: British patrons and neapolitan viewpainters*, « Country Life », II, May 30, 1985.
Tecce, A., *L'eruzione del Vesuvio nelle gouaches del XVII e XIX secolo*, in Naples: exhibition catalogue, *Gouaches napoletane del settecento e dell'ottocento*, Naples 1985, pp. 89-97.
Venice: exhibition catalogue, *Le Venezie possibili*, Venice 1985.
Vitale, G., *Una residenza nobiliare napoletana tra cinque e settecento*, in *Palazzo Corigliano tra archeologia e storia*, Naples 1985, pp. 93-115.
Washington: exhibition catalogue, *The Treasure houses of Britain. Five hundred years of Private Patronage and Art Collecting*, Washington 1985.

1985-1986

London-Manchestern-Lousanne: exhibition catalogue, *Louis Ducros: Images of the Grand Tour*, Geneva 1985-1986.

1986

Alessandro Baratta. Fidelissimae Urbis Neapolitanea cum omnibus viis accurata et nova delineatio, edited by Cesare De Seta, Naples 1986.
Borghero, G., *Collezione Thyssen-Bornemisza. Catalogo ragionato delle opere*, Milan 1986.
Ciudades del Siglo de Oro. Las vistas españolas del

Anton van den Wyngaerde, edited by R. L. Kagan, Madrid 1986.
Cora, G.-Zanfani, A., *La porcellana dei Medici*, Milan 1986.
De Seta, C., *La città nella storia d'Italia*, Rome-Bari 1986.
Haverkamp-Begemann, E., *Las vistas de España de Anton van den Wyngaerde*, in *Ciudades del Siglo de Oro. Las vistas españolas del Anton van den Wyngaerde*, edited by R. L. Kagan, Madrid 1986.
Il Palazzo Reale di Napoli, edited by Marina Causa Picone e Annalisa Porzio, Naples 1986.
Il Quarto del Priore. Museo delle Certosa di S. Martino, edited by Luciana Arbace e Rita Pastorelli, Naples 1986.
Knight, C., *Il Casino del Chiatamone*, « Napoli Nobilissima », XXV, 1986, pp. 16-27.
Kochel, V., *Proposta per la identificazione ed il contesto storico del centrotavola del servizio per la Duchessa di Parma*, in Naples: exhibition catalogue, *La porcellana dei Borbone di Napoli*, Naples 1986, pp. 404-406.
Krönig, W., *Jacob Philipp Hackert: View from the Solfatara onto the Gulf Pozzuoli*, « The Bulletin of the Cleveland Museum Art », 1986, 71, pp. 14-23.
Leone de Castris, P., *Arte di corte nella Napoli Angioina*, Florence 1986.
Lorenzetti, C., *G. Vanvitelli*, in *I precedenti del vedutismo settecentesco: immagini di repertorio archeologico. Corso di storia dell'arte moderna*, Rome 1986, pp. 24-39.
Lausanne: exhibition catalogue, *A. R. L. Ducros (1748-1810)*.
Paysages de Italie à l'époque de Goethe, edited by Pierre Chassex, Geneve 1986.
Marshall, D., *A view of Poggioreale by Viviano Codazzi and Domenico Gargiulo*, « Journal of the Society of Architectural Historians », XLV, 1986, pp. 32-46.
Milan: sale catalogue, *Salamon-Augustoni-Algranti*, Milan May 8, 1986.
Naples: exhibition catalogue, *Le porcellane dei Borboni di Napoli: Capodimonte e Real Fabbrica Ferdinandea 1734-1806*, edited by Angela Carola Perrotti, Naples 1986.
Nappi, M. R., *Il Filippo Napoletano di Roberto Longhi. Scipione Compagno e Cornelio Busco*, « Prospettiva », 1986, 47, pp. 24-37.
Padula: exhibition catalogue, *La fortuna di Paestum e la memoria moderna del dorico 1750-1830*, edited by Joselita Raspi Serra, 2 voll., Florence 1986.
Pane R., *Costumi e scene popolari di Napoli nelle incisioni di Vianelli e Lindström*, Naples 1986.
Pisani, M., *Gaetano De Simone un ignoto pittore napoletano della seconda metà del Settecento*, « Prospettiva », 1986, 47, pp. 69-74.
Richard, J. C.-Fragonard, J. H., *Panopticon Italiano. Un diario di viaggio ritrovato 1759-1761*, edited by P. Rosenberg, Rome 1986.
Siracusano, C., *La pittura del settecento in Sicilia*, Rome 1986.
Sloan, N., *Alexander John, and Robert Cozens: The poetry of landscape*, London 1986.
Spinosa, N., *Pittura napoletana del settecento dal Barocco al Rococò*, Naples 1986.
Stumpf, C., *Richard Payne Knight: Expedition into Sicily*, London 1986.
Wagner, A., *Freude an Ruinen*, « Die Kunst », 1986, 98, pp. 356-361.
1987
Bang Lødrup, M., *Johan Christian Dahl 1788-1857. Life and Works*, Arlöv 1987.
Busiri Vici, A., *Peter, Hendrik e Giacomo Van Lint: Tre pittori di Anversa del '600 e '700 lavorano a Roma*, Rome 1987.
Copenhagen: exhibition catalogue, *J. C. Dahl i Italien 1820-1821*, Copenhagen 1987.
De Seta, C., *Real Teatro di San Carlo*, Milan 1987.
Knight, C., *Il giardino inglese di Caserta: storia e prospettiva*, in Caserta: exhibition catalogue, *Il giardino inglese nella Reggia di Caserta – La storia e i documenti – Le piante, le fabbriche*, Naples 1987.
Krönig, W., *Vedute di luoghi classici della Sicilia Il viaggio di Philipp Hackert del 1777*, preface by Georges Vallet, Palermo, 1987.
Les récentes acquisitions des musées internationaux, « Revue du Louvre », 1987, 3, pp. 207-216.
Mancini, F., *Il teatro di S. Carlo: 1737-1987, la storia, la struttura*, Naples 1987.
Martorelli, L., *Smargiassi e il suo tempo*, in Francavilla a Mare 1987.
Naples: exhibition catalogue, *Il miracolo dipinto* edited by M. Rak, A. E. Giordano, Naples 1987
New York: exhibition catalogue,*The treasure of San Gennaro – Baroque Silver from Naples*. Naples 1987.
Paris: exhibition catalogue, *Nouvelles acquisitions du Département des Peintures (1983-1986)*, Paris 1987.
Paris-Lyon-Capri: exhibition catalogue, *Realtà e fantasia nella pittura napoletana (XVIII-XIX)*, edited by Roberto Middione, Brigitte Daprà. Naples 1987.
Pompeii: exhibition catalogue, *Pio IX a Pompei – Memorie e testimonianze di un viaggio*, Naples 1987.
Powell, C., *Turner in the South*, New Haven-London 1987.
Roland-Michel, M., *Le dessin français au XVIII siècle*, Paris 1987.
Rome: exhibition catalogue, *Ducros 1748-1810. Paesaggi d'Italia all'epoca di Goethe*, edited by Pierre Chassex, Rome 1987.
Rosenberg, P.-Stewart, M., *French paintings*, « The Fine Arts Museums of San Francisco » 1987, pp. 197-199.
Schade, G., *Berlin Porzellan*, Munich 1987.
Spinosa, N., *Pittura napoletana del settecento dal rococò al classicismo*, Naples 1987.
Sudbury: Gainsborough's House, *Joseph Wright of Derby in Italy 1773-1775*, exhibition catalogue by David Fraser, Sudbury 1987.
Thiery, Y., *Les peintres flamands de paysage au XVII siècle*, 2 voll., Bruxelles 1987.
Venice-Milan: exhibition catalogue,*Vedute italiane nel '700 in collezioni private italiane*, edited by Marco Magnifico, Mariella Utili, Venice 1987.
Williams, C., *Lusieri's masterpiece?*, « The Burlington Magazine », CXXXIX, 1987, 1012, pp. 475-459.
1987-1988
Rome-Milan-Naples: exhibition catalogue, *Le stanze della memoria. Vedute di ambienti, ritratti in interni e scene di conversazione della collezione Praz*, edited by Stefano Susinno, Elena Di Mayo, Rome-Milan 1987-1988.
1988
Börsch-Supan, H., *Die deutsche Malerei 1760-1870*, Munich 1988.
Catello, E., *La carrozza napoletana del XVIII secolo*, in *Scritti di storia dell'arte in onore di Raffaello Causa*, Naples 1988, pp. 351-358.
Cioffi, R., *Aspetti e problemi dell'attività artistica a Napoli in relazione alle vicende rivoluzionarie del 1799*, in *Scritti di storia dell'arte in onore di Raffaello Causa*, Naples 1988, pp. 359-366.
De Seta, C., *L'immagine di Napoli dalla Tavola Strozzi a Jean Brueghel*, in *Scritti di storia dell'arte in onore di Raffaello Causa*, Naples 1988, pp. 105-117.
Di Majo, E., *Un dipinto di Pitloo alla Galleria Nazionale d'Arte Moderna di Roma: attorno ad una committenza*, in *Studi di storia dell'arte in onore di Raffaello Causa*, Naples 1988, pp. 383-386.
Edinburgh: exhibition catalogue, *Reality and imagination in neapolitan Painting of the 17th. to 19th. centuries*, edited by Roberto Middione, Brigitte Daprà, Edinburgh 1988.
Florence: exhibition catalogue, *Disegni tedeschi da Schongäuer a Liebermann*, edited by Keith Andrews, Florence 1988.
Fusco, M. A., *Sulla formazione tecnica di Giacinto Gigante*, in *Studi di storia dell'arte in onore di Raffaello Causa*, Naples 1988, pp. 387-392.
Goethe, J. W., *Philipp Hackert: la vita*, edited by Novelli Radice, Naples 1988.
Il mito e l'immagine. Capri, Ischia e Procida nella pittura dal '600 ai primi del '900, Turin 1988.
Knight, C., *I palazzi di Mergellina*, « Napoli Nobilissima », 1988 pp. 29-40, 122-123.
Krapf, M., *Rebell*, J., in *Österreichisches Biographisches Lexicon*, Vienna 1988, IX, pp. 2 sgg.
Madrid: exhibition catalogue, *Carlo III y la illustracion*, Madrid 1988.
Manchester: exhibition catalogue,*Travels in Italy 1776-1783: Based on the « Memoirs » of Thomas Jones*, edited by Francis Hawcroft, Manchester 1988.
Mancini, F., (ed), *Philipp Hackert alla corte di Napoli*, Naples 1988.
Marshall, D., *Ascanio Luciani: a neapolitan follower of Viviano Codazzi*, « Paragone », XXXIX, 1988, pp. 21-43
Naples: exhibition catalogue, *La città di Napoli tra vedutismo e cartografia*, edited by Giulio Pane, Vladimiro Valerio, Naples 1987.
Nappi, M. R., *F. De Nomé un problema di fortuna critica*, in *Scritti di storia dell'arte in onore di Raffaello Causa*, Naples 1988, pp. 167-174.
Russel, F., *Canaletto and Joli at Chesterfield house*, « The Burlington Magazine », CXXX, 1988, 1025, pp. 627-630.
Spinosa, N., *Il Vesuvio in fiamme*, « Casa-Vogue-Antiques », May 4, 1988, pp. 48 sgg.
Susinno, S., *Riflessi di storia artistica napoletana in alcuni dipinti della collezione Praz*, in Milan-Naples: exhibition catalogue, *Le stanze della memoria. Vedute di ambienti, ritratti in interni e scene di conversazione della collezione Praz*, edited by Stefano Sussino, Elena Di Majo, Milan-Rome 1988, pp. 107-115.
Utili, M., *Capri*, in *Il mito e l'immagine. Capri, Ischia e Procida nella pittura dal '600 ai primi del '900*, Turin 1988, pp. 59-128.
Zwolle: exhibition catalogue, *Loosdrechts Poselein*, Zwolle 1988.
1989
Amalfi: exhibition catalogue, *Alla ricerca del sud. Tre secoli di viaggio ad Amalfi nell'immaginario europeo*, edited by Dieter Richter, Florence 1989.
Belli, C. (edited by), *Archivio storico della Augustissima Compagnia della Santa Croce*, Naples 1989.
Bologna, F., *Ritorno al Maestro di San Severino Apostolo del Norico*, in Naples: exhibition catalogue, *Il polittico di San Severino Apostolo. Restauri e recuperi*, edited by F. Bologna, Naples 1989.
Brilli, A., *Die Kulturgeschichte der Klassischen Italienreise*, Cologne 1989.
Carughi, U.-Martorelli, L.-Porzio, A., *Il Palazzo della Prefettura*, Naples 1989.
Colletta, T., *Storia del Reame di Napoli*, Milan.
De Seta, C., *Tetti rossi a Napoli. Francesco Roselli e la Tavola Strozzi*, « F. M. R. », 1989, 75.
Di Mauro, L., *Osservazioni sugli allineamenti dell'edilizia religiosa nella parte più antica del centro storico di Napoli*, in *Il cantiere della Conoscenza. Il Cantiere del Restauro*, Atti del Convegno di Studi Bressanone June 27-30, 1989, Padova 1989, pp. 603-611.
Fino, L., *Il vedutismo a Napoli nella grafica dal XVII al XIX secolo*, Naples 1989.
Fraser, F., *Lady Hamilton*, Milan 1989.
Guerra, A. M.-Guerra, G., *Iconografia e realtà della Casina Reale del Chiatamone*, « Atti dell'Accademia Pontaniana », XXXVII n.s., 1989.
Krems: exhibition catalogue, *Michael Wutky 1739-1822, Zur Wiederkehr des 2500. Geburtstages*, edited by Kuhn, H. Kühnel, Krems 1989.
London[1]: sale catalogue, *Paintings and Drawings sculpture works of art*, Chaucer Fine Arts, London 1989.
London[2]: sale catalogue, *Sotheby*, London, December 6, 1989.
Lossky, B., *La terrasse à Sorrento de Silvestre Chtchedrin (1791-1830) au Louvre*, « Revue du Louvre et des Musées de France », 1989, 5/6, pp. 353-356.
Madrid: exhibition catalogue, *Carlos III en Italia, Itinerario italiano de en monarca español 1731-1759*, edited by J. Urrea Fernandez, Madrid 1989.
Mammucari, R., *Napoli e i suoi odori. Dai Campi Phlegraei di W. Hamilton alla scuola di Posillipo*, Velletri 1989.
Mormone, M. S., *Gaetano De Simone*, in Naples: exhibition catalogue, *Napoli e la Repubblica del '99. Immagini della rivoluzione*, Naples 1989, pp. 134 sgg.

Naples[1]: exhibition catalogue, *Capolavori della collezione d'arte del Banco di Napoli*, Naples 1989.
Naples[2]: exhibition catalogue, *Napoli e la Repubblica del '99. Immagini della rivoluzione*, Naples 1989.
Negro Spina, A., *Napoli nel Settecento. Le incisioni di Antonie Alexandre Cardon*, Naples 1989.
Ricci, G., *Città murate e illusione olografica. Bologna e altri luoghi (se. XVI-XVIII)*, in *Le città e le mura* edited by Cesare De Seta, Jacques Le Goff, Rome-Bari 1989.
Riccio, V., *Un capolavoro del gusto rococò a Napoli. La chiesa nella Nunziatella a Pizzofalcone*, Naples 1989.
Rome[1]: exhibition catalogue, *Arte e scienza nella perestrojka*, Rome 1989.
Rome[2]: exhibition catalogue, *IRIARTE, Antico e moderno nelle collezioni del gruppo IRI*, Milan 1989.
Rome[3]: exhibition catalogue, *Vedute romane di Lievin Cruyl*, edited by B. Jetta, J. Connors, Rome 1989.
São Paulo-Rio de Janeiro: exhibition catalogue, *O século de ouro de Pintura Napolitana*, Rome 1989.
Spinosa, N., *La pittura del Seicento nell'Italia meridionale*, in *La pittura in Italia - Il Seicento*, Milan 1989, vol. II, pp. 461-517.
Spinosa, N.-Di Mauro, L., *Vedute napoletane del Settecento*, Naples 1989.
Urrea Fernandez, J., *Carlos terzero soberano y cazador*, Madrid 1989.

1990

Madrid: exhibition catalogue, *El Arte de la Corte de Nàples en el siglo XVIII*, Madrid 1990.

Forthcoming publications

Gaskell, I., *Painting XVII century dutch and flemish paintings. The Thissen-Bornemisza Collection.*
Pisani, M., *De Simone Gaetano*, in *Dizionario Biografico degli Italiani.*

Published by Electa Napoli in October 1990

Typeset by Fotocomporre
Printed by Incisivo Salerno and Centro dms
Bound by Legatoria Tonti